Mastering AGILE Project Management

Pass Your APMG Foundation & Practitioner Exams with Confidence!

Filled with Case Studies for a Vibrant Understanding of the Concepts

Morgan Carter

British Library cataloguing in the publication data is available.

ISBN: 978-1-916720-12-1

May 'Mastering Agile Project Management' illuminate your journey, empower your learning, and prepare you for success in the Agile world.

Table of Contents

WELCOME

In the contemporary world where adaptability to change is not just a virtue but a requisite, Agile project management has emerged as a crucial key to unlocking organizational success. Whether you are a seasoned project manager, a budding professional in the project management sphere, or an organization aiming to scale new heights in project delivery, "Mastering Agile Project Management: A Comprehensive Guide to Success with the Agile Project Management Framework" is crafted to be your compass in the journey toward Agile Project Management certification and beyond.

Hello and welcome, dear reader! I am Morgan Carter, and I am thrilled to accompany you on this enlightening venture into the dynamic universe of Agile Project Management through the lens of Agile Project Management. This book was conceived and designed with an unwavering commitment to illuminating the path toward mastery in Agile Project Management, guided by the Dynamic Systems Development Method (DSDM).

Why Agile Project Management? Agile Project Management offers a meticulous and structured framework that enables organizations to navigate through the complexities and uncertainties of the agile project management world while adhering to established principles and practices. Agile Project Management harmoniously marries flexibility with governance, agility with assurance, and innovation with method—factors that are pivotal to driving successful projects in a volatile, uncertain, complex, and ambiguous (VUCA) environment.

In "Mastering Agile Project Management," we embark together on a voyage from the foundational principles to the intricate nuances of the Agile Project

Management framework. Through rich, detailed content, practical insights, and real-world scenarios, this book aims to equip you not only with the theoretical knowledge needed to pass the Agile Project Management Foundation and Practitioner exams but also with pragmatic skills and understanding to apply this knowledge in the professional arena.

What to Expect?

The first half of the book delves into the Agile Project Foundations, exploring the underlying philosophy, principles, processes, roles, and products within DSDM. This section will establish a robust foundational understanding of the Agile Project Management framework, providing you with a solid base upon which to build your expertise.

The second half ventures into an immersive exploration of the Agile Project Management framework from the project manager's viewpoint. It not only deepens the understanding developed in the first half but also introduces concepts and strategies pivotal to those aiming to assume a project management role in an agile context.

Each chapter is thoughtfully designed to weave through the theoretical and practical aspects of each topic, facilitating a learning experience that is both engaging and enriching. Real-world examples and case studies have been integrated to enable you to apply your learning and prepare effectively for the certification exams.

"Mastering Agile Project Management" extends beyond certification preparation, aiming to be a continuous reference point throughout your Agile Project Management journey. Whether you're preparing for your exam or grappling with real-world project challenges, this book aspires to be your go-to guide.

Your Companion in Mastery

Your decision to explore and master Agile Project Management could be the catalyst propelling your career and your organization toward unparalleled project success. In this journey of mastery, I am not just an author but a fellow traveler, exploring alongside you, navigating through the challenges, and celebrating the triumphs.

Let's embark on this journey toward mastering Agile Project Management together, exploring, learning, applying, and achieving success in the captivating world of Agile Project Management.

Chapter One

Exploring the Philosophy and Fundamentals

Unpacking the Core Tenets of DSDM: Philosophy, Principles, and Ethos

The Philosophy of DSDM: A Holistic Approach

The Dynamic Systems Development Method (DSDM) adheres to a holistic philosophy that extends beyond mere product delivery. It concentrates on harmonizing project outcomes with business objectives while fostering collaboration and empowerment among the stakeholders. The philosophy comprises several key aspects:

Alignment with Business Vision

Ensuring that the project's goals align with the broader business objectives is paramount. This lends purpose and direction to the entire endeavor.

Empowerment and Autonomy

By empowering individuals involved in the project to make decisions within their areas of expertise, DSDM encourages quick and agile decision-making.

Stakeholder Collaboration

DSDM advocates for ongoing, multi-dimensional collaboration, which harnesses diverse perspectives and skills, enriching the final project outcome.

Adaptability to Change

Being flexible to change is essential as it acknowledges the possibility of evolving requirements as the project progresses and better solutions become evident.

Stakeholder Involvement

Whether internal or external, stakeholders' active involvement and feedback are crucial to the project's success.

The Eight Pillars: Supporting Principles of DSDM

These eight guiding principles serve as the backbone of DSDM's philosophy, each reinforcing a different aspect of the framework:

Focus on the Business Need

Prioritizing what is most essential for the business ensures that the project remains aligned with organizational goals.

Deliver on Time

Timely delivery is not just an operational efficiency; it's a strategic advantage that maximizes value.

Foster Collaboration

Active collaboration among all stakeholders ensures that the project benefits from diverse inputs and skills.

Never Compromise on Quality

Upholding set quality standards ensures that the project outcome meets or exceeds expectations.

Build Incrementally from Firm Foundations

Starting with a strong base ensures that further development can proceed more smoothly and efficiently.

Develop Iteratively

A cyclical development approach allows for ongoing refinement and adaptation.

Ensure Clear and Continuous Communication

Open channels for communication are crucial for effective coordination and timely decision-making.

Demonstrate Control

Regular validation checks and governance mechanisms ensure that the project remains on track.

Underlying Ethos: Common Sense and Pragmatism

At its core, DSDM values practical wisdom and a results-driven approach:

Common Sense

By relying on intuitive decision-making and practical judgment, DSDM negates the need for excessive formality or specialized training.

Pragmatism

Being pragmatic means prioritizing effective outcomes over strict adherence to theory or method. Results are the ultimate yardstick for success.

Concluding Remarks

DSDM stands as a multi-faceted, agile framework that is underpinned by a rich philosophy, robust principles, and a common-sense ethos. Together, these elements create a flexible, stakeholder-centric, and outcome-oriented approach to project management. The framework is built to produce efficient and effective results when applied with the understanding and commitment it necessitates.

Case Study: Implementing DSDM in a Digital Transformation Project

Background: Navigating Complexity

Imagine a large organization embarking on a comprehensive digital transformation journey. This project is not just about updating software; it aims to realign business processes, customer experiences, and overall corporate strategy. Given the complexity and the myriad stakeholders involved, selecting an agile project management approach becomes critical.

Utilizing DSDM's Philosophy and Principles

Alignment with Business Vision

The project kicks off by defining its goals in line with the company's broader business strategy. Executives, IT leaders, and other key stakeholders establish these foundational aspects early on, adhering to DSDM's focus on business vision alignment.

Empowerment and Decision-making

Various teams across different departments are empowered to make decisions relevant to their expertise. This operational autonomy fast-tracks many aspects of the project, streamlining decision-making processes.

Collaboration among Stakeholders

Cross-functional teams are formed, consisting of members from IT, marketing, operations, and customer service departments. These teams collaborate intensively, breaking down silos and fostering a culture of shared ownership.

Adaptability and Flexibility

As the project progresses, it becomes apparent that customer preferences are shifting, requiring a change in some functionalities of the digital interface. Due to the flexibility ingrained in DSDM's philosophy, these new requirements are integrated seamlessly into the ongoing cycles.

Priority-based Development

Using the MoSCoW prioritization technique, essential features and modules are developed and rolled out first, ensuring that the project provides immediate value to the business and the end-users.

Continuous Communication

Regular stand-up meetings, reviews, and updates are integral parts of the project, ensuring everyone is aligned and aware of the project's status and any emerging issues.

Quality Assurance

Quality benchmarks are established early in the project and monitored continuously. Teams are diligent in adhering to these quality standards, ensuring that the project does not just complete on time but excels in meeting its objectives.

Results

The digital transformation project is rolled out successfully within the stipulated timeline and budget. Most importantly, it aligns perfectly with the business objectives and receives positive reception from both internal stakeholders and customers.

Lessons Learned

The organization realizes the immense value of adhering to a disciplined yet flexible approach like DSDM. Its core philosophy and principles act as guiding lights throughout the project, ensuring that it not only meets but exceeds expectations.

Conclusion

This case study exemplifies how DSDM's philosophy and principles can guide a complex project to success. By embedding the philosophy and principles into its project management approach, the organization achieved a digital transformation that was timely, within budget, and highly aligned with its strategic business objectives.

Navigating the Treacherous Waters of Project Management: How DSDM's Approach Offers a Beacon of Clarity

The Universal Dilemma in Project Management

Managing a project invariably involves juggling various conflicting demands, namely time, cost, features, and quality. Traditional project management approaches often make the error of trying to set all these parameters in stone at the onset. This rigidity is problematic because it does not account for the dynamic nature of business environments, unexpected challenges, or shifts in project understanding.

Comparing Traditional and DSDM Approaches

The Traditional Fixation

In conventional project management, the feature set (scope) is usually predetermined and fixed. However, time and cost estimates often exceed their original limits, and as a result, quality can get compromised. This compromise typically occurs when testing phases are crammed into the end of a project, leading to inadequate scrutiny and evaluation.

DSDM's Paradigm Shift

Dynamic Systems Development Method (DSDM) upends this traditional model by fixing the time, cost, and quality parameters at the beginning of the project. The variable element becomes the feature set or scope. Through prioritization techniques like MoSCoW and practices such as Timeboxing, DSDM introduces flexibility where it's most needed— in the features or requirements of the project. When challenges arise, rather than stretching timelines or sacrificing quality, DSDM allows for the least critical features to be deferred or dropped altogether.

Key Benefits of Adopting DSDM's Approach

Guaranteed Delivery with a Minimum Usable Subset

By focusing on the most critical requirements first and keeping time, cost, and quality as fixed factors, DSDM assures that, at the very least, a Minimum Usable Subset (MUST) of features will be delivered.

Assurance of Quality

Quality isn't relegated to the last minute but is maintained throughout the development lifecycle. High-priority features are built and tested to meet predefined quality standards before moving on to less critical elements.

Flexibility and Adaptability

DSDM's approach allows for adaptive course corrections without requiring major overhauls. This feature-specific flexibility makes the methodology particularly resilient to changes and unforeseen challenges.

Satisfaction of Stakeholders

By delivering within predefined boundaries of time, cost, and quality, stakeholders have a clearer idea of what to expect, thereby increasing their satisfaction level.

Conclusion

In an ever-changing project landscape, DSDM offers a pragmatic and effective approach to balancing conflicting demands. By flipping the traditional project management triangle and fixing time, cost, and quality while keeping features flexible, DSDM offers a well-suited framework for contemporary project environments that require adaptability, without compromising on essential project factors.

Balancing Conflicting Demands in Projects: A Practical Example with DSDM

The Scenario: Developing a Mobile App for a Retail Business

Imagine a retail business aiming to develop a mobile application to enhance customer engagement and improve online sales. The project must be completed within six months, with a budget not exceeding $200,000, and must meet high quality standards.

Traditional Approach and Its Shortcomings

In a traditional project management framework, the project may begin with a fixed set of features or functionalities that need to be included in the app. However, as development progresses, various challenges such as technical hurdles, scope creep, and budget overruns may begin to surface. The result could be either a delay in project delivery, an overshooting budget, or compromises in the quality of the final product.

DSDM's Approach and How It Addresses the Dilemma

Prioritization Using MoSCoW

DSDM starts by employing the MoSCoW method to prioritize the features. This ensures that all 'Must-have' features are built and tested first. Once they meet the predefined quality standards, only then are the 'Should-have' and 'Could-have' features addressed.

Timeboxing to Ensure Timely Delivery

The project timeline is divided into fixed time boxes, where each box is dedicated to delivering a particular set of features. This mechanism helps ensure that the project stays on schedule.

Handling Changes and Unforeseen Challenges

Suppose, during the third month, a competitor launches an app with a new, engaging feature that wasn't initially considered. Instead of throwing the whole project into chaos, the DSDM approach would review the remaining 'Should-have' and 'Could-have' features. The least important could be deferred or dropped to make room for this new market-driven requirement, without affecting the overall project timeline or budget.

Stakeholder Involvement

Regular reviews with stakeholders at the end of each timebox ensure that the project remains aligned with business objectives and can adapt to any new insights or market developments.

Conclusion: The Strength of DSDM in Real-world Application

In this hypothetical example, the DSDM approach proves its mettle by maintaining a delicate balance between time, cost, quality, and features. By employing prioritization techniques, setting clear boundaries, and involving stakeholders, DSDM ensures that the project not only meets its objectives but is also agile enough to adapt to changing market conditions.

This practical example underscores the robustness and adaptability of DSDM in managing conflicting project demands effectively.

Chapter Two

Unveiling the Underpinning Principles

Decoding the Eight Core Principles of DSDM: The Foundation of Agile Project Management

Dynamic Systems Development Method (DSDM) is a framework in agile project management that leans heavily on a set of eight core principles. These principles not only guide the behavior and decision-making of project teams but also ensure that projects are well-aligned with business objectives. Here, we will delve into each principle to understand its importance and the role it plays in successful project delivery.

1. Focus on the Business Need

Concentrating on the business need is pivotal for the efficient allocation of resources. This principle ensures that every decision made, and every action taken, contributes towards fulfilling essential business requirements. It is the cornerstone that keeps the project aligned with the overarching objectives of the business.

2. Deliver on Time

Time is often a non-negotiable constraint in project management. Adhering to timelines is crucial for the rapid realization of business benefits. Fixed deadlines help in the effective prioritization of features and tasks, which allows for the delivery of a Minimum Viable Product (MVP) within the stipulated timeframe.

3. Collaborate

The essence of DSDM lies in collaboration. It facilitates a synergetic relationship between business representatives and development teams. Such collaboration is essential for crafting a solution that is not only technically sound but also meets the business needs effectively.

4. Never Compromise Quality

The DSDM approach views quality as a multi-dimensional attribute. It is not just about a defect-free product but also about a solution that fully meets its intended purpose. A defined set of quality criteria must be adhered to, ensuring that the end product is in line with business expectations.

5. Build Incrementally from Firm Foundations

Jumping headlong into the build phase without a clear understanding of objectives can be risky. It is crucial to lay down a solid foundation of what the project aims to achieve. Once this foundation is laid, incremental development allows for the delivery of smaller, value-adding solutions that evolve into the final product.

6. Develop Iteratively

Embracing an iterative development approach acknowledges the reality that not all requirements can be fully understood at the project's onset. This principle facilitates ongoing refinement of the solution based on iterative feedback, tailoring the end product more closely to user needs.

7. Communicate Continuously and Clearly

DSDM emphasizes the need for regular and transparent communication among all stakeholders. It not only keeps everyone on the same page but also fosters an environment where stakeholders are more engaged and informed, thereby contributing to the project's success.

8. Demonstrate Control

Transparency and control go hand-in-hand in DSDM projects. Regular reviews and tracking mechanisms show stakeholders that the project is proceeding as planned, thereby establishing trust and opening the door for feedback and adjustments.

Conclusion

DSDM's eight core principles are more than just guidelines; they are the bedrock upon which successful project implementation rests. By embedding these principles into the project lifecycle, organizations can ensure alignment with business goals, timely delivery, and a collaborative environment that leverages collective expertise. It's an approach that understands the complexities of the modern business landscape and offers a robust framework for navigating it successfully.

Practical Example: Implementing DSDM Principles in a Software Development Project

Overview

Let's consider a hypothetical software development project aimed at creating a mobile application for online retail. The project faces typical constraints: a tight timeline, a set budget, and high-quality expectations. The development team decides to employ the DSDM framework to navigate these challenges effectively.

1. Focus on the Business Need

The team collaborates with business stakeholders to identify the most critical features that will drive customer engagement and sales. Based on this, they prioritize functionalities like secure payment options, an intuitive user interface, and fast load times.

2. Deliver on Time

A release date coinciding with a major shopping season is set. The team adheres to this timeline rigorously, using time-boxing techniques to ensure that the most critical features are developed and tested first.

3. Collaborate

Regular meetings between the business and technical teams are scheduled. During these sessions, the project's progress is reviewed, and insights from both sides are integrated into the development process.

4. Never Compromise Quality

Quality gates are established at each iteration. Features move to the next stage only if they meet the predefined quality standards, ensuring that the final product is robust and reliable.

5. Build Incrementally from Firm Foundations

The initial sprints focus on establishing a strong architectural foundation for the app. Once this is in place, the team starts building additional features, layering them onto the established core.

6. Develop Iteratively

The application goes through several iterations, each followed by a round of user testing. Feedback from these tests is integrated into the subsequent development cycles.

7. Communicate Continuously and Clearly

The project manager sends out weekly status updates to all stakeholders. These updates include accomplishments, upcoming milestones, and any potential risks, keeping everyone well-informed.

8. Demonstrate Control

The team holds a monthly review meeting with all stakeholders to showcase the developed features and gather feedback. This transparency assures stakeholders that the project is well-managed and on track for successful completion.

Conclusion

By adhering to DSDM's core principles, the project team can navigate the intricate maze of constraints and expectations. They successfully deliver a high-quality mobile application on time and within budget, meeting both technical and business requirements. This example illustrates the transformative power of DSDM's principles when applied effectively in a real-world scenario.

The Core Tenets of the Principle "Focus on the Business Need"

Overview

The "Focus on the Business Need" principle serves as a foundational pillar in DSDM and agile methodologies at large. It stresses the significance of aligning every facet of a project with the underlying business objectives. This principle acts as a guiding light, ensuring that all project efforts and resources are directed towards achieving the highest impact on business goals.

Detailed Exploration

Alignment with Business Objectives

The alignment between business objectives and project activities is a crucial aspect of this principle. It serves as a cornerstone that dictates the features, functionalities, and overall scope of the project, ensuring the realization of tangible value for the business.

Avoid Gold-Plating

The temptation to add extraneous features, commonly known as "gold-plating," can be a detrimental diversion. Such additions may extend timelines and consume resources, ultimately diluting the project's focus on the core business needs.

Regular Validation of Business Value

Periodic evaluations of how well the project aligns with business objectives are essential. These checkpoints, built into the project lifecycle, serve as reality checks, reaffirming the project's relevance and value to the business.

Stakeholder Engagement

Stakeholders, including business representatives and product owners, must be involved throughout the project. Their input provides the project team with essential insights into the business's evolving needs, allowing for more informed decision-making.

Prioritization Techniques

Effective prioritization methods, such as the MoSCoW technique, are invaluable tools for keeping the project aligned with business objectives. By categorizing features into 'Must-Have,' 'Should-Have,' 'Could-Have,' and 'Won't-Have,' teams can channel their efforts towards the most business-critical tasks first.

Flexibility and Adaptability

As the business landscape is continuously evolving, a rigid approach to project management can be counterproductive. Adaptability and flexibility are key to ensuring that the project remains aligned with shifting business needs.

Outcome Over Output

The project should aim not merely to produce outputs but to achieve specific business outcomes. This differentiation is critical for ensuring that project efforts translate into real-world business benefits.

Conclusion

The principle of "Focus on the Business Need" is more than a guideline; it's a fundamental doctrine that shapes project activities and decisions. By adhering to this principle, project teams can ensure they are continuously aligned with business objectives, thereby maximizing value and relevance. This principle acts as a critical compass, guiding projects toward outcomes that have a significant and positive impact on the business.

Illustrative Case Study: Implementing the "Focus on the Business Need" Principle

Scenario: Implementing a Customer Relationship Management System

Background

Suppose a retail company aims to improve customer retention and loyalty through the implementation of a Customer Relationship Management (CRM) system. The primary business need is to increase customer engagement and foster more personalized interactions.

Aligning with Business Objectives

From the get-go, the project team aligns the CRM system's features with the primary objective of enhancing customer engagement. For instance, they focus on developing modules for targeted promotions and customer segmentation.

Avoiding Gold-Plating

During the development phase, the team contemplates adding a sophisticated machine learning algorithm to predict future buying behavior. While intriguing, this feature doesn't directly align with the immediate business need of improving customer engagement. Therefore, it's marked as a 'Could-Have' or even a 'Won't-Have' in the MoSCoW prioritization.

Regular Business Value Validation

The project team schedules bi-weekly check-ins with business stakeholders to validate the system's features against the defined business objectives. Any divergence is promptly identified, and course correction is initiated if necessary.

Stakeholder Engagement

Throughout the project, key business stakeholders, including sales and marketing representatives, are continuously consulted. Their insights are invaluable in fine-tuning the CRM system to ensure it meets actual business requirements.

Prioritization Techniques

The project employs the MoSCoW method to prioritize features. Segmentation and targeted promotions are marked as 'Must-Have' features, as they directly impact customer engagement, the primary business objective.

Flexibility and Adaptability

Midway through the project, the retail landscape shifts due to external market factors. The company realizes that an online chat feature would now be extremely beneficial for customer engagement. The project team adapts the scope to incorporate this new feature without disrupting the primary objective.

Outcome Focus

Finally, the team doesn't just focus on launching the CRM system (output) but also tracks how the system impacts customer engagement levels in the subsequent months (outcome).

Conclusion

By adhering to the "Focus on the Business Need" principle, the project successfully delivers a CRM system that not only meets the technical specifications but, more importantly, fulfills the primary business objective of enhancing customer engagement.

The principle served as a navigational aid, ensuring that every aspect of the project, from feature development to stakeholder consultation, was aligned with delivering the most significant business impact.

Exploring the "Deliver on Time" Principle in Depth

Importance of Timely Delivery in DSDM Projects

The Role of Time-Criticality

Timely delivery often determines a project's ultimate success, especially in industries where speed to market is a competitive advantage. The delayed implementation could lead to missed business opportunities and undermine stakeholder confidence.

Demonstrating Control and Predictability

Consistently meeting or beating deadlines is not just a matter of ticking boxes. It creates a sense of predictability and control, crucial for building trust with stakeholders and establishing a robust project management reputation.

Key Techniques to Ensure On-Time Delivery

Fixed Time, Flexible Features

The DSDM framework advocates for the principle of fixing time but allowing flexibility in features. By prioritizing essential features and being willing to defer or drop less critical ones, projects can maintain their commitment to deadlines.

Regular, Incremental Deliveries

The use of incremental deliveries, often broken down into Timeboxes, allows for a phased approach to project delivery. This provides regular milestones that serve as both progress markers and opportunities for feedback and course correction.

Efficient Stakeholder Expectation Management

Keeping stakeholders engaged and informed through on-time delivery minimizes the risk of project derailment due to unexpected interventions or changes in direction from business leaders.

Resource Management and Continuous Learning

Resource Efficiency

One benefit of sticking to deadlines is the efficient utilization of resources. Delayed projects not only drain financial resources but can also lead to attrition, as team members may be needed for other pressing organizational initiatives.

Feedback Loops and Continuous Learning

On-time delivery, particularly through incremental phases, allows for more frequent validation of project assumptions and quicker feedback loops. This paves the way for iterative learning and ongoing improvements.

Conclusion

The "Deliver on Time" principle is integral to the successful implementation of DSDM projects. By adhering to fixed timeframes while allowing features to remain flexible, projects are more likely to meet business objectives, earn stakeholder trust, and optimize resource usage. The emphasis on regular, incremental deliveries not only facilitates better project control but also promotes a culture of continuous learning and improvement.

Unpacking the "Deliver on Time" Principle: A Practical Example

Scenario: Software Development for a Healthcare Provider

Imagine a healthcare provider planning to roll out a patient management system to streamline appointment scheduling, medical records storage, and billing. The system needs to be fully operational before the start of the new fiscal year to align with organizational financial planning and reporting requirements. Missing the deadline would not only affect financial metrics but also disrupt patient care and staff workflow.

Implementing the "Deliver on Time" Principle

Initial Planning and Timeboxing

The project team establishes an aggressive but realistic timeline broken down into Timeboxes. Each Timebox is designed to deliver specific features that cumulatively build up the full system.

Prioritization Using MoSCoW

The team adopts the MoSCoW method to prioritize features. Essential elements like appointment scheduling and medical record storage are tagged as "Must-Haves" and are prioritized for the earliest Timeboxes. Additional functionalities, such as billing integration and patient portals, are categorized as "Should-Have" and "Could-Have."

Stakeholder Communication

To manage stakeholder expectations, regular project status meetings are scheduled. These meetings serve as platforms for the team to demonstrate completed functionalities, thereby building confidence and trust in the project's progress.

Regular, Incremental Deliveries

As planned, the team delivers "Must-Have" functionalities in the initial Timeboxes. The system starts undergoing real-world testing well before the final deadline, allowing for critical evaluation and adjustments.

Flexibility and Adaptability

As the project progresses, some features initially thought to be "Could-Have" or "Should-Have" are reevaluated based on user feedback and emerging needs. Some are promoted to higher priority levels, while others are deferred to future Timeboxes or even to a phase two roll-out.

Outcomes and Benefits

Met Deadlines and Preserved Stakeholder Trust

The system is rolled out before the start of the new fiscal year, meeting the essential deadline. This on-time delivery strengthens stakeholder trust and establishes a track record of reliability for the project team.

Optimized Resource Utilization

By meeting the planned deadlines, the organization avoids the cost overruns that typically accompany delayed projects.

Enhanced Capacity for Future Projects

The success of delivering on time, in alignment with the DSDM principles, serves as a template for future projects. Lessons learned are codified, and best practices are integrated into the organization's project management methodology.

Conclusion

The practical application of the "Deliver on Time" principle within this healthcare scenario underscores its significance. By adhering to this DSDM principle, the project team was able to meet business-critical deadlines, optimize resource utilization, and build a strong foundation for future initiatives.

The Integral Role of the "Collaborate" Principle in Project Success

Shared Vision and Ownership: The Bedrock of Collaboration

When team members actively collaborate, they align themselves with the project's goals and objectives. This alignment manifests in collective ownership, where everyone takes responsibility for the project's success. Each team member sees the big picture and recognizes their role in achieving it.

Facilitating Knowledge Sharing and Cross-Functional Synergy

One of the most significant benefits of collaboration is the sharing of expertise and skills. In a collaborative environment, the free flow of ideas and perspectives fosters innovative problem-solving and ensures that the team capitalizes on its collective knowledge.

Accelerated Problem-Solving: The Collective Mind at Work

The synergistic effects of collaboration allow for efficient problem-solving. Teams can brainstorm, pool their knowledge, and leverage collective experiences to navigate challenges more effectively than individuals working in isolation.

Building Trust: The Foundation of Effective Teams

Active collaboration naturally leads to an environment of trust among team members. This trust is essential for open dialogue, constructive criticism, and the willingness to take calculated risks—all of which contribute to a project's success.

The Feedback Loop and Continuous Improvement

A collaborative team sets up regular touchpoints for sharing feedback. These feedback loops facilitate reflective practices that help the team adapt, improve, and refine their approaches continuously.

Broadening the Scope: Stakeholder Engagement

A collaborative approach extends beyond the core project team. It involves key stakeholders, such as customers, end-users, and organizational leaders. Their active participation ensures that the developed solutions align with both business needs and user expectations.

Navigating Cultural Shifts

The principle of collaboration often requires an organizational culture change. This change involves moving from a more traditional, siloed work environment to one that is open, transparent, and focused on team-centric collaboration.

Conclusion

The "Collaborate" principle underpins the conviction that collective efforts yield superior results compared to isolated actions. It champions the ideals of shared ownership, knowledge transfer, and continuous improvement. By adopting this principle, projects can not only achieve their stated objectives but often exceed them, delivering solutions that are innovative, robust, and closely aligned with stakeholder needs.

Unpacking the Practical Example: Developing a Mobile Banking Application Through Collaboration

The Cross-Functional Team: A Melting Pot of Expertise

In the context of developing a mobile banking application, the project assembles a team of developers, designers, testers, business analysts, and customer representatives. The team is not merely a collection of individuals but a well-coordinated unit. They conduct joint workshops, brainstorming sessions, and daily stand-ups to align their efforts and keep the project on track.

Seamless Integration of Design and Development

The designers and developers work in close collaboration from the project's inception. This alignment ensures that the application's design is not just visually appealing but also technically feasible. Developers get a clearer understanding of the design vision, while designers gain insights into technical constraints, allowing for a balanced and effective solution.

Testers as an Integral Part of the Development Process

In a collaborative setup, testers are actively involved from the early stages of development. Their close interaction with developers ensures that bugs and issues are identified and rectified promptly. This dynamic minimizes delays and ensures a higher quality output.

Continual Feedback from Business Analysts and Customer Representatives

The collaboration extends to include business analysts and customer representatives, who act as the voice of the market and the end-users. They provide continuous feedback, ensuring that the mobile app is aligned with market needs and expectations. This two-way communication channel allows for timely adjustments and refinements.

Collective Problem-Solving and Decision-Making

Whenever challenges or roadblocks arise, the collaborative team pools their collective expertise to find solutions. The varied perspectives contribute to a more comprehensive understanding of the issues, leading to more effective and innovative solutions.

Conclusion

In this practical example, the principle of "Collaborate" manifests as a powerful enabler for project success. Through active collaboration among cross-functional team members and key stakeholders, the project successfully delivers a mobile banking application that is robust, user-friendly, and market-ready. This approach not only fulfills the technical requirements but also resonates strongly with the end-users and meets business objectives.

Diving Deeper into the "Never Compromise Quality" Principle

The Imperative of Clear Acceptance Criteria

One of the cornerstones of ensuring quality is establishing clear, measurable, and agreed-upon acceptance criteria before the project even begins. This foundational step provides a benchmark that aligns stakeholders and serves as the yardstick against which all deliverables will be measured.

Quality Over Quantity: A Focused Approach

Quality and feature-set are not synonymous. While it's tempting to include as many features as possible, doing so can dilute the focus on each feature's quality. The principle advises a more disciplined approach: better to have fewer features of high quality than to have a multitude that are unreliable or substandard.

Iterative Checks: A Safeguard Against Quality Slippage

Consistent, iterative feedback loops serve as a safeguard against any degradation of quality. By continually measuring deliverables against the set acceptance criteria, the project can make timely adjustments, thus ensuring that quality is never compromised.

The Pitfall of Over-Engineering

Striking a balance between quality and pragmatism is crucial. Over-engineering can introduce unnecessary complexity, leading to delays and cost overruns. The principle advises that solutions should be "fit for purpose" – meeting business needs within the boundaries of agreed-upon criteria.

Transparent Decision-Making: The Backbone of Quality Assurance

Transparency in decision-making processes, particularly when it comes to quality, fosters trust among stakeholders. It ensures that quality remains a collective responsibility, rather than the domain of a select few. This collective oversight ensures adherence to the established quality benchmarks.

The Role of Balanced Testing

A comprehensive and balanced testing strategy plays a crucial role in upholding quality standards. A mix of unit tests, integration tests, and user acceptance tests allows for thorough validation against the predefined criteria. It ensures that the delivered solution not only works in isolation but also functions seamlessly within the broader ecosystem.

Conclusion

The "Never Compromise Quality" principle forms a robust framework for ensuring that the quality of the delivered solution aligns with business expectations. By focusing on clear acceptance criteria, prioritizing quality over sheer feature quantity, and adopting a transparent and iterative approach, the project safeguards its deliverables against both over-engineering and mediocrity. It guarantees that the final product is reliable, fit for its intended purpose, and provides consistent value to the business.

Practical Example Unveiled: The Case of an E-Commerce Platform

Setting the Stage

In the development of a new e-commerce platform, the primary acceptance criteria include user-friendliness, robust security measures, and a response time of under three seconds for primary user actions like searching for products, adding items to the cart, and checkout processes.

The Temptation of the Advanced Recommendation Engine

During development, the team comes across an enticing opportunity: the integration of an advanced recommendation engine. On paper, this engine could potentially increase user engagement and sales. However, there's a catch: implementing it would slightly extend the project timeline and, more critically, could compromise the response time, one of the primary acceptance criteria.

Adhering to the "Never Compromise Quality" Principle

Faced with this dilemma, the team returns to the core principle: "Never Compromise Quality." After a thorough evaluation, they find that adding the recommendation engine would risk breaching the agreed-upon response time threshold.

The Decision

In line with the principle, the team chooses to prioritize the original quality criteria, particularly the response time, over the added feature. This decision aligns with the predefined acceptance criteria and ensures that the platform remains user-friendly and efficient, meeting both the stakeholders' expectations and business objectives.

The Outcome

By staying true to the principle, the team successfully delivers an e-commerce platform that is both robust and meets all the original quality criteria. Though the advanced recommendation engine was appealing, the team's commitment to never compromising on quality ensures the platform's reliability and user satisfaction, thereby delivering consistent value to the business.

The application of the "Never Compromise Quality" principle in this scenario underscores its utility as a decision-making framework, guiding teams in balancing feature addition against the vital necessity of adhering to predetermined quality standards.

The Quintessence of "Build Incrementally from Firm Foundations"

A Holistic Approach to Navigating Project Complexity

Overview

The principle "Build Incrementally from Firm Foundations" champions the dual significance of establishing a robust base and facilitating gradual progress throughout the project. This philosophy aligns seamlessly with business goals, minimizes the risk of veering off track, and nimbly adapts to changing conditions, all the while skirting the potential hazards of extensive upfront planning.

In-depth Analysis

Setting the Cornerstones: Firm Foundations

Initially, the project's scope, objectives, and the business problem it aims to solve must be clearly defined. Importantly, this doesn't imply the need for a minutely detailed list of requirements. The focus is on crystallizing the project's overarching goals and vision.

Striking the Right Balance: Avoid Analysis Paralysis

Though a comprehensive understanding of the problem and its prospective solutions is crucial, an excessive focus on analytical deliberation could become an obstacle to progress. The emphasis should be on achieving a balanced approach between foundational knowledge and iterative learning.

Taking Measured Steps: Incremental Delivery

In lieu of delivering a monolithic solution in a single stroke, the DSDM methodology advocates for subdividing the project into smaller, digestible increments. Each successive increment serves as an extension of its predecessor, thus continually enhancing the project towards its ultimate objective.

Learning as You Go: Feedback and Adaptation

The incremental approach paves the way for frequent feedback loops with stakeholders, providing valuable insights to improve subsequent development phases. This establishes a self-correcting mechanism that aligns the project with business imperatives while maximizing value.

Immediate Value Adds: Early Business Benefit

The segmented delivery model allows certain functional components of the project to be rolled out and operationalized ahead of full completion, thus offering immediate business value and bolstering stakeholder confidence.

Agile Adaptability: Flexibility and Responsiveness

Constructing the project incrementally upon a sturdy foundational base ensures that it retains the flexibility to adapt to shifts in business priorities, technological innovations, or fresh insights that may come to light as the project evolves.

Conclusion

The principle of "Build Incrementally from Firm Foundations" serves as a beacon for steering projects with finesse and precision. It lays emphasis on the virtue of grounding projects in a well-defined vision and objectives, followed by a process of iterative enhancements. This multifaceted approach assures alignment with business goals, offers the flexibility to adapt, and ensures that tangible benefits are delivered consistently throughout the project lifecycle.

The Practical Application of "Build Incrementally from Firm Foundations"

A Real-World Scenario: Developing a New CRM System

Setting the Stage

Let's consider a hypothetical situation where a company aspires to construct a new CRM (Customer Relationship Management) system. The immediate impetus is to focus on elevating customer service levels and making the sales process more efficient.

Establishing Firm Foundations

Before engaging in full-scale development, the company ascertains the core objectives of this new CRM system, thereby setting up the foundational pillars for the project. It is vital that this stage is not bogged down by over-analysis but instead achieves a crisp understanding of what the CRM system needs to accomplish.

Proceeding Incrementally

The first increment focuses on essential features pivotal to the sales process. This segment of the software is then promptly delivered to the sales team, providing them with functional tools to enhance their operations.

Facilitating Feedback Loops

Once the sales team has had an opportunity to interact with the new system, their feedback is gathered. This feedback is invaluable in making iterative improvements to the system and also plays a crucial role in shaping the next increment aimed at optimizing the customer service department.

Early Business Benefit Realized

By strategically releasing the sales-related functionalities ahead of the full project completion, the company achieves an early win by augmenting the sales process. This not only delivers immediate value but also fortifies stakeholder confidence in the project's potential for success.

Remaining Agile

As the development proceeds in these manageable increments, the project has the latitude to adapt to any emerging changes in business priorities, technological advancements, or unforeseen challenges, making it resilient and responsive.

In Summary

Through its staged, incremental approach built upon clearly defined foundational elements, the project adheres closely to business requirements. More importantly, by enabling early utilization and ongoing refinements, it offers a spectrum of benefits across different phases of its lifecycle. This amplifies stakeholder confidence and aligns the project seamlessly with organizational objectives, substantiating the efficacy of the "Build Incrementally from Firm Foundations" principle.

Develop Iteratively: A Deep Dive

Overview

The "Develop Iteratively" principle is a cornerstone of the DSDM framework, advocating that the journey to the perfect solution is usually paved with cycles of development and refinement. The primary advantage of an iterative development process is that it creates room for ongoing alignment with business objectives, thus ensuring the solution is not just technically feasible, but also business-relevant.

Components of Iterative Development

The Iterative Process

Iterative development is a dynamic process of recurring revisits and refinements to various aspects of a solution. With each cycle, the solution is adjusted and perfected, edging it closer to the ultimate goal. This method of incremental improvements allows for a highly adaptive and responsive project structure.

Frequent Demonstrations

Conducting regular demonstrations of the solution's current state serves multiple purposes. It provides stakeholders with a tangible understanding of the project's progress, facilitating more informed discussions. Moreover, it can be a crucial tool for identifying any misunderstandings, gaps, or emerging requirements.

Comprehensive Review

The cycle of each iteration concludes with a thorough review that assesses the developed solution against the established business goals and objectives. This step is critical for confirming alignment and directing future development efforts.

Feedback-Driven Model

Feedback acts as the cornerstone of iterative development. It is gathered from various sources—be it end-users, stakeholders, or team members—and is used to inform changes in the subsequent iterations, keeping the project perpetually aligned with business objectives.

Embracing Change

Understanding and accepting that change is not only inevitable but also valuable is an integral part of this principle. As projects evolve and business landscapes shift, an iterative approach allows for the necessary flexibility to adapt and remain relevant.

Convergence on the Optimal Solution

The cyclic nature of iterative development leads to a gradual convergence on the most effective and relevant solution. This results in a solution that is not just functional but also finely tuned to meet the needs of the business throughout the project lifecycle.

In Conclusion

The "Develop Iteratively" principle is a testament to the importance of a dynamic and adaptive approach, one that embraces ongoing refinements and frequent stakeholder feedback. It fosters a development environment where the project is continually optimized to remain aligned with the ever-changing needs and objectives of the business.

The Power of Iterative Development: A Practical Example

In the context of a financial institution aiming to develop a new mobile banking application, the principle of "Develop Iteratively" manifests itself through multiple development cycles. Each of these cycles adds new layers of functionality and refinement to the app.

First Iteration: Laying the Groundwork

In the initial phase, the team focuses on building basic functionalities such as checking account balances and enabling money transfers. This iteration serves as a baseline that fulfills the most essential user needs.

Feedback and Refinement

After a demonstration of the first iteration to stakeholders and potential users, feedback reveals an additional requirement: the users express a desire for a feature that allows them to set and monitor savings goals.

Second Iteration: Meeting Evolving Needs

Incorporating this feedback, the next iteration involves the development of the "Savings Goals" feature. This additional layer enriches the app's value proposition and brings it closer to user preferences.

Subsequent Iterations and Further Refinement

Later reviews and feedback loops indicate yet another user requirement—insights into spending patterns. Consequently, future iterations focus on developing an analytics dashboard that provides users with spending insights.

Final Product

By the time the app is ready for market launch, it's not just a transactional tool but a comprehensive financial management platform that aligns closely with the users' needs and preferences. It exemplifies how iterative development leads to a product that is both functional and finely attuned to user expectations.

Concluding Thoughts

This practical example illustrates how the "Develop Iteratively" principle aids in the creation of a product that isn't just built to specifications, but evolves to meet emerging needs. The iterative process, underpinned by regular feedback and comprehensive reviews, ensures that the app remains aligned with business objectives and user expectations throughout its development lifecycle.

The Art of Seamless Communication in DSDM Projects: A Closer Look

Continuous Flow of Information: The Lifeline of a Project

In a rapidly changing environment, timely and frequent communication is indispensable. Constant updates on project developments keep all stakeholders in the loop, enabling more informed decision-making. This is particularly vital in DSDM projects, which often require rapid responses to emerging challenges or opportunities.

The Nuance of Clarity

Merely sending out messages is not effective communication; the clarity of those messages is equally critical. Clear and unambiguous communication minimizes misunderstandings and sets the stage for more effective collaboration. It ensures that stakeholders not only receive information but understand it in the context in which it was intended.

Two-Way Dialogue: A Symbiotic Relationship

Effective communication is not a one-way street. It should involve a two-way dialogue that incorporates feedback from all parties involved. Establishing feedback loops helps clarify uncertainties, provides valuable insights, and maintains alignment between business and technical teams.

The Power of Visual Aids

While words can convey meaning, visual aids like flowcharts, diagrams, or mock-ups can often do so more succinctly. They offer a tangible focal point for discussions, enabling stakeholders to visualize complex scenarios or interrelationships more easily.

The Primacy of Face-to-Face Interaction

Though written and electronic communication are useful, there is no substitute for face-to-face interactions when possible. Such engagements allow for immediate feedback, foster stronger interpersonal relationships, and create an environment conducive to collaborative problem-solving.

Inclusive Communication: Leaving No One Behind

DSDM's emphasis on comprehensive communication ensures that all stakeholders, from developers to end-users, are continuously engaged and have a clear understanding of the project's objectives and status. This fosters a sense of ownership and commitment, making the journey towards project completion more collaborative and efficient.

Conclusion

The principle of "Communicate Continuously and Clearly" isn't just an ancillary part of DSDM projects; it's a cornerstone. It establishes a framework for consistent, clear, and collaborative dialogue among all stakeholders. This facilitates a unified vision and a well-coordinated approach, factors that are instrumental in driving the project to its successful completion.

Diving Into Real-World Communication in DSDM: A Practical Insight

Setting the Scene

Consider a project that aims to overhaul a company's e-commerce platform. The stakeholders are diverse, encompassing teams from marketing, sales, IT, and customer support. The project has an ambitious goal: to enhance user experience, streamline navigation, and integrate advanced analytics.

Daily Stand-ups: A Dev Team Ritual

As the development team dives into the work, they maintain a ritual of daily stand-up meetings. These brief, focused discussions allow the team to share what they accomplished the previous day, what they plan to work on next, and any challenges they are facing. This continuous communication loop enables quick problem-solving and keeps everyone aligned with the project's pace and direction.

Marketing' s Role: Regular Pulse Checks

The marketing team isn't just a passive recipient of updates; they also provide feedback based on customer preferences and market trends. This information is invaluable for aligning the platform's features with real-world needs.

Prototyping and Demonstrations: Tangible Milestones

Midway through the project, a prototype of the new platform is ready. It is then presented to the stakeholders in a highly interactive session. Visual aids and demos serve to make the presentation more engaging, facilitating richer feedback and more meaningful conversations.

Keeping Everyone in the Loop: Townhalls and Workshops

To make sure that the broader organization is aligned, regular townhall meetings and workshops are organized. These sessions serve multiple purposes: they update everyone on the project's progress, allow for broader organizational input, and serve as a forum for addressing any concerns that may arise.

Final Thoughts

By the time the e-commerce platform is ready for launch, a robust communication strategy has ensured that every department within the company not only understands the new features but also appreciates the benefits they will bring. This unified understanding is not just a byproduct of effective communication; it is a critical success factor that has been cultivated deliberately.

This practical example illustrates how the principle of "Communicate Continuously and Clearly" can serve as a linchpin for successful project execution, ensuring that all stakeholders are informed, aligned, and engaged from inception to completion.

The Essence of Demonstrating Control in DSDM Projects

What Demonstrating Control Entails

The principle of "Demonstrate Control" focuses on managing and monitoring a project scrupulously to ensure it aligns with its objectives, optimally utilizes resources, and effectively manages risks. This principle goes beyond just maintaining control; it also entails displaying that control transparently to stakeholders, thereby fostering trust, accountability, and confidence in the project's success.

Pillars of Control

High-level Plans and Designs

The foundation of control lies in planning. High-level plans and designs act as the architectural blueprint of a project. They delineate what needs to be achieved and lay down the parameters within which the team should operate. These plans are essential for setting the vision, defining objectives, and marking key milestones.

Regular Monitoring and Reporting

Ongoing surveillance and evaluation of a project's status compared to its plans are crucial. Regular updates and reports act as a barometer of control, offering stakeholders an evidence-based look at how well the project is progressing.

Risk Management

A project without risk management is like a ship without a compass. Continually identifying, assessing, and mitigating risks ensures that the project stays its course and reaches its destination. It's a way of demonstrating control over the uncertainties that any project inevitably faces.

Transparent Work Practices

Transparency breeds trust. Employing transparent operational practices ensures that all stakeholders have a clear understanding of the project's status. Tools like dashboards, team boards, and burn-down charts serve as visual aids to represent the project's state clearly and objectively.

Feedback and Adjustments

Control isn't rigid; it's adaptable. Seeking feedback and making real-time adjustments assures stakeholders that the project isn't just on autopilot but is being actively managed to meet its objectives.

Stakeholder Engagement

Consistent engagement with all stakeholders—end-users, sponsors, team members—provides opportunities for displaying control. Platforms such as demonstrations, reviews, and retrospectives offer windows into the project's progress and governance.

Final Thoughts

In summary, the "Demonstrate Control" principle places great emphasis on the active and transparent management of the project, ensuring that it stays aligned with its objectives, utilizes resources judiciously, and manages risks effectively. It is a cornerstone for building stakeholder confidence and ensuring a project's successful outcome.

Demonstrating Control in Action: A Practical Example

The Project Scenario

Let's consider a healthcare organization aiming to develop a telemedicine platform. The high-level plan outlines key functionalities like video consultations, prescription management, and electronic medical records, along with user experience benchmarks and a stringent launch deadline due to increased demand for remote healthcare services.

Control Mechanisms in Play

Planning and Milestones

The project team lays out a roadmap that sets milestones for each major functionality. These serve as guideposts for assessing whether the project is on track and for demonstrating control to stakeholders.

Weekly Demonstrations

Each week, the project team showcases the current state of the telemedicine platform. This not only serves to keep stakeholders in the loop but also as a tangible means of displaying control over the project's development.

Risk Register

A continuously updated risk register is maintained, listing potential challenges like compliance with healthcare regulations, data security concerns, and technical difficulties. This register is reviewed in stakeholder meetings, showcasing the team's control over possible project risks.

Transparency through Dashboards

An online dashboard accessible to all stakeholders provides real-time information on project status, budget utilization, and risks. This transparency serves as a demonstration of control, showing that nothing is being hidden and that the project is in capable hands.

Customer Beta Testing

As the project nears completion, a beta version is tested among a select group of healthcare providers and patients. The feedback collected leads to final tweaks, ensuring the platform meets user needs and industry standards.

Concluding Insights

By consistently employing these control mechanisms, the healthcare organization demonstrates effective project governance, earning stakeholders' trust and confidence. When the telemedicine platform eventually launches, it meets the stringent deadlines, adheres to industry regulations, and satisfies both healthcare providers and patients—all indicators of a project well-controlled.

The "Demonstrate Control" principle, in this case, proves crucial in not only guiding the project towards its intended goals but also in validating that direction for all those involved. It's an affirmation that good control mechanisms are more than just a managerial necessity; they're a lynchpin for project success.

Chapter Three

Preparing for Success: A Proactive Approach to Implementation

The Essence and Implications of Embracing the DSDM Approach

The Dynamic Systems Development Method (DSDM) is an agile project management framework that places a premium on flexibility, collaboration, and a keen focus on achieving concrete business objectives. By marrying traditional and agile best practices, DSDM aims to provide a holistic approach to project management.

Key Tenets of DSDM

Alignment with Business Goals

Under DSDM, projects are not just about technological achievements; they are strategically aligned to serve business objectives. The premise is that technology should be a means to an end, not an end in itself.

Frequent Deliveries

DSDM advocates for frequent, incremental deliveries of usable products. This provides stakeholders with tangible evidence of progress and allows for early feedback, contributing to a more refined final output.

Empowered Collaboration

This approach relies on the collective competence of team members who are not just technically skilled but also empowered to make decisions. This encourages ownership and accountability.

Acceptance of Sub-Optimal Solutions

DSDM recognizes the reality that waiting for a 'perfect' solution might lead to missed opportunities. Instead, it promotes delivering the 'good enough' that meets immediate needs and aligns with current business objectives.

Advantages and Practical Implications

Increased Stakeholder Satisfaction

When projects are tightly aligned with business objectives, the probability of meeting or exceeding stakeholder expectations is high.

Adaptability and Responsiveness

The iterative cycles of DSDM provide room for quick adjustments, enabling organizations to better adapt to changes in technology, market dynamics, or stakeholder requirements.

Risk Management

Early deliveries mean that risks are identified and dealt with at an earlier stage, thus offering better risk mitigation strategies.

Efficient Resource Utilization

The collaboration of empowered and competent individuals ensures that resources are utilized in the most effective manner, aligning directly with project goals.

Enhanced Communication

DSDM fosters a culture of clear and continuous communication, creating a shared understanding among all stakeholders.

Challenges in Adopting DSDM

Need for a Mindset Change

The shift from traditional to agile practices involves a cultural change, particularly in the acceptance of less-than-perfect yet value-adding solutions.

Empowerment Challenges

Hierarchical organizations may find it difficult to embrace the level of team empowerment that DSDM necessitates.

Frequency Overload

The rapid cycles of delivery and feedback may be overwhelming for teams or stakeholders accustomed to a more linear, waterfall approach.

Conclusion

Adopting the DSDM approach is not without its challenges, including shifts in mindset and operational adjustments. However, its potential benefits—such as increased stakeholder satisfaction, greater adaptability, and efficient resource utilization—make it a compelling choice for organizations aiming to be more agile and responsive to business needs.

Would you like this elaborated through a practical example or case study?

Practical Illustration of the DSDM Approach in Action

Setting the Scene

Suppose a financial institution aims to digitize its customer service operations. The project involves creating an AI-driven chatbot that can handle customer queries, thereby reducing the workload on human agents and increasing efficiency. Senior management, IT experts, customer service representatives, and even some selected customers are identified as key stakeholders.

Application of DSDM Principles

Aligning with Business Goals

From the outset, the project is aligned with specific business objectives: to improve customer satisfaction rates and reduce operational costs in customer service.

Frequent Deliveries

The project is broken down into several sprints, each focused on developing specific functionalities of the chatbot. After each sprint, a working version is shared with stakeholders for feedback.

Collaboration of Empowered Teams

A cross-functional team comprising software developers, data scientists, and customer service experts is formed. This team is empowered to make significant decisions regarding the project, without waiting for higher managerial approval.

Accepting Sub-Optimal Solutions

Initial versions of the chatbot may not be able to handle all types of queries but can deal with the most frequent ones. Instead of waiting for a version that can handle all possible queries, the initial 'good enough' versions are rolled out.

Advantages Realized

Stakeholder Satisfaction

The early and incremental releases ensure that stakeholders see real progress. This constant visibility increases confidence in the project.

Adaptability

The chatbot's design evolves based on the feedback from the sprints. When a sudden regulatory change occurs requiring stricter data handling, the project can adapt quickly.

Risk Management

The frequent check-ins and stakeholder feedback loops enable early identification of potential bottlenecks or issues, allowing for timely remediation.

Resource Optimization

The project utilizes both technological and human resources efficiently. For instance, customer service agents whose workload is reduced by the chatbot are reskilled to handle more complex customer issues.

Clear Communication

Regular status updates, sprint reviews, and stakeholder meetings ensure everyone has a clear understanding of what is happening, thereby adhering to DSDM's principle of clear and continuous communication.

Conclusion

In this example, the DSDM approach provided the structure, flexibility, and stakeholder engagement necessary to make the project a success. The organization was able to meet its business objectives while remaining agile, thus validating the effectiveness of DSDM as a project management methodology.

Building an Effective Solution Development Team in DSDM: A Comprehensive Guide

In the realm of Dynamic Systems Development Method (DSDM), the Solution Development Team serves as the bedrock of project success. As the entity responsible for transforming ideas into deliverables, its effectiveness is paramount. This guide explores key principles that define an effective Solution Development Team within the DSDM framework.

Principle 1: Empowerment of the Solution Development Team

Overview

Empowerment within DSDM is centered on granting the team the autonomy to make decisions related to their domain and within the purview of the project's foundational agreements.

Significance

Speed

Empowerment accelerates decision-making processes, positively impacting project timelines.

Ownership & Accountability

Empowerment nurtures a sense of responsibility and ownership, augmenting team commitment and dedication.

Expertise Utilization

By empowering team members in their areas of expertise, the project benefits from optimal decision-making.

Principle 2: Stability of the Solution Development Team

Overview

Stability, as emphasized by DSDM, discourages frequent rotations of team members, which can disturb the team's rhythm and introduce inefficiencies.

Significance

Continuous Communication

A stable team enhances the communication flow, an indispensable attribute in agile environments.

Cohesiveness & Trust

Stability fosters mutual trust and camaraderie, crucial for cohesive team operations.

Consistent Progression

A stable team mitigates knowledge gaps, ensuring a more consistent project progression.

Principle 3: Skills within the Solution Development Team

Overview

DSDM promotes a balanced skill set within the team, without mandating a "jack-of-all-trades" requirement for each member.

Significance

Holistic Development

A balanced skill set ensures comprehensive solution development, covering all facets of the project.

Flexibility & Adaptability

A variety of skills allows the team to adapt to changing requirements or unforeseen challenges.

Collaborative Synergy

Each team member's unique skills contribute to a synergistic problem-solving approach.

Principle 4: Size of the Solution Development Team

Overview

DSDM proposes an ideal team size of seven members, allowing for a deviation of two. For larger needs, multiple teams are recommended.

Significance

Efficient Communication

Smaller teams simplify communication, minimizing the risks of misinterpretation or oversight.

Team Dynamics

A smaller group allows for better coordination and understanding among team members.

Manageability

A more compact team size facilitates easier oversight and efficient management.

Conclusion

Creating an effective Solution Development Team is a nuanced task that requires a well-calibrated blend of empowerment, stability, skill diversity, and optimal size. Adhering to these DSDM principles offers a robust framework for assembling a team that is not only competent but also committed to achieving project success.

Case Study: Implementing the Principles for an Effective Solution Development Team in a DSDM Project

Background

Let's consider a hypothetical scenario involving the development of an e-commerce platform. The project aligns with key business objectives, including boosting online sales and enhancing user experience. For this project, the organization adopts the DSDM framework, focusing on forming an effective Solution Development Team.

Applying Principle 1: Empowerment of the Solution Development Team

Actions Taken

The team is empowered to make critical decisions within their domain, such as choosing technology stacks and determining feature priorities.

Outcome

Empowerment fosters a quicker decision-making process, and team members display increased ownership and dedication to their tasks.

Applying Principle 2: Stability of the Solution Development Team

Actions Taken

The core team remains unchanged throughout the project duration, with members only being replaced under extreme circumstances.

Outcome

Stability ensures that the team builds a strong communication framework, fostering mutual trust, which significantly contributes to project consistency and progression.

Applying Principle 3: Skills within the Solution Development Team

Actions Taken

The team is composed of members with a balanced skill set, including front-end and back-end developers, a UX designer, and a data analyst.

Outcome

This diversity enables the team to address the project's needs holistically. When unforeseen challenges arise, the varied skill set allows the team to adapt rapidly.

Applying Principle 4: Size of the Solution Development Team

Actions Taken

The team size is kept within the DSDM recommended range of 5 to 9 members. For this project, a team of seven was chosen.

Outcome

The chosen team size proves to be manageable and facilitates efficient communication. The team works cohesively, and each member understands their role clearly.

Conclusion

By adhering to DSDM principles, the Solution Development Team successfully develops and launches the e-commerce platform within the stipulated timeline and budget, meeting all key business objectives. The effectiveness of the team was significantly boosted by empowering members, maintaining stability, ensuring a balanced skill set, and optimizing team size.

Amplifying the Role of Business Engagement in DSDM Projects

The Dynamic Systems Development Method (DSDM) mandates a multi-dimensional approach to project management, and at the forefront of this approach is business engagement. Unlike traditional frameworks where business input may be primarily front-loaded or sporadic, DSDM insists on sustained and active business engagement as a critical success factor. This article delves into the nuances and critical aspects of business engagement in DSDM projects, shedding light on its various tenets and implications.

Tenet 1: Commitment of Business Time Throughout

Overview

The principle of "Commitment of Business Time Throughout" does not merely imply token representation of business stakeholders in project meetings. It demands sustained, active engagement from the project's inception to completion.

Significance

Direction & Vision

A project not aligned with business objectives is akin to a ship without a compass. Continuous business involvement acts as this compass, ensuring that the project sails in the direction intended by the business.

Stakeholder Buy-in

Sustained commitment from business stakeholders ensures continuous resource allocation and circumvents roadblocks, as these stakeholders act as project champions within the larger business ecosystem.

Anticipating Changes

An agile environment is characterized by flux. A project may need to change course based on emerging business requirements. Active business involvement aids in preemptively identifying these shifts and planning for them.

Tenet 2: Active Involvement of Business Roles

Overview

DSDM stipulates that it's not just the project managers or business analysts who need to be involved; various business roles must participate actively throughout the project.

Significance

Real-time Feedback

When diverse business roles are involved, it creates an immediate feedback mechanism, ensuring that the project output remains continually calibrated to business needs.

Skill Leveraging

DSDM projects often require multifaceted expertise. Active involvement of professionals from different business roles ensures a composite skill set, conducive for resolving complex issues that may arise.

Ensuring Quality

Quality is not an isolated phase but an ongoing process. Constant business participation ensures that the project output meets the desired quality benchmarks.

Tenet 3: Supportive Commercial Relationship

Overview

In instances where external vendors or partners are involved, DSDM emphasizes the need for supportive commercial relationships, which are inherently designed to foster collaboration.

Significance

Facilitating Collaboration

A collaborative commercial agreement not only sets the stage for mutual benefits but also eliminates roadblocks that typically occur due to rigid contractual obligations.

Flexibility

Agile frameworks like DSDM require room for change. A supportive commercial relationship facilitates this by allowing changes to be made without complex administrative hurdles.

Trust & Transparency

In the agile world, trust and transparency aren't just buzzwords; they are necessities. A harmonious commercial relationship fosters these elements, making it easier to navigate the complexities of agile projects.

Conclusion

Business engagement in DSDM is not an optional feature but an integral part of the framework's DNA. Through continuous commitment, multi-role involvement, and supportive commercial relationships, DSDM projects achieve a level of synergy and alignment with business objectives that sets them apart from projects managed using more traditional methods.

Case Study: Transforming Business Engagement in a Financial Services DSDM Project

In a leading financial services organization, the implementation of a new customer relationship management (CRM) system was conducted using the DSDM framework. The project was initially facing challenges in alignment with business objectives and timely delivery. However, the active and consistent engagement of business stakeholders transformed the project into a success story. Below are the aspects of business engagement that played a pivotal role.

Tenet 1: Commitment of Business Time Throughout

How It Was Applied

Key stakeholders from the business side were identified early on, and their calendars were booked for all critical project meetings, reviews, and decision-making processes.

Impact

Direction & Vision

The constant presence of business stakeholders ensured that every aspect of the CRM system was in line with the strategic objectives of the financial services organization.

Stakeholder Buy-in

Because stakeholders were continuously involved, there was never a shortage of resources or internal support for the project.

Anticipating Changes

Being in the financial services sector, compliance requirements could change rapidly. The business stakeholders were crucial in signaling any such changes in real-time.

Tenet 2: Active Involvement of Business Roles

How It Was Applied

Beyond executives and project managers, personnel from sales, customer service, and compliance were also roped in for regular project involvement.

Impact

Real-time Feedback

Having multiple business roles involved led to a comprehensive feedback mechanism, ensuring that the CRM system was robust and covered all bases.

Skill Leveraging

Each department contributed its expertise, making the CRM system more holistic and aligned with diverse business functions.

Ensuring Quality

Regular involvement of diverse business roles made quality checks more stringent and relevant.

Tenet 3: Supportive Commercial Relationship

How It Was Applied

The contract with the CRM system vendor was designed to be flexible, with room for changes and iterations.

Impact

Facilitating Collaboration

The flexible contract enabled both the organization and the vendor to work as partners rather than mere client and supplier.

Flexibility

The contract allowed for changes in project scope and requirements without invoking complex change management processes.

Trust & Transparency

Because the commercial relationship was built on trust and flexibility, the entire project could proceed more smoothly and efficiently.

Conclusion

The financial services organization successfully implemented its CRM system, thanks to the robust business engagement as mandated by the DSDM framework. By investing time, involving diverse roles, and fostering a collaborative commercial relationship, the project not only met but exceeded business expectations.

Amplifying Success Through Iterative Development, Integrated Testing, and Incremental Delivery in DSDM

Dynamic Systems Development Method (DSDM) encapsulates a set of best practices designed to deliver efficient and effective software solutions. Among its key tenets are Iterative Development, Integrated Testing, and Incremental Delivery. These are not standalone concepts but tightly interwoven strategies aimed at enhancing project outcomes. Below is an elaborative discussion on these core principles.

1. Iterative Development

Overview

Iterative Development in DSDM is not merely a repetitive act but a structured methodology where each iteration contributes to a progressively refined end product.

Significance

Feedback Loops

Iterative Development encourages constant feedback from users and stakeholders, thereby ensuring that the solution evolves to meet business needs precisely.

Risk Management

The iterative nature of DSDM allows teams to identify problems and challenges early on, enabling proactive risk management measures.

Enhanced Quality

Because the solution undergoes multiple cycles of design, development, and testing, it gets refined and optimized with each iteration, leading to a high-quality end product.

2. Integrated Testing

Overview

Unlike traditional approaches that treat testing as a distinct phase, DSDM incorporates testing as an integral part of the development lifecycle.

Significance

Continual Verification

Integrated testing signifies that every piece of code is continually verified against pre-defined quality criteria, ensuring a high standard of product integrity.

Cost and Time Effective

Catching defects early on eliminates the expensive and time-consuming process of redoing large sections of the project at a later stage.

Boosts Confidence

Regular testing cycles instill confidence among stakeholders as they can witness the solution meeting quality and functional requirements in real-time.

3. Incremental Delivery

Overview

DSDM champions the delivery of the solution in manageable increments, each contributing tangible value to the business.

Significance

Early ROI

The ability to deploy usable features early in the project lifecycle enables the business to realize a quicker return on investment.

User Feedback

Small, usable increments allow for real-world user testing, which can be invaluable in guiding the development of subsequent features.

Adaptability

Incremental delivery makes it easier for the project to adapt to changing business requirements, thereby maximizing its responsiveness and agility.

Conclusion

The emphasis on Iterative Development, Integrated Testing, and Incremental Delivery in the DSDM framework forms a trifecta that significantly contributes to project success. This strategic trio fosters quality, adaptability, and timeliness, aligning closely with both the technical and business objectives. Organizations employing DSDM are thus better equipped to deliver high-quality solutions that yield immediate and long-term business value.

Case Study: Implementing DSDM Principles in a Financial Services Project

Context

A leading financial services company embarked on a project to overhaul its existing customer management system. Given the competitive nature of the financial industry and the high expectations for system reliability and user experience, the company adopted the DSDM framework. The focus here will be on how the principles of Iterative Development, Integrated Testing, and Incremental Delivery were meticulously applied.

Iterative Development in Action

Scoping and Feedback Loops

The project commenced with a discovery phase, resulting in a prototype that encapsulated core features. This prototype underwent a series of iterations based on stakeholder feedback, which helped refine its functionality and interface.

Risk Management

Each iteration also included a formal risk assessment, during which any issues with scalability, security, or data integrity were flagged and addressed.

Ensuring Quality

As the prototype progressed through successive iterations, features were not merely added but refined, resulting in a robust system optimized for both performance and user experience.

Integrated Testing Unveiled

Continuous Testing Cycle

An automated testing suite was integrated into the development environment. Every code check-in triggered a battery of tests, ranging from unit tests to complex system simulations.

Real-Time Issue Resolution

By integrating testing, the development team was able to catch defects early, significantly reducing the cost and complexity of late-stage fixes.

Confidence Building

Each successful test cycle was communicated to stakeholders, reinforcing their confidence in the system's reliability and functionality.

Mastering Incremental Delivery

Phase-wise Rollout

Instead of a single, monolithic release, the system was rolled out in phases, beginning with a limited set of features.

Early Benefit Realization

The phased approach allowed end-users to start realizing the benefits of the new system, even while other features were still in development.

Adaptability in Deployment

As each phase was rolled out, user feedback and real-world usage data were collected. These insights were invaluable in shaping the next set of features to be developed.

Conclusion

The application of Iterative Development, Integrated Testing, and Incremental Delivery within the DSDM framework ensured that the financial services company could navigate complex business and technical landscapes. The project was not only completed within time and budget but also exceeded stakeholder expectations in terms of functionality, reliability, and user experience.

This case study serves as a testament to the efficacy of DSDM's key principles in driving project success, mitigating risks, and delivering exceptional business value.

Amplifying the Role of Transparency in DSDM Projects

Transparency in DSDM projects is not an optional element; rather, it's a core tenet that enriches the fabric of project execution and stakeholder engagement. The focus on transparency performs specific functions and provides a myriad of benefits that can significantly impact the outcome of a project. Let's delve deeper into its facets.

Significance of Transparency in DSDM Projects

Trust as a Cornerstone

Transparency serves as a powerful catalyst in building trust among stakeholders, team members, and project sponsors. By eliminating ambiguity, it minimizes the room for speculation and mistrust, thereby creating a foundation of credibility upon which the project can thrive.

Decision-Making Grounded in Facts

Transparency also ensures that stakeholders have access to real-time data, thereby providing the necessary informational substratum for more nuanced and prompt decision-making.

Promoting Enhanced Collaboration

With open communication channels and the clear visibility of work, team members can actively collaborate to resolve challenges and mitigate risks.

Cultivating Accountability and Ownership

Lastly, by clearly delineating roles, responsibilities, and expectations, transparency fosters a sense of accountability and ownership among project participants.

Tools and Practices to Foster Transparency

Demonstrative Power of the Evolving Solution

Regular demonstrations at the end of each Timebox not only validate the work done but also serve as platforms for stakeholders to assess progress and offer valuable feedback.

Utility of Team Boards

Visual boards serve as an immediate snapshot of the project's pulse, depicting ongoing tasks, their status, and any potential bottlenecks or challenges.

The Importance of Daily Stand-ups

These meetings act as pivotal junctures for real-time information sharing among team members. They foster open communication, facilitate immediate problem-solving, and keep everyone aligned with project objectives.

Linkage with Principle 8 - "Demonstration of Control"

Early Mitigation of Risks

By maintaining transparent processes, potential risks are identified at an earlier stage, thus facilitating timely preventive or corrective actions.

Heightened Stakeholder Engagement

Transparency feeds into stakeholders' comfort and trust, encouraging their continued engagement and support throughout the project lifecycle.

Driving Operational Efficiency

Clear visibility into the project's state allows for more efficient allocation of resources, thereby increasing operational effectiveness.

Conclusion

In summary, transparency in DSDM projects is not just a good practice but an indispensable tenet. It enriches stakeholder relationships, fine-tunes decision-making, and optimizes operational efficiency. More than just a way to keep everyone informed, it is a strategic lever that helps steer projects towards successful outcomes.

Case Study: Implementing Transparency in a DSDM Project for a Financial Institution

Background

A major financial institution decided to upgrade its customer relationship management (CRM) system and chose the DSDM framework for project execution. The size and complexity of the project, along with a diverse set of stakeholders, made transparency an essential component for its success.

Utilizing Tools and Practices

Team Boards

The project team implemented visual team boards that were digitally accessible to all stakeholders. This enabled real-time tracking of tasks and helped in identifying bottlenecks early, thereby allowing for prompt corrective actions.

Daily Stand-ups

Daily stand-up meetings were held without fail. These were brief, focused, and ensured that each team member was aware of the project's current status, challenges faced, and action plans.

Demonstrations

At the end of each Timebox, a demonstration was organized to showcase the evolving solution. This acted as a factual progress report and allowed stakeholders to provide immediate feedback.

Outcomes

Trust and Stakeholder Engagement

The transparency measures established trust among stakeholders and kept them actively engaged. Their feedback during the demonstrations often provided invaluable insights that helped refine the project's direction.

Efficient Risk Mitigation

Potential issues were identified early due to the transparent procedures, and appropriate mitigation plans were promptly activated. This early identification reduced the severity and impact of risks on the project.

Improved Decision-Making

The availability of real-time data enabled stakeholders and the project management team to make informed decisions swiftly, keeping the project aligned with its objectives.

Conclusion

In this case, the focus on transparency not only kept stakeholders engaged but also created an environment conducive to proactive problem-solving and effective decision-making. The experience demonstrated that transparency is not merely a procedural requirement but a strategic asset in DSDM projects.

A Deep Dive into the Project Approach Questionnaire (PAQ) in DSDM

The Project Approach Questionnaire (PAQ) is not merely an optional tool but a cornerstone in the DSDM framework. Its importance lies in its structured design to evaluate multiple facets of a project, offering insights into whether the chosen approach aligns with DSDM principles, potential risks, and viable action plans.

Objectives Unpacked

Assess Project Alignment

The PAQ serves as a litmus test for ensuring that the project's goals, resources, and methodologies align with DSDM principles. This initial alignment sets the stage for how well the rest of the project will follow the DSDM framework.

Identify Risks Early

Early identification of risks offers a preemptive strike capability. The PAQ ensures that potential challenges, whether they pertain to resources, stakeholders, or methodologies, are highlighted before they escalate into significant roadblocks.

Foundation for the Foundations Phase

DSDM's Foundations phase serves as a blueprint for the project. The PAQ feeds into this phase, providing much-needed clarity and direction that influence the overall development and delivery plans.

Key Areas Scrutinized

Project Environment

The PAQ goes beyond a superficial examination to delve into the stability, resource availability, and stakeholder structure of the project environment. These insights enable better resource planning and stakeholder engagement strategies.

Business Commitment

In DSDM, the business side is not just an observer but an active participant. The PAQ evaluates the degree of business commitment, which is often crucial for the successful implementation of agile principles.

Technological Compatibility

The flexibility and adaptability of the technology stack in use are assessed. This ensures that the project's technology is conducive to the iterative and incremental nature of DSDM.

The PAQ Process

Initiation and Re-assessment

The PAQ is initially filled out during the Feasibility phase and revisited at the end of the Foundations phase. This two-tiered approach allows for ongoing alignment and course corrections.

Outcome-Driven

The PAQ culminates in a set of actionable insights. Whether it is affirming the alignment with DSDM, identifying challenges, or proposing changes, the PAQ sets the tone for the project's trajectory.

Conclusion

The Project Approach Questionnaire (PAQ) is a potent strategic tool that brings method to the agile madness in DSDM projects. By assessing alignment, pinpointing risks, and helping to shape the Foundations phase, it adds multiple layers of safeguards and clarity, aiming for a successful project outcome.

The Vitality of PAQ in a DSDM Project: A Case Study

Introduction

While the theoretical underpinnings of the Project Approach Questionnaire (PAQ) are well-established, its practical application further substantiates its significance. This case study outlines a real-world project scenario where the PAQ was used as a pivotal tool in the DSDM methodology.

Project Background

The project in question aimed to develop a cutting-edge e-commerce platform for a fashion retail giant. The development process was scheduled to span eight months and involved various stakeholders, including product managers, developers, and marketing teams.

The Role of the PAQ

Initial Assessment

At the Feasibility phase, the PAQ identified several potential risks, including unclear business commitment and technology stack incompatibility. These early insights led the team to reevaluate their approach before moving forward.

Foundations Phase Re-assessment

The PAQ was revisited at the end of the Foundations phase, confirming that the previously identified risks had been mitigated. It also provided additional insights into resource allocation for the remaining phases.

Outcomes

Aligned Objectives

The PAQ helped align the project objectives with DSDM principles, leading to a more structured and effective approach.

Mitigated Risks

Thanks to the early identification of potential challenges, the project team was able to proactively address these issues, averting major roadblocks.

Informed Stakeholders

The PAQ played a vital role in keeping all stakeholders informed and aligned, thereby fostering a collaborative and transparent environment.

Conclusion

The application of the PAQ in this project not only substantiated its theoretical significance but demonstrated its practical utility. It acted as a crucial navigational tool that guided the project through its various phases, ensuring alignment with DSDM principles, effective risk management, and stakeholder alignment.

Chapter Four

Navigating the Process: A Detailed Guide

Overview of DSDM: Aligning Business Value, Iterative Development, and Integrated Project Management

Dynamic Systems Development Method (DSDM) stands as a stalwart in the realm of Agile methodologies. Its unique features and flexibility make it a comprehensive tool for modern projects that require an intricate blend of business alignment, iterative development, and seamless project management.

Philosophical Foundation

The guiding philosophy of DSDM is deeply rooted in delivering optimal business value. The method emphasizes aligning the project with well-articulated business objectives while fostering a collaborative environment. Unlike some other methodologies that focus mainly on task completion or technical challenges, DSDM places a premium on achieving business outcomes through iterative and incremental approaches. It does so by prioritizing the most critical business requirements for immediate attention, thus maximizing early returns and stakeholder satisfaction.

Unique Features of DSDM

Integrated Framework

What sets DSDM apart is its integrated framework, which accommodates both project management and product development under a single umbrella. This cohesiveness allows for an unparalleled synergy between various project components, thereby ensuring a more harmonized and efficient delivery process.

Compatibility with Other Frameworks

Another compelling feature of DSDM is its designed compatibility with other methodologies, such as PRINCE2 and PMI, as well as software engineering practices like eXtreme Programming (XP). This adaptability makes it an excellent choice for organizations with existing processes and governance models, providing them the agility they require without mandating a complete overhaul of existing systems.

Process Model as a Baseline

The DSDM process model serves not as a rigid structure but as a flexible template. It delineates the key phases and their interconnections, offering a standardized yet customizable roadmap. Each project can tailor this baseline model to suit its unique requirements and constraints, making DSDM a truly adaptable framework.

Practical Example: Financial Services Platform Modernization

Without diving into details, a project of this nature underscores the multifaceted utility of DSDM. The integrated framework would be invaluable in juggling the diverse aspects of such a project, including software development and inter-departmental change management. Moreover, if the organization is already employing other project management frameworks, DSDM can be seamlessly integrated, proving its interoperability and enhancing overall project governance.

Conclusion

DSDM emerges as a comprehensive framework capable of tackling the complexities and uncertainties inherent in modern projects. Its focus on aligning projects closely with business goals, coupled with its seamless integration of project management and product development processes, sets it apart. Additionally, its compatibility with other frameworks and methodologies enhances its adaptability, solidifying its position as a robust choice for organizations that seek a balanced, flexible approach to project management and product development.

Case Study: Leveraging DSDM for a Healthcare Digital Transformation Project

Background

Consider a healthcare organization embarking on a digital transformation journey with a complex project aimed at enhancing patient engagement through a new mobile application. The stakes are high, with multiple stakeholders involved, including doctors, administrative staff, and patients. The challenges are multifaceted, encompassing technological changes, data security concerns, and the need for organizational culture shifts.

Utilizing DSDM's Philosophical Foundation

In line with DSDM's core philosophy, the project starts by aligning its objectives with the healthcare organization's overarching business goals—improving patient engagement and care quality. To ensure maximum business value, the project team prioritizes functionalities like appointment scheduling and prescription refills for early development and release.

Advantages of the Integrated Framework

Given the multiple dimensions of the project, including software development, data security, and process re-engineering, DSDM's integrated framework proves to be instrumental. It allows for effective collaboration between the technology development teams and the organizational change management teams, thereby facilitating more holistic project governance.

Compatibility with Existing Frameworks

The healthcare organization was previously using PMI for managing projects. DSDM’s compatibility feature allowed for a seamless integration with PMI processes, thus providing an agile layer to the existing project governance model.

Customizing the Process Model

Building upon DSDM's baseline process model, the project team customizes it to incorporate unique healthcare compliance requirements and security protocols. This ensures that the project is not just a technological success but also adheres to the critical industry-specific mandates.

Outcome

The iterative cycles, guided by DSDM, result in early and consistent deliveries, much to the satisfaction of stakeholders. The integrated framework and compatibility features enable a well-coordinated effort, achieving the desired synergy between different project components. Risks are identified and mitigated in a timely manner, contributing to the project’s overall success.

Conclusion

Through DSDM, the healthcare organization successfully navigates the complexities of digital transformation. By focusing on business value, enabling integrated project management, and offering adaptability through compatibility with existing frameworks, DSDM proves its mettle as a comprehensive, flexible, and robust methodology. The end result is a project that not only meets its technological objectives but also achieves broader business goals, validating DSDM's efficacy as a holistic project management approach.

Detailed Insights into the Pre-Project Phase in DSDM

The Pre-Project phase in the Dynamic Systems Development Method (DSDM) is a pivotal juncture that sets the trajectory for the entire project. Unlike the subsequent phases where focus shifts to implementation and delivery, this phase is predominantly concerned with ensuring the project's alignment with organizational goals and its overall viability. The emphasis is on rigorous evaluation, ensuring only the most strategic and feasible projects move forward.

Essential Activities of the Pre-Project Phase

Initial Identification of the Project

Here, the embryonic concept of a project surfaces, usually in response to a business need, an identified gap in operations, or a market opportunity. The objective is to identify if there's a genuine problem or an opportunity worth exploring.

Feasibility Assessment

This step is integral for screening projects, where technical, financial, and operational feasibilities are meticulously assessed. The goal is to avert any initiation of projects that may be either technically unviable or financially impractical.

Business Case Development

A comprehensive business case is drawn up, detailing the expected returns on investment (ROI), cost structure, and an inventory of risks and mitigation plans. This document becomes the cornerstone for justifying the project and securing approvals.

Stakeholder Analysis

The influence and interest of all stakeholders are evaluated. This information is crucial for tailoring communication plans and for understanding how to manage different stakeholders throughout the project.

Initial Governance Setup

The governance framework is outlined, specifying key roles and responsibilities. The configuration is generally flexible but formal enough to provide the needed structure for decision-making.

Terms of Reference

The Terms of Reference (ToR) is a seminal document that encapsulates the project's raison d'être. It outlines the objectives, scope, constraints, and expected deliverables, providing a blueprint for what the project aims to achieve.

Approval and Funding

Once the preparatory work is deemed satisfactory, approval is sought from the relevant authority, generally a board or a steering committee. Concurrently, the necessary financial resources are allocated to commence the project.

Summary and Conclusion

The Pre-Project Phase is essentially the gatekeeper in the DSDM framework. It employs a set of rigorous evaluative activities that determine whether a project should be given the green light. By meticulously assessing feasibility, developing a robust business case, and establishing clear governance mechanisms, this phase performs the crucial function of aligning the project with organizational objectives. Its successful execution sets the foundation for an organized, risk-mitigated, and business-aligned project lifecycle.

Case Study: Employing the Pre-Project Phase in a Healthcare System Overhaul

Scenario

Consider a healthcare organization that aims to overhaul its existing patient management system. The objective is to implement an integrated solution that improves patient experience and streamlines operations across multiple departments.

Initial Identification of Project

Leadership identifies lapses in patient care coordination and inefficiencies in the administrative process as a key challenge that requires immediate attention.

Feasibility Assessment

A preliminary feasibility study estimates a significant improvement in operational efficiency and patient satisfaction. It also assesses technical requirements and confirms that the existing infrastructure can support the new system.

Business Case Development

The business case is structured around the primary goal of enhancing patient experience while optimizing resources. It projects a 20% reduction in administrative costs and a 25% improvement in patient satisfaction ratings. The expected ROI is calculated to be achieved within 24 months.

Stakeholder Analysis

Key stakeholders include department heads from medical, administrative, and IT divisions. Their roles, interests, and influence levels are carefully mapped to ensure proper communication and decision-making throughout the project.

Initial Governance Setup

A governance committee is formed with a diverse set of stakeholders, including a Business Sponsor from the medical department, a Project Manager from IT, and subject matter experts from various units.

Terms of Reference

A Terms of Reference document is prepared, detailing the scope of the system overhaul, objectives, expected outcomes, and key milestones. This document serves as the formal agreement that sets the project's boundaries.

Approval and Funding

Armed with a well-defined business case, clear Terms of Reference, and stakeholder consensus, the project receives board approval. Subsequently, a budget is allocated, paving the way for the project to proceed to the next phase.

Summary

By meticulously following the activities outlined in the Pre-Project Phase of DSDM, the healthcare organization ensures that their ambitious project is not just a conceptual idea but a well-vetted, organizationally aligned initiative. The thorough vetting process mitigates early risks and sets a strong foundation for the subsequent phases of the project. The Pre-Project Phase thus serves its role as an essential preparatory stage, confirming the project's alignment with both technical feasibility and organizational objectives.

Unpacking the Feasibility Phase in DSDM

Philosophical Foundation

The Dynamic Systems Development Method (DSDM) follows an agile philosophy, advocating a business-driven approach to projects. While agility and flexibility are emphasized throughout the lifecycle, it is during the Feasibility Phase that the viability and practicability of a project are put to the test. This phase serves as a robust validation mechanism, allowing organizations to gauge whether the project aligns with their technical capabilities and business objectives.

Detailed Examination of Key Activities in the Feasibility Phase

Technical Feasibility Assessment

This is where the rubber meets the road for any project. Teams need to scrutinize the technical resources at their disposal, from hardware to software and the skillsets available within the organization. This involves:

Hardware Requirements: Confirming whether existing hardware can support the project or if new purchases are needed.

Software Necessities: Analyzing if current software packages are up-to-date and fit-for-purpose, or if new licenses need to be acquired.

Skillset Analysis: Evaluating if the in-house team has the skills required to implement the project or if external consultants need to be hired.

Business Feasibility Assessment

The business feasibility assessment provides a refined outlook on the project's financial viability. More comprehensive than the initial business case developed during the Pre-Project Phase, this assessment aims to:

Cost-Benefit Analysis: Weigh the projected costs against expected benefits in a quantifiable manner.

ROI Metrics: Calculate key financial indicators such as Return on Investment (ROI), Net Present Value (NPV), and Internal Rate of Return (IRR).

Budget Compliance: Ensure that the estimated project budget is in alignment with organizational financial constraints.

Risk Assessment

This activity is integral to the Feasibility Phase as it serves to identify, quantify, and prioritize potential project risks. Elements typically assessed include:

Technical Risks: Such as software compatibility issues, data migration challenges, and hardware malfunctions.

Business Risks: Including market volatility, ROI concerns, and stakeholder disengagement.

Operational Risks: Like project delays, budget overruns, and resourcing challenges.

Feasibility Report

Upon the completion of the technical and business feasibility assessments, along with the risk assessment, a comprehensive feasibility report is prepared. This document summarizes:

Findings: Data collected from the technical and business assessments.

Risks: Identified risks and their categorization in terms of impact and likelihood.

Recommendations: Suggestions on the project's direction, whether to proceed, pivot, or terminate.

Decision Making

Based on the insights gathered in the feasibility report, stakeholders make informed decisions about the future of the project. The outcomes could be:

Proceed: Move forward to the next phase if the project is deemed viable.

Pivot: Modify the project scope or approach based on the findings.

Terminate: Halt the project if it is determined to be unfeasible.

Stakeholder Communication

After a decision is made, it is critical to communicate the findings and recommendations to all relevant stakeholders. This ensures that everyone is aligned and understands the next steps in the project's journey.

Conclusion

The Feasibility Phase in the DSDM framework is pivotal for ensuring that a project is technically sound and business-wise rational before any significant investments of time and resources are made. By taking a comprehensive approach to assess technical aspects, business viability, and potential risks, this phase serves as a robust mechanism for informed decision-making.

Case Study: Implementing the Feasibility Phase in a Smart City Initiative

A metropolitan government was contemplating a Smart City initiative aimed at integrating various digital technologies into its existing urban infrastructure. The goal was to improve the quality of life for residents, streamline municipal operations, and reduce costs. Given the complex and multi-faceted nature of the project, the decision-makers chose to employ the DSDM framework, particularly focusing on the Feasibility Phase to validate the project's viability.

Technical Feasibility Assessment

Hardware Requirements
An inventory was taken of the existing digital infrastructure, which revealed that additional IoT sensors and data servers would be needed to support the Smart City functions.

Software Necessities
The team evaluated software requirements, concluding that new Smart City management software would need to be developed to integrate with the existing municipal systems.

Skillset Analysis
An evaluation of the existing workforce revealed that additional training in data analytics and IoT management would be required.

Business Feasibility Assessment

Cost-Benefit Analysis
The financial analysis revealed that the project would require a substantial investment but projected significant long-term savings through automation and more efficient use of resources.

ROI Metrics
Calculated ROI indicated that the project would break even in approximately five years, with continuous benefits expected after that point.

Budget Compliance
The initial cost estimates were aligned with the municipal budget for infrastructure projects, confirming financial feasibility.

Risk Assessment

Technical Risks

The assessment identified risks associated with the integration of new and existing hardware and software.

Business Risks

Market research indicated that public reception could be a concern if not properly managed.

Operational Risks

Potential for delays in project timelines and budget overruns were identified and factored into the project plan.

Feasibility Report

A comprehensive feasibility report was prepared, including the data collected, a risk assessment matrix, and multiple scenarios on project execution approaches.

Decision Making

Given the positive but cautiously optimistic feasibility report, the decision was made to proceed with the project in a phased manner, with pilot programs leading the way.

Stakeholder Communication

The government held a series of town halls and released public documentation to ensure all stakeholders, including residents and municipal employees, were informed and could offer feedback.

Conclusion

The Feasibility Phase was instrumental in assessing the project's viability, thereby giving stakeholders the confidence to proceed. Through meticulous planning and analysis, the city was able to make an informed decision, ensuring that their Smart City initiative was both ambitious and achievable.

Understanding the Foundations Phase in DSDM

Overview

The Foundations Phase is an integral part of the Dynamic Systems Development Method (DSDM) framework, serving as a bridge between the Feasibility Phase and the functional iterations of the project. While the Feasibility Phase verifies whether the project should be done, the Foundations Phase concentrates on how it should be done. This phase aims to achieve a high-level yet firm understanding of what the project will entail, without getting caught up in detailed specifications. It acts as a blueprint that sets the guidelines for how the project will proceed.

Key Objectives and Activities in the Foundations Phase

Scope Definition

One of the first objectives in the Foundations Phase is to clearly define the scope of the project. This involves establishing what the project will address and, perhaps just as importantly, what it will not. Scope definition provides the boundaries that keep the project focused and manageable.

High-Level Planning

This activity entails laying down a high-level roadmap of the project. It involves estimating timelines, identifying milestones, and allocating resources in a broad sense. This does not replace the detailed planning that occurs later but serves as a strategic guide for the project's direction.

Roles and Responsibilities

Determining who is involved in the project and what they will be doing is a crucial step in this phase. This involves identifying key stakeholders and defining their roles and responsibilities. This setup ensures that everyone knows their place and purpose in the project, promoting better coordination and accountability.

Project Lifecycle Customization

While DSDM provides a generic process model, every project has its unique set of requirements and challenges. During the Foundations Phase, the generic DSDM process is adapted to fit the specific project, making allowances for its individual complexities and nuances.

Governance Model

The governance model outlines the decision-making processes, risk management strategies, and quality assurance mechanisms. This model ensures that the project remains aligned with business objectives while adhering to quality standards and managing risks effectively.

Delivery Approach

Lastly, the method of development and delivery of the solution is determined. Given DSDM's iterative nature, this usually involves deciding the increments in which the solution will be developed and the iterations that will be employed for its refinement.

Conclusion

The Foundations Phase in DSDM is vital for setting the course of the project. By establishing the scope, roles, governance model, and high-level plans, it serves as a foundational blueprint for the entire project lifecycle. Executed effectively, this phase enables teams to embark on the project with a clear sense of direction, adequate preparation, and a solid plan, thereby significantly enhancing the probability of the project's success.

Case Study: Foundations Phase in a Financial Software Implementation Project

Background

A financial services company seeks to implement new software to improve its risk analysis capabilities. After determining the project's feasibility, the company moves into the Foundations Phase to establish how the project should be carried out.

Objectives and Activities

Scope Definition

The scope includes the implementation of new risk analysis software within the existing IT infrastructure, training for analysts, and integration with current data sources. Explicitly excluded from the scope are any changes to the existing accounting software and customer databases.

High-Level Planning

A high-level timeline is laid out, proposing a 12-month project cycle with quarterly milestones to evaluate progress. An initial budget is allocated, and departments that will contribute resources are identified.

Roles and Responsibilities

Key stakeholders, such as the CFO, IT Manager, and Lead Risk Analyst, are identified. Their roles and responsibilities are outlined to include decision-making authority, resource allocation, and oversight.

Project Lifecycle Customization

Given the specific requirements and constraints of financial compliance, the generic DSDM process is tailored to include additional checkpoints for regulatory approval.

Governance Model

A governance committee is formed, comprising members from the finance, IT, and risk departments, along with an external consultant for compliance verification. They establish a decision-making process that includes escalation paths for risk and dispute resolution.

Delivery Approach

The decision is made to implement the software in three iterations, each dealing with different modules. This approach allows for incremental improvement and easier troubleshooting.

Conclusion

By meticulously executing the Foundations Phase, the financial services company set clear directives for the scope, planning, roles, and governance of the project. This preparation served as a robust foundation, enabling the project to navigate complexities while staying aligned with organizational objectives. The phase provided the team with clarity, focus, and a shared understanding of the project's trajectory, thereby enhancing the likelihood of successful project delivery.

Delving Deeper into the Evolutionary Development Phase in DSDM

Overview

The Evolutionary Development Phase is a pivotal component in the DSDM framework. This phase is essentially where the rubber meets the road, transitioning from strategic planning to tactical execution. Here, Agile best practices are leveraged to build the actual solution incrementally while ensuring that it aligns with both business and technical imperatives.

Key Objectives and Activities

Iterative Development

This is the core activity in the Evolutionary Development Phase. The team undergoes repetitive cycles of planning, coding, and testing, progressively refining the solution. This iterative approach allows for prompt feedback and facilitates early detection of issues, thereby reducing the risk and improving the quality of the final output.

Timeboxing

Timeboxing helps to keep the project on schedule and within budget. Each Timebox is a pre-defined, fixed time period during which specific objectives must be achieved. By constraining the time for work, the process encourages focus and productivity, enabling the team to concentrate on high-priority tasks.

MoSCoW Prioritization

The MoSCoW method allows the team to classify the requirements into Must-haves, Should-haves, Could-haves, and Won't-haves. This categorization assists in determining the work that needs to be tackled in each Timebox. It ensures that critical functionalities get developed first, while less crucial features can be deferred, providing flexibility in project execution.

Modelling and Facilitated Workshops

These tools are indispensable for enhancing communication and ensuring everyone is on the same page. Visual models help to crystallize complex concepts, while facilitated workshops offer a structured environment for team members and stakeholders to collaborate, resolve issues, and make informed decisions.

Continuous Testing

The practice of constant testing serves as a quality gatekeeper throughout the development process. It ensures that each incremental piece of the solution adheres to both functional and non-functional criteria. This continuity in testing not only assures quality but also allows for early corrections, thereby avoiding costly late-stage changes.

Solution Increments

Each Timebox culminates in a Solution Increment — a usable fragment of the overall solution. These increments progressively contribute to the full scope of the project, each one building upon the last. By the end of this phase, the assembled Solution Increments coalesce into a cohesive, well-tested product or system that meets the business requirements.

Conclusion

The Evolutionary Development Phase is the linchpin of a DSDM project, bridging the gap between planning and execution. Its structured yet flexible approach allows for a nuanced, iterative development process that is deeply aligned with business objectives. It ensures that the solution not only meets technical specifications but is also practical and beneficial from a business standpoint. This phase offers the rigorous structure and adaptive latitude necessary for executing complex projects successfully.

Case Study: Evolutionary Development Phase in a Retail E-commerce Platform Upgrade

Background

A leading retail company decided to upgrade its existing e-commerce platform to enhance user experience and integrate new features like AI-based recommendations and chat support. Having navigated through the Feasibility and Foundations Phases, the project team enters the Evolutionary Development Phase with well-defined objectives.

Objectives and Activities

Iterative Development

The Solution Development Team undertakes multiple iterative cycles to build the e-commerce platform. Each cycle focuses on a specific set of features, such as the shopping cart functionality, user interface, and recommendation engine.

Timeboxing

The team sets up 2-week Timeboxes, each aimed at achieving a particular milestone. For instance, one Timebox is devoted to implementing a secure payment gateway, while another focuses on optimizing page load speeds.

MoSCoW Prioritization

Critical features like secure transactions and inventory management are categorized as Must-haves. Additional features like chat support are listed as Should-haves, and elements like social media integration fall under Could-haves. The team prioritizes development work accordingly.

Modelling and Facilitated Workshops

Several workshops are conducted to iron out design intricacies and resolve any ambiguities. Flowcharts and wireframes are created to visualize the navigation and layout, ensuring that everyone understands the proposed enhancements.

Continuous Testing

Each feature undergoes rigorous testing after its development cycle. Automated testing tools are used to perform functional, performance, and security tests to ensure that the platform adheres to specified quality standards.

Solution Increments

The team successfully creates several Solution Increments throughout this phase. Each Increment is reviewed and assessed for quality and functionality, contributing to the overall robustness of the new e-commerce platform.

Conclusion

By methodically applying the practices and guidelines of the Evolutionary Development Phase, the project team was able to successfully develop an upgraded e-commerce platform that met both business and technical requirements. The phase's iterative and incremental approach ensured that the solution was continually refined, allowing for course corrections and adaptations as needed. This ultimately led to a more effective and seamless upgrade, enabling the retail company to provide a superior user experience to its customers.

The Deployment Phase in DSDM: A Deep Dive

Overview

The Deployment Phase in DSDM serves as the culmination of all the previous phases and is critical for ensuring that the solution transitions smoothly from a development setting to a live environment. This phase is multifaceted, encompassing various activities that range from final testing to project closure. Its primary objective is to ensure that the deployed solution is not only technically sound but also adds value to the business by meeting all predetermined criteria.

Key Objectives and Activities

Deployment Preparation: More Than Just Final Checks

This is not just a last-minute review but a comprehensive series of activities that set the stage for a successful deployment. It includes final system and acceptance testing to ensure that all elements are functioning as expected. Often overlooked, data migration is another crucial aspect, ensuring that existing data is transferred accurately to the new system. Lastly, user training is vital; the most technically perfect solution can still fail if end-users are not comfortable using it.

Release Management: Aligning with the Bigger Picture

The deployment of a new solution rarely occurs in a vacuum. Companies usually have a release calendar that outlines when different system upgrades or releases will occur. Aligning the project's deployment with this calendar is essential to minimize disruption to other projects and ongoing business operations.

Operational Transition: The Handover

At this juncture, the developed system transitions from the project team to the operational teams. These are the people who will be using or maintaining the system daily, and therefore, it's essential to ensure a seamless handover. This involves not just transferring access and controls but also providing comprehensive documentation and training.

Post-Deployment Review and Feedback: Confirming Success

Once the system is live, a rigorous post-deployment review is indispensable. It evaluates whether the system meets all the acceptance criteria defined in earlier phases and whether it aligns with the business objectives. Feedback is collected from various stakeholders, including end-users and operational staff, to assess the deployment's real-world efficacy.

Project Closure: The Final Lap

The closure of the project is just as crucial as its initiation. Formal project closure activities are necessary to evaluate what went well and what didn't. This often includes a post-implementation review, financial reconciliation, and documentation of lessons learned. These insights are valuable not only for auditing purposes but also for future projects.

Summary

The Deployment Phase in DSDM is not just a technical exercise but a multidimensional process that aligns technological deployments with business needs. By following a structured approach that includes preparation, alignment, transition, review, and closure, organizations can ensure a successful deployment that brings the project to a satisfactory conclusion while delivering maximum business value.

Case Study: Deployment Phase in a Healthcare Software Implementation

Background

A healthcare provider decides to implement a new patient management software system to improve operational efficiency and patient care. After successfully navigating through the earlier DSDM phases, the project enters the Deployment Phase.

Objectives and Activities

Deployment Preparation

The final testing is conducted in a simulated live environment, replicating the actual hardware and software configurations. Concurrently, data from the old system is migrated to the new one, ensuring data integrity and compliance with healthcare regulations. A training program is rolled out for doctors, nurses, and administrative staff who will be using the new software.

Release Management

The deployment is scheduled in sync with the hospital's annual system upgrade cycle to minimize operational disruptions. Notifications are sent out well in advance to all staff, and a downtime window is planned to carry out the actual deployment.

Operational Transition

The newly developed patient management system is handed over to the operational teams. Comprehensive documentation, including user manuals and troubleshooting guides, is provided to facilitate a smooth transition.

Post-Deployment Review and Feedback

After the system goes live, a series of audits and reviews are conducted to assess its performance against the acceptance criteria and business objectives. Feedback is collected from medical staff and patients to gauge the system's efficacy in a real-world setting.

Project Closure

A formal closure meeting is held, involving all key stakeholders. Financials are reconciled, and a final report is generated, outlining the project's successes and areas for improvement. The documentation serves as a valuable resource for future projects.

Conclusion

The Deployment Phase was executed meticulously, ensuring that the new patient management system was not only technically sound but also aligned well with the organization's operational needs and long-term objectives. By adhering to the DSDM framework, the healthcare provider was able to transition smoothly from a legacy system to a more efficient and effective solution, enhancing both operational efficiency and patient care.

Unlocking the Value of the Post-Project Phase in DSDM

Overview

The Post-Project Phase in the Dynamic Systems Development Method (DSDM) serves as the reflection and evaluation stage that follows the Deployment Phase. It stands as an essential mechanism for determining how effectively the project has translated into real-world benefits. Unlike other phases that lean heavily on technical and developmental aspects, this phase emphasizes assessing value delivery, stakeholder satisfaction, and the realization of business benefits, thereby wrapping up the project life cycle.

Key Objectives and Activities

Benefits Realization Review

The cornerstone of this phase is the Benefits Realization Review, which aims to validate whether the anticipated business benefits have materialized or are in the process of realization. It's an evaluative step that compares the forecasts outlined in the initial business case with the actual outcomes.

Post-Implementation Audit

A comprehensive Post-Implementation Audit is conducted to examine the complete set of project activities, from inception to deployment. This encompasses a review of the development processes, adherence to timelines, and the effectiveness of the deployment strategy.

Stakeholder Feedback

Understanding the perspectives of those impacted by the project is critical. Feedback is systematically gathered from end-users, stakeholders, and project team members to gauge satisfaction levels, identify bottlenecks, and flag any areas requiring improvement.

Performance Metrics Evaluation

The project's success isn't merely qualitative; it needs to be quantified to present a complete picture. To this end, performance metrics that were defined at the project's outset are evaluated against the actual data. This quantitative assessment provides a clear measurement of project success and ROI.

Lessons Learned

Finally, a structured 'Lessons Learned' exercise is conducted. This involves compiling insights about what went well and what could be improved. This invaluable knowledge is then documented for the benefit of future projects and contributes to the organization's knowledge base.

Summary

The Post-Project Phase is a vital step in the DSDM framework, offering a comprehensive evaluation of the project's lifecycle. By focusing on benefits realization and stakeholder satisfaction, this phase ensures that projects do not just end with deployment but culminate in the delivery of real value to the organization.

Case Study: Post-Project Phase in a Healthcare System Upgrade

Background

A healthcare organization had recently completed the deployment of a new patient management system. The Post-Project Phase was initiated to evaluate the effectiveness of the new system and to assess whether the projected benefits were realized.

Objectives and Activities

Benefits Realization Review

The organization had aimed to achieve a 20% reduction in patient wait times and a 15% improvement in staff productivity. A review indicated that they had realized a 18% reduction in patient wait times and a 14% increase in staff productivity, closely aligning with the initial objectives.

Post-Implementation Audit

An audit was carried out to evaluate the project's alignment with initial plans, timelines, and resource allocation. The audit concluded that while the project had mostly stayed within budget, there were slight delays due to unforeseen complexities in data migration.

Stakeholder Feedback

Feedback was collected from healthcare providers, administrative staff, and patients. Overall, the satisfaction rate was high, although some users pointed out areas where the interface could be more user-friendly.

Performance Metrics Evaluation

Metrics such as system uptime, speed, and error rates were monitored. The new system had a 99.5% uptime and had significantly lower error rates compared to the previous system.

Lessons Learned

Among the lessons learned were the need for more rigorous pre-deployment testing, especially for data migration, and the importance of user training programs to boost the system's effective utilization.

Conclusion

The Post-Project Phase served as an effective tool for the healthcare organization to measure the success of the new patient management system. It provided a detailed analysis of the extent to which the project achieved its goals and offered insights for improvement. The organization could thus close the project with a comprehensive understanding of its impacts, both positive and negative, thereby ensuring continuous improvement for future initiatives.

DSDM Lifecycle: A Flexible Yet Governed Approach to Project Management

Understanding the Lifecycle Structure

The Dynamic Systems Development Method (DSDM) framework is often presented as a sequential process that runs from the Pre-Project Phase to the Post-Project Phase. While this linear representation is conceptually convenient, the real-world application of DSDM is inherently more dynamic. Arrows that trace back from the "Deployment Phase" to earlier phases like the "Foundations Phase" and the "Evolutionary Development Phase" exemplify the cyclic nature of DSDM. These return paths are explicitly designed to accommodate the uncertainties and constant changes that characterize many project environments.

Key Features of the DSDM Lifecycle in Practice

Agility

The return paths embedded in the DSDM lifecycle signify its agile characteristics. When significant new insights are gained, particularly during the Deployment Phase, the project can revisit earlier phases for fine-tuning and adjustments. This looping back is not viewed as a failure but as an agile response to new information or changed circumstances.

Lifecycle Customization

The DSDM framework serves as a foundational model that can be customized to fit the unique characteristics of each project. During the Foundations Phase, the project team tailors the generic DSDM lifecycle to meet project-specific needs, requirements, and constraints. This customization ensures that the lifecycle is optimally aligned with the project's objectives and operational context.

Incremental and Iterative Approach

The non-linear nature of the DSDM lifecycle supports incremental development and iterative learning. This flexibility allows project teams to adapt their approaches and even revisit previously 'completed' phases for course correction or further development. By doing so, the project can more closely align with evolving business objectives and technical requirements.

Governance

Even with its adaptability, the DSDM lifecycle does not compromise on governance. Any change in direction or iteration back to a previous phase is performed within the governance framework established during the Foundations Phase. This approach ensures that all changes or iterations are well-justified, systematically evaluated, and consistent with project and organizational goals.

Summary

The DSDM Lifecycle is a sophisticated framework that marries flexibility with governance. Its agile characteristics, coupled with the ability for customization and robust governance protocols, make it a powerful tool for managing projects in dynamic, uncertain, and complex environments.

Case Study: Implementing DSDM Lifecycle in a Healthcare Project

Background

A healthcare institution embarks on a project to develop an electronic health record (EHR) system. Given the regulatory complexities and the need for a flexible yet controlled environment, the project team opts for the DSDM framework.

Objectives and Activities

Agility

In the middle of the Deployment Phase, new healthcare regulations are introduced, requiring additional data fields in the EHR system. The project team takes this as an opportunity to loop back to the Foundations Phase to reassess the scope and make necessary adjustments.

Lifecycle Customization

During the Foundations Phase, the team customizes the DSDM lifecycle to include extra milestones for regulatory approvals and third-party assessments, given the sensitive nature of healthcare data.

Incremental and Iterative Approach

The team adopts an incremental approach, aiming to roll out the EHR system department by department. After each incremental deployment, the team iterates back to the Evolutionary Development Phase to integrate lessons learned and user feedback.

Governance

A Project Governance Committee comprising senior management, legal advisors, and clinical experts is set up. This committee oversees all major decisions, including those related to looping back to previous phases. Strict governance protocols ensure that every iteration or course correction is well-documented and justified.

Conclusion

The healthcare institution successfully implements the EHR system by capitalizing on the inherent flexibility and robust governance structure of the DSDM lifecycle. The system not only meets regulatory requirements but is also well-received by its users. The project serves as a shining example of how the

DSDM lifecycle can be applied in a complex, regulated environment to deliver value and maintain control.

Navigating the Symbiosis of Scalability and Formality in DSDM

Understanding the Balance

The unique architecture of DSDM creates a powerful synergy between agile methodologies and governance structures. This allows projects to be agile while meeting the formal requirements dictated by various external and internal factors such as compliance, financial governance, and organizational constraints. DSDM becomes an invaluable asset when dealing with multi-faceted projects that require both agility and formal control mechanisms.

Key Configuration Strategies

Lifecycle Customization

DSDM's lifecycle is an adaptable structure. Its flexibility allows it to be tailored to projects of varying sizes and complexities, thus ensuring that governance needs are adequately met. For small projects, the framework can be simplified, cutting down on unnecessary formalities. In contrast, larger, more complex projects may require a more detailed lifecycle with additional governance checks and milestone reviews.

Level of Formality

The DSDM framework offers versatility in the level of formality for its artifacts and deliverables. This enables the project team to make pragmatic decisions about how detailed or simplified documents need to be. For instance, in a less formal environment, Solution Architecture Definitions and Management Approach Definitions may be quite streamlined. Conversely, in a project requiring stringent governance, these documents could be more exhaustive.

Role Adaptation

Scalability in DSDM extends to roles as well. In projects with multiple teams or larger scale, roles can evolve to include additional responsibilities. For instance, a coordinator role could be introduced to ensure seamless interaction among various sub-teams, thereby preserving the integrity of governance across the project.

Product Elaboration

As the scale and complexity of a project grow, it often necessitates more elaborate planning and control mechanisms. DSDM products like the Delivery Plan and Timebox Review Records can be expanded to accommodate these needs, thus providing a more granular level of planning, tracking, and control.

Conclusion

DSDM's adaptability makes it an ideal framework for projects that need to strike a balance between agility and governance. Through intelligent configuration strategies, DSDM can be scaled and formalized to meet a diverse range of project requirements, thereby offering a structured yet flexible approach to project management.

Case Study: Implementing DSDM in a Large Healthcare Organization

Background

A large healthcare organization decided to adopt DSDM for its electronic health records (EHR) implementation project. Due to the sensitive nature of health data and stringent compliance requirements, the project had to navigate a complex governance landscape while remaining agile enough to adapt to evolving healthcare standards.

Strategies Employed

Lifecycle Customization

Given the complexity and high stakes, the organization opted for a detailed DSDM lifecycle that included additional governance checkpoints for compliance with healthcare regulations.

Level of Formality

The project generated formal and exhaustive versions of key documents, such as the Solution Architecture Definition and Management Approach Definition, to ensure complete compliance with healthcare regulations.

Role Adaptation

The role of the Project Manager was expanded to include a Compliance Officer who was responsible for ensuring that all regulatory requirements were met. Additionally, coordination roles were introduced to manage interactions between the multiple teams involved in the project, ranging from healthcare professionals to IT specialists.

Product Elaboration

Due to the scale of the project and its critical nature, Delivery Plans and Timebox Review Records were elaborated to include comprehensive tracking metrics and control mechanisms.

Conclusion

By effectively configuring DSDM to its unique project environment, the healthcare organization successfully navigated the challenges posed by regulatory compliance and complex stakeholder needs. The project was delivered on time, met all compliance requirements, and effectively adapted to changes in healthcare standards, thereby proving the value of DSDM's adaptable framework in balancing agility with robust governance.

Chapter Five

Demystifying Roles and Responsibilities

Diving Deeper into the DSDM Team Model

Understanding the Model' s Underpinning Philosophy

The DSDM Team Model aims to be more than just a distribution of tasks; it embodies the Agile principle of creating empowered, self-organizing teams. The model encourages collaboration among various stakeholders, minimizes hierarchical constraints, and promotes a holistic view of the project by integrating business, technical, and managerial perspectives.

The Significance of Role Color Scheme

The color scheme serves as a visual tool to immediately identify the primary area of concern for each role. This aids in aligning expectations and facilitates more effective communication among team members. The usage of mixed colors for certain roles underscores the multi-faceted nature of Agile projects, where individuals often wear multiple hats.

The color scheme in the DSDM Team Model delineates areas of interest:

Orange: Represents roles focused on business interests

Green: Represents roles dedicated to technical or solution aspects

Blue: Represents roles focused on management and leadership

Grey: Represents roles concentrated on process optimization

Mixed Colors: Indicates roles that span multiple areas of interest

Dissecting Categories of Roles

Project-Level Roles

Project-level roles are the custodians of the project's vision and governance. They steer the project strategically, setting the direction and making high-level decisions. Their roles are essential in ensuring that the project stays aligned with business goals and adheres to governance protocols.

Solution Development Team Roles

These are the operational roles responsible for executing the vision set by the project-level roles. They engage in the hands-on tasks of planning, development, testing, and delivery. Their primary focus is the project's tactical and practical aspects, ensuring that the solution meets both business and technical requirements.

Supporting Roles

The supporting roles provide expertise that may not be continuously required but is essential for project success. Their involvement can be intermittent and specialized, depending on the project's demands.

Fluidity in Role Fulfillment

The flexible nature of role assignment in DSDM accommodates varying project sizes, complexities, and skills available within the team. This fluidity allows for both vertical and horizontal scaling, making DSDM a versatile framework that can adapt to different project environments.

Summary

The DSDM Team Model is meticulously designed to offer a balanced blend of strategic oversight, tactical execution, and specialized expertise. It achieves this through a mix of well-defined roles and responsibilities that can adapt to the unique challenges and opportunities that each project presents.

Case Study: Implementing the DSDM Team Model in a Large Enterprise

Scenario Overview

In a large financial organization, there was a need to overhaul an existing software infrastructure that had become outdated and was not meeting business requirements efficiently. The organization chose the DSDM framework for this complex, enterprise-level project.

Role Allocation and Interactions

Project-Level Roles

- The Business Sponsor was a high-ranking executive who provided financial backing and strategic direction.
- The Business Visionary was an experienced manager from the business unit most affected by the project.
- The Project Manager was an Agile-experienced individual responsible for keeping the project on track.

These individuals formed the project board and met regularly to review progress and provide direction.

Solution Development Team Roles

Multiple Solution Development Teams were formed, each led by a Team Leader and comprising of Solution Developers, Solution Testers, and Business Ambassadors. These teams were responsible for different modules of the software.

Supporting Roles

- Business and Technical Advisors were consulted during critical milestones.
- A DSDM Coach was brought in to guide the teams in adhering to DSDM principles.

Role Flexibility

The Business Analyst role was one that saw dual responsibilities. They engaged in both strategic planning with the Project Board and day-to-day activities with the Solution Development Team.

Outcomes and Lessons Learned

- The Project Board was effective in providing clear strategic goals, allowing the development teams to operate with a high degree of autonomy.
- The flexible nature of role assignment allowed the project to adapt to unforeseen challenges.
- The DSDM Coach played a pivotal role in keeping the project aligned with Agile principles, especially when challenges arose.

Summary

This case study demonstrates how the DSDM Team Model can be successfully implemented in a large, complex project environment. The well-defined roles and responsibilities, combined with the flexibility to adapt, proved crucial in the project's success.

The Role of the Business Sponsor in DSDM

In-Depth Overview

The Business Sponsor in the Dynamic Systems Development Method (DSDM) framework holds a pivotal role that transcends mere project oversight. Occupying the apex of the project's business hierarchy, the Business Sponsor serves as a linchpin that connects the operational aspects of the project with the strategic imperatives of the organization. This role is characterized by a multi-dimensional set of responsibilities that go beyond traditional project management to include elements of strategy, governance, and organizational alignment.

Expanded Key Responsibilities

Business Case Ownership

While the Business Case is a foundational document for any project, in DSDM it is an ever-evolving entity requiring constant monitoring and adjustment. The Business Sponsor is not just its creator but its custodian, continually evaluating it against shifting organizational goals and market realities.

Budget Oversight

Financial stewardship entails more than just budget allocation. The Business Sponsor must balance fiscal prudence with the agility required in a DSDM project. This means making real-time decisions on resource allocation based on the project's immediate needs and long-term objectives.

Issue Resolution

The Business Sponsor is often the court of last resort for issue resolution, especially for issues with far-reaching business implications. Their high position in the organizational hierarchy equips them with the authority and influence necessary to make or facilitate decisions quickly.

Governance and Decision-Making

Governance is not just about compliance but also about steering the project in a way that it remains aligned with organizational strategy. The Business Sponsor collaborates with other governance bodies like the Project Board, offering insights that only a senior organizational position can provide.

Championing the Project

The role is not passive; it's proactive. Being the project's primary advocate, the Business Sponsor is responsible for ensuring visibility, securing resources, and gaining organizational buy-in.

Stakeholder Management

The Business Sponsor often acts as a conduit between the project team and the upper echelons of the organization, serving as both an information disseminator and a feedback collector.

Qualification Criteria and Organizational Position

The Business Sponsor is typically a senior executive with substantial organizational influence. This ensures that they have the latitude to make decisions that are binding, not just on the project but also across functional areas of the organization. The role requires a mix of technical acumen, strategic foresight, and leadership skills to effectively balance the myriad responsibilities it entails.

Summary

The Business Sponsor's role in a DSDM project is multi-faceted and vital for ensuring that the project not only meets its technical objectives but also aligns closely with organizational strategy and business goals. This is achieved through a blend of strong governance, financial oversight, and dynamic leadership.

Case Study: The Multi-Dimensional Role of the Business Sponsor in a Large-Scale DSDM Project

Background

In a hypothetical organization embarking on a large-scale digital transformation project using the DSDM framework, the role of the Business Sponsor becomes particularly challenging. The project aims to overhaul the company's entire customer relationship management (CRM) system. Given the project's scale and strategic importance, the Business Sponsor must navigate a complex web of responsibilities.

How Business Case Ownership Evolves

Initially, the Business Sponsor collaborated with various stakeholders to formulate a compelling Business Case. As the project progressed through its various phases, the Business Sponsor revisited the Business Case multiple times, adjusting it to reflect changes in market conditions and internal priorities.

Dynamic Budget Oversight

Financial governance in this case was not about merely setting a budget cap. The Business Sponsor had to make strategic decisions about resource reallocations to meet unexpected challenges, such as a sudden shift to remote work due to a pandemic. The role required dynamic financial management skills.

Issue Resolution in Real-Time

In one instance, a major business issue arose when a key supplier threatened to pull out. Given the Business Sponsor's organizational clout, they were able to negotiate a resolution directly, without causing a project standstill.

Governance Beyond Compliance

The Business Sponsor led the formation of a Project Board comprising key organizational stakeholders. The governance process was enhanced by introducing regular strategy alignment sessions, ensuring the project stayed on course vis-a-vis organizational objectives.

The Art of Championing

As the project reached its final stages, there was a risk of "project fatigue" setting in. The Business Sponsor reignited organizational enthusiasm by actively championing the project's successes and forthcoming benefits in various internal forums.

Stakeholder Management

Being at the top rungs of the organizational ladder, the Business Sponsor effectively engaged with C-level executives, securing necessary support and alignment. They also ensured that the project was well-represented at board meetings and other high-level gatherings.

Conclusion

The Business Sponsor's role in this large-scale DSDM project illustrates the complexity and multi-dimensionality involved. The role is not static but evolves in response to the project's needs and organizational dynamics. Effective fulfillment of this role can make the difference between a project that is merely completed and one that truly adds value to the organization.

Exploring the Multifaceted Role of the Business Visionary in DSDM Projects

A Strategic Liaison

The Business Visionary is not just another managerial role but serves as a crucial interface between the Business Sponsor and the project team. This individual ensures that the Business Sponsor's strategic vision is seamlessly transformed into tactical actions and objectives that guide the project team. Given the significance of this role, it is designed to be held by one person to maintain a consistent and clear vision throughout the project's lifecycle.

Key Responsibilities Demystified

Interpretation and Communication

One of the Business Visionary's pivotal responsibilities is to be an effective communicator. They must translate high-level business objectives into actionable goals that the project team can work towards. This involves not only interpreting the needs of the Business Sponsor but also conveying these interpretations unambiguously to the team.

Strategic Direction

The Business Visionary is like the project's compass, consistently guiding it in alignment with strategic organizational goals. They are responsible for making course corrections if the project shows signs of deviating from its strategic path. This ensures that the final deliverables resonate well with the organizational objectives and the Business Case.

Business Case Integration

This role works closely with the Business Sponsor to ensure that the Business Case accurately reflects the project's goals and scope. In addition, they help to incorporate any adjustments or shifts in organizational strategy into the Business Case, thereby keeping it dynamically aligned with organizational realities.

Ongoing Involvement

What sets the Business Visionary apart from other roles is their sustained involvement throughout the project lifecycle. From its inception to closure, the Business Visionary remains engaged, providing much-needed continuity and focus.

Benefits Realization

One of the crucial end-games for any project is the realization of benefits. The Business Visionary is responsible for ensuring that the project's deliverables are shaped in a manner that enables the tangible realization of the benefits outlined in the Business Case.

Qualifications: The Balanced Skill Set

The role of the Business Visionary demands a unique blend of skills. It requires a deep understanding of the business domain and the ability to think both strategically and tactically. Given the role's multifaceted nature, the individual must excel in high-level thinking while also having an eye for detail.

Delving Deeper into the Role of the Business Visionary: A Case Study Approach

Context Setting

Imagine a financial services company that is embarking on a digital transformation journey. The Business Sponsor has laid down the overarching vision of becoming a digital-first organization that offers unparalleled customer service. Here's how the Business Visionary role comes into play to ensure that this strategic vision is achieved through the project.

Interpretation and Communication

The Business Visionary takes the first critical step of translating this vision into a more detailed set of objectives. For instance, they might set the goal of achieving a 20% increase in digital customer engagements over the next year. They communicate these specific objectives to the project team to set the direction.

Strategic Direction

As the project moves forward, emerging technologies like blockchain start becoming more relevant in the financial services space. The Business Visionary acknowledges this change and guides the project to include blockchain capabilities, ensuring alignment with both current market trends and the Business Sponsor's vision.

Business Case Integration

The Business Visionary works with the Business Sponsor to continuously update the Business Case, incorporating the addition of blockchain technology as a new objective. They ensure that the Business Case remains a living document, reflecting the dynamic nature of business and technology landscapes.

Ongoing Involvement

The Business Visionary remains involved throughout the project's different phases. When a pilot test of the new digital platform shows lower customer engagement than expected, they take proactive steps to understand the reasons behind this and suggest corrective measures, ensuring the project stays on track.

Benefits Realization

Once the project is completed and the digital platform is launched, the Business Visionary shifts their focus towards measuring the actual benefits.

They compare the pre-defined objectives with the actual performance metrics to evaluate if the project has realized the expected benefits. If there's a gap, they identify the reasons and suggest a plan to close it.

Summary

Through the case study, it's evident how the Business Visionary serves as a critical connector and guide, ensuring that the project not only aligns with but also achieves the strategic vision laid down by the Business Sponsor. This role, therefore, is not merely operational but profoundly strategic, requiring a balanced skill set that spans business acumen, strategic thinking, and tactical execution.

Role of the Technical Coordinator in DSDM: Bridging Technical Aspects with Business Goals

The role of the Technical Coordinator in a DSDM project is one of technical stewardship and leadership. This role safeguards the technical integrity of the project, ensuring that technology solutions are not only robust and scalable but also aligned with the business objectives.

Key Responsibilities Explained

Technical Coherence

The Technical Coordinator ensures that all elements within the project's technical ecosystem are consistent. This means that the technologies, frameworks, and coding standards chosen at the start are adhered to throughout the project, minimizing fragmentation and improving efficiency.

Technical Standards Compliance

In this capacity, the Technical Coordinator ensures that the project follows accepted industry best practices and internal corporate guidelines. This includes everything from data security protocols to quality assurance methods, which are crucial for the long-term viability of the project.

Decision-Making and Innovation

The Technical Coordinator is empowered to make critical decisions concerning the technical aspects of the project. This could involve choosing between different architectural patterns, databases, or even programming languages. They are also responsible for fostering a culture of innovation, exploring cutting-edge technologies that could potentially bring value to the project.

Cross-Functional Coordination

One of the essential responsibilities of this role is to collaborate closely with the Business Visionary. This ensures that the technical solutions being developed are in complete alignment with the business objectives, creating a harmonious relationship between the technical and business aspects of the project.

Technical Advisory

As the project's primary technical authority, the Technical Coordinator serves as a reservoir of technical expertise. The project team looks to this individual for guidance, and their recommendations are generally considered decisive in resolving technical challenges.

Required Qualifications and Position

The Technical Coordinator must have in-depth expertise in the project's domain, be it e-commerce, healthcare, finance, or any other sector. They should be well-versed in the technologies and methodologies that are pertinent to the project. Their reputation for sound technical judgment, backed by a history of successful project implementations, is also crucial for this role.

Case Study: The Technical Coordinator in a Large E-Commerce Project

Context

In a large-scale e-commerce project powered by the DSDM framework, the role of the Technical Coordinator was highly pivotal. The project aimed to build a sophisticated online platform capable of handling millions of users and integrating with various third-party services like payment gateways, inventory management systems, and customer relationship management (CRM) software.

Challenges

Technical Complexity: Multiple technology stacks were under consideration, including varying databases and programming languages.

Business-Technical Alignment: The project had to meet aggressive business targets for customer engagement and conversion rates.

Compliance: Security and data protection were significant concerns, given the sensitive customer data involved.

Actions Taken by the Technical Coordinator

Decision Framework

The Technical Coordinator created a decision framework to evaluate different technologies, taking into account scalability, performance, and cost.

Standardization

To ensure compliance with industry standards and best practices, the Technical Coordinator worked on creating a set of internal guidelines that covered everything from code quality to data encryption protocols.

Innovating with AI

Given the project's scale, the Technical Coordinator saw an opportunity to leverage Artificial Intelligence for personalized customer recommendations. After a thorough assessment, they decided to implement a machine learning model that would enhance user experience.

Business Liaison

Throughout the project, the Technical Coordinator met regularly with the Business Visionary to ensure that technical choices were in sync with business goals, particularly around customer experience and revenue targets.

Outcome

Technical Excellence: The project was developed using a tech stack that was both cutting-edge and practical, balancing immediate needs and future scalability.

Business Impact: The machine learning model significantly improved customer engagement, contributing to higher conversion rates.

Compliance and Security: The platform was built to high security standards, passing multiple third-party audits and compliance checks.

The Technical Coordinator's role was pivotal in navigating the project through complex technical landscapes while ensuring that the end product met all business objectives. Their actions stand as a testament to the critical importance of this role in a DSDM project.

The Comprehensive Role of the Project Manager in DSDM

Overview

In the Dynamic Systems Development Method (DSDM) framework, the role of the Project Manager is not merely administrative; it is a multifaceted position that embodies the essence of agile leadership. Responsible for harmonizing the diverse components of a project, the Project Manager navigates between high-level management tasks and a nuanced understanding of both technical and business imperatives.

Key Responsibilities

High-Level Coordination

The Project Manager orchestrates high-level activities, ensuring a seamless integration of timelines, budgets, and resources. This is crucial for the alignment of the project's objectives with its execution plan.

Agile Leadership

Rooted in Agile principles, the leadership style of the Project Manager is designed to encourage team collaboration and enable rapid development cycles. This is central to achieving a flexible and responsive project environment.

Environment Management

One of the often-overlooked aspects of project management is the creation and maintenance of a conducive working environment. The Project Manager ensures that the Solution Development Team has all the necessary tools and resources for effective functioning.

Empowerment and Delegation

Aligning with DSDM's emphasis on team empowerment, the Project Manager acts more as a facilitator than a dictator. The role involves delegating detailed planning to the Solution Development Team, thereby creating a sense of ownership and accountability among team members.

End-to-End Responsibility

The role of the Project Manager is expansive, covering the entire lifecycle of the project from the Foundations Phase through to the Deployment Phase. This end-to-end responsibility is necessary for ensuring that both business and technical dimensions are effectively managed.

Required Qualifications and Position

A qualified Project Manager in a DSDM environment should be well-versed in Agile methodologies, with a particular focus on DSDM. Additionally, the role requires a balanced understanding of both business and technical aspects, strong communication skills, and a proven track record in managing complex projects. These qualifications equip the Project Manager to make informed decisions that are aligned with the project's objectives and the organization's strategic goals.

Case Study: The Agile Project Manager in a DSDM Environment

Context

In a hypothetical technology firm, the project at hand is the development of a new cloud-based application. Given the complex nature of the project, involving multiple stakeholders and technical intricacies, the organization opts for DSDM as the project management framework. A seasoned Project Manager, skilled in Agile methodologies, is appointed to steer the project.

Challenges Faced

Timeline Conflicts: Different departments have varying timelines, creating synchronization issues.

Resource Allocation: Technical and business teams vie for the same pool of resources.

Stakeholder Expectations: Balancing the often conflicting expectations of technical and business stakeholders.

Steps Taken by the Project Manager

Implementing High-Level Coordination

The Project Manager starts by constructing a detailed yet flexible project plan that aligns the different timelines. Periodic alignment meetings are scheduled to ensure that everyone is on the same page.

Fostering Agile Leadership

To create a flexible environment, the Project Manager introduces regular "sprint review" meetings. These meetings foster a culture of continuous feedback and adaptation.

Ensuring Environment Management

To facilitate effective work, the Project Manager arranges for the procurement of essential tools and creates an internal documentation system to keep track of resources.

Promoting Empowerment and Delegation

The Project Manager allows the Solution Development Team to take ownership of their respective components, thereby encouraging proactive problem-solving and innovation.

Maintaining End-to-End Responsibility

The Project Manager stays involved in every phase of the project, from conceptualization to deployment, ensuring that both the business and technical aspects are in alignment with the project's objectives and the organization's strategic goals.

Outcome

As a result of the Project Manager's adept handling, the project is completed within the estimated timeline and budget, meeting the key performance indicators and fulfilling stakeholder expectations.

This case study exemplifies the multifaceted role of a Project Manager in a DSDM environment and how effective leadership can influence the outcome of a complex project.

Unveiling the Multifaceted Role of the Business Analyst in DSDM

Your comprehensive description captures the essence of the Business Analyst's role within the DSDM framework. This role serves as a keystone in balancing the technical and business aspects of a project, ensuring a cohesive and effective outcome.

Key Functions of the Business Analyst in DSDM

Facilitation and Mediation

The Business Analyst operates as the fulcrum, balancing the technical and business objectives. This ensures a more streamlined decision-making process, enriched by perspectives from both sides of the organization.

In-depth Business Analysis

Through rigorous analysis, the Business Analyst helps shape the project by articulating business needs that are understandable, actionable, and integrated into the solution.

Continuous Decision Support

In the constantly evolving environment of a DSDM project, the Business Analyst's ongoing engagement in decision-making is indispensable for maintaining alignment with business objectives.

Open Communication

Contrary to roles that may act as mere conduits of information, the Business Analyst nurtures a culture of open dialogue, facilitating better understanding and collaboration among team members.

User-Centric Focus

By ensuring the active involvement of business users in the development process, the Business Analyst helps to align the project outcome closely with real-world business requirements.

Required Qualifications and Skills

The Business Analyst should be adept in business processes, technology, and solution development. They must excel in stakeholder communication, be proficient in data analysis, and have strong problem-solving skills. Their adaptability in fast-paced Agile environments is another essential qualification.

Conclusion

In summary, the Business Analyst plays an instrumental role in DSDM projects. Their unique dual responsibility not only bridges the gap between business and technical dimensions but also elevates the quality of interaction among team members, thereby contributing to a more effective and harmonious project outcome.

Zooming In: Practical Insights on the Business Analyst in an E-commerce Platform Upgrade

Your case study brings to life the pivotal role of the Business Analyst in the context of an e-commerce platform upgrade, a project that inherently demands a harmonious balance between technical capabilities and business objectives.

Key Activities of the Business Analyst in This Scenario

Data-Driven Decision-Making

One of the primary tasks would be to analyze sales data and user behavior. The insights drawn could set the stage for the entire project, helping to identify not just areas of improvement but also potential opportunities for innovation.

Facilitation of Collaborative Workshops

These workshops serve as multi-disciplinary arenas where stakeholders from marketing, sales, and development converge. The Business Analyst facilitates these sessions, ensuring that all voices are heard and integrated into a unified project vision.

Continuous Review and Alignment

The role doesn't end at the planning stage. The Business Analyst remains engaged, continuously reviewing development stages to ensure alignment with the identified business objectives.

Prioritization Based on Business Value

Here, the Business Analyst shifts from being a technical liaison to a business strategist, helping to prioritize features that offer the highest business value.

Enhancing Interdisciplinary Communication

The Business Analyst fosters effective communication among designers, developers, and business stakeholders. This ensures that the resulting solution is not just technically sound but also sharply focused on fulfilling business objectives.

Conclusion: The Business Analyst as a Catalyst

In this setting, the Business Analyst does more than just connect two disparate worlds. They act as a catalyst for effective dialogue, smarter decision-making, and ultimately, a more successful project outcome. Their involvement ensures that the upgraded e-commerce platform aligns seamlessly with overarching business goals and meets, if not exceeds, customer expectations.

Unpacking the Multifaceted Role of the Team Leader in DSDM Projects

Overview: The Servant-Leader in Action

In the context of Dynamic Systems Development Method (DSDM) projects, the Team Leader emerges not as a conventional taskmaster but as a servant-leader. This role is essential within the Solution Development Team and is geared towards enabling the team to meet project objectives efficiently and effectively.

Key Responsibilities: A Balanced Act

Servant Leadership: The Cornerstone

The primary responsibility of fostering an environment of trust, collaboration, and high performance falls under the purview of the Team Leader. They aim to facilitate rather than dictate, making sure that the team is empowered to reach its full potential.

Detailed Planning: A Collaborative Endeavor

While they do not interfere in individual tasks, the Team Leader collaborates with team members to plan and coordinate product delivery at a detailed level. This ensures that the project remains on track without compromising team autonomy.

Objective Alignment: Bridging Visions

Another significant responsibility involves ensuring that the team's efforts align with the overall project objectives and milestones. The Team Leader helps in translating the broader goals into actionable tasks for the team.

Peer-Elected Leadership: A Badge of Trust

In an ideal DSDM setting, the Team Leader is elected by the team members, which serves as a vote of confidence and indicates a mutual understanding of the individual's capability to lead effectively.

Dual Role: Wearing Multiple Hats

It's common for the Team Leader to also perform another role within the team. This dual role can range from a Business Analyst or Business Ambassador to a Solution Developer or Solution Tester, depending on the project's needs.

Required Qualifications and Skills: The Ideal Candidate

The Team Leader should possess an arsenal of leadership qualities, such as excellent communication skills and the ability to inspire and motivate the team. A deep understanding of Agile methodologies and domain-specific expertise are equally beneficial. Experience in other roles within the Solution Development Team adds another layer of versatility to this role.

Conclusion: The Team Leader as an Enabler

The Team Leader serves as a pivotal role within the Solution Development Team, acting as both an enabler and a facilitator. By focusing on servant leadership and fostering an environment of collaboration and trust, the Team Leader ensures that the team is well-equipped to meet the project's objectives in a harmonious and effective manner.

Case Study: The Team Leader's Impact on a DSDM-Driven Software Development Project

Context: Setting the Stage

In a hypothetical software development project adopting the DSDM framework, the objective is to build a state-of-the-art customer relationship management (CRM) system. The Solution Development Team comprises individuals with a diverse skill set, including Business Analysts, Solution Developers, and Solution Testers. A Team Leader is elected by the team members, signifying trust and an endorsement of the individual's capability to guide the team effectively.

Challenges Encountered: The Obstacles

The team faces several challenges, including:

Complex Technical Requirements: The CRM system must integrate seamlessly with existing platforms.

Short Timelines: The project must be completed within a tight timeframe.

Diverse Team Skills: The team comprises members with varied levels of experience and expertise.

Actions Taken by the Team Leader: Navigating Through Challenges

Fostering Servant Leadership

The Team Leader initiates regular one-on-one sessions and team meetings to discuss issues and concerns openly, thereby building a supportive work environment.

Collaborative Detailed Planning

The Team Leader collaborates with the team to develop detailed sprints, breaking down the tasks required to meet the technical specifications. This ensures that the project remains on schedule without sacrificing quality.

Aligning Objectives

To make sure that everyone is aligned with the project's broader objectives, the Team Leader holds alignment meetings at the beginning of each sprint.

Dual Role as a Solution Developer

In this scenario, the Team Leader also takes on the role of a Solution Developer, contributing to the codebase while also steering the team.

Outcome: Success Through Effective Leadership

Under the Team Leader's effective guidance, the team manages to complete the CRM system within the stipulated timeframe and with adherence to technical specifications. The project is deemed a success, and the team members credit much of this success to the effective servant leadership and coordination provided by the Team Leader.

Conclusion: The Team Leader as a Catalyst

This case study illustrates how a Team Leader, through servant leadership, detailed planning, and effective communication, can act as a catalyst in the successful delivery of a DSDM project. It underscores the multifaceted nature of the Team Leader's role, emphasizing how they can both enable and elevate team performance.

The Integral Role of the Business Ambassador in DSDM Projects

Overview

Within the framework of the Dynamic Systems Development Method (DSDM), the Business Ambassador functions as a critical conduit between the business goals and the technical execution carried out by the Solution Development Team. This role is not merely ceremonial but is deeply ingrained in the project lifecycle, particularly during the Foundations and Evolutionary Development phases.

Key Responsibilities

Requirements Gathering

In the Foundations phase, the Business Ambassador takes an active role in defining and prioritizing the business requirements. This phase sets the stage for the entire project, making the Business Ambassador's input vital for long-term alignment with business objectives.

Day-to-Day Guidance

During the Evolutionary Development phase, which encompasses the timeboxed sprints, the Business Ambassador offers ongoing and nuanced articulation of business requirements. This continuous guidance ensures that the Solution Development Team is in sync with the changing and often complex business needs.

Decision-Making

In line with the DSDM principle of empowered teams, the Business Ambassador serves as the primary decision-maker on business-related aspects during the Evolutionary Development phase. This ensures that tactical decisions align with strategic business objectives.

Consultation with Business Advisors

To make well-informed decisions, the Business Ambassador may consult Business Advisors. These advisors provide specialized or broader business perspectives that enrich the decision-making process.

Fit-for-Purpose Evaluation

Finally, it is the Business Ambassador's responsibility to ascertain that the evolving solution is fit for its intended business purpose. This involves a continuous loop of validation against business objectives, a critical part of which occurs during the internal reviews at the end of each sprint.

Required Qualifications and Skills

The Business Ambassador is generally a senior member of the organization with sufficient authority and credibility to make impactful decisions. Key qualifications include a profound understanding of the business landscape, excellent decision-making abilities, and effective communication skills to articulate business requirements to the Solution Development Team.

Case Study: The Business Ambassador in a DSDM-Driven E-commerce Upgrade

Context

In a fictional scenario where a company aims to upgrade its e-commerce platform, the role of the Business Ambassador is particularly influential. The project involves various stakeholders—from developers to marketers—and has implications for diverse aspects of the business, such as customer experience, sales, and data security.

Challenges Faced

Requirements Alignment

Given the variety of stakeholders involved, consolidating and prioritizing their diverse requirements present a significant challenge.

Decision Agility

The fast-paced development cycles necessitate prompt and informed decision-making to keep the project on track.

Inclusive Communication

Ensuring that both technical and business stakeholders are on the same page is critical for the success of the project.

Steps Taken by the Business Ambassador

Proactive Requirements Gathering

At the Foundations phase, the Business Ambassador engages with different business units to create a comprehensive list of requirements for the upgrade.

Continuous Day-to-Day Guidance

During the Evolutionary Development phase, the Business Ambassador actively participates in sprint planning sessions, offering granular details about each feature based on the latest business objectives.

Rapid Decision-Making

Throughout the development cycles, the Business Ambassador makes agile, on-the-spot decisions. For example, prioritizing a secure payment gateway feature over a new recommendation engine could be a crucial decision based on emerging business needs.

Consultation with Advisors

The Business Ambassador collaborates with Business Advisors specializing in fields like cybersecurity and customer experience to ensure a holistic approach to the upgrade.

Final Evaluation

In the concluding stages, the Business Ambassador reviews the completed features to validate their alignment with the original business objectives. This final review ascertains that the upgraded platform serves the intended business purpose effectively.

Outcome

Due to the Business Ambassador's proactive involvement and effective decision-making, the e-commerce platform upgrade is executed successfully, meeting all predefined business objectives while staying aligned with the company's broader goals.

This case study showcases the dynamic role of the Business Ambassador in a DSDM project, highlighting how this role's strategic involvement can significantly influence the project's success.

Unpacking the Role of the Solution Developer in DSDM Projects

Overview

Within the framework of Dynamic Systems Development Method (DSDM), the Solution Developer is a cornerstone of the Solution Development Team. This role transcends mere coding; it entails understanding and interpreting business requirements to transform them into functional aspects of the evolving solution, also known as Solution Increments. In this endeavor, the Solution Developer collaborates extensively with the Business Ambassador, Business Analyst, and Solution Tester among other roles.

Key Responsibilities

Technical Implementation

This is the core of the Solution Developer's role, encompassing coding, testing, and integrating different elements to form coherent Solution Increments.

Understanding Business Requirements

In DSDM, it's not just about writing code. The Solution Developer actively collaborates with roles like the Business Ambassador and Business Analyst to fully understand what the business seeks to accomplish.

Ensuring Solution Quality

Quality is a multi-faceted criterion, touching upon functionality, performance, usability, and security. The Solution Developer ensures these attributes align with the guidelines set by the Technical Coordinator and meet business objectives.

Collaborative Engagement

Collaboration isn't optional. Working hand in hand with Solution Testers and other team roles, the Solution Developer helps validate that what's being built aligns well with business needs.

Fostering Continuous Improvement

The concept of 'learning while doing' is ingrained in Agile methodologies like DSDM. Solution Developers participate in retrospectives to evaluate and improve their practices.

Required Qualifications and Skills

Technical Competency: Mastery over relevant programming languages, frameworks, and tools is a given.

Business Acumen: While not business analysts, Solution Developers should have a grasp of business processes and objectives to align their technical solutions accordingly.

Collaboration and Communication: Soft skills like collaboration and effective communication are equally essential, given the cross-functional nature of DSDM projects.

Agile Mindset: The ability to work in fast-paced, iterative cycles, adapting to changes as they come along, is a hallmark of a competent Solution Developer.

Case Study: Role of the Solution Developer in a DSDM Project for a Healthcare App

Setting the Context

In a project aimed at creating a healthcare app that provides remote consultation and medical history tracking, the Solution Developer plays a multifaceted role. Let's examine the role in the context of some of the key responsibilities and tasks performed by the Solution Developer in this DSDM project.

Technical Implementation

The core task of writing and optimizing the code for features like video conferencing and medical history databases falls on the Solution Developer. This also involves continuous testing and integration to ensure smooth functioning and user experience.

Interpreting Business Requirements

Understanding the criticality of patient data and regulatory compliance, the Solution Developer works closely with the Business Ambassador to align the security features of the app with these high-stakes business requirements.

Ensuring Solution Quality

Here, the Solution Developer collaborates with the Technical Coordinator to ensure the app meets the necessary standards, including compliance with healthcare regulations such as HIPAA (Health Insurance Portability and Accountability Act).

Collaborative Engagement

Collaboration with the Solution Tester becomes crucial when validating whether the app's features meet the defined business requirements. This could involve multiple iterations of testing, debugging, and quality assurance.

Continuous Improvement

Participation in retrospectives leads the Solution Developer to suggest implementing more efficient algorithms and updating the tech stack for better performance, thus contributing to the project's continuous improvement.

In this healthcare app project, the Solution Developer's role goes far beyond coding. It encompasses interpreting and implementing complex business requirements, adhering to strict quality standards, and actively engaging in collaboration and continuous improvement. This multidimensional involvement ensures that the app is not just functional but also aligns closely with the critical business objectives and compliance needs.

The Vital Role of the Solution Tester in DSDM Projects: Ensuring Business Objectives Translate to Functional Solutions

The Solution Tester in a Dynamic Systems Development Method (DSDM) framework plays an essential role in ensuring that the solution developed meets the requisite business and technical standards. While most Agile methodologies emphasize testing, the DSDM approach uniquely situates the Solution Tester as a key member of the Solution Development Team, charged with the comprehensive task of aligning technical development with business objectives.

Core Responsibilities

Test Planning

A well-structured test strategy serves as the blueprint for all testing activities. The Solution Tester is responsible for developing or contributing to this strategy, ensuring it aligns well with both the technical requirements and business objectives. This might include identifying the types of tests to be conducted, such as unit tests, integration tests, and acceptance tests.

Test Execution

The Solution Tester takes on the hands-on role of conducting the various tests as per the plan. The tests range from unit tests that focus on individual components, to acceptance tests that ascertain if the solution as a whole meets the business objectives.

Quality Assurance

Through these rigorous testing procedures, the Solution Tester assures that the solution is of high quality and is in accordance with the project's standards and business requirements. This involves not only validating functionalities but also scrutinizing non-functional aspects like performance, security, and user experience.

Continuous Feedback

The role is not isolated to simply finding defects but extends to providing immediate feedback to Solution Developers and Business Ambassadors. This continuous feedback loop enables the team to make rapid adjustments, ensuring that the solution aligns closely with business requirements.

Documentation

Meticulous documentation of test plans, test results, and any identified areas for improvement or defects discovered, contributes to both project transparency and subsequent retrospective analyses. This serves as a repository that can be revisited for future projects and for ongoing maintenance.

Necessary Qualifications and Skills

The Solution Tester should possess:

Expertise in Testing Methodologies: Knowledge of various testing frameworks and tools is essential.

Business Acumen: An understanding of the business requirements and objectives helps in aligning the test strategies effectively.

Analytical Skills: Detail orientation and strong analytical skills are critical for identifying issues and evaluating the quality of the solution.

Adaptability: The Agile environment of DSDM requires the Solution Tester to be highly adaptable to changes in requirements or project scope.

Communication Skills: Effective communication is key to ensure that feedback is properly understood and implemented by the team.

Conclusion

The Solution Tester serves as a cornerstone in DSDM projects, bridging the gap between business objectives and technical deliverables through structured and rigorous testing. Beyond mere defect identification, this role contributes to the project's overall success by aligning every aspect of the solution with business objectives, while ensuring that it meets established quality standards.

A Practical Case Study: Ensuring Software Quality in a Financial Application

Scenario

In a DSDM project aimed at developing a financial management application, the Solution Tester's role becomes critical. This application has complex functionalities like real-time stock updates, budget planning, and tax computations.

Test Planning

The Solution Tester would start by devising a comprehensive test strategy. Given the financial nature of the application, aspects like data accuracy, security, and performance would be of paramount importance. The tester could decide to employ various testing techniques such as white-box testing, black-box testing, and stress testing to cover these facets.

Test Execution

Following the plan, the Solution Tester would then execute the tests. The scope could range from unit testing individual financial calculations to system testing the application's overall performance under peak load conditions. Special attention might be given to areas that handle sensitive financial information, where both functionality and security are thoroughly vetted.

Quality Assurance

At this stage, the Solution Tester ensures that all components meet the stipulated business requirements and technical standards. Any deviation would be documented and communicated back to the Solution Developer and Business Ambassador for immediate correction.

Continuous Feedback

Feedback loops are initiated where the tester provides real-time reports on the test findings. This may lead to crucial design changes, like restructuring the algorithm for tax computation to align it more closely with current tax laws, or enhancing security protocols to ward off potential data breaches.

Documentation

All test scenarios, outcomes, and defects are meticulously documented. This provides a transparent view into the system's quality and helps in future maintenance or when planning for application upgrades.

Final Thoughts

The Solution Tester's role in this project would be instrumental in ensuring that the financial application is not only functionally robust but also meets all the standards for security and performance. Through planned testing, continuous feedback, and stringent quality assurance, the tester helps in delivering a product that aligns closely with both technical and business objectives.

This case study highlights how integral the role of the Solution Tester is in ensuring that DSDM projects meet the desired quality standards and business objectives.

Deep Dive: The Multifaceted Role of the Business Advisor in DSDM Projects

Within the Dynamic Systems Development Method (DSDM), the Business Advisor is a unique yet peripheral role that offers a blend of subject matter expertise and strategic input to guide the Solution Development Team. Unlike roles that are involved in the daily grind of the project, the Business Advisor's involvement is more sporadic but highly impactful, bringing in nuanced perspectives in areas like regulatory compliance, domain-specific knowledge, and risk assessment.

Key Areas of Influence and Responsibility

Expert Consultation

The Business Advisor is often the go-to expert when the Solution Development Team needs specialized knowledge. This expertise could range from understanding industry-specific technologies to complex business processes. The Advisor's input is particularly crucial in navigating the project through complex landscapes, which require specialized knowledge that the team may not possess.

Regulatory Guidance

In projects that are subject to legal and compliance requirements, the Business Advisor becomes a vital player. They are responsible for ensuring that every aspect of the project, from data handling to customer interaction, complies with the relevant laws and regulations. This is not just about adhering to rules but also about protecting the business from potential legal risks.

User Perspective

Although the Business Ambassador generally handles the representation of business needs, the Business Advisor brings additional depth by offering specialized perspectives from an end-user or stakeholder point of view. This ensures that the solution developed is not just aligned with the business needs but also caters to the specific requirements of distinct user groups or stakeholders.

Risk Assessment

The Business Advisor plays an instrumental role in identifying and assessing specialized risks that the general team might overlook. These risks can often be domain-specific, regulatory, or even related to the project's technical aspects. Their insights into these risks can save the project from costly mistakes and delays.

Documentation

Another area where the Business Advisor's expertise becomes invaluable is documentation. This can range from contributing to the development of compliance checklists to reviewing technical specifications and documents that require a deep understanding of specific areas.

Required Skills and Qualifications

Subject Matter Expertise

The Business Advisor should be a seasoned expert in relevant business or technical domains. This not only adds credibility but also ensures that the advice given is well-grounded and applicable.

Business Acumen

Understanding the broader business objectives and constraints is essential for this role. The Business Advisor must be able to align their specialized advice with the overarching goals of the project.

Consultative Skills

The Advisor's role is consultative in nature, often requiring them to work closely with different team members in a short span of time. Hence, the ability to work in a consultative capacity within an Agile framework is essential.

Communication Skills

Given the often complex and specialized nature of their advice, excellent communication skills are vital. They need to articulate complex concepts in a manner that is easily understandable to people without a background in the subject matter.

Conclusion

The Business Advisor in a DSDM project is an auxiliary yet powerful role that provides the Solution Development Team with specialized insights across various facets of the project. Their role serves to enhance the depth of knowledge within the team, providing a nuanced layer of expertise that helps in steering the project towards success in a compliant and efficient manner.

Case Study: Navigating Regulatory Complexity with a Business Advisor in a DSDM Project for a Healthcare Application

Context

In a DSDM project aimed at developing a healthcare application, the role of the Business Advisor becomes exceptionally crucial given the regulatory labyrinth that healthcare projects often entail. This app was intended to facilitate remote consultations and patient record management. With patient data being sensitive, the project had to comply with a variety of regulations, including HIPAA (Health Insurance Portability and Accountability Act) in the United States and GDPR (General Data Protection Regulation) in Europe.

Expert Consultation

The Business Advisor, in this case, was a legal expert specializing in healthcare laws and data privacy. They provided key advice on how patient data should be stored, transmitted, and accessed, thereby guiding the Solution Development Team in implementing features in compliance with these complex regulations.

Regulatory Guidance

The Advisor conducted a detailed review of the project's compliance checkpoints and ensured that each feature adhered to the stipulated rules. They also guided the project team in preparing for audits and ensured that compliance documentation was in order.

User Perspective

The Business Advisor also brought in a nuanced understanding of the healthcare ecosystem, adding layers of specific user requirements, such as the need for emergency access to patient records by authorized medical professionals. This enriched the feature set to align more closely with user needs and expectations.

Risk Assessment

Data breaches in healthcare can have dire consequences. The Business Advisor helped identify various potential risks related to data security and guided the Solution Development Team in implementing additional layers of security measures to mitigate these risks.

Documentation

They were instrumental in drafting and reviewing legal disclosures, consent forms, and the data management policy. Their involvement in documenting these crucial aspects ensured that the project would stand up to regulatory scrutiny.

Conclusion

In the complex and highly regulated field of healthcare, the Business Advisor played a vital role in guiding the project through a web of legal, ethical, and business-specific considerations. By addressing these multiple facets, the Advisor significantly contributed to the project's success in delivering a solution that was not just technically sound but also legally compliant and closely aligned with user needs.

This case study illustrates the depth and breadth of impact that a Business Advisor can have in specialized and regulated environments.

Expanding the Horizons: The Role of the Technical Advisor in DSDM Projects

Overview

Within the DSDM (Dynamic Systems Development Method) framework, the Technical Advisor stands as a pillar of specialized technical wisdom for the Solution Development Team. Unlike roles that are continuously active in the day-to-day development cycles, the Technical Advisor steps in at critical junctures to provide expert opinions. This role plays a significant part in making sure that the technical aspects of the project are not just theoretically sound but are also practically sustainable over the long term.

Key Responsibilities

Technical Consultation

The Technical Advisor offers nuanced expertise in specialized areas that are vital to the project. These areas could range from database optimization to cloud architecture, or even cybersecurity. The role ensures that technical strategies employed are efficient, effective, and fit for purpose.

Operational Change Management

Transitioning a solution from the development phase to the operational phase often involves considerable change. The Technical Advisor provides crucial insights into aspects like deployment mechanisms, roll-back plans in case of failures, and versioning strategies. This ensures that operational transition happens smoothly, reducing risks and enhancing operational efficiency.

Operational Support

Understanding how a developed solution fits into the existing operational frameworks is essential for its success. The Technical Advisor guides the team on how the solution should be monitored, debugged, and troubleshot, ensuring a seamless integration into existing or planned operational support mechanisms.

Maintenance Guidance

Software maintenance can often be a costly and complex process. The Technical Advisor helps in preempting these challenges by offering advice on constructing a solution that is modular, upgradeable, and accumulates minimal technical debt over time.

Risk Assessment

Every technical choice comes with its own set of risks. The Technical Advisor identifies these potential hazards and offers mitigation strategies, thus ensuring that the technical aspects of the project are as foolproof as possible.

Required Qualifications and Skills

Deep Technical Expertise: Proficiency in the technical domains relevant to the project is non-negotiable.

Operational Landscape Understanding: An in-depth knowledge of how the developed solution will be deployed and maintained in an operational environment is critical.

Consultative Capability: The ability to work in an advisory capacity, especially within the fluidity of an Agile framework, is a must-have skill.

Communication Skills: The role often involves translating complex technical issues into language that non-technical stakeholders can understand, making excellent communication skills essential.

Conclusion

The role of the Technical Advisor in DSDM projects is a multifaceted one, straddling the domains of deep technical expertise and operational pragmatism. By acting as a bridge between these domains, the Technical

Advisor ensures that the project not only meets its development objectives but is also operationally sustainable and efficient.

A Closer Look: Practical Insights into the Role of the Technical Advisor in DSDM Projects

The Situation

In a hypothetical DSDM project aimed at developing a robust cybersecurity solution for financial institutions, the project team was composed of Business Ambassadors, Solution Developers, and Solution Testers. However, they encountered challenges related to ensuring the long-term sustainability and scalability of the cybersecurity solution they were developing.

The Involvement of the Technical Advisor

Technical Consultation

The Technical Advisor was brought in to provide expert guidance on cryptography methods, intrusion detection systems, and secure data transmission protocols. Their involvement led to the selection of more advanced and sustainable cybersecurity technologies.

Operational Change Management

Given that financial institutions are highly regulated and cannot afford downtime, the Technical Advisor outlined a phased deployment strategy that would allow the new cybersecurity solution to be rolled out without disrupting existing operations. This included a comprehensive roll-back plan in case of deployment failures.

Operational Support

The Advisor also consulted on how the solution would fit into the existing cybersecurity monitoring frameworks of financial institutions. They helped the team to design features that would facilitate easier monitoring and faster incident response.

Maintenance Guidance

Technical Advisors played a critical role in advising on how to construct the solution in a modular fashion. This modularity would make it easier to implement future upgrades and patches, thereby extending the lifespan of the solution.

Risk Assessment

They also conducted a thorough technical risk assessment that identified potential vulnerabilities and challenges that could arise during the operational phase. This allowed the team to proactively address these issues, making the project more robust.

The Impact

The inclusion of the Technical Advisor significantly improved the technical robustness and operational sustainability of the cybersecurity solution. Their contributions ensured that the solution was not only cutting-edge but also practical and sustainable in a real-world operational environment.

Conclusion

The role of the Technical Advisor was instrumental in elevating the project from being merely good to exceptionally great. Their specialized knowledge filled critical gaps in the team's expertise, ensuring that the developed solution was both technically sound and operationally viable.

Exploring the Workshop Facilitator: The Conductor of DSDM Collaboration

Overview

Within the context of Dynamic Systems Development Method (DSDM) projects, the Workshop Facilitator stands out as an essential role that doesn't directly contribute to the content or technical requirements of the project but focuses instead on the process and structure of collaboration. Their role is likened to that of a conductor in an orchestra, synchronizing various instruments (team members in this context) to produce a harmonious outcome.

Key Responsibilities

Planning: Blueprinting the Workshop

Ahead of the actual workshop, the Facilitator takes charge of setting the scene. This involves detailing the workshop's objectives, defining the agenda, and deciding on the participants. The planning phase serves as the blueprint that will guide how the workshop unfolds, ensuring that the activities within align with the project's broader goals.

Organizing: Setting the Stage

This phase is where the Workshop Facilitator turns plans into actionable logistics. From booking an appropriate venue to ensuring that the necessary materials are available, the Facilitator ensures everything is in place for a smooth-running workshop.

Facilitating: Orchestrating the Event

Perhaps the most visible part of their role, facilitating involves keeping conversations focused, time managed effectively, and the workshop's objectives met. They employ various techniques to stimulate discussion and encourage participation from all attendees, ensuring that the workshop generates meaningful output.

Conflict Resolution: The Neutral Arbiter

Conflicts and disagreements are almost inevitable in any collaborative endeavor. The Workshop Facilitator steps in here as an impartial mediator, guiding discussions back to a more constructive course. Their neutrality is crucial in preserving the workshop's integrity and ensuring its objectives are met.

Outcome Documentation: The Record Keeper

Once the workshop is complete, it's essential to capture the decisions made, ideas generated, and any other relevant information. The Workshop Facilitator ensures that this documentation is both accurate and distributed to the appropriate parties, serving as a vital reference point for future activities.

Required Qualifications and Skills

Expertise in Facilitation Techniques: Mastery over various facilitation tools and techniques is vital, as this equips them to guide discussions effectively.

Strong Organizational Skills: The logistical aspects of planning and running a workshop require a meticulous level of organization.

Neutrality: A capability to remain impartial ensures that the facilitation process is unbiased and focused solely on achieving the workshop's objectives.

Excellent Interpersonal Skills: The Facilitator interacts with various team members who have different views and interests; thus, interpersonal skills are vital.

Documentation Skills: The ability to accurately capture the outcomes of a workshop is crucial for transparency and for informing subsequent phases of the project.

Case Study: Implementing the Role of Workshop Facilitator in a DSDM Project

Scenario Overview

In this hypothetical case study, a mid-sized fintech company is undertaking a DSDM project to develop a new mobile banking application. Various team members from different departments, including business analysts, solution developers, and compliance officers, are involved. Given the complexity and the need for cross-functional collaboration, the role of a Workshop Facilitator is considered essential.

Pre-Workshop Planning: Aligning with Business Objectives

The Workshop Facilitator, named Sarah, begins by discussing the workshop's objectives with the project manager and the Business Ambassador. The primary goal is to align the technical features of the new application with compliance requirements. Sarah crafts an agenda that outlines discussion topics, time allocations, and identifies key participants, including compliance officers and solution developers.

Workshop Logistics: Building the Framework

Sarah secures a conference room fitted with necessary AV equipment and collaboration tools. She arranges for printed materials, such as compliance guidelines and technical specifications, to be distributed during the workshop. Pre-workshop briefings are sent out to all participants to bring them up to speed on what to expect and what is expected from them.

Facilitation: Managing Dynamics and Time

On the day of the workshop, Sarah ensures that discussions stay on topic and time is managed judiciously. When a debate arises between a compliance officer and a solution developer regarding data encryption standards, Sarah skillfully intervenes. She redirects the conversation back to the workshop's objectives, ensuring that a common ground is reached that satisfies both technical and compliance requirements.

Conflict Resolution: Maintaining Neutrality

During the workshop, conflicts arise, primarily around the stringency of certain compliance measures and their impact on user experience. Sarah remains impartial, steering the discussion towards constructive resolutions. Her neutrality helps in arriving at a balanced viewpoint that serves both the business objectives and the technical possibilities.

Outcome Documentation: Sealing the Deal

After the workshop, Sarah promptly captures the decisions made, areas of agreement, and action items in a comprehensive document. This is shared with all participants and other key stakeholders, serving as an essential guide for the project's next steps.

By skillfully fulfilling her role, Sarah ensures that the workshop serves its intended purpose, helping the team to align on complex issues that require cross-functional insights. Her contributions highlight the indispensable value of the Workshop Facilitator in achieving effective collaboration within DSDM projects.

Unpacking the Role of the DSDM Coach in DSDM Projects

Background

The DSDM Coach serves as a linchpin in DSDM projects, especially when the team has limited familiarity with the DSDM framework. Acting as an internal consultant, mentor, and trainer, this role ensures that the team adopts and adapts the DSDM principles effectively. Through educational initiatives, mentoring, consultative support, and continuous feedback, the DSDM Coach ensures that the project not only complies with the DSDM framework but also tailors it to the organizational context.

Key Areas of Responsibility

Educational Guidance

The DSDM Coach is a repository of knowledge and expertise in DSDM practices. They provide ongoing training to the team, ensuring that the principles and practices are not just understood but also efficiently applied. These educational sessions can range from formal training modules to informal lunch-and-learn sessions.

Mentoring

One-on-one or group mentoring sessions are organized by the DSDM Coach to tackle specific challenges or knowledge gaps that team members may encounter. The mentoring role is less about instructional dissemination and more about individualized guidance, ensuring that team members can apply DSDM principles in their specific roles effectively.

Consultative Support

The DSDM Coach offers advice that spans across various project roles, including the Solution Development Team. Whether it's about adopting the right practices for requirements elicitation or effective collaboration strategies, the DSDM Coach brings in a consultative lens that helps align activities with DSDM principles.

Process Oversight

One of the fundamental tasks is to ensure that the project remains compliant with the DSDM framework. To this end, the DSDM Coach monitors project activities closely, scrutinizing them against DSDM guidelines to ensure that deviations are either corrected or consciously adapted.

Feedback and Adaptation

The DSDM Coach takes an iterative approach, constantly collecting feedback on how DSDM is being implemented in the project. This allows them to recommend adjustments or improvements, ensuring that the DSDM practices are not just followed but also adapted to better fit the organizational context.

Required Qualifications and Skills

- A robust understanding of the DSDM framework is non-negotiable. The DSDM Coach must be well-versed in DSDM principles, practices, and the lifecycle phases to guide the team effectively.
- Educational prowess is essential, as the DSDM Coach will need to design and deliver training programs that are both effective and engaging.
- Exceptional communication skills are crucial, given the need to convey complex concepts clearly and persuade team members to adopt best practices.
- The ability to adapt DSDM practices to the specific organizational context is vital. This calls for an understanding of both the framework and the unique challenges and constraints of the organization.

Case Study: Enhancing Project Success with a DSDM Coach

Scenario

Imagine a mid-sized software development firm undertaking a project to develop a new inventory management system for a retail client. The project team has a mix of experienced developers, but they are new to the DSDM framework. The management decides to bring in a DSDM Coach to facilitate the adoption of DSDM practices.

Actions Taken by the DSDM Coach

Educational Initiatives

The DSDM Coach starts by conducting a two-day workshop to familiarize the team with the DSDM framework's principles and lifecycle phases. The sessions are interactive, with case-based discussions to facilitate better understanding.

Mentorship Program

After the initial training, the DSDM Coach establishes a mentorship program. Team members are paired based on their roles and challenges, allowing for focused guidance. Bi-weekly mentorship sessions are scheduled to discuss problems and find solutions.

Consultative Approach

As the project progresses, the DSDM Coach holds weekly meetings with project leaders and the Solution Development Team. In these sessions, the Coach provides specific advice on aligning their activities with DSDM practices. For instance, they assist the Business Analyst in optimizing requirements prioritization techniques and guide the Solution Developer in implementing timeboxing effectively.

Compliance Monitoring

The DSDM Coach regularly reviews project artifacts and attends key meetings to ensure that the team is adhering to the DSDM guidelines. Any deviations are promptly addressed, and the rationale for specific adaptations is well-documented.

Feedback Loop

At the end of each iteration, the DSDM Coach conducts a retrospective meeting. The objective is to gather feedback on what went well and what didn't. Based on this, the Coach refines the training modules and consultative strategies for the next iteration.

Outcomes

- Enhanced adherence to DSDM practices, which results in more predictable delivery timelines.
- Improved collaboration among team members, facilitated by the DSDM Coach's mentorship and consultative roles.

- Minimized deviations from the DSDM framework, thanks to active monitoring and real-time adjustments.

The inclusion of a DSDM Coach significantly smoothened the team's transition to the DSDM framework, leading to a successful project completion within scope, time, and budget constraints.

Chapter Six

A Comprehensive Guide to Products

Unveiling the Intricacies of DSDM Products in Agile Project Frameworks

Overview

DSDM Products in the Agile Project Framework are multifaceted elements that contribute significantly to the project's success. These products are not monolithic; instead, they can be broadly categorized into three primary groups: Solution-Related, Process-Related, and Governance-Related. They serve to not only create the primary project deliverables but also to navigate through the process and comply with governance protocols.

Classification of DSDM Products

Orange Products

These products are geared toward meeting business requirements and satisfying stakeholder interests. Their primary function is to align the project output with overarching business objectives, which could range from revenue generation to compliance or process optimization.

Green Products

Green Products form the technical backbone of the solution being developed. They often include software components, technical documentation, and system architectures. These products are pivotal in shaping the functional and technical aspects of the project.

Blue Products

Focused on project governance and control, Blue Products are integral to project management. These may include items like project plans, risk assessments, and compliance checklists. They provide the framework within which the project operates, ensuring alignment with regulatory and organizational standards.

Factors Influencing Product Formality

Contractual Relationships

The nature of the contractual obligations between involved parties can heavily influence the formality of DSDM Products. For instance, a strict contract may necessitate highly detailed technical documentation as a Green Product.

Corporate Standards

The prevailing organizational standards can also dictate the level of formality and the specific structure of these products. In organizations with a mature project management office (PMO), Blue Products like project plans and risk assessments may require a higher level of detail and standardization.

Governance Requirements

Governance needs, either from an internal or regulatory standpoint, could demand specific kinds of DSDM Products. For example, a financial services project might require detailed compliance reports as a Blue Product to satisfy regulatory scrutiny.

Governance and Compliance

Governance and Compliance often become the rationale for specific types of DSDM Products. They serve as milestones for governance gateways, enabling project managers and stakeholders to evaluate the project's health and compliance level. This feature makes them invaluable in projects that are subject to stringent regulatory oversight or internal governance structures.

Case Study: Navigating DSDM Products in a Financial Services Project

Scenario Overview

In a hypothetical financial services organization, a DSDM project is undertaken to develop a new customer relationship management (CRM) system. The project is subject to rigorous governance due to industry regulations and internal compliance requirements. Let's explore how DSDM Products manifest in this setting.

Classification of DSDM Products in Context

Orange Products

In this case, Orange Products would encompass business requirement documents and stakeholder analysis reports. These products would serve to ensure that the new CRM aligns with business objectives like customer satisfaction and regulatory compliance.

Green Products

The codebase of the new CRM system, along with its architectural documentation and API guides, would fall under Green Products. They would be the technical linchpins that bring the project to life.

Blue Products

Blue Products in this scenario could include risk assessment reports focusing on data security and compliance, as well as project plans outlining milestones tied to governance gateways. These would help in steering the project within the constraints of financial regulations.

Factors Influencing Product Formality

Contractual Relationships

Given the high-stakes nature of financial services, the contract between the development team and internal stakeholders would likely stipulate formal documentation, especially for Green and Blue Products.

Corporate Standards

Being a financial institution, the corporate standards would undoubtedly require rigorous project management. This means that Blue Products like project plans would need to adhere to PMO standards and likely be more formal.

Governance Requirements

Given the regulated environment, governance requirements would play a significant role. Blue Products like compliance reports would be essential, not only as internal guiding documents but also as records for regulatory bodies.

Governance and Compliance Considerations

For this project, Blue Products would be critical in enabling the organization to pass through internal and external governance gateways. Documents such as compliance checklists and risk assessment reports would serve as key artefacts in demonstrating the project's alignment with industry regulations.

Through this case study, we can see that the necessity, formality, and function of DSDM Products are highly contextual, influenced by a myriad of factors including industry, regulatory landscape, and organizational culture.

An In-depth Look at the Terms of Reference in the DSDM Agile Project Framework

The Importance of Terms of Reference

Definition

In the DSDM Agile Project Framework, the Terms of Reference (ToR) document is not just a formality, but a critical governance asset. It acts as a contract of sorts between stakeholders and the project team, crystallizing the understanding of what the project is expected to deliver.

Purpose and Scope

The ToR serves multiple, interconnected purposes. Firstly, it acts as a scope-defining mechanism, providing a framework that specifies what will and will not be tackled in the project. This limits scope creep and ensures that the team remains focused on delivering what is essential. Secondly, it serves as an initial justification tool, used to validate whether the project aligns well enough with organizational strategy to warrant the investment of resources.

Governance and Strategic Alignment

Governance Implications

In the realm of governance, the ToR gains a different level of importance. It becomes an instrument of prioritization within a portfolio of projects. By clearly stating the project's objectives and how these align with organizational goals, it becomes easier to prioritize this project relative to others. Further, it sets the stage for performance metrics, tying the hands of stakeholders and making them accountable for the project's success or failure based on predefined criteria.

Strategic Alignment

The ToR not only serves governance functions but also acts as a tool for ensuring that the project remains strategically aligned throughout its lifecycle. The document can be revisited at different phases to ensure that the course being taken still fits within the scope and objectives initially set out, thereby maintaining a clear line of sight to the organization's strategic goals.

Key Components Explored

Components of Terms of Reference

A well-crafted ToR document generally encompasses several key sections, each serving a specific purpose:

Project Title and Description: The essence of the project, summarily described, serves as a quick reference and framing device.

Business Objectives: These are the lighthouses guiding the project, essential for ongoing alignment checks.

Key Stakeholders: Knowing who is involved, and what their interests are, helps in communication planning and conflict resolution.

Constraints and Assumptions: These shape the project's environment, impacting everything from resource allocation to timeline estimates.

Initial Budget and Timeline: While these are subject to refinement, initial estimates set the stage for future project planning and execution.

Risk Assessment: An initial risk profile can help in proactive problem-solving, allowing for contingencies to be built into the project plan.

Through its multiple functions and components, the Terms of Reference in a DSDM project serves as a vital tool for governance, strategic alignment, and informed decision-making.

Case Study: Implementing the Terms of Reference in a DSDM Project

Setting the Stage

In this hypothetical case study, a financial services company is gearing up to launch a new digital payment platform. They decide to use the DSDM Agile Project Framework. At the initiation stage, the project manager drafts the Terms of Reference (ToR) document, understanding its critical role in project governance and strategic alignment.

Crafting the ToR: A Closer Look at Components

Project Title and Description

The ToR starts with a concise project title, "Digital Payment Platform Implementation," followed by a brief description outlining the purpose and scope of the project.

Business Objectives

The business objectives are clearly stated to include improving customer experience, increasing market share in the digital payments sector, and ensuring high-level security and compliance with regulatory standards.

Key Stakeholders

The stakeholders range from the CEO and board members to the IT department and customer service representatives. Their roles, interests, and levels of influence are clearly defined.

Constraints and Assumptions

Budget constraints, compliance requirements, and assumed market readiness for a digital solution are listed here to set the environmental context for the project.

Initial Budget and Timeline

A preliminary budget is estimated, alongside a tentative project timeline divided into sprints, aligning with the Agile framework.

Risk Assessment

Initial risks like potential data breaches, project overruns, and non-compliance issues are identified along with potential mitigation plans.

Governance and Ongoing Alignment

Prioritization and Accountability

The ToR is used in executive meetings to prioritize this project in the company's project portfolio. It serves as the basis for allocating resources and setting performance metrics.

Strategic Revisits

As the project progresses through its sprints, the ToR is regularly revisited during governance meetings to ensure that the project's current status aligns with the initial business objectives and organizational goals.

Conclusion: The Impact of the ToR

The Terms of Reference played a critical role throughout the project lifecycle. It guided decision-making, informed governance, and kept the project strategically aligned. Any deviations or scope creeps were quickly identified and addressed, keeping the project on track and ensuring its successful completion.

Through this case study, it becomes evident how crucial the Terms of Reference is, not just as a starting document but as an ongoing tool for effective project management within the DSDM framework.

The Significance of the Business Case in DSDM Projects

Definition and Contextual Importance

In DSDM (Dynamic Systems Development Method) Agile projects, the Business Case is a cornerstone document that serves as a governance instrument. It justifies the initiation and continuation of a project by assessing its alignment with business objectives, financial viability, and risk considerations. Far from being a static document, the Business Case undergoes multiple revisions throughout the project lifecycle.

Multiple Roles of the Business Case

Vision Statement

The Business Case is the narrative that illustrates the intended future state of the business, a transformation that the project seeks to enable. This vision aids in steering the team's efforts toward a cohesive objective.

Financial Justification

Crucially, the Business Case contains an investment appraisal that scrutinizes the financial aspects of the project. It meticulously calculates the Return on Investment (ROI) and evaluates whether the projected benefits validate the estimated costs of development, ongoing support, and future maintenance.

Risk Assessment

Beyond just financial figures, the Business Case provides a comprehensive risk analysis. This covers various potential roadblocks, from market fluctuations to technical limitations, and outlines mitigation strategies.

Review and Update Mechanism

The Business Case is not a 'set-and-forget' artifact. It incorporates a mechanism for periodic reviews to assess whether the project remains viable and aligns with the business goals.

Components that Build a Business Case

Project Objectives and Cost Estimates

These provide the baseline for what the project seeks to accomplish and at what estimated cost. They serve as the initial metrics against which project performance is gauged.

Benefit Analysis and Risk Evaluation

A detailed account of the projected benefits is laid out, along with a thorough evaluation of risks. These sections help in decision-making processes throughout the project.

ROI Calculation and Stakeholder Analysis

The ROI calculation quantifies the expected benefits in relation to the costs, while stakeholder analysis identifies the interests and influence levels of different parties involved in the project.

Governance and Milestone Significance

Project Feasibility and Foundations Approval

The Business Case is pivotal at the outset. An outline is prepared during the Feasibility phase, which is crucial for moving to the Foundations phase. The fully fleshed-out Business Case, upon review and approval, enables the project to transition into the development stage.

Incremental Reviews

In alignment with Agile principles, the Business Case is revisited at the end of each Project Increment. This ensures that the project remains financially viable and strategically aligned, allowing for timely corrections or even termination if necessary.

The Business Case is therefore not just a document but an active tool for strategic alignment, financial accountability, and risk management in DSDM projects.

A Deep Dive: Case Study on Utilizing a Business Case in a DSDM Project

Context Setting: The Project Scenario

In a hypothetical DSDM project at XYZ Corp, the team is entrusted with developing an AI-based customer service platform. The Business Case is prepared during the Feasibility phase and presented to the steering committee for approval to move on to the Foundations phase.

Leveraging the Business Case at Various Stages

Feasibility Phase: Initial Validation

An outline of the Business Case is created, emphasizing the vision of an AI-driven transformation in customer service. Initial cost estimates and anticipated benefits in terms of improved efficiency and customer satisfaction are presented. This preliminary Business Case helps the committee decide whether to proceed to the Foundations phase.

Foundations Phase: Detailed Elaboration

The Business Case is elaborated with more accurate cost estimates, detailed benefit analysis, and an in-depth risk assessment. This becomes the basis for formally initiating the development process.

Evolutionary Development: Periodic Reviews

After each Project Increment, the Business Case is revisited. ROI is recalculated based on the actual costs and realized benefits. For instance, after the first increment, the AI platform successfully handles 20% of all customer inquiries, confirming the projected benefits. However, the costs run 10% higher than anticipated due to unforeseen technical challenges.

Project Close: Final Assessment

Upon project completion, the Business Case serves as a benchmark for evaluating the project's success. Did it meet its financial expectations? Was the vision realized to the extent planned? The Business Case provides the metrics for this final assessment.

Outcome and Lessons

The Business Case proved to be an invaluable governance tool throughout the project. It set the strategic direction and was crucial for ongoing assessments. Moreover, the periodic reviews allowed the team to make course corrections, such as budget adjustments and risk mitigation strategies, thereby ensuring that the project remained aligned with its initial objectives and justified the investments made.

In summary, the Business Case at XYZ Corp served not just as a static document but as a dynamic tool that actively guided the project at every key milestone. It offered a structured framework for decision-making and helped maintain alignment between the project execution and organizational objectives.

The Prioritised Requirements List (PRL) in DSDM Agile Project Framework

Importance of a Baseline PRL

The Governance Perspective

The establishment of a baseline PRL by the end of the Foundations phase serves not just as a procedural requirement but as a robust governance mechanism. This baseline PRL becomes the "ground truth" against which all future changes, milestones, and deliveries are evaluated.

Preventing Scope Creep

Having a baseline PRL is instrumental in preventing scope creep. Scope creep can derail projects, leading to increased costs and timelines. By having a clear scope defined through the PRL, stakeholders have a reference point that ensures alignment with the intended business objectives and strategic goals.

Intricacies of Requirements Prioritization

The Ongoing Process

The task of assigning priority to each requirement is not a static or one-time affair; it's a dynamic process that may be revisited as new insights emerge during the project lifecycle. Prioritization needs to take into account various facets, including technical complexity, stakeholder urgency, and dependencies among different requirements.

Prioritization Methodologies

In most instances, formal methodologies like MoSCoW (Must-have, Should-have, Could-have, and Won't-have) are employed to provide a structured approach to prioritizing requirements. Such methodologies enable objective evaluation and agreement among stakeholders, ensuring that the most critical aspects are not compromised.

Change Management and the PRL

Organic vs. Formal Changes

While DSDM Agile allows for organic evolution and changes to requirements, any change that affects the "breadth" of the project—essentially adding or removing high-level requirements—must be formally managed through adjustments to the PRL.

Governance Through Ongoing Review

Changes to the high-level requirements need formal approval. This iterative approval process ensures that any shift in direction or scope still aligns with the business vision and has the necessary governance oversight to proceed.

Case Study: Implementing the Prioritised Requirements List (PRL) in a DSDM Agile Project

Project Background

Scenario

Imagine a financial services organization embarking on a project to develop a new online banking platform. The team adopts the DSDM Agile Project Framework, as it is flexible yet robust enough to manage the complexities involved. The Prioritised Requirements List (PRL) is developed early on as a part of the Feasibility phase and then finalized in the Foundations phase.

Governance Through PRL

Initial Collation

During the Feasibility phase, key stakeholders, including business analysts, domain experts, and potential users, contribute to an initial list of high-level requirements. These are collated into a draft PRL.

Baseline Development

In the Foundations phase, the draft PRL is rigorously examined, and priorities are assigned using the MoSCoW method. The PRL is then baselined, providing the definitive scope of the project.

Change Management

Requirement Changes

Midway through the project, a new regulatory requirement necessitates the addition of more stringent user authentication mechanisms. This change affects the "breadth" of the project, as it involves adding a new high-level requirement to the PRL.

Governance Procedure

Before making this change, a formal review is initiated. Key stakeholders assess the impact of this new requirement on the project's budget, timeline, and other high-priority requirements. After thorough analysis and receiving necessary approvals, the PRL is updated, and the new requirement is integrated into the project scope.

Project Milestones and Reviews

Incremental Verification

After each Project Increment, the baselined PRL serves as a reference for assessing what has been delivered versus what was initially scoped. This ensures the project remains aligned with its original objectives.

Final Validation

At project completion, the final deliverables are cross-referenced with the PRL to validate that all high-priority requirements have been fulfilled, thereby confirming the project's success according to initially agreed upon scopes and priorities.

The PRL, in this case, played a critical role in governance, scope definition, and change management, ensuring the project remained aligned with both strategic objectives and operational constraints.

The Intricacies of Solution Architecture Definition in the DSDM Agile Project Framework

The Essence of Solution Architecture Definition

The Solution Architecture Definition serves as a blueprint for the entire project in the context of the DSDM Agile Project Framework. It is instrumental in guiding both the business and technical teams, ensuring that they work in a unified manner toward the achievement of the project goals.

Multifaceted Roles

Clarifying the Project Scope

One of the essential functions of the Solution Architecture Definition is to make explicit the scope of the solution. This clarification is vital as it sets the expectations right for all stakeholders involved, from project managers to technical teams and business analysts.

Technical Steering

This document serves as a compass for the technical side of the project. It outlines the high-level architectural design, which forms the basis for more detailed technical specifications and decisions as the project unfolds.

Business Synergy

By incorporating business objectives and requirements into the architecture, the document ensures that the technical execution remains closely aligned with business goals. This is particularly important for avoiding costly misdirection and ensuring that the project delivers real business value.

Flexibility and Evolution

Crucially, while the Solution Architecture Definition provides an essential framework, it is not overly prescriptive. It gives room for the evolutionary development of the solution, facilitating adaptability to new insights, requirements, or constraints that may arise as the project progresses.

Key Components

The Building Blocks

Common elements that often form part of the Solution Architecture Definition include an outline of business objectives, high-level technical architecture, data models, and constraints. It may also delve into the interactions between different system components and interfaces, offering a more comprehensive view of the envisioned solution.

Governance Highlights

Foundations Phase

Usually, the Solution Architecture Definition is crystallized by the end of the Foundations phase. It acts as a pillar for the subsequent phases of the project, offering a well-defined architectural lens through which the entire project is viewed.

Periodic Reviews

As the project matures, the Solution Architecture Definition might need to be revisited and potentially revised. These review points are vital for ensuring that the document remains aligned with the project's evolving nature, ensuring coherent governance across all phases.

Case Study: Implementation of Solution Architecture Definition in a Hypothetical DSDM Project

Setting the Scene

Project Overview

Imagine a company that aims to develop a comprehensive Customer Relationship Management (CRM) system to enhance customer engagement and drive sales. The organization adopts the DSDM Agile Project Framework to govern the project.

Crafting the Solution Architecture Definition

Key Stakeholder Involvement

During the Foundations phase, architects, business analysts, and key stakeholders collaborate to draft the Solution Architecture Definition. This document lays out a high-level view of how the CRM system will work, from business objectives such as "Increase Customer Engagement by 20%" to technical elements like "Microservices Architecture."

Initial Components

The document includes high-level objectives, technical architecture blueprints, data models, and interfaces between the CRM and existing systems. It also outlines known constraints, such as budget limitations and compliance requirements.

Governance Through Milestones

Finalizing the Document

By the end of the Foundations phase, the Solution Architecture Definition is finalized and approved. It serves as the architectural cornerstone upon which the entire project will be built.

Review Points

As the project moves into the Exploration and Engineering phases, the team revisits the Solution Architecture Definition. These review points serve as 'sanity checks,' confirming that ongoing work remains aligned with the initial architecture and business objectives.

Evolution and Adaptability

During one of these review points, the team realizes that a planned integration with an external email marketing tool would bring immense value but was not included in the initial document. After a formal governance meeting, the Solution Architecture Definition is updated to incorporate this component, demonstrating its flexibility and ability to adapt to new insights.

Conclusion

In this hypothetical DSDM project, the Solution Architecture Definition not only provided the initial guiding framework but also allowed for adjustments aligned with real-world challenges and opportunities. It proves to be an indispensable tool for steering the project from both a technical and business standpoint, proving its vital role in the DSDM Agile Project Framework.

Unlocking the Potential of Development Approach Definition in DSDM Agile Projects

Overview and Purpose

What It Is and Why It Matters

The Development Approach Definition is a pivotal element in the DSDM Agile Project Framework, acting as the go-to reference for the developmental side of a project. Essentially, it outlines the roadmap for how the solution will evolve from concept to reality, emphasizing on the standards and quality assurance practices to be followed.

Key Components

Methodological Choices

The document stipulates which development methodologies are appropriate for the project—be it Agile, DevOps, or perhaps a hybrid model. This sets the stage for the practices, activities, and rituals the team will use throughout the development lifecycle.

Toolkit Essentials

Technological underpinnings are addressed by specifying the software and hardware tools that will be employed. This can range from development environments to version control systems.

Best Practices and Norms

This section is particularly significant for establishing team norms and ensuring consistent application of standards. It discusses standard coding practices, the correct forms of documentation, and even data management strategies.

Quality: More than Just a Buzzword

Given its emphasis on quality assurance, the document outlines both qualitative and quantitative metrics that the project aims to achieve. This sets the quality expectations and provides benchmarks for ongoing assessment.

Testing, Not Guessing

A well-defined testing strategy is outlined, specifying the various levels of testing to be performed—unit, integration, system, and user acceptance tests—to ensure the solution meets its quality metrics.

Review Mechanisms

Processes for both code and architectural reviews are delineated, often setting forth the frequency and types of reviews that will take place.

Governance and Lifecycle Relevance

Initial Drafting and Ongoing Adaptability

Typically created during the Foundations phase, the Development Approach Definition isn't just a one-off artifact. It's a living document that evolves with the project, reflecting changes in methodology, tooling, or even quality metrics.

Governance Touchpoints

As an essential document for technical governance, it provides a foundation for decision-making in governance meetings and periodic reviews. Its elements are often cited when assessing the technical soundness and quality of the project's evolution.

Exploring a Case Study: Application of Development Approach Definition in a Hypothetical DSDM Project

Setting the Stage

Project Scenario

Let's consider a hypothetical financial services company looking to develop a new mobile application aimed at facilitating easier access to investment portfolios. The project is governed by the DSDM Agile Project Framework.

How the Development Approach Definition Comes into Play

Initial Creation

At the outset, during the Foundations phase, the project team drafts the Development Approach Definition. Given that they decide on a hybrid Agile-DevOps model, this becomes the first component to be documented.

Tooling

For this particular project, the team opts for specific sets of software and hardware that are geared toward mobile application development and financial data security. This information is laid out in the "Tools and Technologies" section.

Best Practices and Standards

Given that they're dealing with sensitive financial data, the best practices outlined are stringent. They specify encryption methods for data storage and secure coding practices to prevent common vulnerabilities.

Quality Metrics

In a field like financial services where the margin for error is minimal, quality metrics are set high. Performance benchmarks and latency metrics are laid out clearly, along with key performance indicators (KPIs) to measure customer satisfaction once the app is rolled out.

Testing Strategy

A multi-layered approach to testing is documented, encompassing unit tests for individual pieces of code, integration tests for data flows, and a series of rigorous user acceptance tests to ensure the app meets end-user needs.

Governance

Given its comprehensive nature, the Development Approach Definition becomes the cornerstone document in technical governance meetings. Whenever there's a shift in development strategies, tools, or even team members, this document is revisited and updated to reflect those changes.

Takeaway

The Development Approach Definition serves as a key governance tool and living document that not only outlines how the solution will be developed but also sets the benchmarks for its quality. It's a cornerstone in the decision-making process and offers a structured pathway for the project to evolve while meeting its business objectives and quality parameters.

The Delivery Plan: Navigating Through DSDM Projects

Overview

Defining the Delivery Plan

The Delivery Plan is a pivotal element in any project managed under the DSDM Agile Project Framework. Unlike a traditional Gantt chart, which is often filled with task-level minutiae, the Delivery Plan takes a higher altitude view. It outlines the timeline and structure for Project Increments and Timeboxes, thereby offering a guiding framework for the agile team.

Key Features

Components that Make Up the Delivery Plan

Project Increments: These are essentially macro-level goals that the project aims to achieve, serving as key deliverables.

Timeboxes: To maintain the agile spirit, the initial or upcoming Project Increment is divided into timeboxed periods. These Timeboxes have specific, albeit adaptable, deliverables attached to them.

Dependencies: In real-world projects, various external factors can influence the delivery. The Delivery Plan accounts for these by identifying dependencies.

Resource Allocation: Some projects may require specialized skills or resources. If such needs are anticipated, they can be incorporated into the Delivery Plan.

Milestones: These are landmark moments in the project timeline that signify important achievements or deliverables.

Governance and Lifespan

How the Delivery Plan Fits into Governance

The Delivery Plan is not just a planning artifact but a governance tool. Created typically during the Foundations phase, this document serves several key governance functions:

Progress Checkpoints: It is regularly consulted in governance meetings to assess if the project is on course.

Data-Driven Decisions: Its milestones and timelines offer tangible data for decision-making.

Adaptability: True to the agile methodology, the Delivery Plan is flexible. It is revisited and possibly revised at the end of each Project Increment.

Lifecycle

The plan's lifecycle is inherently iterative, being updated at various stages, particularly at the end of each Project Increment. This keeps it aligned with the project's evolving requirements and constraints.

A Closer Look: Case Study on Implementing a Delivery Plan in a DSDM Project

The Scenario

Project Background

In this hypothetical case, a software company is working on a cloud-based customer relationship management (CRM) system. They have chosen to manage the project using the DSDM Agile Project Framework.

The Delivery Plan in Action

Foundations Phase

During the Foundations phase, a high-level Delivery Plan was created. It outlined three key Project Increments:

User Authentication and Dashboard

Contact Management

Reporting and Analytics

Timeboxing

The first Project Increment, 'User Authentication and Dashboard,' was further divided into three Timeboxes:

User Sign-Up and Verification

Basic Dashboard Features

Security Measures

Governance Reviews

The Delivery Plan was then used in governance meetings to set expectations and make adjustments as necessary. After the first Timebox, the team realized that they were ahead of schedule and decided to pull in a few features from the second Timebox.

Milestones and Dependencies

Two critical milestones were identified in the Delivery Plan:

Completion of User Authentication: Essential for early beta testing.

First Complete Draft of Contact Management Features: Needed before a demo to potential investors.

Dependencies like API approvals from third-party services were also included in the Delivery Plan.

Outcome

Flexibility and Adaptability

Because they had a clear but flexible Delivery Plan, the team could make informed decisions, like accelerating certain features when they found they were ahead of schedule.

Governance Benefits

The Delivery Plan was an invaluable tool during governance meetings. It helped stakeholders understand the project's progress and make data-driven decisions.

Continuous Updates

The Delivery Plan was updated after the completion of each Project Increment, keeping it aligned with actual progress and any new dependencies or requirements that emerged.

Through this case study, it becomes clear how vital the Delivery Plan is for both planning and governance in projects managed under the DSDM Agile Project Framework.

In-Depth Exploration: The Role of Management Approach Definition in DSDM Agile Projects

Understanding the Essence

The Fundamental Premise

The Management Approach Definition is a linchpin in the structure of a DSDM Agile project. It sets the managerial tone and operational strategy, ensuring that everyone involved understands the "how" of managing the project, not just the "what" of the project's deliverables.

Key Components Dissected

Organizational Structure

This segment lays out the governance hierarchy within the project. It allocates roles and responsibilities, providing a roadmap for who is accountable for what. It's essential for avoiding conflicts and streamlining the decision-making process.

Planning Approach

Planning is the backbone of project management. This section provides guidelines on how the work will be organized, from defining Project Increments to setting Timeboxes. It's instrumental in ensuring the project stays on course and aligns with the overarching business objectives.

Stakeholder Engagement

Effective communication is vital for a project's success. This part outlines how stakeholders will be kept in the loop. It addresses communication methods, frequency, and avenues for feedback, ensuring that stakeholder expectations are managed and met.

Progress Reporting

Here, the focus is on visibility. Key performance indicators (KPIs) are defined, along with a reporting schedule. This ensures that both the project team and stakeholders have a clear understanding of the project's status at all times.

Review Mechanisms

Reviews serve as health checks for the project. This section spells out how and when these reviews will occur, what will be examined, and who will be involved, allowing for data-driven adjustments to the project strategy.

Governance and Project Lifecycle

Initial Drafting and Baseline

The Management Approach Definition is initially drafted during the Feasibility phase and then finessed and finalized—or "baselined"—during the Foundations phase. This baseline document becomes the governing manifesto for how the project will be managed.

Evolution and Flexibility

While the document is considered final post-baselining, it is not set in stone. If significant shifts in project conditions occur, or if governance reviews suggest updates are needed, the document can be revised accordingly.

Case Study: Implementing Management Approach Definition in a DSDM Agile Project

Scenario Overview

In our hypothetical example, a financial services company embarks on a DSDM Agile project to overhaul its online banking system. The project faces complex challenges, including regulatory compliance, multiple stakeholder groups, and a mix of legacy and new technologies. A well-crafted Management Approach Definition document becomes crucial to navigate these challenges.

Key Components Applied

Organizational Structure

In this project, a robust governance hierarchy was set up, comprising executive sponsors, project managers, Agile coaches, development teams, and QA teams.

Each role was explicitly defined in the Management Approach Definition to avoid overlaps and ambiguities.

Planning Approach

Given the complexity and regulatory requirements, the planning section outlined a series of Project Increments focused on specific compliance goals. Timeboxes were designed to be flexible but rigorous, allowing the team to adapt without compromising on quality or compliance.

Stakeholder Engagement

The document delineated a multi-channel communication strategy for stakeholders, including monthly town-halls, weekly status reports, and an online portal for asynchronous updates. This helped manage expectations and kept everyone informed.

Progress Reporting

Custom KPIs, like 'Compliance Milestones Reached,' 'Defects per Increment,' and 'Stakeholder Engagement Levels,' were established. A bi-weekly reporting cadence was set, targeting different audience layers, from executive leadership to operational teams.

Review Mechanisms

Quarterly governance reviews were scheduled, involving internal audit teams and external regulatory bodies. These were built into the project calendar and used to update or validate the existing management approach.

Governance Through the Lifecycle

Baseline and Beyond

Initially drafted in the Feasibility phase, the document was baselined at the end of the Foundations phase. Post-baselining, it was considered the ultimate guide for managing the project.

Adaptability in Action

When the project encountered a significant regulatory change, the Management Approach Definition was revisited and updated to align with the new requirements. This ensured that the project remained compliant while still maintaining its Agile essence.

This case study illustrates the indispensable role played by the Management Approach Definition in setting the project's managerial and governance framework, especially in complex and dynamically changing environments.

The Indispensable Role of Feasibility Assessment in DSDM Agile Projects

The Feasibility Assessment stands as a cornerstone in the DSDM Agile Project Framework. Conducted at the end of the Feasibility phase, this assessment serves as a rigorous evaluative tool to gauge the project's viability across business, technical, and managerial dimensions. Below we delve into its key elements, structure, and governance implications.

Key Elements Explored

Business Feasibility

The first pillar of the Feasibility Assessment is an exhaustive evaluation of how the project aligns with organizational objectives. Crucial financial metrics like cost-benefit analysis and potential ROI are assessed at this juncture.

Technical Feasibility

Ensuring technical feasibility involves assessing whether the organization has the necessary technological infrastructure and skills. Aspects like software compatibility, hardware requirements, and scalability are thoroughly evaluated.

Management Feasibility

This portion of the assessment looks into the managerial aspects like governance structure, resource availability, and stakeholder buy-in. Essentially, it examines whether the organization is capable of managing the project effectively from a governance perspective.

Format and Structure

Baselined Collection

The assessment may compile baselined versions of critical documents such as the Terms of Reference and Business Case. These matured documents provide a reliable foundation for decision-making.

Executive Summary

In some instances, the Feasibility Assessment is synthesized into an executive summary. This concise document encapsulates key findings, associated risks, and strategic recommendations, offering a streamlined guide for stakeholder review.

Governance and Lifecycle

Initial Stage Importance

The assessment's role is most salient at the initial stages of the project. Its findings provide the rationale to move from the Feasibility phase into the Foundations phase.

Decision-making Authority

The Feasibility Assessment serves as a critical decision-making instrument. It can influence whether the project advances, undergoes re-scoping, or is terminated, thus acting as a gatekeeper to resource allocation and project initiation.

In conclusion, the Feasibility Assessment is not merely a bureaucratic requirement but a strategic tool designed to offer an empirical basis for project initiation, planning, and governance. Would you like to hear about a case study that elaborates on the Feasibility Assessment in the DSDM Agile Project Framework?

Case Study: Implementing Feasibility Assessment in a DSDM Agile Project for a Financial Institution

Overview

A financial institution sought to modernize its legacy systems to improve operational efficiency and customer experience. The firm decided to adopt the DSDM Agile Project Framework to guide the project. One of the critical early steps taken was a comprehensive Feasibility Assessment.

Key Elements Explored

Business Feasibility

Given the financial stakes involved, a meticulous cost-benefit analysis was conducted. Projections indicated a positive ROI, aligned with the institution's long-term revenue growth targets.

Technical Feasibility

A technology audit revealed that although the existing infrastructure was outdated, it was compatible with the proposed solutions. The assessment also highlighted the additional resources needed, giving the organization a clear roadmap for technical preparedness.

Management Feasibility

The governance structure was scrutinized to assess if it could support Agile processes. While stakeholder buy-in was largely positive, it was recommended that a more agile-aware management structure should be put in place.

Format and Structure

Baselined Collection

The project team collated baselined versions of essential documents like the Business Case and Terms of Reference. These were included in the Feasibility Assessment for higher management review.

Executive Summary

A high-level executive summary was crafted, capturing essential findings, risks, and next steps. This document was circulated among key stakeholders, providing a quick but thorough understanding of the project's viability.

Governance and Lifecycle

Steering Committee Review

The completed Feasibility Assessment was presented to a steering committee comprising senior executives, technical leads, and project managers.

Decision-making Outcome

Armed with the insights from the Feasibility Assessment, the steering committee green-lighted the project, approving the resources for the Foundations phase. Importantly, it was agreed that governance structures would be adapted to be more agile-responsive.

Conclusion

The Feasibility Assessment served as a pivotal element in initiating the project. By systematically evaluating business, technical, and managerial feasibilities, the institution made an informed decision that effectively navigated risks and aligned with organizational goals.

This case study demonstrates how the Feasibility Assessment in the DSDM Agile Project Framework is not just a theoretical exercise but a practical tool that can have a tangible impact on a project's outcome.

Foundations Summary in the DSDM Agile Project Framework

Definition

The Foundations Summary is an essential evaluative artifact produced at the close of the Foundations phase in the DSDM Agile Project Framework. It aggregates the salient insights gleaned from various documents and assessments carried out during this phase. The document is geared towards informing stakeholders on the project's alignment with organizational goals and readiness across technical and managerial facets.

Key Elements

Business Alignment

The Foundations Summary meticulously scrutinizes how well the project dovetails with the organizational objectives. It helps in ascertaining that the project is not a standalone endeavor but is synergistically aligned with the broader strategic aims.

Technical Readiness

A key aspect reviewed is the preparedness of the technical infrastructure. It examines whether the existing or proposed technical architecture is robust enough to handle the anticipated project demands.

Management Approaches

The project's governance and managerial aspects are also assessed. This includes an evaluation of risk management protocols, resource planning, and other administrative procedures that will be essential for the successful execution of the project.

Format and Structure

Baselined Collection

The Foundations Summary often encapsulates the finalized, or 'baselined,' versions of crucial foundational documents. These may include the Business Case, Prioritised Requirements List, and Solution Architecture Definition among others.

Executive Summary

In certain cases, instead of a comprehensive document, the Foundations Summary may be presented as an executive summary. This brief outline extracts and synthesizes the core conclusions and recommendations from the foundational documents, providing a digestible overview for stakeholders.

Governance and Lifecycle

Decision-making

The Foundations Summary stands as a pivotal juncture in the project lifecycle. It informs the decision on whether to transition from the Foundations phase to the Evolutionary Development phase, based on a holistic understanding of the project's feasibility and alignment with organizational goals.

Stakeholder Communication

One of the indispensable functions of this document is to offer stakeholders a transparent, consolidated view of the project's foundational elements. This enhances communication and contributes significantly to informed decision-making processes.

Foundations Summary: A Hypothetical Case Study

Context

In this hypothetical scenario, a medium-sized software company aims to develop a new Customer Relationship Management (CRM) system. At the end of the Foundations phase, the project management team compiles a Foundations Summary to evaluate the project's alignment with organizational objectives, technical readiness, and management approaches.

Business Alignment

Examination

The Foundations Summary begins with an examination of the project's alignment with the organization's key business goals, such as revenue growth, customer retention, and market expansion. The project aims to create a CRM that not only improves internal operations but also enhances customer engagement and, ultimately, profitability.

Findings

The summary establishes that the project is in line with the organization's ambition to capture a more significant market share in the SME sector. It is designed to be scalable, allowing it to grow in parallel with the business.

Technical Readiness

Evaluation

The technical team reviews the existing architecture to determine if it can accommodate the new CRM system's demands. They explore various factors like scalability, performance, and integration with existing systems.

Findings

The summary reports that the current architecture is robust enough to accommodate the new system but recommends the adoption of a microservices architecture for better scalability and easier maintenance.

Management Approaches

Assessment

The project's management methods are scrutinized next. This includes an evaluation of the planned governance structure, the effectiveness of the chosen Agile methodology, and how well risks and resources have been assessed and planned for.

Findings

The summary concludes that while the management approaches are sound, there is room for improvement in stakeholder engagement and communication.

Decision-making and Stakeholder Communication

Governance

Based on the findings, the summary informs the decision to proceed to the Evolutionary Development phase. It provides specific recommendations for the identified areas of improvement.

Communication

The Foundations Summary is then circulated among stakeholders, providing a transparent view of the project's readiness and alignment with organizational objectives. This step is crucial for stakeholder buy-in and ensures that everyone is on the same page as the project progresses into its next phase.

This case study serves as a practical illustration, providing a structured view of what a Foundations Summary might encompass in a real-world scenario.

The Essence of the Evolving Solution in the DSDM Agile Project Framework

Definition and Conceptual Overview

The Evolving Solution is an adaptive and iterative ensemble of artifacts that collectively form the developing output of a DSDM Agile project. Unlike a static project deliverable, the Evolving Solution is a fluid entity, constantly updated and refined throughout the project's lifecycle. It serves as a manifestation of the project's progress and a baseline for each iteration, enabling an incremental and Agile approach to solution development.

Key Components of the Evolving Solution

Complete Components

These are fully realized elements that have undergone all necessary development and testing phases. They are considered complete and can be part of the Deployed Solution.

Solution Increments

These are stable versions of the solution that are ready for deployment or additional development. Solution Increments serve as checkpoints, providing a stable basis for future iterations.

Work-in-Progress Components

These elements are under active development and are expected to evolve into Complete Components. Their status is often tracked in a backlog.

Supporting Materials

These may include various forms of documentation, models, and prototypes that assist in detailing requirements, specifying designs, and aiding in the construction of the solution.

Testing and Review Artifacts

To ensure quality and functionality, the Evolving Solution includes elements such as test cases, test results, and records of peer reviews, adhering to the quality assurance guidelines defined in the Development Approach Definition.

Lifecycle and Governance in Relation to the Evolving Solution

Project Increments

At the conclusion of each Project Increment, the most mature Solution Increment is typically deployed, thereby becoming part of the final Deployed

Solution. This milestone is critical for demonstrating project progress and is typically a focus during governance reviews.

Quality Assurance

Each component in the Evolving Solution undergoes a strict regime of quality assurance activities. These activities are generally outlined in the Development Approach Definition and are rigorously implemented to ensure that the evolving components meet the project's quality standards.

Case Study: Implementing the Evolving Solution in a DSDM Agile Project

Project Context

In an enterprise software development project aimed at building an Inventory Management System, the concept of the Evolving Solution was pivotal. The project was managed under the DSDM Agile Project Framework, and involved multiple teams including development, quality assurance, and business analysis.

Initial Setup

The project began with a strong emphasis on establishing baseline requirements and initial architectures. These formed the first iteration of the Evolving Solution. It consisted of rudimentary database designs, initial code for core functionalities, and elementary UI/UX designs.

Iterative Development and Solution Increments

Throughout the project lifecycle, multiple iterations (or Project Increments) were executed. At the end of each, a Solution Increment was identified. This served as a 'snapshot' of the Evolving Solution at that point, and was made up of the most stable and mature components developed thus far. These Solution Increments were the primary deliverables evaluated during the project's governance reviews.

Testing and Quality Assurance

All elements in each Solution Increment underwent extensive testing, ranging from unit tests to user acceptance tests. Any identified issues were logged, prioritized, and planned for resolution in subsequent iterations.

Governance Focus

The Evolving Solution served as a focal point during governance meetings. The stability and maturity of the Solution Increment were assessed against predetermined quality metrics, ensuring alignment with the overall project objectives. Any deviations triggered corrective actions, including scope adjustments and timeline realignments.

Final Deployment

By the end of the project, the last Solution Increment became the Deployed Solution after undergoing a final round of testing and validation. It served as the final, approved version of the Inventory Management System, satisfying all initial objectives and requirements.

Conclusion

The Evolving Solution, in the context of the DSDM Agile Project Framework, facilitated a structured yet flexible approach to software development. By providing a clear framework for incremental development and continuous quality assurance, the concept was crucial for meeting project milestones and ensuring a high-quality final deliverable.

The Timebox Plan: A Detailed Examination in the DSDM Agile Project Framework

Definition and Importance

The Timebox Plan is an essential artifact in the DSDM Agile Project Framework, structured to provide a focused, short-term roadmap for the Solution Development Team. It lays out the specific objectives, deliverables, tasks, and resources assigned for a particular Timebox—usually a fixed period in which the team aims to accomplish certain goals. By delineating these elements, the Timebox Plan allows for a structured yet flexible approach to project development, ensuring that the team remains aligned, efficient, and effective in delivering incremental value.

Key Components of the Timebox Plan

Objectives

The primary goals or targets that the team aims to achieve within the Timebox. These are clearly articulated to ensure that everyone understands what success looks like for this specific period.

Deliverables

The tangible outputs or artifacts that are expected to be produced by the end of the Timebox. These could range from code modules to documentation or any other type of project asset.

Activities

The specific tasks and processes that need to be executed to produce the aforementioned deliverables. Activities are the actionable items that the team members will be engaged in throughout the Timebox.

Resources

Identification and allocation of necessary resources, including team members, tools, and other assets that will be essential for the successful completion of the Timebox.

Governance and Daily Operations

Daily Stand-ups

The Timebox Plan is a living document frequently reviewed and updated during daily stand-up meetings. These meetings allow the team to discuss the status of various tasks, identify blockers, and realign if necessary.

Team Board

To further facilitate tracking and transparency, the Timebox Plan often employs a visual board, either physical or digital. This board categorizes tasks into different statuses such as 'To Do,' 'In Progress,' and 'Done,' serving as a visual indicator of the team's progress and what still needs to be accomplished.

Case Study: Implementing the Timebox Plan in a Software Development Project

In a software development project guided by the DSDM Agile Project Framework, the project team was tasked with delivering a new feature—User Authentication—within a two-week Timebox. This case study explores how they successfully utilized the Timebox Plan to manage their tasks, resources, and deliverables efficiently.

Objectives

The primary objective was to implement a secure and user-friendly authentication system that would allow users to log in via email or social media accounts. Secondary objectives included ensuring high-quality code, optimizing database queries, and preparing comprehensive documentation.

Deliverables

1. User Authentication Code Modules
2. Database Schema for User Data
3. Unit Tests and Integration Tests
4. Technical Documentation

Activities

The activities were divided among the front-end developers, back-end developers, and Quality Assurance (QA) testers.

- Front-end developers were responsible for creating the login page and integrating it with the back-end API.
- Back-end developers were tasked with writing secure and efficient code for user authentication and data storage.
- QA testers had to prepare and execute unit and integration tests to validate the functionality and security of the authentication system.

Resources

Human Resources

- 2 Front-end Developers
- 3 Back-end Developers
- 1 QA Tester
- 1 Technical Writer

Tools and Technologies

- Front-end: React.js
- Back-end: Node.js
- Database: MySQL
- Testing: Jest

Governance and Daily Operations

Daily Stand-ups

The team had daily stand-up meetings every morning to discuss the tasks completed, identify any blockers, and plan for the day ahead.

Team Board

A digital Kanban board was used to track the status of various tasks. Every team member was responsible for updating the board at least once a day, ensuring that it accurately reflected the team's progress.

Outcome

By adhering strictly to the Timebox Plan and leveraging agile practices, the team successfully implemented the User Authentication feature within the two-week Timebox, meeting all the primary and secondary objectives.

The Timebox Plan was instrumental in keeping the team aligned and focused, thereby contributing to the project's success.

The Significance of Timebox Review Record in DSDM Agile Project Framework

Definition and Purpose

The Timebox Review Record is a quintessential component of the Dynamic Systems Development Method (DSDM) Agile Project Framework. It functions as a repository for a range of critical information resulting from the review process within a Timebox. By encapsulating the results, feedback, and learnings, the Timebox Review Record aids in two significant aspects: reflection on what has been achieved and strategic planning for future iterations or phases.

Key Components of the Timebox Review Record

Achievements

This section outlines the key objectives met and the artifacts delivered during the Timebox. It serves as a factual account of what has been accomplished, thereby offering a measurement criterion for performance and success.

Feedback

Feedback from multiple sources is compiled to evaluate the quality, functionality, and suitability of the work delivered. This could be from internal team members or external stakeholders like Business Advisors, and may touch upon technical, business, or managerial aspects.

Influence on Future Plans

Based on what has been achieved and the feedback received, this section delves into the implications for ongoing and future tasks or iterations. It assists in identifying course-corrections or refinements that could be beneficial in enhancing project outcomes.

Governance and Compliance

Formal Records in Regulated Industries

In industries that necessitate compliance with specific governance norms or standards, the Timebox Review Record gains additional importance. It serves as an auditable document capturing formal remarks and assessments from experts and Business Advisors, thereby fulfilling the governance requirements.

Governance Role in Project Management

The Timebox Review Record holds value in governance meetings, offering insights that could influence important project decisions. It serves as an evidence-based instrument for gauging the project's standing and what adjustments may be required moving forward.

Case Study: Implementing Timebox Review Record in a Financial Services Project

Project Overview

In a large financial services organization, a project was initiated to develop a new customer management system using the DSDM Agile Project Framework. The project had multiple Timeboxes, each focusing on different functionalities like customer onboarding, transaction management, and compliance checks.

Utilization of Timebox Review Record

Achievements Section

After the completion of the first Timebox aimed at developing the customer onboarding feature, the Timebox Review Record listed all the accomplished objectives, such as the successful integration of identity verification services and the automation of the account creation process.

Feedback Section

The record included feedback from the Solution Development Team who pointed out minor bugs, Business Advisors who assessed the user experience, and compliance officers who verified the alignment with regulatory requirements.

Influence on Future Plans Section

The feedback received indicated that while the automation worked well, the user interface needed slight improvements for a better customer experience. This was documented in the "Influence on Future Plans" section, serving as an input for the next Timebox that would focus on enhancing the user interface.

Governance and Compliance Role

Being in the financial sector, regulatory compliance was a critical aspect. The Timebox Review Record was rigorously maintained to capture all formal remarks from compliance officers, and it served as an auditable asset during internal audits and governance meetings.

Conclusion

In this manner, the Timebox Review Record proved to be an invaluable tool for the project. Not only did it facilitate reflective analysis and future planning, but it also played a pivotal role in governance and regulatory compliance.

This case study demonstrates the multifaceted utility of the Timebox Review Record in successfully navigating complex project environments.

In-depth Analysis of the Project Review Report within the DSDM Agile Project Framework

The Project Review Report is a cornerstone in the DSDM Agile Project Framework's governance structure. Acting as a dynamic document, it plays a dual role of offering retrospective evaluations and proactive planning guidelines. Updated at the close of each Project Increment, this tool is instrumental for continuous improvement and alignment with strategic business aims.

Vital Elements of the Project Review Report

Feedback on Delivered Solution

This facet of the report provides a meticulous comparison between the delivered project components and the initially defined objectives. More than a mere progress report, it offers critical insights into areas of overachievement and underperformance. These evaluations are pivotal for steering ongoing and future Project Increments.

Learning Points

This segment serves as a rich repository of experiential knowledge, garnered from different phases of the project. It offers an avenue for capturing insights on various elements such as procedural adjustments and team interactions. The gleaned lessons become invaluable assets for both the existing project and subsequent endeavors.

Business Benefits

This section demystifies the tangible and intangible rewards harvested from the project. Whether they relate to cost-efficiency, superior customer engagement, or internal workflow enhancements, these quantified benefits are crucial for securing stakeholder support and continued allocation of resources.

Core Aims of the Project Review Report

Continuous Learning

One of the foremost goals of the Project Review Report is to embed a culture of incessant learning within the project milieu. Regular updates to the report empower the team to adapt and refine strategies, thus thwarting the stagnation that can afflict long-drawn projects.

Alignment with Business Objectives

The Project Review Report serves as an ongoing alignment check with the organization's larger strategic framework. By facilitating regular reviews, the report ensures that the project stays on track, fully harmonized with broader business objectives.

Governance and Accountability

In the context of increasing compliance and governance oversight, the Project Review Report stands as an essential governance artifact. It not only caters to internal stakeholder requirements but is often a mandatory component for industries that are regulated.

Case Study: Implementing the Project Review Report in a DSDM Agile Project

Background

Imagine a financial technology startup embarking on a DSDM Agile Project to develop a next-generation mobile payment app. The team has just completed the first Project Increment, and it's time to produce the Project Review Report.

Application of Vital Elements

Feedback on Delivered Solution

The report starts by reviewing what was achieved versus the initial objectives. For instance, while the user interface was delivered with high-quality, the backend APIs for payment processing took longer than expected to develop. This section provides an opportunity for the team to discuss bottlenecks and suggests that additional resources may be needed in the upcoming Project Increments.

Learning Points

The team noticed that adopting a DevOps approach significantly streamlined the deployment process. However, they also discovered that the chosen programming language had some limitations for specific financial calculations. This section documents these insights, providing valuable data for future phases.

Business Benefits

The developed app's prototype was tested among a focus group, receiving positive feedback, especially for its user interface. These early signs suggest that the app could potentially capture a significant market share and bring revenue benefits to the company.

Core Aims Achieved

Continuous Learning

The retrospective analysis ensures that the lessons learned in this Increment are embedded into the planning for the subsequent Increments. With clearly documented setbacks and successes, the team is better prepared for future challenges.

Alignment with Business Objectives

The report reveals that while there have been some delays, the project is fundamentally on track to achieve the business goals of providing a next-generation payment solution.

Governance and Accountability

As a startup in the financial technology space, compliance with regulatory standards is crucial. The Project Review Report serves as a record that can be presented to regulatory bodies to demonstrate due diligence and adherence to quality standards.

By thoroughly applying the Project Review Report, the team sets the stage for ongoing improvements and ensures that the project aligns with organizational and regulatory standards.

Unpacking the Benefits Assessment in the DSDM Agile Project Framework

Overview

The Benefits Assessment in the context of the DSDM Agile Project Framework is a critical tool for gauging the success of a project beyond its technical implementation. By focusing on real-world outcomes and aligning them with initial business objectives, it ensures that the project serves the broader organizational goals.

Key Elements of the Benefits Assessment

Benefit Metrics

This section details the specific metrics—both qualitative and quantitative—that were initially defined in the Business Case. For example, metrics might include percentage increase in customer engagement, reduction in operational costs, or the speed of service delivery.

Benefit Realization Timeline

The timeline offers a snapshot of when benefits began to materialize and when they are expected to reach full realization. This timeline enables the project team and stakeholders to understand the pacing of value creation over time.

Benefit Owners

Identification of benefit owners assigns accountability. It indicates which individual or department is responsible for ensuring that each benefit is realized and measured according to the predefined metrics.

Performance Analysis

This component delves into a comparison of actual versus expected benefits. It's the core analysis section that indicates whether the project has been successful in delivering its proposed value. Any variances are identified and scrutinized for their root causes.

Recommendations

Based on the performance analysis, recommendations are made to correct course or to enhance benefit realization. This might include changes to technology, additional training, or strategic realignment.

Core Objectives Fulfilled by the Benefits Assessment

Accountability

One of the most critical functions of the Benefits Assessment is to establish accountability for project outcomes. It helps in validating that the project has successfully delivered on its promises and justifies the initial investment made.

Continuous Improvement

By analyzing what worked well and what didn't, the Benefits Assessment serves as a learning tool. The insights gathered are invaluable for refining future project plans or even adjusting current ongoing phases.

Strategic Alignment

Finally, the Benefits Assessment ensures that the project's real-world outcomes are aligned with the organization's overarching strategic objectives. This ensures that the project is not just a one-off success but contributes to long-term organizational value.

Case Study: Utilizing Benefits Assessment in a DSDM Agile Project

Context

Imagine a large healthcare organization that has just completed a significant project to modernize its electronic health record (EHR) system. The project was undertaken using the DSDM Agile Project Framework. After the system was deployed and in use for six months, the project team conducted a Benefits Assessment.

Elements of the Benefits Assessment

Benefit Metrics

Key metrics included the speed of patient data retrieval, the rate of data entry errors, and clinician satisfaction levels.

Benefit Realization Timeline

The timeline indicated that significant benefits, like a 20% increase in data retrieval speed, were realized within the first three months after deployment.

Benefit Owners

The IT department was the benefit owner for technical aspects like data retrieval speed, while the clinical departments owned the clinician satisfaction metric.

Performance Analysis

The assessment revealed that while data retrieval speeds met expectations, clinician satisfaction was lower than anticipated.

Recommendations

The Benefits Assessment suggested targeted retraining programs for clinicians and interface tweaks to address the identified issues.

Core Objectives Achieved

Accountability

The organization could clearly see that the IT department had met its objectives, establishing a high degree of accountability.

Continuous Improvement

The insights gained led to immediate remedial measures, making this an excellent learning experience for the organization.

Strategic Alignment

The Benefits Assessment affirmed that the EHR modernization project aligned well with the healthcare organization's strategic goal of enhancing patient care through technology.

Thus, the Benefits Assessment played an indispensable role in validating the project's success and guided data-driven decisions for future initiatives.

Navigating the Balance: DSDM Products in Governance and Communication

The Dual Role of Documentation in Agile Environments

The Paradox of Agility and Documentation

DSDM Agile Project Framework underscores the value-driven philosophy that endorses generating only those products or documents that truly add meaningful contributions to the project or the final solution. However, the Agile ethos of 'working software over comprehensive documentation' often collides with the conventional wisdom favoring extensive documentation for governance and compliance reasons. Therefore, it's essential to recognize that the degree of documentation formality is not a one-size-fits-all criterion; rather, it is influenced by organizational contexts, governance mandates, and stakeholder communication needs.

Significance in Governance and Regulatory Compliance

Audit Trail

In environments where strong governance is not merely an option but a requirement, formal documentation acts as the backbone of the audit trail. When well-maintained, these documents stand as credible records that can be reviewed during internal or external audits. In particular, they help ensure that a project aligns with legal requirements and industry best practices.

Risk Mitigation

The value of formal documentation is accentuated when considering risk management, especially in contentious or complex scenarios such as contractual disputes or legal challenges. Documents substantiate the due diligence exercised in project planning and execution and act as verified records of agreed-upon plans and outcomes.

Stakeholder Accountability

DSDM's well-articulated products provide a mechanism for delineating responsibilities clearly. These products are instrumental in defining roles and responsibilities, thereby facilitating an accountability structure among stakeholders. This is especially beneficial in larger teams or in projects involving multiple external partners, where a lapse in accountability could potentially derail the project.

Case Study: Balancing DSDM Products and Governance in a Financial Institution

Overview

The Setting

A financial institution initiated an Agile project for implementing a new customer management system. The institution is subject to stringent regulatory compliance, requiring a robust governance structure. Using DSDM's Agile Project Framework, the project team had to find the right balance between agility and documentation for effective governance and compliance.

The Challenge: Striking the Right Balance

Documentation Quandary

The project team faced the challenge of complying with both the Agile tenet of minimizing documentation and the organizational governance protocols that called for extensive documentation for audit trails.

Stakeholder Dynamics

Various stakeholders, including auditors, business advisors, and upper management, had different expectations regarding the level of documentation, further complicating the balance.

Solution & Outcomes

Customized Documentation

After thorough risk assessment and stakeholder analysis, the project team decided to produce DSDM products like the Timebox Review Record and Project Review Report in a formal, auditable manner. This not only satisfied governance requirements but also met the needs of diverse stakeholders.

Accountability and Compliance

The formally produced DSDM products became the go-to artifacts for roles and responsibilities, ensuring stakeholder accountability. They also served as the basis for the audit trail, aiding in internal and external audits.

Agility Preserved

By selectively formalizing only those DSDM products that were critical for governance and compliance, the team preserved the agility inherent in the DSDM framework. Less critical documents were kept informal, aligning with Agile principles.

Lessons Learned

Flexibility in Approach

This case study underscores the need for flexibility in adapting the documentation strategy according to project-specific governance and stakeholder requirements.

Importance of Stakeholder Analysis

Incorporating a stakeholder-centric approach when deciding the level of formality for each DSDM product is crucial for ensuring both governance compliance and project success.

The Art of Balance

Achieving a balance between agility and governance is more an art than a science, requiring thoughtful deliberation and contextual understanding.

Chapter Seven

Mastering Planning and Control

DSDM Agile Planning: Striking a Harmony Between Flexibility and Structure

High-Level Planning within the DSDM Framework

The Agile-Planning Dichotomy

DSDM's Agile Project Framework achieves a nuanced balance between the agile ethos of adaptability and the indispensable need for planning. It escapes the fallacy of considering planning as restrictive, instead framing it as a tool that allows agility to coexist with structure. In this context, planning acts as a framework within which adaptability can flourish, as opposed to being a constraint.

Dual Focus: What, How, and Why

While traditional agile methodologies may solely center on the operational aspects—the 'how'—DSDM amplifies the importance of the 'what' and the 'why.' This dual focus sets the stage for not just the development activities but also for achieving business alignment and strategic objectives.

Core Concepts in DSDM Planning

Agile Project Planning Concepts

Incremental Delivery

DSDM believes in breaking down the solution into manageable Project Increments and Timeboxes. This strategy allows for rapid deployment and iterative improvement, fostering a responsive and adaptive project environment.

Quality Assurance

Quality is not an afterthought; instead, it is weaved into the fabric of the development process. Various mechanisms, such as continuous testing and reviews, are integrated throughout the project lifecycle to maintain high quality.

Strategy Agreement

Before plunging into the whirlpool of project activities, DSDM mandates an agreement on the strategy for evolving the solution. This agreement acts as the project's North Star, guiding all subsequent phases and ensuring alignment with business goals.

Testing Concepts

DSDM employs six unique testing concepts aimed at creating a robust solution that closely aligns with business requirements. These testing measures range from unit testing to end-user validation, providing a comprehensive approach to quality assurance.

Tracking and Control Concepts

To maintain a clear line of sight on project progress and to pivot when necessary, DSDM utilizes four specific tracking and control mechanisms. These mechanisms facilitate real-time visibility into project status, allowing for swift adjustments to maintain alignment with strategic objectives.

Case Study: Implementing DSDM Agile Planning in a Financial Services Project

In this hypothetical case study, a leading financial services company aims to launch a new digital banking platform. With a need for both agility and compliance, the firm adopts the DSDM Agile Project Framework to marry flexibility with structure.

High-Level Planning

Choosing the 'What' and 'Why'

The company sets clear business objectives—such as increasing the user base by 20% and improving customer satisfaction by 15 points within a year—alongside the functional requirements. These objectives act as the guiding metrics throughout the project.

Core Concepts in Action

Agile Project Planning Concepts

Incremental Delivery

The project is broken down into quarterly Project Increments, each focusing on a core set of features like account management, fund transfers, and customer support. This approach allows for periodic assessment and course correction, if needed.

Quality Assurance

The firm adopts automated testing suites that are run at the end of each Timebox. Additionally, each Project Increment undergoes a security audit to ensure compliance with financial regulations.

Strategy Agreement

Before initiating the first Project Increment, a strategy document is agreed upon. This outlines the key performance indicators (KPIs), timelines, and the general development approach, ensuring that all stakeholders are aligned.

Testing Concepts

A variety of testing methods—unit tests, integration tests, user acceptance tests—are employed throughout each Project Increment. This rigorous approach guarantees that the solution is both technically sound and business-ready.

Tracking and Control Concepts

The firm uses a combination of traditional Gantt charts for high-level tracking and agile boards for Timebox-level activities. Dashboards displaying real-time KPIs are made available to all stakeholders, ensuring transparent tracking and control.

Conclusion

By employing DSDM's unique approach to agile planning, the financial services company successfully delivers the digital banking platform within the targeted time frame while achieving all strategic objectives. The project serves as a compelling testament to the benefits of marrying agility with structured planning under the DSDM framework.

Outcome-Based Planning in DSDM: A Paradigm of Empowerment and Accountability

The Hierarchical Structure of Empowerment

An Orchestrated Approach

In DSDM, empowerment isn't just a buzzword; it's a structured mechanism that ensures project success. At the highest level, the Business Sponsor wields the ultimate decision-making power and is responsible for empowering the project roles. This top-down empowerment ensures that the project not only has a clear directive but also the backing needed for execution.

Project Roles and their Empowerment Matrix

In a cascading effect, project-level roles like the Business Visionary and Technical Coordinator further empower the Solution Development Team. This ensures that decision-making ability is distributed, but still aligned with higher-level objectives.

Roles and Responsibilities: The Cornerstones of Outcome-Based Planning

Project Manager: The Strategic Navigator

Defining the Course

The Project Manager operates at a macro level, liaising with the Business Sponsor to set overarching goals and establish the project's framework. One of the key responsibilities is to map out the incremental delivery of the solution, essentially constructing the project's roadmap.

Solution Development Team: The Tactical Executors

Task-Level Planning and Execution

Operating on the micro-level, the Solution Development Team is endowed with the responsibility of meticulous planning for each Timebox. They break down objectives into tasks, delegate responsibilities, and maintain the tactical pulse of the project.

Synergistic Outcomes

By entrusting specific roles with particular planning responsibilities, DSDM creates a harmonious balance. The Project Manager is empowered to focus on aligning the project with business objectives, while the Solution Development Team can concentrate on the details, ensuring that each Timebox is a step toward those objectives. This mutual empowerment results in a cohesive, outcome-based approach to project delivery.

Case Study: Implementing Outcome-Based Planning in a DSDM Project

The Project Context

Scenario Overview

Imagine a fintech company embarking on a project to develop a new mobile banking app. The Business Sponsor is the company's CFO, and the Project Manager has been tasked with overseeing the development. The Solution

Development Team comprises software developers, designers, and QA testers. The Business Visionary and Technical Coordinator also play key roles.

Empowerment Structure in Action

The Business Sponsor's Mandate

The CFO, serving as the Business Sponsor, outlines the strategic importance of the app and empowers the Project Manager to lead the initiative, aiming to disrupt the mobile banking market and significantly boost user engagement.

Project Roles and Responsibilities

The Project Manager works in tandem with the Business Visionary to define the broader business goals and sets up a roadmap for incremental delivery. Simultaneously, the Technical Coordinator reviews the technical aspects to ensure feasibility and scalability.

Outcome-Based Planning by the Solution Development Team

Timebox Planning

For each Timebox, the Solution Development Team receives a set of objectives from the Project Manager. They then divide these objectives into specific tasks and allocate them among team members.

Execution and Adaptability

As the team progresses, they adapt their approach based on real-time feedback and outcomes, without losing sight of the strategic objectives set by the Business Sponsor and the Project Manager.

Synergy and Final Outcomes

Cohesion Leads to Success

The structurally-defined empowerment and clear demarcation of roles and responsibilities ensure that everyone knows what they need to do and have the authority to do it. This results in a successful project that not only delivers a cutting-edge mobile banking app but also achieves its intended business outcomes.

This case study illustrates the effective application of Outcome-Based Planning within the DSDM framework, showcasing how empowerment and accountability can coexist to drive project success.

Diving Deeper into Planning Horizons in DSDM

Understanding the Layers of Planning

DSDM distinguishes between long-term and short-term planning through the concepts of Delivery Plans and Timebox Plans. Each represents a different planning horizon, allowing for a modular and responsive approach to project management.

What Are Planning Horizons?

Planning horizons serve as temporal scopes within which planning exercises occur. These horizons are not merely timelines; they are also indicative of the granularity and specificity with which planning should be approached at different phases of the project.

Core Features of Delivery and Timebox Plans

Delivery Plan: The Long-Term Perspective

Planning Horizon

The Delivery Plan typically looks ahead over an extended period, often ranging from six weeks to six months. This longer horizon allows for strategic alignment with overarching business objectives.

Content and Scope

While it does outline Timeboxes and specific objectives, the Delivery Plan does so at a high level. It offers a macro view, laying out Project Increments and establishing milestones to gauge progress.

Level of Detail

The Delivery Plan is intentionally less detailed, focusing instead on setting the trajectory for the project as a whole.

Timebox Plan: The Granular Approach

Planning Horizon

In contrast, the Timebox Plan is short-term, extending usually between two to four weeks. This narrow window promotes agility and adaptability.

Content and Scope

The Timebox Plan is task-oriented and provides a micro view of the project. It outlines the specific activities, tasks, and objectives that must be accomplished within that Timebox.

Level of Detail

Being short-term in nature, the Timebox Plan is highly detailed. It frequently specifies not only the tasks to be accomplished but also designates who is responsible for each task and the time frame within which it should be completed.

Synthesizing Planning Horizons: A Balanced Approach

Both types of plans are pivotal in creating a balanced planning framework. While the Delivery Plan ensures that the project stays aligned with long-term business goals, the Timebox Plan ensures that short-term tasks are aligned with these goals. This dual-layered approach allows for both strategic planning and agile execution, offering a balance between foresight and adaptability.

Case Study: Implementing Planning Horizons in a DSDM Project

Background

Imagine a software development company undertaking a six-month project to create a customer relationship management (CRM) solution for a client. The Project Manager and the Solution Development Team are well-versed in DSDM methodology.

Application of Delivery Plan

Planning Horizon and Objectives

The Delivery Plan was created at the outset, laying out the high-level objectives and the Project Increments spanning the entire six-month period. Milestones were set for the completion of critical modules of the CRM software.

Role in Governance

The Delivery Plan was shared with stakeholders, providing a long-term view of the project. It served as an essential governance tool, giving the Business Sponsor and stakeholders an understanding of what to expect.

Application of Timebox Plans

Planning Horizon and Granularity

Every two weeks, a Timebox Plan was generated, detailing the activities to be undertaken by the Solution Development Team. Each plan specified the objectives for the Timebox, the tasks, and who would be responsible for each.

Daily Stand-Ups and Adaptability

These Timebox Plans were revisited in daily stand-up meetings. Adjustments were made as needed to tackle unforeseen challenges or to incorporate feedback from the client, ensuring agility.

Outcome and Lessons

Synergy Between Plans

The Delivery Plan provided a strategic scaffold, while the Timebox Plans ensured that tactical objectives were met. Both types of planning horizons informed and complemented each other.

Adaptability and Alignment

By having both long-term and short-term plans, the project team was able to adapt to changing requirements without losing sight of the strategic objectives.

This case study illustrates the efficacy of employing both Delivery and Timebox Plans in a DSDM project, ensuring a balance between long-term vision and short-term agility.

Estimation and Re-Estimation Strategies in DSDM

Navigating the Complex Landscape of Project Estimation

The process of estimation is pivotal in the DSDM Agile Project Framework, as it provides a basis for planning, resource allocation, and stakeholder communication. Because DSDM operates in an agile environment, the approach to estimation is not static. It is reiterative and responsive to the evolving nature of the project.

Lifecycle Phases and Their Influence on Estimation

Initial Estimation

The earliest estimates are formulated during the project's inception and are inherently speculative. These are high-level estimates, serving as placeholders until more detailed information becomes available.

Foundations Phase

Upon reaching the Foundations Phase, the availability of more concrete details allows for more accurate estimates. These refined figures then become committed items that shape the project's trajectory.

During Project Increments

The ongoing Project Increments serve as periodic reassessment points where existing estimates are fine-tuned. This iterative reassessment reflects the agile principle of adapting to change and continuously improving.

Principles for Robust Estimation in DSDM

Iterative Refinement

Estimates in DSDM are not set in stone. They are subject to revisions based on the actual performance and outcomes of the project. Each iteration offers an opportunity to recalibrate the estimates to match the reality more closely.

Methodological Diversity

Utilizing a variety of estimation techniques provides a more nuanced and accurate picture. Methods like expert judgment, analytical models, and historical data can be used in conjunction to achieve more reliable estimates.

Collective Wisdom

The process of estimation should involve multiple stakeholders, including team members and subject matter experts, to harness a range of perspectives. This collective approach ensures that the estimates are well-rounded and consider various facets of the project.

Case Study: Utilizing DSDM Estimation Principles for Effective Project Planning

Setting the Scene

Imagine a software development company that has adopted the DSDM Agile Project Framework for an upcoming project aimed at creating a new customer relationship management (CRM) system. The project is complex, involving various teams and stakeholders, and is expected to last for six months.

How Estimation Principles Are Applied

Initial Estimation

During the project's feasibility stage, initial estimates are formulated based on limited information. These are considered rough guidelines, mainly serving to provide a ballpark figure for budget allocation and initial scheduling.

Foundations Phase

As the project moves into the Foundations Phase, more specific information is collected. The project team, now with better-defined user stories and initial prototypes, revises the initial estimates. These figures are then committed to, shaping the project's planning and stakeholder expectations.

During Project Increments

Each Project Increment provides an opportunity to assess the validity of the existing estimates. Lessons learned from each increment are applied to update the estimates for the following phases. For example, if a particular module took longer than expected to develop, this insight would be used to adjust future estimates.

Iterative Refinement

Throughout the project, the estimates are continuously refined based on real-world results. This iterative process enables the project to adapt and change course as needed, staying agile while maintaining alignment with business objectives.

Methodological Diversity

The project employs various estimation techniques like expert judgment, where senior developers provide their insights, and parametric models, using mathematical formulas to predict outcomes. This multi-faceted approach enhances the accuracy of the estimates.

Collective Wisdom

The estimation process includes inputs from multiple team members and stakeholders, such as developers, testers, business analysts, and customer representatives. This collective involvement ensures that the estimates are comprehensive, considering various perspectives and types of expertise.

Conclusion

By adhering to the principles of estimation outlined in DSDM, the project team maintains a balance between agility and structured planning. The iterative process of estimation and re-estimation enables the project to remain adaptable while keeping stakeholders informed and aligned.

The Intricacies of Testing Concepts in DSDM: A Comprehensive View

The Primacy of Early Testing Strategy

Why Planning Matters

In the DSDM framework, the planning stage is not just a preliminary step; it's a foundational element that directly influences the success of the project.

Establishing a testing strategy early on brings forth clarity in roles, responsibilities, and the methodologies to be used. A clearly defined roadmap prevents ambiguity and ensures that the team members can align their activities toward common quality objectives.

Components of a Robust Testing Strategy

A robust testing strategy typically encompasses several key elements, including but not limited to:

Quality Criteria: Establishing the parameters that the solution must meet to be considered acceptable.

Resource Allocation: Identifying and allocating the human and technical resources that will be involved in the testing process.

Testing Tools: Selecting the appropriate testing tools and frameworks that align with the project's technological stack.

Timelines: Outlining a schedule for testing activities in relation to the development cycle.

Integrating Testing into Iterative Development

Symbiotic Relationship with Development

Integrating testing activities into the iterative development cycle, often within the same Timebox as development tasks, establishes a symbiotic relationship between development and testing. This relationship facilitates a seamless transition between building and validating the solution, thereby enhancing the project's overall efficiency.

The Multi-Faceted Benefits of Integrated Testing

Quick Identification of Defects

By incorporating testing into the development process, defects are identified almost as soon as they occur. This timeliness not only makes the resolution quicker but also reduces the associated costs.

Operational Efficiency

The integration allows for a fluid workflow, reducing the time and effort required to switch between development and testing. This arrangement also eliminates the need for prolonged periods of isolated testing, thus expediting the project timeline.

Continual Quality Assurance

Consistent testing activities throughout the development cycle ensure that the quality of the solution is never compromised. Regular checks against the predefined quality criteria enable adjustments to be made in real-time, thus preserving the integrity of the end product.

End-of-Timebox Objectives: A Pragmatic Approach

Balancing Idealism with Realism

While the ultimate objective at the end of each Timebox is to have a fully tested and deployable solution, DSDM takes a pragmatic approach. It acknowledges that various constraints such as limited resources, tight timelines, or the inherent complexity of the solution could sometimes make this idealistic objective unattainable. In such instances, the framework offers the flexibility to adapt plans and extend testing into subsequent Timeboxes.

Case Study: Implementing Integrated Testing in a DSDM Project

Project Overview

Context and Objectives

In a hypothetical DSDM project aimed at developing a healthcare application, the primary objective was to ensure the secure and efficient management of patient data. Due to the sensitive nature of the data, quality assurance was a top priority, making a robust testing strategy essential.

Early Testing Strategy: Laying the Groundwork

Initial Planning

Right from the Feasibility phase, the project team, along with QA analysts, outlined the testing strategy. They determined the quality criteria, allocated resources, and decided on the testing tools and frameworks. The timeline for testing activities was also set in relation to the project's overall schedule.

Iterative Development and Integrated Testing: A Seamless Flow

Timebox Activities

For each Timebox, a sprint backlog was created that included both development and testing tasks. This integrated approach provided a two-fold benefit:

Quick Detection of Defects: As soon as a feature was developed, it underwent immediate testing. This approach helped in identifying defects at the earliest stage, allowing for quick resolutions.

Efficiency Gains: The absence of a 'hard switch' between development and testing phases contributed to smoother operations and less downtime, positively impacting the project's pace.

End-of-Timebox Review: Realism Meets Objectives

Adapting to Constraints

While the team aimed for a fully tested and potentially deployable solution at the end of each Timebox, they encountered challenges like resource constraints and complex integrations. As a result, some testing activities had to spill over into subsequent Timeboxes. The DSDM framework provided the flexibility to adapt and re-plan, without compromising the project's strategic objectives.

This case study demonstrates the practical application of integrated testing within a DSDM framework and highlights how early planning and continuous execution can contribute to project success.

Collaborative Testing in the DSDM Framework

The Imperative for a Multi-Stakeholder Approach

Aligning with DSDM Core Principles

Collaborative testing in a Dynamic Systems Development Methodology (DSDM) environment is not an optional activity but an integral component that aligns perfectly with the framework's core principles, particularly the emphasis on collaboration. The practice orchestrates the collective skills and perspectives of various stakeholders to conduct testing activities, thereby ensuring a rounded approach to quality assurance.

Stakeholder Involvement in Collaborative Testing

Achieving a Balanced View

While traditional testing methods often involve only a select group of quality assurance professionals, DSDM recommends a broader involvement. Business representatives ensure the alignment of the solution with organizational objectives and can articulate the user perspective more accurately. Technical team members bring the much-needed expertise on system capabilities and limitations. The Solution Development Team, having been intricately involved in building the solution, offers invaluable insights into potential problem areas that may require focused testing. Lastly, specialized testing representatives bring methodologies and techniques that help in performing a detailed evaluation. Together, this diverse group ensures that all aspects—functional, technical, and business—are well-scrutinized.

The Tangible Advantages of Collaborative Testing

Realizing Multi-faceted Benefits

Collaborative testing offers numerous benefits that contribute to both the efficiency and effectiveness of the project. By fostering comprehensive coverage, the process ensures that both business and technical requirements are equally vetted. This minimizes the risk of overlooking important aspects and enhances the reliability of the end product. Reduced redundancy is another critical advantage; with multiple eyes scrutinizing the test plans, there's a higher chance that duplicate or irrelevant tests will be eliminated, thus saving time and resources.

Moreover, involving multiple stakeholders speeds up the feedback loop, making the process of applying corrections and re-tests more agile. This faster feedback mechanism contributes to a more dynamic and responsive project environment. Last but not least, collaborative testing serves as a catalyst for enhanced communication among team members, which is fundamental in agile frameworks like DSDM where fluid and transparent communication is vital for success.

Case Study: Implementing Collaborative Testing in a DSDM Project

Project Overview

A Complex Web Application Development

Consider a project where a team is developing a complex web application for a healthcare provider. The primary stakeholders include the Business Sponsor representing the healthcare organization, Technical Team Members specialized in software development and database design, a dedicated Solution Development Team of developers and designers, and Testing Representatives who are quality assurance professionals.

Phase-Wise Collaborative Testing

Starting Early and Iterating

The team started implementing collaborative testing right from the Feasibility phase. Each phase of the project included specific test scenarios based on the objectives and deliverables of that phase. For instance, during the Foundations phase, Business Representatives helped define tests that would validate the business logic and user experience. Technical team members devised tests to assess system performance, database integrity, and API functionality.

Unveiling the Benefits

Quality, Speed, and Cohesion

Because the team was cross-functional and involved in collaborative testing, the test-fix-retest cycle was much more efficient. Early detection of defects led to quicker resolutions and lesser impact on project timelines. Due to the multi-stakeholder involvement, test scenarios were more comprehensive, reducing the risk of late-stage defects considerably.

Eliminating Redundancy

At every Timebox review meeting, the group collectively scrutinized the test results and test scenarios. This collective scrutiny led to the removal of several redundant tests, thereby streamlining the testing process and saving time.

Improved Communication

The team members found that the practice of collaborative testing had a significant positive impact on communication. Technical team members gained a better understanding of the business logic and requirements, while Business Representatives got a clearer picture of technical constraints, leading to more informed and realistic decision-making.

This case study exemplifies the multi-faceted benefits of implementing collaborative testing in a DSDM project. Through this approach, the team could achieve a more robust and reliable web application while ensuring that both business and technical aspects were thoroughly vetted.

The Imperative of Repeatable Testing in DSDM: A Deeper Look

Repeatable testing in DSDM projects is not just a best practice; it's an essential aspect of ensuring the software's robustness and stability over time. Let's delve deeper into its components and benefits.

Essential Components for Achieving Repeatability

Standardized Test Scripts

The foundation of repeatable testing lies in the standardization of test scripts. These are pre-defined sets of instructions that guide how each test should be performed. Standardized test scripts minimize human error and bring uniformity to the testing process, making it easier to compare results over multiple iterations.

Data Consistency

Data plays a pivotal role in testing. Using the same or equivalent test data across iterations ensures that the conditions under which the software is tested remain constant. This makes it easier to identify if a newly introduced feature or code change is the cause of any anomalies in test results.

Automation

While manual testing has its place, automation is key to achieving true repeatability. Automated tests can be run at any time without human intervention, ensuring that tests are performed consistently. Automation not only frees up valuable human resources but also significantly speeds up the testing process.

Advantages of Emphasizing Repeatable Testing

Assurance of Quality

One of the primary benefits of repeatable testing is the assurance it provides in terms of software quality. By rerunning the same tests over each iteration or Timebox, teams can quickly identify if a newly added feature has caused any regression in existing functionalities. This proactive identification helps in maintaining the quality of the software throughout its development lifecycle.

Efficiency in Time and Cost

Inconsistent testing often leads to incorrect results, which can be time-consuming and costly to rectify. Standardized, repeatable tests offer more accurate results and help in early identification of defects. This saves both time and costs associated with late identification and rectification of issues.

Enhanced Traceability and Accountability

Repeatable testing also enhances traceability. With a set of standardized test scripts, it becomes much easier to trace back any defects or issues to their source. Moreover, it also aids in creating a comprehensive audit trail that can be invaluable for compliance and governance purposes.

Conclusion

Repeatable testing is integral to the DSDM methodology, serving as a quality gatekeeper that ensures the end-product is both reliable and robust. By adhering to standardization, maintaining data consistency, and leveraging automation, DSDM teams can realize the manifold benefits of repeatable testing, from quality assurance to operational efficiency and compliance facilitation.

Case Study: Implementing Repeatable Testing in a DSDM Project

Overview

In a DSDM project for developing a healthcare application, the team faced challenges in maintaining a high level of software quality while meeting tight deadlines. They decided to focus on implementing a robust repeatable testing strategy to improve quality and streamline the development process.

Implementation Steps

Standardization of Test Scripts

The team began by creating standardized test scripts for all critical functionalities of the application. These were stored in a central repository that was easily accessible to all team members.

Data Consistency

To maintain data consistency, they created a separate test database that mirrored the production environment. The test database was updated to reflect any schema changes in the production database, ensuring that tests would run in conditions as close to the live environment as possible.

Automation

The team selected a test automation tool compatible with their tech stack and started automating the standardized test scripts. They also integrated these automated tests into their Continuous Integration/Continuous Deployment (CI/CD) pipeline, ensuring that the tests would run automatically at key points in the development process.

Outcomes

Quality Assurance

Implementing repeatable testing led to significant improvements in software quality. The team was able to identify and fix issues early in the development process, reducing the risk of defects making it to the production environment.

Time and Cost Efficiency

Automation and standardization reduced the time needed for test preparation and execution. This allowed the team to allocate more time to other crucial activities like code review and feature development, thereby increasing overall productivity.

Traceability and Compliance

The standardized and automated tests generated logs and reports that were stored in a central location, enhancing traceability. This not only made it easier to identify the root cause of defects but also provided an audit trail that proved invaluable during compliance reviews.

Conclusion

The team's focus on implementing repeatable testing provided multi-faceted benefits that improved software quality, operational efficiency, and compliance readiness. It served as a compelling example of how repeatable testing is integral to achieving a successful outcome in DSDM projects.

Prioritized Testing in DSDM: Elevating Risk-Based Approach to Maximize Value

An In-depth Exploration of Prioritized Testing

Prioritized testing within the DSDM Agile Project Framework refines the traditional approach to testing by focusing on both the sequence and scope of testing activities. This approach aims to maximize project value while optimizing the allocation of resources. The nuances of prioritized testing within DSDM extend beyond merely identifying what to test; it delves into the 'when,' 'how,' and 'to what extent' aspects as well.

Understanding the Multiple Layers Influencing Test Prioritization

Risk Assessment: The Pinnacle of Prioritization

In prioritized testing, risk is not just a technical or functional parameter. It is a composite measure that takes into account various dimensions including user experience, compliance, and market variables. The risk profile of each project component guides its position in the testing queue.

Business Value: The Economic Underpinning

Beyond technical merit, a feature's alignment with business objectives significantly influences its priority in testing. The consideration of economic metrics like ROI ensures that testing activities are not just technically sound but also financially sensible.

Complexity: The Complicating Factor

Features can be overtly or covertly complex. Both types of complexities need adequate representation in the testing regimen. Complexity often harbors hidden defects, making it a critical consideration in test prioritization.

MoSCoW Methodology in Prioritized Testing

Demystifying the MoSCoW Categories

Must-Have: The Non-Negotiables

Tests in this category are indispensable. They cover components with the highest business value and risk, setting the go/no-go benchmarks for project increments.

Should-Have: The Important Yet Manageable

These tests, while not as urgent as 'Must-Have' tests, are far from optional. They focus on areas that, if deferred, would not derail the project but would lead to lost opportunities or increased risks.

Could-Have: The Beneficial Add-ons

These are the non-critical, nice-to-have tests. They typically focus on aesthetic or incremental functional enhancements and are not mission-critical.

Won't-Have: The Deferable Aspects

These are the lowest-priority tests that either provide minimal immediate value or carry the least amount of risk. These tests might be postponed to future project increments or skipped altogether if resources are constrained.

In summary, DSDM's prioritized testing approach, enriched by the multi-dimensional factors and the MoSCoW methodology, aims to deliver a solution that is not just functional but also strategically aligned and risk-mitigated. This sophistication distinguishes DSDM as a mature and effective Agile framework.

Case Study: Implementing Prioritized Testing in DSDM for a Financial Services Application

The Project Context

The project in question aimed to revamp an existing online banking platform for a leading financial services company. The DSDM Agile Project Framework was chosen to facilitate rapid and iterative development.

Objectives

1. Ensure top-grade security features
2. Enhance the user experience
3. Implement machine learning for fraud detection

Methodology: Adopting Prioritized Testing in DSDM

Given the scope and objectives, the project team decided to adopt a prioritized testing approach that aligned with DSDM principles.

Risk Assessment: The Pinnacle of Prioritization

Given that the application involved financial transactions, security features were deemed to be of the highest risk and, therefore, given top priority in the testing queue.

Business Value: The Economic Underpinning

The machine learning algorithms, intended to provide a competitive edge in fraud detection, were identified as having high business value and were therefore given significant attention in the test plan.

Complexity: The Complicating Factor

The user experience components, although not risky or high-value, were complex due to the multitude of supported platforms and devices. Hence, they were also included in the prioritized tests.

MoSCoW Methodology

- Must-Have: Security features
- Should-Have: Machine learning algorithms
- Could-Have: User interface improvements
- Won't-Have: Some of the least used features like theme customization.

Results: Outcomes of the Prioritized Testing

- All the security features passed the 'Must-Have' tests, and the project received the green light for the next increment.
- The machine learning algorithms, although complex, were successfully implemented and validated.
- Some 'Could-Have' and 'Won't-Have' elements were deferred to the next release cycle, freeing up resources for more critical aspects.

Conclusion: Impact of Prioritized Testing

The prioritized testing approach ensured that the most crucial and high-value aspects of the application were rigorously evaluated and optimized. The project was not only delivered on time but also exceeded stakeholder expectations in terms of both functionality and quality.

Independent Testing in DSDM: A Pillar for Objectivity and Comprehensive Validation

The Role of Independent Testing in DSDM

Independent testing stands as a cornerstone in the DSDM framework to ensure that a product meets both its technical specifications and business requirements. By delegating the testing activities to parties other than the solution developers, the approach aims to ensure a well-rounded, objective evaluation of the product.

The Imperative for Independent Testing

Objectivity: Distancing from Creation

Developers may unwittingly have blind spots concerning their own work. Independent testing eliminates the emotional or cognitive biases that might prevent the identification of defects, ensuring a more objective evaluation.

Requirement Validation: Bridging Understanding and Implementation

An independent tester serves as a check against misunderstandings or misinterpretations of requirements. When the testing is separated from development, there is a built-in control to confirm that what was understood and built truly aligns with what was required.

Enhanced Coverage: Expanding the Testing Horizon

An independent tester may consider different testing scenarios or focus areas that the developer might have overlooked, thereby providing more comprehensive test coverage.

Roles and Responsibilities Within the DSDM Framework

Solution Developer

This individual or team is tasked with constructing the feature or component under development. However, their role stops short of validating the quality and functionality of what they have built, which is where the independent tester comes in.

Solution Tester

The Solution Tester undertakes the independent tests and is not involved in the development of the features being tested. Their role is to provide an unbiased, thorough evaluation of the solution component to ensure it meets both functional and non-functional requirements.

Business Ambassador and Business Advisor

These roles represent the business interests in the project and are critical in ensuring that the solution meets the intended business outcomes. They often work closely with the Solution Tester to ensure that the tests cover all the business-centric scenarios and requirements.

Conclusion: The Multi-Faceted Benefits of Independent Testing

The notion of independent testing in DSDM not only provides a safety net for ensuring technical quality but also serves as a governance mechanism for aligning the solution with business requirements and expectations. The practice brings together technical and business stakeholders in a harmonious yet independent validation process, ensuring that the final solution is both technically sound and business-wise relevant.

Case Study: Implementing Independent Testing in a DSDM Project for a Financial Services Firm

Background and Context

A mid-sized financial services firm decided to adopt the DSDM framework for the development of its new customer relationship management (CRM) system. The project was considered high-stakes given the sensitivity of financial data and the need for a robust, secure, and user-friendly system. Independent testing was identified as a cornerstone practice to meet these requirements.

Key Stakeholders

Solution Developer Team: Responsible for coding the features based on set requirements.

Solution Tester Team: A third-party firm specializing in financial software testing.

Business Ambassador: Senior Manager from the client services division.

Business Advisor: A regulatory compliance expert.

Phase I: Establishing Testing Objectives and Metrics

The first step was defining what "success" meant in the context of independent testing. The Business Ambassador and Business Advisor collaborated with the Solution Tester Team to set the objectives, which included:

- High-level security

- Seamless integration with existing databases
- Intuitive user interface

Phase II: Crafting the Test Strategy

The Solution Tester Team crafted a detailed test strategy, outlining the methodologies, tools, and timelines. Test scripts were prepared for each feature, and key performance indicators (KPIs) were set for evaluating the testing process.

Phase III: Execution of Independent Tests

The Solution Tester Team began executing the tests as the Solution Developer Team completed each feature. They adhered strictly to the test strategy and liaised closely with the Business Ambassador and Business Advisor for feedback.

Key Findings:

- Several security loopholes were identified and flagged for immediate rectification.
- UI elements that were initially deemed intuitive by the developers were found to be confusing during user acceptance testing.
- Some issues related to database integration were discovered, requiring rework by the Solution Developer Team.

Phase IV: Feedback and Iterative Improvements

The findings were discussed in a feedback session, and an action plan was created. The Solution Developer Team implemented the necessary changes, after which the Solution Tester Team performed a retest.

Conclusion: Outcomes and Lessons Learned

The independent testing phase was deemed successful in identifying both technical and business-oriented issues that might not have been apparent if testing had been conducted by the Solution Developer Team. The process ensured that the CRM system was not only technically sound but also aligned with business objectives and regulatory compliance requirements.

By implementing independent testing, the financial services firm was able to achieve a higher level of quality assurance, thereby greatly reducing the risk associated with deploying a new, critical system.

Test-Driven Development in DSDM: Elevating Quality Assurance Through Pre-Emptive Measures

The Changing Landscape of Quality Assurance: Introduction to TDD in DSDM

Test-Driven Development (TDD) marks a paradigm shift in software quality assurance, positioning testing as a preemptive rather than a reactive exercise. This forward-thinking approach is particularly synergistic with Agile frameworks like DSDM, where quick iterations and adaptability are key. TDD offers a structured methodology for converting requirements into precise, executable specifications, thereby minimizing the chances of misinterpretation and the subsequent development of flawed features.

Sequential Steps for Implementing TDD within a DSDM Project

Preliminary Test Design: The Forethought

The TDD process within a DSDM environment begins with the development of an initial test case that provides a definitive set of criteria for the feature under consideration. This is an imperative step, as it forces stakeholders to delineate the expected behavior and outcome of a given requirement with unparalleled clarity.

The Trial Run: Confirming the Inevitable Failure

The initial run of the test is designed to fail since the code to fulfill the specified criteria has not been developed yet. This failure is actually a positive affirmation of the testing process, serving as a control measure that the test is capable of identifying an incomplete or defective feature.

Code Creation: Breathing Life into Requirements

After confirming the failure of the initial test, the development phase begins. During this stage, the feature is developed with the sole aim of meeting the specific criteria set forth in the initial test.

Reassessment Through Test Execution

The test is executed a second time following the coding phase. If the code is correctly implemented, the test should now pass, confirming the feature's integrity.

Iterative Refinement: The Pursuit of Perfection

If the test does not pass in the second execution, it signals the need for code refinement. This iterative process continues, looping through code modification and retesting until the test passes successfully.

The Art of Refactoring: Code Optimization

Once the test is successfully passed, developers have the opportunity to optimize the code. The goal here is to improve its structural integrity and performance, without altering its behavior.

The Tangible Benefits of Adopting TDD in DSDM

Eliminating Ambiguity: Clear Definition of Requirements

Formulating tests before diving into coding forces both developers and stakeholders to arrive at a mutual understanding of what is required. This eliminates ambiguity and serves as a protective measure against scope creep or feature drift.

Instantaneous Feedback: The Agile Advantage

TDD offers developers immediate feedback on the accuracy and efficacy of their code. This not only accelerates the development cycle but also enhances its agility, aligning perfectly with the iterative nature of DSDM.

Upholding Code Quality: A Long-Term Investment

TDD inherently fosters higher code quality. With each iteration scrutinized against predefined criteria, the resultant code is both robust and maintainable. This long-term view on code quality ensures easier future modifications and extensions, thus making the codebase more sustainable.

Case Study: Implementing Test-Driven Development in a DSDM Project for a Financial Services Application

Project Overview

This case study examines a project within a financial services company where DSDM and Test-Driven Development (TDD) were integrated. The objective of the project was to develop a new customer portal for online banking. Due to the sensitive nature of financial transactions and the complexity involved, ensuring high-quality code was a paramount requirement.

Phase 1: Requirement Analysis and Initial Test Design

The project kicked off with an intense requirement gathering session, including stakeholders like business ambassadors, domain experts, and the technical team. Based on the collated requirements, initial test cases were developed, focusing on core features such as authentication, transaction processing, and data encryption.

Phase 2: The Trial Runs and Initial Failures

Each test case was executed against an empty codebase, resulting in expected failures. This established the validity of each test as a mechanism for detecting incomplete or faulty features.

Phase 3: Iterative Development and Testing

Development proceeded in Timeboxes, following the DSDM framework. After coding for each feature was completed, the corresponding test was executed. Whenever a test failed, the team followed an iterative process of code refinement and retesting until each test passed successfully.

Phase 4: Code Refactoring

Once all core features were developed and their respective tests were passed, a code refactoring phase was initiated. During this phase, developers optimized the code for better performance, readability, and maintainability, all without affecting its behavior. This was performed under the safety net of the already-passed tests, ensuring that refactoring did not introduce any regressions.

Outcome and Benefits Realized

Elevated Code Quality

TDD ensured that every line of code was scrutinized against pre-defined, exacting criteria, resulting in high-quality code that was robust and reliable.

Agile Adaptability

The immediate feedback loop provided by TDD perfectly complemented the agile nature of DSDM, allowing the team to adapt quickly to changing requirements without sacrificing quality.

Business and Technical Alignment

The TDD approach ensured that both technical and business aspects were considered from the get-go, resulting in a product that was not only technically sound but also aligned with business objectives.

In summary, the integration of TDD within a DSDM framework led to the successful development of a customer portal that met stringent quality, security, and functionality requirements, thereby delivering exceptional value to the business.

Timeboxing and Outcome-Based Measurement in DSDM: Crafting a Robust Framework for Project Success

A Closer Look at Timeboxing in DSDM

The Anatomy of a Timebox

A Timebox in DSDM isn't just a schedule; it's a commitment. Each Timebox is rigorously planned and bounded by a specific timeframe, within which a predetermined set of features or requirements must be developed. This ensures that the project remains on track, irrespective of the complexities encountered.

The Rule of Discipline

The unfaltering adherence to Timeboxes adds an extra layer of accountability and control. If specific tasks are not completed within a given Timebox, these tasks are not merely extended or deferred. Instead, they undergo a reevaluation process, ensuring that priority and resources are reassigned in a manner consistent with the project's evolving needs.

Peeling the Layers of Outcome-Based Measurement

The Paradigm Shift from Process to Product

Outcome-based measurement steers clear from the traditional model of gauging project success by adherence to process metrics. It propels the focus towards the end-products or solution increments, compelling teams to envision the tangible impacts of their work.

Business Affirmation: The Final Seal of Approval

When a Timebox concludes, the resultant increment undergoes rigorous assessment by Business Ambassadors or Business Visionaries. This ensures that every piece of the developed solution not only meets the technical criteria but also aligns perfectly with business objectives.

Real-Time Analytics: Actual vs. Planned

The delivered solution increment is compared against original plans to provide an evidence-based performance appraisal. This comparison offers the team and stakeholders a transparent look at the project's health, assisting in more informed decision-making for future Timeboxes.

The Synergy of Timeboxing and Outcome-Based Measurement

Building a Culture of Accountability

The rigidity of Timeboxes and the focus on measurable outcomes act as double-layered checks. Teams are not only responsible for adhering to schedules but also for ensuring that their efforts culminate in meaningful outcomes.

Adaptive Maneuverability

This dual methodology accommodates agile responsiveness. Timeboxes are short enough to allow for course correction, and outcome-based measurements ensure that these corrections are not whimsical but are data-backed.

Transparency: The Cornerstone of Stakeholder Trust

The focus on demonstrable outcomes, combined with the timeline discipline of Timeboxing, offers stakeholders an unparalleled level of transparency into the project's progression, facilitating enhanced trust and engagement.

Operational Efficiency: Doing More with Less

By aligning activities with a focused set of outcomes within fixed timelines, the project team can work in a leaner manner, cutting down on time and resource wastage.

In summation, Timeboxing and Outcome-Based Measurement in DSDM offer a well-rounded framework for achieving project success. By balancing disciplined execution with outcome-oriented evaluation, they serve as navigational beacons guiding the project toward its ultimate objectives.

Case Study: Implementing Timeboxing and Outcome-Based Measurement in a DSDM Project for a Financial Institution

Project Context

A leading financial institution was looking to upgrade its legacy customer management system. The project was critical, not just from a technology standpoint but also in terms of regulatory compliance and customer experience. The DSDM framework was chosen for its agility and robustness, and Timeboxing and Outcome-Based Measurement were implemented as key control methodologies.

Timeboxing Strategy

Planning the Timeboxes

Given the complexity of the project, Timeboxes were carefully planned, each lasting two weeks. Specific features and regulatory requirements were assigned to individual Timeboxes to ensure that the most critical aspects of the project were addressed first.

Adhering to Discipline

As Timeboxes concluded, incomplete tasks were not rolled over to the next Timebox blindly. Instead, they were reevaluated to check if their priority had changed due to new insights or shifts in regulatory landscapes.

Outcome-Based Measurement Techniques

Focus on Business Objectives

Key performance indicators (KPIs) were established that directly aligned with the business objectives. These included compliance rate, transaction speed, and customer satisfaction scores.

Validation by Business Units

At the end of each Timebox, Business Ambassadors reviewed the developed increment against the defined KPIs to ensure alignment with business goals and compliance standards.

Synergistic Benefits

Enhanced Accountability

Teams were more conscious of their roles and contributions, knowing that they were accountable both for the timely delivery and the quality of the outcomes.

Adaptive Strategy

The two-week Timebox allowed the project to adapt to new regulatory guidelines that were introduced midway through the project, without causing major disruptions.

Stakeholder Trust

Transparent reporting on both time adherence and outcome achievement led to greater stakeholder confidence and facilitated subsequent phases of investment for project expansion.

Conclusion

The implementation of Timeboxing and Outcome-Based Measurement offered a balanced approach to project management. It ensured that not only were project deliverables achieved on time, but they also met the highest standards of quality and business alignment. The project was hailed as a success, meeting all its objectives and even exceeding some, especially in the areas of customer satisfaction and regulatory compliance.

The case study demonstrates how Timeboxing and Outcome-Based Measurement, when properly implemented within the DSDM framework, can significantly elevate project outcomes and stakeholder satisfaction.

Advanced Strategies for Ensuring Transparency in DSDM Projects

Utilizing Team Boards and Daily Stand-ups for Optimal Transparency

Transparency in DSDM is not just a best practice; it is a foundational principle that can significantly influence project outcomes. As a mechanism for both internal and external communication, transparency serves a variety of functions, from fostering collaboration and trust among team members to keeping stakeholders informed.

Team Boards: More Than a Tracking Tool

While many understand the Team Board as primarily a tracking tool, its functions extend far beyond this singular role.

Catalyst for Accountability

By assigning tasks clearly and transparently, the Team Board helps in attributing accountability. A well-maintained board creates an environment where team members are compelled to follow through on their commitments, knowing that their performance is publicly displayed.

Risk and Issue Flagging

Blockers and other issues are not just notations on the board; they serve as public acknowledgments that require action. The designated owner has the public responsibility to address and resolve the issue, making this a powerful tool for proactive risk management.

Daily Stand-up Meetings: A Ritual of Transparency

Integrating Multidisciplinary Insights

The inclusion of both business and technical team members provides a rounded perspective during stand-ups. It prevents the project from becoming too skewed toward either business objectives or technical requirements.

Transparency in Real-Time

The routine nature of daily stand-ups ensures that transparency is not a periodic activity but a constant feature of the project landscape. This facilitates immediate action and allows for the agility that is at the heart of DSDM.

The Symbiotic Relationship Between Team Boards and Daily Stand-ups

Complementary Tools for Transparency

These tools are not mutually exclusive but are, in fact, deeply interdependent. The Team Board serves as a static reference point, continually updated to reflect the dynamic discussions and agreements made during the Daily Stand-ups.

Enabling Dynamic Adjustments

One of the core benefits of this symbiotic relationship is the ability for real-time project adjustment. Decisions aren't postponed to a future meeting but can be made on the spot, thanks to the comprehensive visibility provided by these tools.

Conclusion

The Team Board and Daily Stand-up meetings are instrumental in achieving the level of transparency that DSDM demands. They work in conjunction to offer a full-fledged system that supports not only tracking and accountability but also real-time adjustments and collaborative problem-solving. Therefore, leveraging these tools effectively is essential for maintaining transparency and thereby contributing to the project's ultimate success.

Case Study: Leveraging Transparency Tools in a DSDM Project for Improved Outcomes

Project Background

A mid-sized technology company embarked on a DSDM project to overhaul its internal communication systems. The project's complexity and the various stakeholder needs made it crucial to maintain a high level of transparency.

Implementation of Team Board and Daily Stand-ups

From the get-go, the company used a digital Team Board accessible to all team members and stakeholders. Daily Stand-ups were scheduled and scrupulously adhered to, involving all relevant team roles.

How Team Board Served Multiple Functions

Rapid Issue Identification and Resolution

Within the first week, the Team Board flagged a significant blocker regarding data migration. The designated owner was able to allocate resources immediately to resolve the issue, thereby averting a potential delay in the project.

Encouraging Accountability

Tasks that were lagging were clearly visible on the Team Board, prompting immediate discussions during the Daily Stand-ups. Team members were motivated to complete their tasks on time, knowing that delays would be visible to all.

The Critical Role of Daily Stand-ups

Unifying Team Objectives

The regular Daily Stand-up meetings ensured that all team members, including business and technical roles, were aligned in their objectives and had a clear understanding of project priorities.

Facilitating Quick Decision-Making

In one instance, a design change was proposed and discussed during a stand-up. Because of the immediate visibility and agreement, the change was implemented on the same day, avoiding delays that are often associated with bureaucratic processes.

The Synergy Effect: Team Board and Daily Stand-ups

Real-time Project Adaptation

The digital Team Board was updated in real-time during Daily Stand-ups. This allowed for a seamless flow of information and immediate updates, facilitating quick adaptations to the project plan.

Strengthening Stakeholder Confidence

The transparency afforded by these tools kept stakeholders informed and engaged, leading to a higher level of trust and confidence in the project's direction and eventual success.

Conclusion

The case underscores the integral roles that Team Boards and Daily Stand-ups play in maintaining transparency in a DSDM project. The effective utilization of these tools resulted in quicker decision-making, better issue resolution, and a greater alignment among team members and stakeholders, contributing to the project's overall success.

Responding to Change in DSDM: Balancing Flexibility and Control

Overview

Adaptability to change is more than a reactive strategy in the Dynamic Systems Development Method (DSDM); it is an embedded feature of the framework. While embracing change is pivotal for keeping a project aligned with shifting business goals, it's equally important to have a structured approach to change control. This ensures that the project retains focus, meets timelines, and upholds quality standards.

Two Levels of Change Control

Project Level: Controlled by the Business Visionary

Role

The Business Visionary takes on the task of ensuring that any alterations to the project remain consistent with the overarching business objectives.

Mechanism

Changes that affect the high-level requirements, as detailed in the Prioritized Requirements List, require formal approval from the Business Visionary.

Type of Change

Such changes generally affect the breadth of the project, including its scope and major features.

Solution Development Team Level: Managed by the Team

Role

The team itself manages the more nuanced changes that arise from a deeper understanding of specific requirements or from shifts in the evolving solution.

Mechanism

These more granular changes don't usually necessitate a formal change in the project scope and are primarily managed at the team's discretion.

Type of Change

The changes at this level focus mainly on the depth or granularity of existing requirements and features.

Key Principles Guiding Change

Focus on Business Needs

Any change must be business-centric, aiming to add value to the business rather than just altering the technical aspects of a project.

Time Constraint

In DSDM, the timeline is fixed, and thus any changes must be accommodated within this pre-defined timeframe.

Quality Non-negotiable

Quality standards cannot be compromised to accommodate changes, ensuring that the end product remains robust and reliable.

Cost Constraint

Lastly, any changes must also respect the fiscal constraints, staying within the project's allocated budget.

Concluding Remarks

Balancing flexibility and control in response to change is a nuanced endeavor in DSDM. While the framework promotes adaptability, it also enforces rigorous change control mechanisms at both the project and team levels. This dual approach ensures that the project not only remains agile but also retains its focus and commitment to quality, time, and cost parameters.

Case Study: Responding to Change in a Financial Services DSDM Project

In a DSDM project undertaken by a financial services company, the need to accommodate changes was constant due to regulatory shifts and evolving customer needs. While the project valued adaptability, it also adhered strictly to change control mechanisms. The following elaboration provides insights into how this financial firm achieved a balanced approach to managing change in a DSDM environment.

Two-Tiered Approach to Change Control

Role of Business Visionary

In this project, the Business Visionary was a senior executive from the finance department. He was responsible for ensuring that all changes at the project level adhered to the firm's broader financial and compliance goals.

The Team's Autonomy

The Solution Development Team had the liberty to tweak details of existing requirements without formal approval from upper management, as long as these alterations did not affect the project's breadth or high-level goals.

Key Principles in Action

Business-Centric Focus

Changes were evaluated based on their capacity to improve the company's compliance with new financial regulations and to enhance customer satisfaction, aligning with the core business needs.

Time-Bound Adaptability

Even when changes were made, they had to fit within the pre-set project timelines. This introduced a disciplined approach to adaptability, ensuring that milestones were met.

Uncompromised Quality

Quality checks were stringent, and any changes had to undergo rigorous testing to make sure they met the established quality benchmarks.

Budget Constraints

The project also had a fixed budget, and any changes were evaluated for their financial implications. This ensured that the project remained financially viable while accommodating changes.

Outcome

The project successfully navigated multiple regulatory changes and shifts in customer expectations while staying on schedule and within budget. The two-tiered approach to change control not only enabled flexibility but also maintained stringent quality and time controls, demonstrating the efficacy of balancing adaptability and control in a DSDM project.

Concluding Remarks

Through structured change control mechanisms and a focus on key principles like business alignment, time, quality, and cost, the financial services firm successfully turned potential challenges into opportunities for improvement.

This case exemplifies how a well-implemented change control process within DSDM can lead to project success, even in a volatile environment like financial services.

A Deeper Exploration of Management by Exception in DSDM: Balancing Autonomy and Oversight

Management by Exception in the DSDM framework represents an intriguing confluence of team autonomy and hierarchical oversight. By providing the Solution Development Team with the independence to make decisions within a predefined scope, while also specifying conditions that necessitate managerial intervention, this approach aims to streamline the project execution without compromising on quality and alignment. Let's delve deeper into the intricate mechanisms and operational nuances that make this approach effective.

The Intricacies of Empowerment

Autonomy as a Motivational Tool

Empowerment in the DSDM context doesn't merely delegate tasks; it instills a sense of ownership and accountability. The team members, knowing that they have the latitude to make important decisions, are motivated to deliver their best performance.

Predefined Boundaries: The Limits of Autonomy

The empowerment is not limitless. Parameters are defined in advance to offer a clear scope within which the team can operate autonomously. This prevents misaligned efforts and ensures that the project remains on course.

MoSCoW Prioritization: More Than a List

A Living Document

Though the MoSCoW list is initially established at the outset, it is not set in stone. It serves as a dynamic tool that can be revisited and revised as the project progresses, particularly for "Could-Have" and "Should-Have" items.

The Art of Sacrifice

One of the benefits of MoSCoW prioritization is the inherent flexibility it offers in sacrificing "Could-Have" items for more critical "Must-Have" or "Should-Have" elements, without the need for bureaucratic delays.

Tolerance Levels and Exception Conditions: The Safety Nets

The Calculus of Tolerance

Tolerance levels are not arbitrarily decided. They are the result of comprehensive risk assessments and deliberations among project-level stakeholders to determine what degree of deviation is acceptable.

Proactive Escalation

When an exception condition is met, the escalation is not merely a reactive measure but a proactive step to bring the project back on track. It serves as an early warning system, enabling timely intervention before issues escalate into more significant problems.

Conclusion

The Management by Exception approach in DSDM elegantly balances the need for speed and flexibility with the imperatives of quality and alignment. By clearly defining the autonomy levels, prioritization mechanisms, and safety nets, it creates a robust framework that allows teams to operate with agility while remaining aligned with the overarching project goals.

Case Study Unpacked: Implementing Management by Exception in a Financial Services DSDM Project

Introduction

In a real-world DSDM project undertaken by a financial services company, the Management by Exception approach played a pivotal role in ensuring a successful outcome. Given the critical nature of the financial domain, where delays can translate to significant revenue loss, the speed of decision-making was crucial. At the same time, maintaining quality and alignment with regulatory standards was non-negotiable. This case study explores how Management by Exception served as the bedrock of this fine balance.

Autonomy in Action: Empowered but Aligned Teams

Aligning with Business Goals

The Solution Development Team was provided with a clearly articulated set of business objectives from the onset. This created a roadmap that guided the team's autonomous actions, ensuring alignment with the company's broader financial strategies.

Risk Mitigation Measures

The team had autonomy but within risk-averse boundaries. The limits were defined in line with the compliance requirements specific to financial services, ensuring that the team's actions remained within regulatory parameters.

Dynamic MoSCoW Prioritization

Frequent Review Cycles

Given the volatility of the financial markets, the MoSCoW list was reviewed on a bi-weekly basis. This allowed the project to remain agile and adapt to sudden market shifts or regulatory updates.

Prioritizing Compliance

In this project, "Must-Have" items often revolved around compliance-related features, due to their non-negotiable nature in the financial industry. This prioritization schema made sure the essential features were always at the forefront.

Exception Handling: Timely Interventions

Real-Time Monitoring

Exception conditions were closely monitored in real-time. This was critical given that lapses in financial data security or compliance could have catastrophic consequences.

The Escalation Protocol

The project had a clearly defined escalation protocol involving immediate involvement from senior compliance officers and legal advisors. This ensured that exception handling was not just swift but also met the stringent industry standards.

Conclusion

In this financial services DSDM project, Management by Exception provided the right blend of autonomy and control. It allowed the Solution Development Team to operate at a high speed, which is a business necessity in the financial sector, while also ensuring that they remained tightly aligned with complex regulatory requirements and business objectives. This duality of speed and compliance served as the cornerstone of the project's success.

Delving Deeper: Planning for Quality and Iteration in DSDM's Lifecycle

In DSDM, the concept of planning is not confined to the early stages of a project but extends throughout its lifecycle. This continuous planning process plays a pivotal role in ensuring quality and robustness in the delivered solution. The following elaboration dissects the integral planning activities associated with each phase of a DSDM project, focusing on quality assurance and iterative development.

The Intricacies of Phases and Planning Activities

Pre-Project: Laying the Groundwork

At this early stage, the project's broad contours are defined, including its fit within the existing portfolio. This step ensures that the project aligns with strategic objectives, setting the stage for a quality-centric approach from the outset.

Feasibility: Beyond Just Viability

The Feasibility phase goes beyond merely ascertaining whether the project is doable. It incorporates high-level risk analyses focusing on elements such as security, performance, and resilience. These considerations set a quality baseline that informs future planning activities.

Foundations: Blueprint for Quality

This phase involves meticulous planning to refine both functional and non-functional requirements. The integration of quality perspectives at this stage lays a solid foundation for the project, ensuring that the subsequent iterations will adhere to high standards.

Evolutionary Development: Adapting Without Compromising Quality

Here, timeboxes are planned iteratively, allowing the project to adapt to emerging requirements without sacrificing quality. Integrated testing is a key feature of this phase, focusing on not just functionality but also other quality attributes such as usability and reliability.

Deployment: More Than Just Delivery

The Deployment phase involves comprehensive planning for rolling out the solution and for tracking the realization of benefits. This ensures that the product not only works as intended but also meets the quality criteria defined earlier in the project.

Post-Project: Quality in Retrospect

The final phase involves a comprehensive assessment of the project's impact on quality and performance. This retrospective view aids in institutionalizing lessons learned and improving quality planning for future projects.

Ensuring Quality Through Planning in DSDM

A Multi-tiered Risk Analysis Approach

Quality planning in DSDM incorporates risk assessments at multiple levels. These analyses extend from high-level identification of quality-related risks in the Feasibility stage to a more nuanced examination of risks associated with specific features during the Evolutionary Development phase.

An Integrated Testing Philosophy

DSDM adopts a testing philosophy that is integrated into the development process itself, rather than being a separate, post-development activity. This ensures that quality assurance is ongoing and not an afterthought.

The Final Seal: End-to-End Testing and Assurance

Before the project closes, a rigorous end-to-end testing process is conducted to validate that all quality benchmarks have been met. This ensures that the deployment process, as well as the delivered solution, stand up to the quality criteria established early in the project.

Conclusion

Planning in DSDM is an ever-evolving process that places a strong emphasis on quality assurance. This iterative planning model, which permeates through the project lifecycle, equips the project to adapt to changing conditions while maintaining a steadfast focus on quality.

Case Study Insights: Quality-centric Planning Across a DSDM Project Lifecycle

Introduction

The case study focuses on a DSDM project executed within the financial services sector. It demonstrates how planning and quality assurance were intertwined at every phase, ensuring not only a successful project outcome but also a solution that met high-quality benchmarks.

Elaboration on Phases and Planning Activities

Pre-Project: Aligning with Business Objectives

The project was positioned within the larger portfolio, ensuring its alignment with the company's strategic goals. Initial planning activities also included identifying key quality parameters such as compliance with financial regulations and data security standards.

Feasibility: Setting a Quality Baseline

In this phase, a high-level risk analysis was carried out to identify quality-related risks, including those pertaining to regulatory compliance and data security. The outcome shaped a quality baseline that would guide future project activities.

Foundations: Engraving Quality in Requirements

Detailed planning in the Foundations phase led to a well-defined Prioritized Requirements List, which included both functional and non-functional elements. The non-functional requirements were particularly focused on ensuring data integrity and transactional security.

Evolutionary Development: Iterative Planning with Integrated Testing

As the project unfolded, each Timebox was planned with an integrated testing component. This approach facilitated the incorporation of immediate feedback, allowing for real-time quality adjustments.

Deployment: Planning for Smooth Transition and Benefits Realization

In the Deployment phase, a comprehensive roll-out plan was developed. This included a set of quality assurance tests to validate the system's readiness for production, focusing on user experience and compliance with industry standards.

Post-Project: Closing the Quality Loop

Upon project completion, a detailed review was undertaken to assess how well the project met the initial quality criteria. The lessons learned were documented for institutional knowledge and to improve quality planning for future projects.

Quality Assurance Highlights

Risk Mitigation Through Planning

The project team utilized risk assessments as a tool for ongoing quality assurance, right from the Feasibility phase through to the Deployment phase.

Embedded Testing

The Evolutionary Development phase included a series of iterative tests, integrated within each Timebox, ensuring that the project was continuously aligned with quality expectations.

Comprehensive Final Testing

Before the deployment, the entire solution underwent a rigorous set of tests to confirm its adherence to the established quality benchmarks, including a focus on regulatory compliance and data security.

Conclusion

The case study underscores the importance of integrating quality assurance into planning activities across all phases of a DSDM project. By doing so, the project not only achieved its functional goals but also delivered a high-quality solution that stood up to stringent industry standards.

Chapter Eight

Unpacking MoSCoW Prioritisation: A Pillar of Agile Project Management

MoSCoW Prioritization Technique in DSDM: A Deeper Dive

Context Matters: MoSCoW within the DSDM Framework

Understanding the context in which MoSCoW operates is crucial for its effective implementation. The categorization of project requirements as "Must Have," "Should Have," "Could Have," or "Won't Have this Time" is not static; rather, it is influenced by various project dynamics like deadlines, stakeholder expectations, and resource constraints.

Adapting to Project Constraints

While MoSCoW provides a robust structure for prioritization, it's vital for the project team to revisit these priorities as constraints evolve. For instance, what is categorized as a "Should Have" might escalate to a "Must Have" if stakeholder requirements change or if business objectives shift.

Navigating Stakeholder Expectations

In practice, MoSCoW also serves as a communication tool between the project team and stakeholders. It's not just about prioritizing work; it's about setting realistic expectations. Open dialogue is essential in clarifying why certain requirements are categorized in a particular way and what the implications are for project delivery.

The Role of the Agile Project Manager

Facilitating MoSCoW Sessions

The Agile Project Manager plays a pivotal role in facilitating MoSCoW prioritization sessions. These are collaborative activities that should involve key stakeholders to ensure that the prioritization aligns with business objectives and stakeholder expectations.

Risk Mitigation through MoSCoW

Proactive risk management is another responsibility of the Agile Project Manager. By ensuring that "Must Have" and "Should Have" items are given priority, the Project Manager can significantly mitigate the risks associated with not meeting key business objectives.

Conclusion

MoSCoW is more than just a technique for prioritizing project requirements; it is a strategic tool that influences and is influenced by various aspects of project management within the DSDM framework. Its effectiveness lies not just in the categorization of work but in its capacity to align stakeholders, manage risks, and adapt to changing project landscapes.

Case Study: Implementing MoSCoW in a DSDM Project for a Healthcare Application

Project Background

The project aimed to develop a healthcare application that allowed patients to book appointments, access medical records, and consult with doctors online. The time frame was strict, with a six-month window for the initial release. The team decided to employ DSDM as the Agile framework, with MoSCoW as the prioritization technique.

Identifying and Categorizing Requirements

Initial MoSCoW Session

An initial MoSCoW session was conducted with stakeholders, including the Business Visionary, Technical Coordinator, and Project Manager. The team identified various features and classified them into MoSCoW categories. For example:

Must Have: Secure login, appointment booking

Should Have: Access to medical records, in-app notifications

Could Have: Online consultations, location-based doctor search

Won't Have this Time: Health trackers, integration with wearables

Revisiting MoSCoW Priorities

As the project progressed, new regulations came into effect, making it compulsory for healthcare apps to provide access to medical records. Thus, "Access to medical records" was moved from the "Should Have" to the "Must Have" category.

Role of the Agile Project Manager

Navigating Changes in Requirements

The Project Manager facilitated a new MoSCoW session to reassess the priorities and communicated the changes to all stakeholders. The development team was realigned to meet the new "Must Have" criteria.

Risk Mitigation

The Project Manager also conducted a risk assessment following the change in requirements. Mitigation strategies were devised to ensure that the newly elevated "Must Have" feature did not affect the project timeline adversely.

Outcomes

The project was delivered within the stipulated time, with all "Must Have" and most of "Should Have" features included. The use of MoSCoW enabled the team to adapt effectively to regulatory changes without derailing the project.

Conclusion

The MoSCoW prioritization technique proved invaluable in ensuring that the healthcare app project not only met its primary objectives but also adapted to external changes swiftly and efficiently. The role of the Agile Project Manager in facilitating MoSCoW sessions and realigning the team was crucial in this success.

Digging Deeper into MUST and "Must Have" in DSDM Projects

The Minimum Usable Subset (MUST) and the "Must Have" category in MoSCoW prioritization serve as twin pillars of certainty in DSDM projects. These concepts are pivotal for steering a project toward success by highlighting non-negotiable requirements that directly impact the solution's viability, safety, legality, and timeliness.

Criteria for Defining "Must Have" Requirements

A Yardstick for Success

Identifying "Must Have" requirements isn't merely a task; it's a meticulous exercise in discernment. Various criteria assist in this categorization, offering teams a standardized framework to make critical decisions.

Critical for Deployment

If a requirement is so vital that its absence renders the solution undeployable, it becomes a "Must Have."

Meeting Legal Obligations

"Must Have" requirements may stem from mandatory legal or regulatory stipulations that the project must fulfill.

Addressing Safety Concerns

Any requirement mitigating safety risks or hazards is categorized as a "Must Have."

Ensuring Solution Viability

If a requirement is the linchpin for the solution's operational effectiveness, it earns a "Must Have" label.

The 60% Rule for Effort Allocation

A Guideline for Prudent Planning

The 60% Rule isn't an arbitrary figure but a strategically calculated guideline. By capping the effort for "Must Have" requirements at 60% of the total project effort, several advantages are unlocked.

Risk Mitigation

This restriction creates a buffer for the project, providing leeway for uncertainties and risks that might surface during the project lifecycle.

Space for Quality and Enhancement

By not exhausting all resources on "Must Have" requirements, the project retains the flexibility to focus on "Should Have" and "Could Have" requirements, thus enhancing the overall quality of the solution.

Change Management Preparedness

Having a reserved pool of effort equips the project to tackle unforeseen changes or challenges, ensuring that core requirements are not compromised.

Conclusion

Understanding and effectively utilizing the concepts of MUST and "Must Have" in DSDM projects form the cornerstone of successful project delivery. These elements serve as critical levers in project planning and execution, ensuring that essential requirements are neither overlooked nor under-resourced. By adhering to the criteria for "Must Have" categorization and respecting the 60% Rule, projects can better navigate the complexities of dynamic systems development.

Unpacking the Case Study: The Role of MUST and "Must Have" in a DSDM-Based Financial Software Project

Introduction

The case study under review revolves around the implementation of a DSDM project in the development of financial software. It particularly focuses on how the concepts of Minimum Usable Subset (MUST) and "Must Have" criteria were utilized to guide the project toward a successful conclusion. The study illuminates how these critical elements helped the team in accurate requirement categorization, risk management, and resource allocation.

Criteria for "Must Have" Requirements in Action

Operational Necessities

The project team identified specific functionalities like real-time transaction tracking and robust security protocols as "Must Have" requirements, given their criticality to the software's core functioning.

Regulatory Compliance

Being a financial software, adhering to specific financial regulations was non-negotiable. Requirements linked to compliance were immediately categorized as "Must Have."

Safeguarding Data Integrity

Given the sensitive nature of financial data, any requirement that contributed to data integrity and safety was identified as a "Must Have."

Implementing the 60% Rule

Risk Buffer

The project initially allocated approximately 58% of its total effort for "Must Have" requirements. This careful allocation created a sufficient risk buffer, enabling the project to absorb uncertainties effectively.

Balancing Quality and Scope

By sticking to the 60% rule, the project team could allocate time and resources to "Should Have" and "Could Have" requirements, like user-friendly interfaces and additional data analytics features, which added value to the end product.

Agility in Change Management

With a 42% effort buffer, the team had the flexibility to adapt to changes in market needs and technology trends without causing disruption in the delivery of "Must Have" functionalities.

Conclusion

The case study offers an insightful look into how the MUST and "Must Have" concepts in DSDM were not just theoretical aspects but practical tools for project success. By diligently applying these principles, the financial software project was delivered on time, within scope, and met all quality benchmarks, thereby validating the importance of these DSDM components in project management.

Delving Deeper into "Should Have" Requirements in DSDM Projects

The concept of "Should Have" requirements in the DSDM (Dynamic Systems Development Method) framework warrants further exploration due to its nuanced role in balancing project scope, quality, and stakeholder expectations. Although these requirements are not as critical as the "Must Have" category, their strategic inclusion or exclusion can significantly impact the project's outcome.

Identifying "Should Have" Requirements: An Analytical Lens

Defining Scope and Business Alignment

Understanding the project's objectives and how each requirement aligns with the business strategy is the first step in identifying "Should Have" items. The aim is to ascertain the level of impact these requirements will have on the project's business value.

Prioritization within Time and Resource Constraints

Given the non-essential nature of "Should Have" requirements, they often compete for the same pool of resources as the "Could Have" items. Prioritization, in this case, becomes an exercise in optimizing resource allocation without compromising the project's primary objectives.

Risks and Trade-offs

The Cost of Exclusion

Although "Should Have" requirements are not critical, their exclusion may lead to sub-optimal results. This could mean anything from reduced user satisfaction to loss of competitive edge.

Balancing Act: Quality vs. Timeliness

Inclusion of too many "Should Have" items without proper planning could jeopardize the project's schedule. Conversely, neglecting them could compromise quality, making it crucial to find the right balance.

Strategies for Effective Management

Periodic Review and Re-prioritization

Given the dynamic nature of projects, it's advisable to periodically reassess the status and importance of "Should Have" requirements. This iterative review process should coincide with major project milestones.

Stakeholder Involvement

Engaging stakeholders in the prioritization process helps in clarifying the business value and potential impact of "Should Have" requirements. This collective decision-making adds another layer of validation to the choices made.

Conclusion

"Should Have" requirements play a nuanced role in DSDM projects, filling the gap between critical essentials and nice-to-haves. Their effective identification, prioritization, and management can be the key to achieving a well-rounded, high-quality project output that meets or exceeds stakeholder expectations. Would you like to hear about a case study or practical example to further elaborate on this topic?

Case Study: Managing "Should Have" Requirements in a DSDM Healthcare Project

Introduction

This case study delves into the management of "Should Have" requirements in a DSDM project for a healthcare provider aiming to digitize patient records. The project had a tight timeline of six months and a limited budget. The focus here is to showcase the challenges and strategies associated with managing these intermediate-level requirements.

Initial Requirement Gathering and Challenges

Volume of Requirements

Initial requirement gathering brought forth a slew of features that ranged from essential functionalities like secure login and record retrieval to advanced features like predictive analytics for patient outcomes.

Balancing Stakeholder Interests

The healthcare provider's management team insisted on advanced analytics capabilities, considering them as "Should Have" elements for the project. However, the development team was cautious about the timeline and available resources.

Prioritization and Trade-offs

Business Value Assessment

An urgent meeting with all stakeholders was conducted to rank the requirements based on business value and resource implications. Advanced analytics, though valuable, was time-intensive.

Outcome of Prioritization

It was decided that while predictive analytics were important, they could be incorporated in a later phase of the project. This allowed the team to focus on essential functionalities without stretching the timeline.

Risk Mitigation and Stakeholder Management

Periodic Reviews

The project was divided into timeboxes, and at the end of each, the status and feasibility of incorporating analytics were reviewed.

Managing Expectations

Regular communication with stakeholders ensured that there were no surprises, and the focus remained on delivering a robust, secure, and user-friendly system in the first phase.

Final Outcome and Lessons Learned

The project was successfully completed within the given timeline and budget constraints. The deferred "Should Have" features were added in the subsequent phase, with a minor increase in budget but a significant uptick in user engagement and satisfaction.

Leveraging "Should Have" Effectively

The project illustrated how judicious management of "Should Have" requirements could result in meeting project goals without compromising on quality or stakeholder expectations.

Conclusion

The case study highlights the importance of meticulous planning, prioritization, and stakeholder engagement in managing "Should Have" requirements in a DSDM project. Balancing the "Should Have" elements effectively can spell the difference between project success and failure.

"Could Have" Requirements in DSDM Projects: Striking the Balance between Desirability and Necessity

In the Dynamic Systems Development Method (DSDM), "Could Have" requirements often constitute elements that enhance the usability or features of a project but aren't essential for its core functionality. These requirements can offer additional value but can also be safely postponed or omitted without jeopardizing the project's primary objectives.

Defining Characteristics of "Could Have" Requirements

Lesser Importance

Unlike "Must Have" or "Should Have" requirements, "Could Have" items don't fundamentally impact the project's success or failure. They are enhancements that improve user experience or add layers of functionality, but their absence is not a deal-breaker.

Low Impact if Omitted

The beauty of "Could Have" requirements lies in their expendability. Omitting them won't hamper the project's essential goals or compromise its deliverables. They are features that are nice to include but not necessary for the project's viability.

Contingency Pool

When a project faces unexpected hurdles, whether in terms of time, budget, or other resources, "Could Have" requirements are usually the first to be sacrificed. They essentially form a contingency pool that project managers can draw from to keep the project on track without affecting its core objectives.

Effort Allocation: The 20% Rule

Strategic Allocation

DSDM guidelines suggest that the effort allocated to "Could Have" requirements should not exceed around 20% of the total project effort. This percentage is deliberately kept low to ensure that the project remains focused on its critical components.

Importance of Flexibility

Keeping the "Could Have" effort to around 20% provides the project with a cushion against unforeseen challenges or changes. This flexibility allows for adjustments to be made to the project scope, timeline, or resource allocation, without affecting the project's crucial elements.

Conclusion

The role of "Could Have" requirements in a DSDM project should not be underestimated. While they may not be critical to the project's success, they often add value that could differentiate a good project from a great one. The key is to manage these requirements strategically, ensuring they don't divert focus or resources from the project's core objectives.

Case Study: Implementing "Could Have" Requirements in a DSDM Project

Background

In a hypothetical software development project aimed at creating a new customer relationship management (CRM) system, the team identified a range of "Could Have" features. These included advanced data analytics capabilities, integration with social media platforms, and an in-app chat support system.

Effort Allocation

Initially, the team allocated approximately 20% of the total project effort toward these "Could Have" requirements. This percentage was in line with DSDM guidelines, providing a balance between focusing on essential features and adding value through these additional functionalities.

Challenges Faced

During the course of the project, the team faced some unexpected delays in the development of "Must Have" features, mainly due to unforeseen technical complexities. This posed a risk to the project timeline.

Decision to De-scope

To address these challenges, the project manager made the strategic decision to de-scope some of the "Could Have" requirements, specifically the advanced data analytics capabilities and social media integration. This freed up resources and time to focus on resolving the complexities surrounding the "Must Have" requirements.

Outcome

The decision to cut back on "Could Have" requirements allowed the team to meet the project deadline without compromising on any of the "Must Have" or "Should Have" requirements. The CRM system was successfully deployed, meeting all its essential criteria. While it lacked some of the advanced features initially planned, the core functionalities were robust, and the project was considered a success.

Lessons Learned

The case underscores the importance of flexibility in DSDM projects. It also validates the DSDM guideline to allocate only around 20% of the effort to "Could Have" requirements, as this leaves room to maneuver when unexpected challenges arise, allowing for a re-focus on essential project elements without substantial negative impacts.

This practical example highlights how "Could Have" requirements, although not critical, need strategic management to ensure that they neither distract from nor jeopardize the main objectives of the project.

Further Exploration of "Won't Have this Time" Requirements in DSDM Projects

Scope Management Through Explicit Exclusions

In any DSDM project, it's not just what you include that counts; it's also what you deliberately exclude. By clearly identifying "Won't Have this Time" requirements, the project team sends a clear message about what will not be delivered. This serves as an anchor for scope discussions and keeps the focus on achieving the essential elements necessary for project success.

Managing Stakeholder Expectations

The categorization of "Won't Have this Time" requirements performs a crucial role in expectation management. Stakeholders often have varying ideas about what is essential for project success. Clearly marking non-essential elements as

"Won't Have this Time" puts everyone on the same page and avoids misunderstandings that could surface later in the project lifecycle.

Preventing Scope Creep

One of the most common pitfalls in project management is scope creep, where additional features or functions are informally added to the project without proper analysis or approval. By formally documenting "Won't Have this Time" requirements in the Prioritised Requirements List, you establish a baseline that prevents these requirements from sneaking back into the project scope. This is crucial for maintaining the integrity of the project and ensuring that it stays on course in terms of time, cost, and quality.

Long-Term Planning and Future Relevance

Just because a requirement is categorized as "Won't Have this Time" doesn't mean it is irrelevant for the long term. Documenting these requirements creates a reference that can be invaluable for future projects or phases. This historical record can serve as a starting point for new initiatives, saving time and effort in the long run.

Organizational Learning and Knowledge Transfer

In addition to serving as a reference for future projects, the Prioritised Requirements List, complete with "Won't Have this Time" entries, can be an essential tool for organizational learning. New team members or stakeholders can quickly understand what was considered and excluded in previous projects, providing context and background that can be invaluable for decision-making and planning.

Case Study: Implementing "Won't Have this Time" Requirements in a DSDM Project for a Healthcare App

Context

A healthcare organization decided to develop a patient management app using the DSDM framework. The project had several stakeholders, including doctors, nurses, administrators, and patients. Each had unique requirements, some of which were conflicting or beyond the scope of the initial project phase.

Initial Requirement Gathering

During the initial requirement gathering process, several features were suggested, such as real-time tracking of patient metrics, an AI-based diagnostic tool, a billing module, and multi-language support.

The Prioritised Requirements List

The project team prepared a Prioritised Requirements List, segregating the requirements into "Must Have," "Should Have," "Could Have," and "Won't Have this Time" categories.

Must Have: Basic features such as patient registration, appointment booking, and medical history tracking.

Should Have: Notification system for appointments, basic billing information.

Could Have: Additional features like reviews for doctors, hospital mapping.

Won't Have this Time: Real-time tracking of patient metrics, AI-based diagnostic tool, multi-language support.

Key Decisions and Outcomes

Scope Clarification

By explicitly stating that real-time tracking of patient metrics and the AI-based diagnostic tool were "Won't Have this Time" requirements, the project team avoided over-committing and clearly defined the scope.

Managing Expectations

This categorization helped manage stakeholder expectations. The doctors, who were initially keen on real-time patient tracking, understood that this feature would not be part of the initial release.

Preventing Scope Creep

During the development phase, there were discussions about reintroducing the AI-based diagnostic tool. However, because it was documented as a "Won't Have this Time" requirement, the feature was not added, thus maintaining the project's scope and focus.

Long-Term Planning

These "Won't Have this Time" items were stored for future reference, paving the way for subsequent phases where more ambitious features could be introduced.

Organizational Learning

The documented requirements became an asset for organizational learning. When a new project for an AI-based diagnostic tool was initiated, the team could refer to this list to understand why it was excluded in the first project, providing invaluable context.

This case study illustrates the value of explicitly defining "Won't Have this Time" requirements in a DSDM project, from scope management to long-term planning.

MoSCoW Prioritization Across Different Timeframes in DSDM Projects: A Deeper Dive

The MoSCoW prioritization model's inherent flexibility finds a unique application within the Dynamic Systems Development Method (DSDM). By being implemented at multiple hierarchical levels—project-wide, within Project Increments, and during individual Timeboxes—this method of prioritization enables both a high-level strategic focus and the agility needed for on-the-ground implementation.

The Anatomy of Hierarchical MoSCoW Prioritization

MoSCoW at the Project Level

When applied to the entire project, MoSCoW prioritization helps the team and stakeholders establish a shared understanding of what is critical, desirable, optional, or completely outside the project's scope. This comprehensive outlook lays the foundation for all subsequent planning and development activities. The project-level MoSCoW acts as the blueprint that guides more refined, phase-specific prioritizations.

MoSCoW for Project Increments

Project Increments, often consisting of multiple Timeboxes, are smaller, manageable portions of the larger project. MoSCoW prioritization at this level is fine-tuned to suit the specific objectives, challenges, and deliverables of the individual increment. This secondary level of prioritization may align closely with the overall project priorities but offers the flexibility to deviate where necessary. The need for such adjustments may arise from lessons learned, changing business landscapes, or emergent risks.

MoSCoW for Individual Timeboxes

The Timebox level represents the most granular application of MoSCoW prioritization. Before starting a Timebox, the Solution Development Team reviews and categorizes each requirement as "Must Have," "Should Have," "Could Have," or "Won't Have," based on what they intend to achieve during this fixed period. This acute focus ensures that each Timebox contributes optimally to the project and aligns with both the Project Increment and broader project objectives.

The Strategic Implications of Timeframe-Specific Prioritization

Agility and Flexibility

By applying MoSCoW prioritization across different timeframes, the DSDM approach inherently builds in agility. Teams can quickly adapt to new information or changing circumstances without causing a ripple effect that disrupts the entire project. This granular approach makes it easier to incorporate late changes or emergent requirements.

Risk Mitigation

Layered prioritization offers a structured method for contingency planning. If a specific requirement cannot be delivered in one Timebox or Project Increment, its priority can be reassessed in subsequent phases, thereby mitigating risks associated with timeline overruns or scope creep.

Alignment and Focus

Perhaps one of the most compelling advantages of this hierarchical MoSCoW method is how it keeps the team aligned with overarching business goals at each phase of the project. Each level of prioritization serves as a check and balance to ensure that immediate actions are consistent with long-term objectives, ensuring a balanced approach that caters to both immediate and future needs.

Case Study: Implementing Hierarchical MoSCoW Prioritization in a DSDM Project for a Healthcare Solution

Background

A healthcare organization embarks on a DSDM project to develop an integrated patient management system. The project has an aggressive timeline of nine months and aims to achieve multiple objectives, including improving patient wait times, enhancing data security, and enabling real-time inventory tracking.

MoSCoW at the Project Level

At the initiation phase, the stakeholders and project team use MoSCoW to define the overall priorities:

- "Must Have": Compliance with healthcare regulations, secure patient data storage.
- "Should Have": Features for real-time inventory tracking.
- "Could Have": An intuitive UI for admin staff.
- "Won't Have this Time": Integration with external fitness tracking devices.

MoSCoW for Project Increments

The project is divided into three Project Increments, each lasting three months.

Increment 1: Regulatory Compliance and Data Security

Given the criticality of healthcare regulations and data security, the team focuses on these "Must Have" features. The MoSCoW for this increment slightly deviates from the project-level prioritization to include enhanced encryption as a "Should Have," recognizing its importance in ensuring data security.

Increment 2: Inventory Tracking and User Interface

This increment concentrates on "Should Have" and "Could Have" features. Real-time inventory tracking is a must, but now, due to user feedback, enhancing the UI is escalated from a "Could Have" to a "Should Have."

Increment 3: Final Touches and Optimizations

This last increment revisits any "Must Have" or "Should Have" features that require refinement and attempts to include some of the "Could Have" items initially set at the project level.

MoSCoW for Individual Timeboxes

Each Project Increment contains multiple two-week Timeboxes. For instance, the first Timebox of Increment 1 prioritizes setting up the secure database as a "Must Have," with secondary tasks like initiating encryption protocols categorized as "Should Have."

Results and Learnings

This hierarchical approach to MoSCoW prioritization provided the team with the flexibility needed to adapt to changes and new information, such as the need to improve the UI after user feedback. It also allowed for more effective resource allocation and risk mitigation, as the team could quickly pivot and adjust their focus based on the granular Timebox-level priorities, all while staying aligned with the project's overall goals.

This case study illustrates the power of applying MoSCoW prioritization across different timeframes in DSDM projects, highlighting the method's ability to balance agility with strategic alignment.

Chapter Nine

Timeboxing in DSDM: A Strategy for Efficient Project Execution

Timeboxing in DSDM: A Comprehensive Look at Management and Control Mechanisms

Definition and Significance of Timeboxing in DSDM

Timeboxing in Dynamic Systems Development Method (DSDM) serves as both a scheduling and a control mechanism. The concept is built around the idea of a fixed period, generally between two to four weeks, dedicated to achieving well-defined objectives that contribute to the development of a Solution Increment. The significance of Timeboxing lies in its capacity to instill discipline, facilitate accurate performance measurement, and guarantee timely delivery, aligning with both the project's micro and macro objectives.

Core Attributes of Timeboxing

Objective-Driven Approach

Each Timebox aims to meet certain objectives, diverging from a task-oriented approach to focus on producing specific and meaningful deliverables.

Determining the Optimal Timeframe

Although Timeboxes usually last between two to four weeks, the duration can be modified, with the minimum being one day and the maximum stretching to six weeks. This flexibility allows for adaptation to specific project circumstances.

Emphasis on Iterative Development

The iterative nature of Timeboxing in DSDM ensures constant review and improvement, aiming at both product excellence and optimized processes.

Hierarchical Integration

Timeboxing is not limited to the granular level of individual tasks; it also scales to the macro level of the overall project and Project Increments, contributing to a harmonious and coordinated project flow.

Categories of Timeboxes in DSDM

DSDM Structured Timebox

This type adheres to the strict framework and guidelines of DSDM, usually involving pre-determined roles and responsibilities.

Free Format Timebox

More versatile than its structured counterpart, the Free Format Timebox adapts to different Agile frameworks and responds to specific project needs, particularly when key personnel are unavailable.

Key Phases in a Timebox Lifecycle

Timebox Kick-Off

This preliminary stage lays the groundwork for the Timebox, setting the objectives, outlining roles, and detailing requirements.

Timebox Close-Out

The conclusion of a Timebox involves an evaluation stage, where the outcomes are reviewed against the initial objectives, and the developed deliverables are formally accepted or revised.

The Control Mechanism of Timeboxing

Timeboxing operates at the grassroots level, offering a detailed view of the project's progression. Successful management of individual Timeboxes indirectly ensures the on-time delivery of larger Project Increments and, ultimately, the entire project. It serves as an effective control mechanism that aligns lower-level activities with higher-level objectives.

Case Study: Implementing Timeboxing in a Large Scale DSDM Project

Project Overview

A multinational corporation decided to migrate its legacy software system to a new platform. The project was monumental, involving multiple teams across different geographical locations and a timeline stretching over two years. To manage this complex undertaking, the organization adopted DSDM and incorporated Timeboxing as a key management and control mechanism.

Application of Timeboxing Strategies

Hierarchical Utilization

Timeboxing was applied not just at the level of individual developers or teams but also for entire Project Increments. The overall project was divided into six major Increments, each assigned multiple Timeboxes based on its specific objectives.

Objective-Driven Development

Each Timebox was designed to fulfill particular objectives contributing to its corresponding Project Increment. For instance, Timeboxes in the first Project Increment mainly focused on architectural setup and basic functionality, while subsequent ones targeted feature enhancement and system optimization.

Iterative Review

Given the project's complexity and extended timeline, iterative review sessions were embedded within each Timebox. This ensured constant alignment with project objectives and allowed immediate course correction when necessary.

Flexible Duration

While the general guideline was to keep Timeboxes within a two-to-four-week range, exceptions were made based on the intricacy of the tasks involved. For example, Timeboxes allocated for foundational architectural work were extended to six weeks to allow for comprehensive testing.

Outcomes and Insights

On-Time Project Delivery

By maintaining rigorous Timebox schedules and constant evaluations, the project was successfully completed within the allocated timeframe.

Adaptability

The Timeboxing technique provided the flexibility to adapt to unforeseen challenges without derailing the project. Whenever issues were identified in a Timebox review, they were promptly addressed in subsequent Timeboxes or escalated to higher management for resolution.

Alignment and Coordination

The hierarchical application of Timeboxing ensured that each layer of project management was in sync. This made it easier to coordinate between diverse teams and facilitated a seamless flow of information.

Conclusion

This case study demonstrates the efficacy of Timeboxing in managing large-scale, complex projects. By applying Timeboxing at different hierarchical levels and emphasizing its core attributes, the organization was able to maintain stringent control over the project's progression, resulting in successful and timely delivery.

The Anatomy of a DSDM Structured Timebox

Intricacies of the Three Main Stages

Investigation: Setting the Stage Right

The Investigation stage serves as the conceptual groundwork for the entire Timebox. While it might seem tempting to skim over this stage to jump directly into the development work, it is critical to ensure that all team members have a shared understanding of what needs to be accomplished. It is at this point that any discrepancies in interpretation of requirements or deliverables should be addressed. Here, aligning expectations with acceptance criteria and measures of success becomes pivotal for the subsequent stages.

Refinement: The Core of the Timebox

The Refinement stage is where the majority of the work happens. Because this stage accounts for a significant portion of the Timebox, effective time management and resource allocation are essential. Given that both technical and business testing occur at this stage, it serves as a vital checkpoint for the project's adherence to technical specifications and business objectives. The review at the end of this stage is not merely a formality but an opportunity to pause and evaluate the Timebox's trajectory.

Consolidation: Tying Up Loose Ends

Although the Consolidation stage may occupy a similar timescale to Investigation, its focus is radically different. This stage is about ensuring that the Timebox deliverables meet the stipulated acceptance criteria. Any lingering issues or tasks are resolved here, making it an essential phase for quality assurance. As with other stages, the review at the end serves as a governance touch-point that has implications for the Close-Out process as well as future Timeboxes.

Significance of Bookend Activities

Kick-Off: More Than a Formality

The Kick-Off is a concise but critical activity that ensures everyone starts on the same page. It sets the tone and expectations for the Timebox, making it essential for effective collaboration and project coherence.

Close-Out: A Forward-Looking Retrospective

The Close-Out is not just about acknowledging the work done but also about understanding what could be improved in future Timeboxes. Here, feedback from key stakeholders like the Business Visionary and Technical Coordinator is invaluable. Their formal acceptance signifies not only the completion of the Timebox but also sets a precedent for the quality and scope of future Timeboxes.

Final Thoughts

A DSDM Structured Timebox is a finely tuned mechanism with clearly defined stages and bookend activities. Each component serves a distinct but interconnected purpose, contributing to the Timebox's overall efficacy. Mastery of this structure offers teams greater predictability and control, essential attributes for achieving project success.

Case Study: Implementing a DSDM Structured Timebox in a Financial Software Project

Background

A fintech company was embarking on a project to enhance its flagship financial software suite. The project involved multiple features but was constrained by a tight schedule. The team decided to use DSDM, opting for Structured Timeboxes to manage each increment effectively.

Investigation Stage

During the initial Investigation stage, the team, including Business Analysts, Developers, and Testers, came together to clarify the objectives. They were aligned with key stakeholders, such as the Business Visionary and Technical Coordinator, to confirm the critical features targeted for the upcoming Timebox.

Governance Touch-Point: Review

A formal review meeting was scheduled with the Steering Committee, where the team presented the confirmed requirements, acceptance criteria, and measures of success. The Steering Committee approved, thereby providing the green light for the team to proceed.

Refinement Stage

Over the course of the Refinement stage, the team dedicated most of their time to developing features that aligned with the requirements confirmed during the Investigation stage. Parallelly, rigorous technical and business testing was conducted to ensure alignment with the acceptance criteria.

Governance Touch-Point: Mid-Refinement Review

A mid-refinement review was conducted to assess the Timebox's trajectory. Though the team was generally on track, they identified a few areas where they could optimize their workflow. These findings were incorporated into the remaining days of the Refinement stage.

Consolidation Stage

During Consolidation, the team addressed minor bugs and performed final tests to ensure that the deliverables met the acceptance criteria. All lingering issues were closed, and a final review confirmed that the objectives were met.

Governance Touch-Point: End-of-Timebox Review

The Business Visionary and Technical Coordinator were present in this final review to accept the deliverables officially. Their feedback was noted for continuous improvement in future Timeboxes.

Bookend Activities

The Kick-Off and Close-Out each lasted approximately two hours. During the Close-Out, a Timebox retrospective was conducted, and the team discussed lessons learned and areas for improvement, setting the stage for the next Timebox.

Conclusion

The Structured Timebox was pivotal in achieving the objectives within the stipulated timeframe. The clearly defined stages, coupled with governance touch-points, ensured that the project remained on track without compromising quality. The methodology offered the team both structure and flexibility, essential for delivering a successful project in a high-stakes, fast-paced environment.

The Free Format Timebox in DSDM

Flexibility as the Core Attribute

In DSDM projects, the Free Format Timebox serves as an alternative to the traditional Structured Timebox, primarily distinguished by its adaptability and flexibility. It caters to environments where a rigid structure might hamper the development process, such as projects that require quick pivots or changes. Unlike its structured counterpart, a Free Format Timebox can more easily adapt to unforeseen challenges and opportunities without the constraints of a fixed framework.

Key Elements Explored

The Significance of the Kick-Off

The Kick-Off phase of a Free Format Timebox is a condensed planning session focused on establishing mutual understanding among team members regarding the objectives and workload for the duration of the Timebox. The underlying intent is to foster collaboration and ensure that the entire team is aligned with what needs to be achieved, thereby setting the stage for a successful implementation.

Iterative Development: Where Flexibility Shines

In a Free Format Timebox, the Iterative Development phase is less structured by design, enabling the team to adapt as they go. While the absence of strict phases might appear chaotic to some, this very flexibility is what makes it ideal for projects with rapidly evolving requirements or those subject to external volatility. Scheduled review points within this phase serve to bring in an element of control, maintaining a balance between freedom and governance.

Close-Out: Concluding with Stakeholder Approval

The Close-Out phase bears the responsibility of bringing the Timebox to an end in a controlled manner. Even in the flexible environment of a Free Format Timebox, formal acceptance of the deliverables by key stakeholders ensures that the project remains aligned with business objectives. It acts as the final checkpoint where the outcomes are measured against the initial goals, followed by a retrospective to draw insights for future endeavors.

The Synergy with Other Agile Methodologies

Given its flexibility, a Free Format Timebox often exhibits similarities with timeboxes in other Agile frameworks like Scrum or Kanban. This makes it easier to integrate into hybrid Agile environments, thereby offering teams the ability to choose the best aspects of multiple methodologies for their specific needs.

Final Thoughts

The Free Format Timebox is an invaluable tool in the Agile practitioner's toolkit, especially for those who operate in dynamic, fast-paced environments. It encapsulates the essence of Agile – the ability to adapt and change as circumstances dictate, all while maintaining a laser-like focus on delivering value to stakeholders.

Case Study: Implementing Free Format Timebox in a Fast-Paced Start-up Environment

Background

Our case study involves a start-up company in the technology sector aiming to rapidly develop a minimum viable product (MVP) for a new application. The project faced frequent changes in requirements due to evolving market conditions and customer feedback. Given these dynamics, the team opted for a Free Format Timebox approach over a traditional DSDM Structured Timebox.

Key Stages and Activities

The Kick-Off: Establishing Agile Alignment

The team held a kick-off session to understand the objectives for the Timebox and to agree on the most critical features for the MVP. The process was streamlined, focusing only on the absolute necessities, given the urgency to bring the product to market.

Iterative Development: Adaptability in Action

Over the next two weeks, the development team worked on the prioritized features. Due to the highly volatile nature of start-up requirements, adjustments were made on the fly. For example, after receiving user feedback on the prototype, the team quickly reprioritized their work to incorporate the suggestions, all without derailing the Timebox.

Review Points: Balance between Flexibility and Control

Scheduled review points were critical in this setting. They provided opportunities to recalibrate the team's focus and ensured that they were on track to meet the Timebox objectives. Reviews also included a rapid assessment of the risks and a validation of the work against the agreed-upon acceptance criteria.

Close-Out: Verification and Retrospective

At the end of the Timebox, the Business Visionary and Technical Coordinator formally accepted the deliverables. This was followed by a retrospective session to evaluate what went well and what needed improvement. The insights gained were immediately incorporated into planning for the next Timebox.

Outcomes and Lessons Learned

The Free Format Timebox approach proved to be invaluable for this start-up. It provided the agility to adapt to rapidly changing conditions, without compromising on governance and control. Stakeholder engagement remained high throughout the process, and the MVP was developed within the expected timeframe, ultimately leading to a successful market launch.

The experience affirmed that Free Format Timeboxes could be highly effective in dynamic environments where rapid adaptability is a crucial success factor.

The Anatomy of the Daily Stand-up in DSDM Timeboxes: A Comprehensive Guide

The Daily Stand-up is an integral practice in DSDM Timeboxes, offering regular opportunities for the Solution Development Team to sync, adjust, and remove roadblocks. This methodological cornerstone aligns with both structured and free format Timeboxes, serving as a tool for daily governance and agile adaptability.

Key Objectives of the Daily Stand-up

Information Sharing: The Lifeline of Team Coordination

In a fast-paced development environment, up-to-date information is crucial. The Daily Stand-up serves as a hub for disseminating key insights about ongoing tasks, new issues, and emerging solutions, ensuring that everyone on the team is aligned.

Re-Planning and Reorganizing: The Essence of Agility

The Daily Stand-up is not just a status update meeting but a decision-making juncture. It serves as an immediate point for re-planning and reorganizing tasks as new challenges come up, ensuring that agility is baked into the daily workflow.

Transparency: Bridging the Gap Between Team and Stakeholders

Transparency is an essential factor in any agile framework, and DSDM is no exception. Daily Stand-ups allow stakeholders such as Business Ambassadors, Business Advisors, and Technical Advisors to gauge the health and progress of the Timebox. This prevents "information silos" and ensures that everyone involved has a clear view of the project's state.

Key Participants: The Contributors to the Stand-up Dialogue

While the core team is invariably present, Daily Stand-ups also offer a unique avenue for Business Ambassadors and Advisors to be directly involved. Their active participation can provide invaluable business perspectives, helping to balance technical considerations against organizational needs.

The Standardized Structure: Enabling Focus and Efficiency

Three-Point Check-In

The meeting is tightly structured around three primary questions, keeping the focus sharp and enabling a rapid exchange of the most crucial information. This "three-point check-in" is a cornerstone that ensures the Stand-up's efficiency and effectiveness.

Synchronization

These three points provide an effective synchronization mechanism, aligning the team's efforts toward the Timebox objectives and enabling the identification of any roadblocks that may need immediate attention.

Duration and Location: Design for Speed and Consistency

Time Conservation

The Daily Stand-up is engineered to be brief, lasting no longer than 15 minutes. The speed is not a mere formality but a practical feature to preserve the team's time for actual development work.

Spatial and Temporal Consistency

Holding the Stand-up at a consistent location and time offers a stable routine, aiding the team's cognitive load management. When conducted near the Team Board, it reinforces the visual elements of project tracking, thus grounding the meeting in the tangible progress and challenges at hand.

Case Study: Implementing Daily Stand-up in a DSDM Project for Optimal Governance

Overview

In a recent DSDM project, the Solution Development Team was struggling with miscommunication, leading to delays and missed objectives in several Timeboxes. Recognizing the need for more effective synchronization and governance, the Project Manager decided to implement a structured Daily Stand-up regimen.

Objectives Set for the Daily Stand-up

Improve Information Flow

The first objective was to streamline communication between team members to avoid any bottlenecks or misunderstandings that could derail progress.

Enable Quick Decision Making

With developers, testers, and Business Ambassadors in the same room, decisions could be made on the spot, avoiding lengthy email chains and meetings.

Increase Stakeholder Engagement

By involving Business Ambassadors and Business Advisors, the aim was to keep them informed and engaged, enabling better alignment with business objectives.

Participants and Structure

The Stand-up included all the core team members and rotating Business Ambassadors. A 'three-point check-in' method was rigorously followed to maintain focus.

Impact

Enhanced Team Coordination

The team found that the consistent sharing of updates and blockers in the Stand-up led to more effective work planning, mitigating delays.

Agile Adaptability

Emerging issues were addressed promptly, and course corrections were made in real-time, thereby maintaining the agile nature of the project.

Elevated Stakeholder Satisfaction

With the business side now more involved and informed, stakeholder satisfaction rates improved, leading to a more harmonious project environment.

Lessons Learned

Consistency is Key

Having a regular, structured Stand-up was crucial for its success.

Multi-Dimensional Benefits

The Stand-up proved beneficial not just for the Solution Development Team but also for the stakeholders, improving the overall project governance and success rate.

Through the disciplined yet flexible approach to Daily Stand-ups, the project managed to resolve communication issues, better align with business objectives, and significantly improve on-time delivery rates.

Chapter Ten

Exploring Other Practices: Beyond MoSCoW and Timeboxing

The Facilitated Workshop as a Catalyst in Project Management: Delving Deeper

Facilitated Workshops are not just ordinary meetings; they are highly focused interactive sessions engineered to achieve particular objectives in a project management environment. With the guidance of an impartial facilitator, these workshops aim to streamline decision-making, foster team cohesion, and expedite issue resolution.

Advanced Objectives of Facilitated Workshops

Creative Ideation

Beyond problem-solving and planning, facilitated workshops can serve as incubators for innovative ideas and approaches that can significantly elevate project quality.

Risk Assessment

Facilitated Workshops can act as platforms for identifying, discussing, and mitigating risks, thereby contributing to the project's overall risk management strategy.

Knowledge Transfer

These workshops are also invaluable for onboarding new team members or stakeholders, serving as a knowledge transfer mechanism and thereby reducing the learning curve.

Deepening the Understanding of Key Characteristics

Time-Efficiency

A well-organized workshop, under the stewardship of an expert facilitator, can be remarkably time-efficient, accomplishing objectives in a fraction of the time compared to traditional meetings.

Facilitator's Toolkit

The facilitator is often equipped with a variety of techniques and tools to guide discussion, manage conflicts, and ensure that the meeting stays on course.

Active Participation

A skilled facilitator ensures that all participants are actively engaged, thereby democratizing the decision-making process and improving the quality of the outcomes.

Augmented Benefits

Resource Optimization

By rapidly achieving consensus and clarifying issues, workshops can help optimize the utilization of resources, including time and human capital.

Emotional Intelligence

Facilitated Workshops can serve as platforms for enhancing the team's emotional intelligence by fostering open dialogue and collaborative problem-solving.

Business Alignment

When key stakeholders are involved in the workshops, it ensures that the project is closely aligned with overarching business objectives and strategies.

Advanced Success Factors

Iterative Improvement

The facilitated workshop process should itself be subject to review and refinement, based on feedback and measurable outcomes from previous sessions.

Stakeholder Management

Successful workshops can act as a tool for stakeholder management, keeping everyone informed and aligned, thereby mitigating potential conflicts down the road.

Contingency Planning

The ability to adapt the workshop's agenda and focus in real-time, based on emerging issues or discoveries, is a critical success factor.

By examining Facilitated Workshops through a more detailed lens, their role as powerful instruments in modern project management becomes increasingly apparent. They offer a multifaceted approach to resolving project challenges, thereby contributing to project success.

Case Study: Implementing Facilitated Workshops in a Software Development Project

Context and Challenges

In a mid-sized software development company, the project management team faced persistent challenges in requirements gathering and scope definition. Despite using Agile methodologies, there was a recurring issue of scope creep and ambiguous requirements, leading to delays and budget overruns.

Decision to Use Facilitated Workshops

Recognizing these issues, the project management decided to incorporate facilitated workshops into their process. The objectives were clear: better define project requirements, involve key stakeholders in decision-making, and expedite the planning phase.

Workshop Execution

Selection of Facilitator

A neutral third-party facilitator with experience in software development projects was chosen.

Participants

The workshop included developers, business analysts, project managers, and client representatives.

Methodology

The facilitator used a blend of brainstorming sessions, SWOT analyses, and user story mapping to guide the discussions.

Outcomes and Benefits

Clarity and Alignment

The workshops led to a much clearer understanding of the project requirements among all stakeholders, effectively aligning everyone's expectations.

Time Savings

By resolving ambiguities and potential conflicts in the initial stages, the team was able to significantly reduce the time spent on revisions and rework later in the project.

Stakeholder Satisfaction

The client, being actively involved in the workshops, expressed a high level of satisfaction with the process and the eventual outcomes.

Lessons Learned

Importance of Skilled Facilitation

The role of the facilitator in steering the group towards productive outcomes was deemed invaluable.

Value of Preparation

The success of the workshops highlighted the need for pre-workshop preparation, including pre-reads and surveys to make the actual sessions more productive.

Integration with Agile Cycles

The team learned to integrate the insights and decisions from the workshops into their regular Agile cycles, thereby making the entire process more cohesive.

In summary, the introduction of facilitated workshops dramatically improved the project management landscape for the software development company. It became a best practice for them, setting a precedent for future projects.

Unlocking the Potential: The Critical Role of Modelling in Project Management

Modelling is an indispensable technique in project management, particularly in the field of Information Technology (IT). It serves as a visual representation of complex processes, systems, or concepts, thereby facilitating better understanding and communication among stakeholders.

The Importance of Modelling in Project Management

Communication Enhancement

Models act as universal languages that transcend technical jargon. They ensure that both technical and non-technical stakeholders can have a unified understanding of the project's goals and scope.

Prompting Questions

Models can provoke critical thinking by highlighting gaps, inconsistencies, or areas that require further clarification. They can serve as a springboard for discussions and problem-solving sessions.

Verification & Validation

Models provide a framework for stakeholders to verify if a particular solution aligns with the project's goals and requirements. This process helps to validate the project's feasibility before entering the development phase.

Efficiency

By converting complex descriptions into digestible visuals, models can considerably expedite the decision-making process.

Abstraction & Focus

Models allow for the abstraction of certain details so that stakeholders can focus on specific elements that are most relevant to their roles or to the problem at hand.

Perspectives in Modelling

The 'WHAT' Perspective

This perspective is concerned with the data and informational aspects of the solution. It delves into data types, their relationships, and the business rules that govern them.

The 'HOW' Perspective

This focuses on the functional and operational aspects of the solution, describing how various components interact or achieve particular outcomes.

The 'WHERE' Perspective

Here, the geographical or virtual spaces that are relevant to the solution are outlined. This could include the layout of physical equipment or the configuration of virtual servers.

The 'WHO' Perspective

This angle looks at the human factors involved in the project. It identifies key roles and responsibilities and illustrates how various stakeholders interact within the project environment.

The 'WHEN' Perspective

This deals with the temporal aspects of the solution, identifying crucial events, schedules, and triggers that impact its operation.

The 'WHY' Perspective

This perspective focuses on aligning the project with the larger business strategy and objectives, exploring the rationale behind its existence.

Navigating the Real World: Case Studies on the Application of Modelling in Project Management

Introduction

In the field of project management, the application of modelling techniques is not merely theoretical but has real-world implications. Multiple case studies have demonstrated how modelling can be instrumental in solving complex problems, facilitating stakeholder communication, and ensuring project success.

Case Study 1: Enhancing Stakeholder Communication in a Software Development Project

In this project, UML (Unified Modeling Language) diagrams were used to facilitate stakeholder understanding. The utilization of Use Case, Sequence, and Class diagrams made it easier for both technical and non-technical stakeholders to grasp the project's scope and objectives.

Case Study 2: Risk Management in Infrastructure Projects

Here, Risk Assessment Models were employed to identify and mitigate risks. These models used various criteria like probability, impact, and exposure to prioritize risks and formulate appropriate risk mitigation strategies.

Case Study 3: Workflow Optimization in Manufacturing

Process modelling techniques were used to map out existing workflows in a manufacturing setting. This provided insights into bottlenecks and inefficiencies, leading to targeted improvements that resulted in a 20% increase in production efficiency.

Case Study 4: Strategic Alignment in a Business Transformation Project

Business Model Canvas and SWOT Analysis models were employed to align the project with organizational strategy. This facilitated the buy-in from executive stakeholders and ensured that the project was in sync with broader business objectives.

Case Study 5: Agile Development in Financial Services

In a project aimed at developing a new financial product, User Story Mapping was used to align the development process with customer needs. This model helped in prioritizing features based on user value, thereby ensuring customer satisfaction.

Conclusion

These case studies illustrate the versatility and effectiveness of modelling techniques in addressing various challenges in project management. Whether it's improving communication, mitigating risks, optimizing workflows, or aligning with business strategy, modelling proves to be an invaluable tool.

Exploring Iterative Development in DSDM: A Detailed Perspective

Iterative Development serves as the backbone of the Dynamic Systems Development Method (DSDM) framework, enabling the project to evolve in sync with business requirements. By applying a sequence of short cycles, the approach assures adaptability, promotes stakeholder engagement, and keeps the focus on meeting project goals.

Key Components of Iterative Development

Cycles of Development

Short, focused cycles constitute the essence of Iterative Development. Each cycle aims at a specific feature or functionality, providing a granularity that enables swift adaptation to changes.

Collaboration

A defining characteristic of this approach is the ongoing collaboration among stakeholders. The Solution Development Team plays a pivotal role, ensuring that the iterative cycles lead to a solution that aligns with business objectives.

Three-Step Process

Every iterative cycle is defined by a three-step sequence:

Thought: Initial planning and envisioning of the work that needs to be accomplished.

Action: Execution of the planned tasks.

Conversation: A review session to examine the work performed and its alignment with project goals.

Planning Iterative Development

Strategic planning is crucial in the initial stages. The planning process should break down the overall project into smaller, manageable segments, typically contained within timeboxes. This aids in effective allocation of resources and time.

Controlling Iterative Development

Iterative Development is designed to facilitate incremental improvements. The approach acknowledges that some cycles may not result in the desired output. A contingency mechanism is in place, allowing the project to revert to a previously approved version and adjust based on new learnings and feedback.

Quality Assurance in Iterative Development

Verification

Continual verification activities ensure that the solution maintains the quality benchmarks set early in the project. This process may include a mix of reviews and tests.

Reviews

Review activities can vary in formality, from casual peer evaluations to structured assessments involving experts in the domain.

Testing

Testing in DSDM is generally divided into three categories:

Positive Tests: To verify the solution's intended functionalities.

Negative Tests: To confirm that the system restricts unwanted actions or features.

Unhappy Path Tests: To scrutinize how the system responds to unexpected or undefined scenarios.

Roles in Quality Assurance

Different roles contribute to the quality assurance process:

Technical Coordinator: Ensures the technical soundness of the solution.

Solution Tester: Primarily responsible for testing, except for business acceptance and unit testing, which are the prerogatives of the Business

Ambassador(s) and Business Advisors, and the Solution Developer, respectively.

Case Study: Implementing Iterative Development in a DSDM Project

Background

In a large financial institution, the IT department initiated a project to revamp its customer service portal. The project adopted the DSDM framework, with a particular focus on Iterative Development. The aim was to improve user experience while integrating new functionalities, such as AI-driven customer support and advanced security measures.

Planning Phase

During the foundational stages, the project team created a strategy that segmented the entire portal overhaul into distinct features. These features were then allocated to specific timeboxes. A project board consisting of a Business Visionary, Technical Coordinator, and other key roles was set up to oversee this process.

Iterative Development in Action

Cycle 1: User Interface

The first cycle focused on improving the user interface. Design mock-ups were created, coded, and reviewed within the team and with stakeholders.

Cycle 2: Security Measures

The second cycle concentrated on integrating new security features, like two-factor authentication. Iterative cycles allowed the team to test different methods, gather feedback, and fine-tune the features.

Cycle 3: AI-Driven Customer Support

The third cycle aimed at implementing an AI-driven customer support chatbot. The team developed a basic version first, then refined it in subsequent cycles based on user feedback.

Quality Assurance

Reviews

Several internal and external reviews were conducted. While internal reviews involved the Solution Development Team, external reviews brought in customer experience experts.

Testing

The project adopted a rigorous testing regimen, covering all three principal categories of tests: Positive, Negative, and Unhappy Path Tests. These tests ensured that the portal not only fulfilled its intended functions but also handled exceptions gracefully.

Roles and Responsibilities

Technical Coordinator: Oversaw the technical aspects, ensuring that the new features integrated well with the existing systems.

Solution Tester: Conducted the bulk of the testing activities, complemented by business acceptance testing by the Business Ambassador.

Outcome

By adhering to the Iterative Development methodology as outlined in DSDM, the project successfully revamped the customer service portal within the stipulated time and budget. The iterative cycles enabled quick adaptations to feedback, ensuring a product that was both high in quality and aligned with user needs.

Chapter Eleven

The Symbiosis of Principles and the Project Manager

Challenges and Solutions in Implementing Principle 1: Focus on the Business Need

Incorporating the first principle of DSDM, "Focus on the Business Need," into project management isn't without its challenges. This principle forms the backbone of the DSDM framework, emphasizing that every aspect of the project must be in harmony with overarching business goals. While the Project Manager is instrumental in operationalizing this principle, navigating its application can be fraught with complexities.

The Complexity of Aligning with Business Objectives

Vague or Evolving Business Needs: It's not uncommon for business objectives to be ill-defined or subject to change as the project progresses.

Divergent Stakeholder Interests: Different stakeholders may have conflicting priorities, complicating MoSCoW prioritization.

Resource Constraints: Achieving all "Must Have" requirements may be unrealistic due to budget or time constraints.

Navigating Complexity

Leverage the Foundations Phase: This is the opportune time to clarify the business objectives and align them with the project scope.

Stakeholder Consensus: Facilitate workshops or decision-making forums to bring alignment among stakeholders.

Adaptive Planning: Make room for flexibility in resources and timelines to cater to evolving business needs.

MoSCoW Prioritization: A Double-Edged Sword

Overemphasis on "Must Haves": While focusing on essentials, some "Should Have" or "Could Have" requirements that offer significant business value may be overlooked.

Inadequate Re-prioritization: Failure to reevaluate priorities can lead to obsolescence.

Ensuring Effective Prioritization

Dynamic Re-prioritization: Consistently revisit the MoSCoW list to accommodate changes in business needs or stakeholder input.

Balanced Focus: While "Must Haves" are non-negotiable, don't ignore requirements that provide additional business value.

Business Case: More Than a One-Time Exercise

Static Business Cases: Often, the business case is developed at the project's onset and then neglected.

Misalignment with Reality: A business case that isn't revisited can become misaligned with actual project execution.

Keeping the Business Case Relevant

Periodic Reviews: Schedule regular reviews of the business case in alignment with project milestones.

Update Mechanisms: Implement a formal process for updating the business case to reflect new learnings or changes in business strategy.

Ensuring Stakeholder Alignment

Communication Gaps: Insufficient communication can lead to misunderstandings and project derailment.

Resistance to Change: Stakeholders may be resistant to changes, even when aligned with business needs.

Bridging the Gap

Transparent Communication: Establish clear communication channels for ongoing stakeholder engagement.

Change Management Strategies: Employ strategies to manage resistance and facilitate stakeholder buy-in.

Case Study: Implementing the Principle of "Focus on the Business Need" in a Tech Start-up

Context

A tech start-up specializing in AI-driven analytics tools initiated a project to develop a new product aimed at small businesses. The Project Manager adopted the DSDM framework and emphasized the principle of "Focus on the Business Need." Despite a promising start, the project faced multiple challenges in adhering to this principle.

Challenge 1: Vague Business Objectives

Situation

The business objectives were vaguely defined at the beginning of the project, mainly due to the start-up nature of the company.

Solution

A Foundations Phase workshop was organized with key stakeholders to refine and clarify business objectives. These were then mapped to specific project deliverables.

Challenge 2: Divergent Stakeholder Interests

Situation

The engineering team was focused on cutting-edge features, while the sales team was concerned about quick market entry.

Solution

A stakeholder meeting was convened, and MoSCoW prioritization was collaboratively conducted. This helped align both teams toward a balanced set of deliverables that catered to urgent market needs while keeping room for innovation.

Challenge 3: Dynamic Business Case

Situation

The initial business case, although robust, did not factor in potential shifts in the market landscape.

Solution

Quarterly business case review meetings were instituted. These included not just the Project Manager but also market analysts who could provide updated insights.

Challenge 4: Communication Gaps with Stakeholders

Situation

There was a lack of effective communication channels between the development team and external stakeholders, such as investors and advisors.

Solution

A monthly stakeholder newsletter was initiated, coupled with quarterly face-to-face meetings to share project updates and gather feedback.

Lessons Learned

Stakeholder Involvement: Early and continuous stakeholder engagement is vital for maintaining a focus on business needs.

Dynamic Planning: The ability to adapt to changing business needs is essential for upholding the principle of "Focus on the Business Need."

Transparent Communication: Effective communication mechanisms can serve as the linchpin for aligning project activities with business objectives.

This case study illustrates the complexities of implementing the principle of "Focus on the Business Need" and offers actionable solutions for overcoming these challenges.

Expanding on Principle 2: "Deliver on Time" in DSDM Project Management

The "Deliver on Time" principle is a fundamental tenet in Dynamic Systems Development Method (DSDM) projects, underlining the critical role of meeting deadlines in achieving project success. This principle is not just a guideline but a strict rule that shapes planning, execution, and tracking activities across the project lifecycle.

Key Responsibilities of the Project Manager in Enforcing This Principle

Strategic Planning and Timeboxing

The Project Manager is tasked with devising a comprehensive project delivery plan during the Foundations phase. This involves creating a realistic schedule divided into manageable timeboxes. Each timebox is aligned with the project's overall objectives and designed to produce a functional solution increment.

Stakeholder Alignment

It is essential that all stakeholders, including team members and business sponsors, agree with the timeboxed plans. At every Timebox Kick-Off, the Project Manager takes on the role of an orchestrator, ensuring that all involved parties are on the same page regarding deliverables, deadlines, and priorities.

Upholding Business Priorities

The "Deliver on Time" principle is intrinsically tied to business needs. While the Project Manager does not dictate business priorities, they ensure that the timeboxes are focused on fulfilling them. This entails a rigorous approach to applying MoSCoW rules for prioritization at the outset of each timebox.

Deadline Enforcement

Consistency in meeting deadlines is not a point for negotiation; it is a requirement. Adhering to the pre-defined schedule is a critical element in maintaining control over the project and providing a clear measure of progress.

Confidence Building Through Predictable Delivery

Timely delivery serves a dual purpose. Apart from aligning with business objectives, it also builds stakeholder confidence. When stakeholders observe a track record of consistent, on-time delivery, it bolsters their faith in the project's successful completion. The Project Manager, therefore, also serves as a steward of stakeholder confidence.

Sustainable Work Pacing

While meeting deadlines is crucial, it should not come at the expense of quality or team well-being. The Project Manager must set a sustainable work pace to prevent burnout and ensure that the team can maintain productivity levels over the long term.

Conclusion

The "Deliver on Time" principle is a cornerstone in the DSDM framework, imposing a disciplined approach to project timelines. It forces a balance between speed and quality, ensuring that the project remains aligned with business objectives while fostering stakeholder confidence through predictability.

Case Study: Implementing the "Deliver on Time" Principle in a Software Development Project

Scenario Overview

In a medium-sized software development company, the Project Manager (PM) is tasked with leading a team to build a customer relationship management (CRM) system for a client. The project is scoped to last six months, and its successful, on-time delivery is crucial for both the client's business objectives and the reputation of the software company.

Strategic Timeboxing

The PM employs DSDM principles and begins by segmenting the project into two-week timeboxes. These timeboxes are strategically aligned with the delivery of critical CRM features, such as user management, data analytics, and customer interaction tracking.

Stakeholder Alignment

Before the onset of each timebox, the PM conducts a Timebox Kick-Off meeting. These meetings serve to reaffirm the objectives of the upcoming timebox, discuss the MoSCoW prioritization of features, and align all stakeholders on what must be achieved. The PM ensures that both the development team and the client's representatives agree on the deliverables and deadlines.

Enforced Deadlines and Business Priorities

The PM diligently tracks the progress of each timebox, ensuring that the development team is adhering to the pre-established timelines. If any delays are anticipated, the PM consults the MoSCoW prioritization list to make informed decisions about which features can be delayed without compromising the business objectives.

Building Stakeholder Confidence

By consistently delivering functional solution increments at the end of each timebox, the PM cultivates a sense of reliability and predictability. This not only strengthens the client's trust but also boosts the morale of the development team.

Sustainable Pace

While the emphasis is on delivering on time, the PM is cautious not to push the team to the brink of burnout. They manage resources wisely, occasionally reallocating tasks among team members to ensure that everyone is working at a sustainable pace.

Lessons Learned

The adherence to the "Deliver on Time" principle enabled the PM to successfully complete the project within the stipulated six months, meeting all critical business objectives. The approach fostered a culture of accountability and efficiency, paving the way for future projects to be managed with similar rigor and discipline.

The principle's successful implementation not only resulted in a satisfied client but also elevated the software company's reputation for being reliable and effective. It reinforced the importance of disciplined time management and strategic planning in achieving project success.

Principle 3 - Collaborate: Deep Dive into Implementation and Management

The principle of "Collaboration" in DSDM encapsulates more than mere teamwork; it's about fostering a unified environment where team members are actively committed to each other's success and, by extension, the success of the project. When correctly implemented, this principle removes barriers between team roles and levels of authority, encouraging active dialogue, co-creation, and shared responsibility.

In-Depth Responsibilities of the Project Manager

Stakeholder Involvement Across Phases

The Project Manager (PM) must cultivate an ongoing dialogue between all stakeholders, from the Business Sponsor and Business Visionary to individual team members. This includes scheduling regular touchpoints that allow for direct feedback and enable adjustments to strategy and scope.

Business Engagement: More than Just Presence

Active business involvement doesn't mean business stakeholders are merely "present"; they should be directly contributing to problem-solving, decision-making, and ideation. The PM's role involves setting the stage for this level of involvement, which may include training sessions on effective collaboration or tools that facilitate joint decision-making.

Power Dynamics: Empowerment with Accountability

Empowering team members isn't a laissez-faire strategy; it's about providing the appropriate autonomy that each role requires to deliver effectively. This involves a balance between freedom and responsibility. The PM must outline what levels of decision-making authority each team member holds and ensure that these levels are respected across the team.

Building an Inclusive Team Culture

Cohesion Through Shared Objectives

A unified team is not built overnight. It takes deliberate effort to align team members around shared objectives and mutual benefits. This often involves facilitating team-building activities that focus on the project's goals and showing how each role contributes to these goals.

Addressing Disruptive Behavior

Team harmony is fragile and can be easily disrupted. The PM, therefore, holds the responsibility for managing interpersonal dynamics and addressing any behavioral issues swiftly and decisively.

Conclusion

The PM's role in fostering collaboration within a DSDM project is multifaceted and extends from high-level stakeholder engagement to the micro-interactions between team members. Effective collaboration does not happen by chance; it requires thoughtful planning, proactive management, and a culture that prioritizes collective success over individual achievements.

Case Study: Navigating the "Collaborate" Principle in a Digital Transformation Project

Introduction

In this illustrative case study, we explore the application of the "Collaborate" principle within a digital transformation project. The project's aim was to modernize the e-commerce platform of a mid-sized retail company. The Project Manager (PM) was tasked with aligning a diverse team, consisting of internal developers, external contractors, business analysts, and high-ranking stakeholders.

Building a Collaborative Culture: The Project Manager's Tactics

Scheduling Routine Stakeholder Updates

The PM initiated bi-weekly "State of the Project" meetings, which incorporated all stakeholders. These platforms offered a venue for open communication, facilitating discussions around current status, evolving priorities, and emerging concerns.

Fostering Active Involvement from the Business Side

To involve business stakeholders actively, the PM organized workshops where both business representatives and developers came together. Here they jointly mapped out user journeys for the forthcoming e-commerce platform. This approach assured that both business and technical teams shared a unified vision of the final product.

Striking a Balance between Empowerment and Responsibility

The PM formulated a "Decision Matrix," clarifying decision-making authority for various roles within the team. For example, developers were entrusted with code-related decisions, while business-centric choices were routed through the Business Visionary or Business Sponsor.

Cohesion and Team Dynamics

Team-Building Activities

Monthly team-building events like hackathons were introduced by the PM, focusing on project-specific objectives. These activities served dual purposes: they improved team cohesion and provided a creative outlet for solving project-specific issues.

Addressing Disruptive Elements

When a team member emerged as a bottleneck due to poor collaborative skills, the PM acted swiftly. After a private discussion with the individual, the matter was brought before the team. A collective decision was made to reassign the person to a role that better suited their skills and interests.

Conclusion

The Project Manager's deliberate effort to build a culture of active collaboration, shared responsibility, and transparent communication was crucial for the project's success. The digital transformation project stands as a testament to the indispensable role effective collaboration plays in achieving project objectives.

Principle 4 - Never Compromise Quality: A Comprehensive Guide

Overview

The "Never Compromise Quality" principle in the Dynamic Systems Development Method (DSDM) stresses the vital importance of upholding specified quality standards throughout a project's lifecycle. It aims not at excessive perfection but at a 'fit-for-purpose' approach. This principle is integral in ensuring that the project deliverables meet or exceed the Minimum Usable SubseT (MUST), as defined by the business requirements.

Key Responsibilities of the Project Manager

Establishing Quality Standards from the Start

Maintainability: Ensure that the project addresses long-term maintainability from its initial phases.

Development Approach and Acceptance Criteria: During the Foundations Phase, these should be precisely defined, setting the standards that will guide the project's quality expectations.

Sustaining Consistent Quality Levels

Prioritization: As the project progresses Timebox by Timebox, the Project Manager (PM) must ensure that the team first addresses the high-priority requirements to the agreed-upon standard before moving onto less critical items.

Technical Coordinator's Role: The involvement of the Technical Coordinator in Timebox reviews is crucial for maintaining quality.

Continuously Upholding Testing Measures

Integrated Testing Approach: The PM needs to establish a methodology that incorporates testing within the development process itself.

Timebox End Reviews: Products delivered at the end of each Timebox must be rigorously reviewed and tested according to both the established development approach and the specific acceptance criteria set forth.

Design and Documentation

Solution Architecture Definition (SAD): The high-level solution design needs to be adequately documented in the SAD. This documentation serves as a guide for the Solution Development Team but should not restrict Iterative Development.

Case Study: Implementing the Principle of "Never Compromise Quality" in a DSDM Project

Adhering to the principle of "Never Compromise Quality" is crucial for the success of projects managed under the Dynamic Systems Development Method (DSDM) framework. This case study offers a deep dive into the effective implementation and management of this principle, focusing on the role of the Project Manager (PM).

Phase 1: Setting Quality Standards

Early Dialogue with Stakeholders

Right from the project's inception, the PM initiated discussions with the Business Sponsor, Business Visionary, and Technical Coordinator. They collectively set maintainability as a long-term objective and established clear acceptance criteria during the Foundations Phase.

Defining a Development Approach

The team adopted a Test-Driven Development (TDD) approach. The PM made sure to communicate this methodology across the team and to align this approach with the overall project strategy.

Phase 2: Maintaining Consistent Quality

Requirement Prioritization

With multiple requirements in the queue, the PM used the MoSCoW method to prioritize. They ensured that high-priority items were developed to the agreed standard before lower-priority items were addressed.

Role of the Technical Coordinator

The Technical Coordinator played an active part in reviewing deliverables at the end of each Timebox. The PM ensured their involvement was appropriately scheduled and managed.

Phase 3: Continuous Testing

Test-Integrated Development

Following the TDD approach, each Timebox included a specific set of tests that the deliverables had to pass. This was not just limited to functional tests but also included performance and security tests.

End-of-Timebox Review

Every deliverable was thoroughly tested against the initial acceptance criteria. The PM organized these reviews and ensured that they were as rigorous as the initial expectations set forth in the project Foundations Phase.

Phase 4: Documentation

Solution Architecture Definition (SAD)

The PM oversaw the documentation of high-level design elements in the SAD. This served as both a guide and a record for the Solution Development Team, ensuring that the project stayed aligned with its original goals without stifling innovation.

Conclusion

The Project Manager's proactive approach to implementing the "Never Compromise Quality" principle was instrumental in the project's success. By setting clear standards, maintaining those standards, and continuously validating the project against those standards, the PM upheld the principle effectively throughout the project lifecycle.

Principle 5: Build Incrementally from Firm Foundations

Comprehensive Overview

The principle of "Build Incrementally from Firm Foundations" sets DSDM apart from other Agile frameworks by emphasizing the critical nature of foundational work before diving into the iterative development phases. This principle safeguards against common project derailments, such as scope creep, by laying down a strong foundational plan upon which the rest of the project can stably develop. It also encourages incremental releases to deliver palpable business value early on, instilling confidence among stakeholders.

Delving into the Responsibilities of the Project Manager

Ensuring a Solid Foundation

While Agile methods often celebrate the concept of "starting before you're ready," this principle suggests a more cautious approach. The Project Manager (PM) is responsible for establishing a firm foundation for the project by ensuring that sufficient planning and initial design have been conducted. During this stage, the PM works closely with the business analysts, architects, and other key stakeholders to define the project's scope, objectives, and critical success factors. This foundational work provides the blueprint for the project, defining not only what needs to be achieved but also how to measure the project's success.

Preemptive Measures Against Scope Creep

Scope creep is a prevalent problem that can gradually divert resources and focus away from the original project objectives. To prevent this, the PM should ensure that the foundational analysis is sufficiently detailed and agreed upon by all stakeholders. This serves as the reference point for all future project activities, helping to keep the project on track and aligned with the original goals.

Importance of Incremental Building

Once a strong foundation has been laid, the next step is to start building incrementally. Rather than aiming to deliver a complete, end-to-end solution in a single phase, the project should be broken down into manageable increments. Each increment should be planned to deliver specific components or features that align with the high-priority business objectives. By doing this, the project starts to deliver value early in its lifecycle, which in turn helps to secure ongoing stakeholder support.

Regular Reassessment of Priorities and Viability

After the completion of each increment, the PM is responsible for leading a reassessment of the project's priorities. This involves revisiting the business case, reviewing the performance metrics, and consulting with key stakeholders to confirm that the project remains aligned with business goals. This exercise also provides an opportunity for the team to reflect on what has been achieved and to identify areas for improvement in subsequent phases.

Conclusion

The "Build Incrementally from Firm Foundations" principle serves as a guiding light for DSDM projects, advocating for a balanced approach that combines thoughtful planning with Agile flexibility. By following this principle, the Project Manager not only ensures that the project is set on a stable course but also maximizes the opportunities for early and continuous delivery of value.

Case Study: Implementing Principle 5 in a Software Development Project

In a software development project for a financial services firm, the principle of "Build Incrementally from Firm Foundations" was meticulously implemented. The objective was to revamp an existing trading platform, aiming to enhance its capabilities and user experience. The challenge was substantial: the platform was complex, featuring multiple integrations with third-party services, real-time data processing, and strict regulatory compliance requirements.

Foundational Work: The Starting Point

Requirement Gathering and Analysis

The Project Manager (PM) led the initial phase of requirement gathering, involving business analysts, user experience experts, and technical architects. An extensive list of user stories, acceptance criteria, and compliance requirements was created. This initial groundwork acted as the foundation for all subsequent project activities.

Consensus Building

Before moving ahead, the PM organized a series of stakeholder meetings to achieve a consensus on the project scope, timelines, and quality benchmarks. This phase culminated in the creation of a detailed Project Initiation Document (PID), setting the stage for incremental development.

Incremental Building: Step by Step

Initial Increment: MVP

The first increment aimed to deliver a Minimum Viable Product (MVP) featuring core trading functionalities. Despite the scaled-down feature set, quality was not compromised. The PM ensured that all components met the predefined quality standards before deployment.

Following Increments: Additional Features

Subsequent increments added layers of complexity, introducing advanced analytics, multi-device compatibility, and third-party integrations. Each increment was carefully planned to align with business priorities, ensuring that the most critical features were developed first.

Reassessment After Each Increment

Stakeholder Reviews

After each increment was deployed, the PM convened a review meeting with key stakeholders. Metrics such as user adoption rates, system performance, and ROI were evaluated to assess the project's ongoing viability.

Priority Realignment

In one such review, it was found that user adoption was lagging due to usability issues. The PM led a realignment of priorities to bring user experience enhancements to the top of the feature development list.

Conclusion

By building incrementally on firm foundations, the project successfully navigated the complexities of a large-scale software overhaul. Every increment brought tangible improvements, boosting stakeholder confidence and engagement. The PM's role in adhering to this principle was pivotal, providing the framework for a project that was both well-planned and agile, delivering high-quality results aligned with business needs.

Principle 6 - Develop Iteratively: Unpacking the Methodology

Overview

The principle of "Develop Iteratively" stands as a cornerstone in the Dynamic Systems Development Method (DSDM) framework. Its inherent philosophy is rooted in adaptability, agility, and constructive feedback loops. It transcends the traditional development approaches that often resist changes, thereby optimizing the project for both flexibility and effectiveness. For the Project Manager (PM), this principle prescribes a set of specific responsibilities designed to make the project more responsive to business needs and emerging requirements.

Key Responsibilities of the Project Manager

Business Feedback Incorporation

In an iterative development framework, feedback is the lifeblood of progress. The PM's role is to ensure active and regular participation from Business Ambassadors and Advisors during each Timebox. These stakeholders provide invaluable business perspectives that guide development efforts. Adequate mechanisms must be in place for gathering and acting upon this feedback in a structured manner.

Foundations Phase: The Right Balance

The Foundations phase can be likened to a roadmap rather than a detailed blueprint. While it sets the general direction and parameters of the project, it should not morph into an exhaustive design and analysis stage. The PM should focus on drawing the boundaries within which the project will evolve, ensuring that these constraints are well-understood but not so detailed as to stifle creativity or adaptability.

Embracing and Managing Change

Change, rather than being a disruptive force, is a constructive element in an iteratively developed project. The PM must possess a nuanced understanding of how to integrate changes effectively. This involves making informed decisions about what changes to incorporate and how to balance them against existing plans. Changes should align with the overarching business goals and should be carefully considered for their impact on the project's scope, time, and resources.

Embracing Iterative Development: The Bottom Line

In summary, iterative development under the DSDM framework empowers the project to be highly adaptable and responsive to both planned and unforeseen changes. The Project Manager plays a critical role in making this principle actionable, setting the tone for a project culture that values feedback, accommodates change, and strives for ongoing improvement.

Case Study: Implementing the "Develop Iteratively" Principle in a DSDM Project

In the fast-paced world of software development, changes in business requirements are often seen as a given. In one particular project for a financial services company, the role of the Project Manager (PM) was instrumental in successfully embodying the DSDM principle of "Develop Iteratively." The project aimed to overhaul the existing customer management system with features that would make it more user-friendly and provide real-time analytics.

The Challenge: Incorporating Emerging Business Needs

The project started with a well-defined scope, but soon the business stakeholders identified new regulatory requirements and user needs that were initially out of scope. The challenge was to integrate these changes without causing delays or going over budget.

Business Feedback Incorporation: A Structured Approach

The PM set up bi-weekly sessions with Business Ambassadors and Advisors. These feedback loops became the mechanism for understanding the implications of the newly identified needs and regulatory changes. The PM then ensured that the most crucial changes were prioritized and fed into the next iteration's planning.

The Foundations Phase: Agility with Guidance

The initial Foundations phase had set up broad parameters for the project, intentionally avoiding excessive detail that could lock the project into a particular path. This foundational flexibility made it easier to integrate the new requirements, even after development had started.

Embracing and Managing Change: A Delicate Balance

Through a transparent process, the PM made it clear which requested changes could be incorporated in the upcoming iteration and which would be deferred for future consideration. This way, the focus stayed on the most business-critical elements while maintaining the project timeline and budget.

Conclusion: Successful Iterative Development

The project was completed on time and within budget, but what stood out was its ability to adapt to new business requirements without compromising its initial objectives. The key to this success was the Project Manager's adept implementation of the "Develop Iteratively" principle, which facilitated the incorporation of real-time feedback and emerging requirements into the project's workflow.

This case study illustrates the versatility and robustness of the DSDM framework when it comes to managing changes in a project environment. It also showcases the pivotal role of the Project Manager in making the principle of "Develop Iteratively" a functional reality.

Principle 7 - Communicate Continuously and Clearly: A Deeper Exploration

Overview

Effective communication isn't just about sharing information; it's about ensuring that the right information reaches the right people at the right time. In the context of a DSDM project, the principle of "Communicate Continuously and Clearly" serves to mitigate the risks associated with poor communication. This principle urges for a seamless flow of information, fostering greater clarity and enhancing collaboration among the team and external stakeholders.

Key Responsibilities of the Project Manager

Utilize DSDM Tools for Optimal Communication

The Project Manager (PM) should not just encourage, but mandate the use of DSDM-specific practices such as Workshops and Timeboxing. These methodologies are not mere tools but integral aspects of the DSDM framework designed to facilitate effective communication.

Maintaining Project Visibility

A hallmark of effective communication is transparency. The PM should ensure that activities, progress, and outputs are not just documented but made openly accessible to all relevant parties. This level of visibility fosters accountability and enables real-time adjustments.

The Art of Lean Documentation

In an agile environment, the emphasis is often on doing over documenting. However, that doesn't mean documentation is unimportant. The PM should instill a culture where documentation is concise but sufficiently detailed, and most importantly, actually used by the team and stakeholders.

Stakeholder Expectations: A Continuous Dialogue

Keeping stakeholders in the loop isn't a one-time event but an ongoing process. The PM should prioritize maintaining an open line of communication with all stakeholders, inviting them to key DSDM practices like end-of-Timebox reviews to foster direct engagement.

Upholding Honesty and Transparency

Lastly, but certainly not least, the PM should act as a role model in championing honest and transparent communication. Whether it's acknowledging challenges or sharing successes, clear and straightforward communication should be the norm, not the exception.

Conclusion

Effective communication is both an art and a science, and the Project Manager's role is pivotal in ensuring that this principle is not just understood but also applied. The Project Manager should actively enforce communication norms, engage stakeholders, and create a transparent environment where information flows freely but purposefully. These are not just best practices; they are imperatives for the success of any DSDM project.

Case Study: Principle 7 - Communicate Continuously and Clearly in Action

The principle of "Communicate Continuously and Clearly" is more than just a guideline; it's a vital component of the DSDM framework. In this case study, we'll explore how a Project Manager (PM) can operationalize this principle in real-world scenarios.

Real-World Challenges and PM Actions

Scenario 1: Fragmented Communication Channels

The project faced a situation where team members were using multiple platforms to communicate—emails, messaging apps, and project management tools. This led to a breakdown in effective communication.

PM Action

The PM standardized communication channels by adopting a unified project management tool integrated with a dedicated communication platform. This streamlined communication and ensured that everyone was on the same page.

Scenario 2: Lack of Stakeholder Engagement

Stakeholders were only sporadically updated on project progress, leading to misunderstandings and misaligned expectations.

PM Action

The PM instituted a structured communication cadence, including monthly stakeholder briefings and direct invitations to end-of-Timebox reviews. This ensured consistent and meaningful stakeholder engagement.

Scenario 3: Overwhelming Documentation

The team was bogged down with excessive documentation, much of which was redundant or irrelevant.

PM Action

The PM led an initiative to review all existing documents and streamline them into a "Lean Documentation" model. Any document that didn't add value was either revised or eliminated.

Lessons Learned

Prioritize Unified Communication Platforms

Having a single, integrated tool for project management and communication can significantly improve information flow and team collaboration.

Engage Stakeholders Proactively

Stakeholder engagement is not a passive activity. The PM should take the lead in ensuring regular and meaningful interactions.

Embrace Lean Documentation

Not all documentation is equally useful. Adopt a lean approach to documentation to focus on value-added activities.

Conclusion

The case study demonstrates that the principle of "Communicate Continuously and Clearly" is not merely theoretical but has practical implications that can make or break a project. The Project Manager plays a critical role in ensuring that this principle is ingrained into the fabric of the project's communication strategy, fostering not just clarity but also contributing to project success.

Principle 8 - Demonstrate Control: A Detailed Exploration

Overview

The principle of "Demonstrate Control" is a cornerstone in the DSDM framework, emphasizing the imperative for transparent and effective project control mechanisms. This principle goes beyond mere management to ensure that control is not just exerted but is also evident to all stakeholders.

Key Responsibilities of the Project Manager

Maintain Transparent Plans and Progress

The Project Manager is entrusted with the vital responsibility of keeping the Delivery Plan current and transparent. This entails maintaining an accessible Timebox Plan that is updated regularly, providing a clear and shared understanding of project progress.

Focus on Product-Based Measurement of Progress

Traditional measurements based on completed activities can be misleading. The Project Manager must steer the team toward a more authentic gauge of progress, emphasizing the delivery of Solution Increments that offer tangible value. This approach aligns well with the project's strategic objectives and ensures a focus on delivering real-world impact.

Strike a Balance in Formality for Tracking and Reporting

Engaging with stakeholders, particularly during end-of-Timebox demonstrations, provides invaluable feedback and keeps everyone informed. However, the Project Manager must ensure that the level of formality in tracking and reporting matches the project's complexity and stakeholder requirements, thereby allowing for a nuanced assessment of project health and viability.

Conclusion

"Demonstrate Control" is not just a theoretical tenet but a practical necessity in the DSDM framework. The Project Manager plays a critical role in operationalizing this principle, instituting transparent planning, focusing on product-based progress metrics, and maintaining an appropriate level of formal reporting. These activities ensure that the project not only remains on track but also visibly so, building stakeholder confidence and contributing to the project's ultimate success.

Case Study: Implementing the Principle of "Demonstrate Control" in a DSDM Project

In any DSDM project, the principle of "Demonstrate Control" is vital for success. For this case study, let's consider a software development project aimed at creating a new customer relationship management (CRM) system for a medium-sized enterprise.

Context and Challenge

The project faced the usual challenges, such as scope changes, resource limitations, and tight timelines. However, the Project Manager realized that stakeholders were increasingly concerned about whether the project was under control, given the many moving parts and inherent uncertainties of software development.

Implementation of "Demonstrate Control"

Transparent Plans and Progress

The Project Manager decided to maintain an open-access digital Team Board that was updated in real-time. This board became the go-to resource for stakeholders to understand the current status of the project.

Product-Based Measurement of Progress

Instead of just listing completed tasks, the digital board also provided visibility into completed Solution Increments. A value score was associated with each Increment to help stakeholders understand the significance of what had been delivered so far.

Balancing Formality in Tracking and Reporting

While informal communication channels were kept open, the Project Manager also instituted a bi-weekly reporting mechanism, which provided an in-depth but concise status update to all stakeholders. This report included key performance indicators, risks, and progress towards the next milestone, offering a rounded view of the project's health.

Results

Stakeholder confidence improved markedly with the visible demonstration of control. Transparency in planning and a focus on value-driven metrics provided a real-world assessment of progress. The bi-weekly reports created a formal cadence that stakeholders could rely on for deeper insights.

Conclusion

In essence, the Project Manager was able to operationalize the principle of "Demonstrate Control" effectively, creating an atmosphere of trust and openness. The visible and transparent controls helped to mitigate risks and navigate challenges, leading to the successful delivery of the CRM system.

By adhering to the principle of "Demonstrate Control," the Project Manager was able to align the team and stakeholders around a common, transparent, and accountable mode of operation, thereby contributing significantly to the project's success.

Agile Project Manager Tips: Navigating DSDM Principles Effectively

Navigating DSDM principles is not merely a matter of acknowledgement; it's about integrating these principles into the very fabric of project execution. As an Agile Project Manager, you have a pivotal role in ensuring that these principles are not just understood but actively applied. Below are some tips to make this a reality.

Tips for Effective DSDM Principle Integration

1. Visibility of Principles

Tip

Make the DSDM principles visibly accessible to everyone involved in the project.

Why it Matters

Visible principles serve as a constant reminder and guide, enabling team alignment and cohesive action towards shared objectives.

2. Encourage Open Discussion

Tip

Actively encourage team members to flag any instances where they think a principle is being compromised.

Why it Matters

Creating an open dialogue fosters shared accountability and promotes early identification and resolution of risks.

3. Risk Management

Tip

Recognize that deviating from one or more principles poses a risk to the project and must be managed accordingly.

Why it Matters

Disregarding principles can lead to inefficiencies, subpar outcomes, or, in the worst case, project failure.

4. Collective Responsibility for Control

Tip

Ensure that the "Demonstrate Control" principle is not viewed as solely the responsibility of the Project Manager.

Why it Matters

Control is a collective endeavor. While procedural aspects might be the purview of the Project Manager, control is inherently tied to team collaboration and individual contributions.

5. Initial Workshop on Principles

Tip

Organize an initial workshop at the onset of the project where the team can agree on how to practically implement each principle.

Why it Matters

Starting with a common understanding paves the way for smoother execution, enabling the team to address challenges more effectively as they arise.

6. Periodic Reviews

Tip

Include a review of the principles' application during each increment or Timebox review.

Why it Matters

Periodic reviews ensure the principles are not relegated to a one-time discussion but continue to be an active part of project evolution.

Conclusion

As an Agile Project Manager, your leadership is instrumental in weaving the DSDM principles into the project's operational framework. These tips serve as actionable guidelines to help you and your team stay aligned with the foundational principles, thereby enhancing project performance and stakeholder satisfaction.

Case Study: Implementing DSDM Principles in Project "Zenith"

Introduction

Project "Zenith" was a software development endeavor aimed at streamlining an organization's internal communication systems. While it started with enthusiastic team members and stakeholders, they soon realized that the project was veering off course. Here, we examine how a seasoned Agile Project Manager utilized tips to navigate DSDM principles effectively and steer the project back to success.

Case Study Highlights

Visibility of Principles

The Project Manager initiated the use of a digital board where each DSDM principle was displayed prominently. This digital board was integrated into daily stand-up meetings.

Encourage Open Discussion

An open channel was created on the project's communication platform exclusively for discussions around DSDM principles. Team members actively used this to raise concerns, which were addressed in real-time.

Risk Management

The Project Manager identified instances where adherence to principles was lacking and classified them as risks. Mitigation strategies were discussed in weekly sprint reviews.

Collective Responsibility for Control

The team was reminded that control was everyone's responsibility, not just the Project Manager's. This led to more proactive status updates and issue flagging from team members.

Initial Workshop on Principles

A one-day workshop was organized where roles, responsibilities, and the practical application of each DSDM principle were agreed upon. This served as a blueprint for project execution.

Periodic Reviews

Every Timebox review included a 10-minute segment dedicated to reviewing how well the DSDM principles had been applied. This kept the principles at the forefront of project activities.

Outcomes

The re-focus on DSDM principles brought a dramatic improvement in project performance metrics, including on-time delivery and stakeholder satisfaction.

Conclusion

This case study demonstrates the tangible impact of systematically integrating DSDM principles into project management. The Agile Project Manager's proactive role was crucial in realigning the project with its foundational principles, leading to its eventual success.

Chapter Twelve

Intersecting Roles and Responsibilities with the Project Manager

The Crucial Role of Team Dynamics in DSDM Projects: A Deeper Dive

The Importance of Team Dynamics in DSDM

Dynamic Systems Development Method (DSDM) inherently acknowledges the profound impact of team roles and dynamics on the project's success. Roles are meticulously defined to enhance communication and orchestrate a more effective collaboration. This not only minimizes misunderstandings but also facilitates the achievement of project objectives.

Four Key Areas of Interest in DSDM Teams

Orange - Business Interests

Roles in this quadrant like Business Ambassador and Business Visionary primarily aim at ensuring that the project objectives align perfectly with the business goals.

Green - Solution/Technical Interests

These roles, such as Solution Developers and Technical Coordinators, are focused on the nitty-gritty of the technical aspects, ensuring that the solution is architecturally sound and technically feasible.

Blue - Management Interests

Roles under this category, such as Project Manager and Team Leader, are geared towards administrative and leadership aspects, ensuring that the project is on course for successful completion.

Grey - Process Interests

Roles like Workshop Facilitator and DSDM Coach are dedicated to the seamless adoption and application of DSDM principles throughout the project's lifecycle.

Mixed Colors - Hybrid Roles

Certain roles, like the Business Analyst, may straddle more than one quadrant, contributing both to business alignment and technical aspects of the project.

Key Principles for Team Members

Respect for Knowledge and Experience

An effective DSDM team leverages the unique skill sets and perspectives of each of its members. This respect for each member's knowledge and experience promotes a collaborative environment.

Personal Responsibility

The culture of personal responsibility is non-negotiable in a DSDM project. Each team member should be aware that their tasks are not performed in isolation but are interdependent on the tasks of others.

Courage to Challenge

A hallmark of a high-functioning DSDM team is the willingness to question existing processes or approaches. This courage to challenge the status quo can lead to significant improvements in team collaboration and overall project outcomes.

Conclusion

Understanding and applying the roles and dynamics specific to DSDM can drastically improve project execution. These roles and principles are not merely procedural requirements but are foundational elements that contribute to the project's overall success.

Exploring a Case Study: Implementing Team Roles and Dynamics in a DSDM Project

Setting the Stage

In a hypothetical DSDM project aimed at developing an eCommerce platform, the organization realized the need for effective team dynamics and clearly defined roles for optimum outcomes. The team was comprised of diverse roles, each fitting into one of the four key areas of interest in DSDM teams—Business Interests, Solution/Technical Interests, Management Interests, and Process Interests.

The Roles in Action

Business Interests

The Business Visionary played a critical role in setting the long-term goals and ensuring the project aligned with the organizational objectives. Meanwhile, the Business Ambassadors were instrumental in representing the needs of end-users and other stakeholders during the development process.

Solution/Technical Interests

Technical Coordinators took the reins of the technical architecture, while Solution Developers were engaged in the actual development of the platform.

These roles ensured that the eCommerce platform was both robust and scalable.

Management Interests

The Project Manager focused on keeping the project on track, ensuring that milestones were met, and navigating any challenges that arose. The Team Leader facilitated the day-to-day operations, ensuring seamless communication between team members.

Process Interests

The DSDM Coach was pivotal in ensuring that the team adhered to DSDM principles. The Workshop Facilitator organized various sessions to brainstorm solutions to emerging challenges.

Outcome

The well-defined roles and strong team dynamics led to an effective and efficient project execution. The eCommerce platform was developed on time, met the business objectives, and was technically sound.

Lessons Learned

Visibility and Clarity: Clearly defined roles led to less overlap and more efficient use of resources.

Accountability: The clarity in roles ensured that each team member was aware of their responsibilities, fostering a sense of personal accountability.

Adaptability: The team was better equipped to adapt to changes because they had a clear understanding of who was responsible for what.

Conclusion

The case study underscores the critical importance of understanding and effectively implementing roles and team dynamics in a DSDM project for successful outcomes. The well-orchestrated interplay of different roles resulted in a project that was not only completed on time but also met all its predefined objectives.

Navigating the Landscape of Role Categories in DSDM Projects: An In-depth Guide

Overview

In the world of Agile methodologies, DSDM stands out for its well-defined framework that categorizes roles into three primary groups: Project-level roles, Solution Development Team roles, and Supporting roles. This structured approach enables a high level of clarity, governance, and efficiency. Let's delve into the key responsibilities, leadership styles, and the impact of each of these roles on a DSDM project.

Project-Level Roles

Key Responsibilities

Business Sponsor

- Provides strategic direction.
- Controls the budget.

Business Visionary

- Holds the overall business vision for the project.

Technical Coordinator

- Shapes the technical vision.

Project Manager

- Manages funds and timelines.

Business Analyst

- Formulates the Business Case.
- Defines requirements.

Leadership Style

- Facilitative and empowering, fostering a culture where Agile teams can adapt and enhance their processes.

Impact on Project

- These roles form the backbone of the governance structure and collectively possess the authority to direct the project.

Solution Development Team Roles

Key Responsibilities

Business Ambassador

- Serves as the voice of the customer.

Solution Developer

- Builds the solution.

Solution Tester

- Ensures solution meets business and quality requirements.

Business Analyst

- Supports ongoing requirement definition and refinement.

Team Leader

- Manages day-to-day activities of the team.

Team Characteristics

- Team members are generally stable throughout the project and share collective responsibility for day-to-day development and fitness for business purpose.

Supporting Roles

Key Responsibilities

Business Advisors and Technical Advisors

- Offer ad hoc expertise in their areas.

Workshop Facilitator

- Manages the workshop process for effective brainstorming and decision-making.

DSDM Coach

- Ensures adherence to the DSDM framework.

Engagement Level

- These roles are involved on an as-needed basis, often during the Foundations phase or during specific Timeboxes where their expertise becomes crucial.

Case Study: Role Categories in Action in a DSDM Project

Context

Imagine a software development project to create an eCommerce platform for a retail company. The project operates under the DSDM framework and has a span of six months, divided into multiple Timeboxes.

Project-Level Roles

Business Sponsor

- The CEO of the retail company, responsible for providing the strategic direction and approving the budget.

Business Visionary

- A senior manager from the marketing department who aligns the project with long-term business goals and the needs of the customer.

Technical Coordinator

- The CTO, ensuring that the technical architecture aligns with the business objectives.

Project Manager

- An experienced Agile Project Manager from the IT department, responsible for managing the timeline and budget constraints.

Business Analyst

- Collaborates with the business sponsor and visionary to develop the initial Business Case and keeps refining the requirements.

Solution Development Team Roles

Business Ambassador

- A representative from the customer service department, keeping the team aligned with customer expectations.

Solution Developer

- A group of skilled programmers responsible for building the eCommerce platform.

Solution Tester

- Works alongside the developers, making sure the solution is of high quality and meets business requirements.

Business Analyst

- Involved in the day-to-day refinement of requirements.

Team Leader

- Coordinates the daily activities and ensures that the team is meeting the objectives set for each Timebox.

Supporting Roles

Business Advisors and Technical Advisors

- Retail experts and database architects are called upon for advice during critical phases.

Workshop Facilitator

- An external Agile consultant facilitating important brainstorming sessions and decision-making workshops.

DSDM Coach

- An internal Agile expert ensures the team follows the DSDM framework correctly.

Outcome

Each role plays a critical part in ensuring the project meets its objectives. The Business Sponsor and Visionary set the strategic direction; the Project Manager and Technical Coordinator ensure alignment; the Solution Development Team builds, tests, and refines the solution; and the Supporting Roles offer targeted expertise. The result is a successful eCommerce platform delivered on time and within budget, aligning with both business and customer expectations.

Navigating Levels of Engagement and Role Fulfillment in DSDM Projects: A Comprehensive Guide

Levels of Engagement in DSDM Projects

Project-level Roles

Engagement Requirement

Project-level roles are primarily responsible for providing strategic direction, vision, and oversight. Their engagement is particularly crucial during high-level reviews, the initiation and conclusion of Timeboxes, and key decision-making points throughout the project.

Nature of Involvement

The involvement of project-level roles is more about governance and ensuring alignment with organizational goals. They do not typically get involved in the day-to-day execution of project tasks but act as high-level overseers to ensure that the project is moving in the right direction.

Solution Development Team Roles

Engagement Requirement

Members of the Solution Development Team are involved daily in the project. They participate in Daily Stand-ups, and their roles are very much operational. They are essential for shaping, building, and refining the solution increment.

Nature of Involvement

The Solution Development Team is on the front lines of the project, making them the primary executors of tasks. They engage in constant, open, and transparent communication among themselves and with other project stakeholders.

Fulfilling the Roles in DSDM Projects

The DSDM framework allows for a degree of flexibility when it comes to fulfilling roles. This flexibility is essential for adapting to different project sizes, complexities, and unique organizational structures. Here are some scenarios:

Role Sharing

In some instances, particularly in smaller projects or resource-strapped environments, it may be necessary for a single individual to fulfill multiple roles.

Multiple Role Holders

Conversely, in larger, more complex projects, a single role may be shared by multiple individuals to distribute the workload and leverage specialized skills.

Adaptability

The DSDM framework is adaptable enough to accommodate these variances, provided that the responsibilities attached to each role are clearly defined and understood by all.

Conclusion

Understanding the varying levels of engagement and the adaptability in role fulfillment is crucial for effectively managing DSDM projects. This nuanced approach ensures that regardless of project size or complexity, roles are effectively filled and team members are adequately engaged, thereby contributing positively to the project outcome.

Case Study: Implementing Levels of Engagement and Role Fulfillment in a Large-scale DSDM Project

In a hypothetical large-scale DSDM project aimed at developing an enterprise resource planning (ERP) system, the complexities involved made it crucial to have multiple individuals sharing roles and a varied level of engagement from both Project-level roles and the Solution Development Team.

Project-Level Roles

Business Sponsor and Business Visionary

The sheer scale of the project necessitated the Business Sponsor and Business Visionary to be actively involved not just at high-level review points but also at certain critical junctions throughout the development phase. The Business Sponsor, for example, was present during important Timeboxes where budget allocation was a significant concern.

Technical Coordinator

Given the technical complexity, the Technical Coordinator engaged with the Solution Development Team more frequently than in smaller projects, especially when architectural decisions were made.

Solution Development Team Roles

Business Ambassadors and Solution Developers

The team had multiple Business Ambassadors and Solution Developers due to the project's size. They were divided into specialized sub-teams focusing on different modules of the ERP system.

Daily Stand-ups

In addition to the general Daily Stand-up involving everyone, specialized Daily Stand-ups were conducted for these sub-teams to address module-specific issues.

Role Fulfillment Adaptability

Role-Sharing among Technical Coordinators

The project's scope was so broad that it was decided to have multiple Technical Coordinators, each specializing in different aspects like database design, user interface, and integration.

Multiple Role Holders in Solution Development Team

Given the range of skills required, several team members took on dual roles. For example, some Solution Developers also acted as Solution Testers, depending on the Timebox focus.

Conclusion

This large-scale ERP project exemplified how varying levels of engagement and flexibility in role fulfillment could co-exist within the DSDM framework. This adaptability ensured that the project could respond effectively to its complexity and size while still adhering to DSDM principles.

Diving Deeper: The Multi-Faceted Role of the Project Manager in DSDM Frameworks

Executive Summary

The role of the Project Manager in the Dynamic Systems Development Method (DSDM) framework is both broad and intricate, covering various domains such as high-level management, environment management, and Agile leadership. By examining each of these focus areas in detail, we can better appreciate the nuanced role that a Project Manager plays in steering a DSDM project to success.

High-Level Management

The Necessity of Macro-Planning

The Project Manager is responsible for setting the overall direction of the project, but refrains from diving into the minutiae of day-to-day activities. The purpose is to create a strategic framework within which the Solution Development Team can operate freely. This allows the team to make dynamic decisions without deviating from the primary objectives.

Coordination Across Project Phases

Given that DSDM projects are inherently iterative and adaptive, the Project Manager must maintain a consistent oversight throughout the various phases. This involves a coordinated approach in transitioning from one phase to another, ensuring that all project artifacts are updated and aligned.

Environment Management

Crafting an Empowering Workspace

Beyond the physicality of the work environment, the Project Manager is tasked with creating a cultural setting conducive to Agile practices. This includes facilitating open communication, encouraging collective decision-making, and instituting mechanisms for rapid feedback.

Technological Infrastructure

A Project Manager needs to ensure that the technological setup adequately supports the development process. This involves coordinating with IT departments and possibly external vendors to secure the necessary hardware and software resources.

Agile Leadership

Facilitation Over Direction

The Project Manager in a DSDM project serves more as a facilitator than a director. The focus is on empowering team members by providing them the autonomy, tools, and information they need to make educated decisions.

Managing the Balance of Power

While an Agile leadership style encourages team empowerment, the Project Manager must also establish clear boundaries and guidelines to prevent chaos. This involves defining clear accountability structures and resolving any conflicts that may arise during the project.

Communication and Reporting

Multi-tiered Communication Strategy

Effective communication is pivotal in any project, more so in an Agile setting. The Project Manager is responsible for setting up and maintaining various channels of communication that serve different audiences—from daily stand-ups with the development team to periodic updates for high-level stakeholders.

Reporting Formalities

The Project Manager needs to tailor the reporting mechanisms to suit the stakeholders involved. While some may prefer a detailed written report, others may be content with a high-level overview in a meeting setting.

Conclusion

Understanding the multifaceted role of the Project Manager in a DSDM framework provides insights into the competencies and strategies needed for effective project governance. Whether it's high-level planning or crafting an empowering work environment, the Project Manager's role is indispensable in navigating the complexities and delivering a successful project.

Case Study & Practical Examples: Unveiling the Depth of the Project Manager's Role in DSDM Frameworks

In the world of DSDM projects, the Project Manager is often the linchpin that holds the various elements together. To shed light on the theoretical aspects discussed earlier, we'll delve into practical examples and case studies that highlight how a Project Manager can successfully navigate the intricacies of a DSDM project.

High-Level Management

Case Study: Transitioning Between Phases

In a recent DSDM project for a financial services company, the Project Manager successfully coordinated the transition from the Feasibility phase to the Foundations phase. By ensuring that key milestones and deliverables were clearly identified and mapped, the team moved to the next phase with an aligned vision and well-defined objectives.

Practical Example: Updating Project Artifacts

One common practice is for the Project Manager to schedule a formal review meeting at the end of each phase. During these meetings, all project artifacts are updated and new deliverables for the upcoming phase are identified and agreed upon.

Environment Management

Case Study: Workspace Transformation

A Project Manager for a healthcare software development project recognized that the physical environment was hindering team communication. By restructuring the workspace to encourage open dialogue and co-location, the team became more collaborative and productivity soared.

Practical Example: Weekly Feedback Loop

Implementing a weekly feedback mechanism where team members can express any concerns about the work environment or tools can be a simple yet effective strategy.

Agile Leadership

Case Study: Empowering Through Autonomy

A Project Manager in a retail software development project employed a decentralized decision-making process, empowering team members to take ownership of sub-projects. As a result, the team was able to respond more quickly to changes, keeping the project on track and within budget.

Practical Example: Conflict Resolution Workshops

When disagreements among team members threatened to derail a project, the Project Manager organized conflict resolution workshops. These sessions helped clarify roles and responsibilities, preventing future conflicts and streamlining the decision-making process.

Communication and Reporting

Case Study: Customized Reporting

For a multi-phased DSDM project in the energy sector, the Project Manager devised a multi-tiered reporting strategy. This involved detailed daily reports for the development team and monthly high-level overviews for the board, resulting in improved stakeholder satisfaction.

Practical Example: Tailored Communication Channels

Implementing different communication channels like daily stand-ups, bi-weekly sprint reviews, and monthly steering committee meetings can serve the unique information needs of various stakeholders effectively.

Conclusion

As illustrated by these case studies and practical examples, the role of the Project Manager in a DSDM project is both versatile and critical. It demands a blend of high-level oversight, environment management, agile leadership, and sophisticated communication skills. Whether it's seamlessly coordinating phase transitions, transforming work environments, empowering teams, or tailoring communication strategies, the Project Manager's competencies are crucial in steering a DSDM project toward success.

Delving Into the Nuanced Role of the Business Sponsor in DSDM Frameworks

The role of the Business Sponsor within the DSDM framework is pivotal for maintaining the alignment of the project with overarching business objectives and financial considerations. It's not just about serving as a high-level overseer; the Business Sponsor takes on specific responsibilities that ensure the project is both business-viable and resource-efficient.

Areas of Focus

Financial Oversight

The Business Sponsor plays a key role in financial governance, keeping a close eye on the project budget and resource utilization. This role typically involves approving budget allocations and adjustments to ensure that financial commitments align with project deliverables and milestones.

Business Case Management

Another significant function of the Business Sponsor is to own the Business Case. This document lays out the rationale behind the project, including its expected business benefits and how these align with organizational goals. The Business Sponsor ensures that this alignment is maintained throughout the project lifecycle.

Decision-making

The Business Sponsor serves as the highest decision-making authority for escalated issues and conflicts within the project. Their judgment is deemed final and is expected to prioritize both immediate project needs and long-term business objectives.

Empowerment

This role involves the empowerment of other business roles within the project. By clearly defining what each role is accountable for, the Business Sponsor helps maintain a structure where decision-making is both quick and effective.

Responsibilities

Business Case Ownership

Maintaining the Business Case isn't a one-time event but a continuous activity. The Business Sponsor reviews and updates the Business Case to reflect any changes in the project scope or business environment, thereby ensuring ongoing viability.

Budget Management

From initial estimates to actual spending, the Business Sponsor manages every financial aspect of the project. This role involves approving changes to the budget and ensuring that funds are allocated in accordance with project priorities.

Decision-making and Conflict Resolution

The Business Sponsor's decision-making responsibility extends to resolving any conflicts that might arise during the project. By serving as the ultimate point of escalation, the Business Sponsor helps prevent bottlenecks that could otherwise delay project timelines.

Resource Allocation

It's not just about money; the Business Sponsor also has a hand in allocating other critical resources like human capital and technological assets. This ensures that the project team has everything they need to meet their objectives.

Empowerment and Monitoring

By empowering various business roles, the Business Sponsor facilitates effective project execution. They also stay informed about project progress through regular updates or by attending milestone meetings, thus ensuring alignment with business goals.

Variability Based on Project Size

In smaller projects, the role of the Business Sponsor may be straightforward, but the complexity increases in larger projects. Here, financial and decision-making responsibilities might be shared with an investment board or an executive committee. Regardless of this complexity, DSDM emphasizes the importance of having a single, identified Business Sponsor to ensure clear accountability.

Case Study: The Multifaceted Role of the Business Sponsor in a Large DSDM Project

Context

In a large-scale DSDM project undertaken by a multinational corporation, the Business Sponsor had a role that was far from straightforward. The company had a centralized investment board and multiple business units with vested interests in the project. Here, the role of the Business Sponsor was nuanced, multi-tiered, and required significant collaboration with other high-level organizational entities.

Balancing Financial Oversight

The Business Sponsor worked closely with the investment board, which held the ultimate authority on financial allocations. However, it was the Business Sponsor's responsibility to negotiate budget needs and to align them with the detailed project requirements. This required both high-level financial acumen and a deep understanding of the project's objectives.

Maintaining the Business Case

Given the project's complexity and its span across different business units, the Business Case was a living document subject to regular reviews. The Business Sponsor coordinated these reviews, collaborating with business analysts, project managers, and business unit heads to ensure the case's continued viability and relevance.

Complex Decision-making

The project had multiple stakeholders, each with their own sets of priorities and objectives. The Business Sponsor acted as the ultimate authority for conflict resolution but did so while orchestrating a complex array of inputs from different business units. This often involved high-stakes negotiations and intricate problem-solving skills.

Resource Allocation in a Multi-Stakeholder Environment

Resource allocation became a complex endeavor involving not just financial but also human and technological resources. The Business Sponsor had to ensure equitable allocation that met the project's overarching objectives, often balancing conflicting demands from different business units.

Empowerment and Monitoring

The Business Sponsor empowered not just individual roles within the project but also facilitated the empowerment of entire business units to make lower-level but critical decisions. This level of empowerment was counterbalanced by a robust monitoring framework, with the Business Sponsor receiving regular, detailed reports on project progress and any emerging issues.

Conclusion

The role of the Business Sponsor in this large, complex DSDM project was multifaceted and required a high level of engagement with both the project team and other organizational authorities. By adeptly managing these complexities, the Business Sponsor was instrumental in steering the project towards its successful completion, while ensuring alignment with business objectives and financial sustainability.

The case study provides a nuanced view of the Business Sponsor's role in larger and more complex DSDM projects, illustrating the adaptability and depth that this role can offer.

The Intricacies of the Business Visionary Role in a DSDM Framework

Understanding the Business Visionary Role

The Business Visionary is not merely a figurehead but a pivotal role in a DSDM project's success. While the Business Sponsor is responsible for high-level governance, the Business Visionary delves deep into the strategic underpinnings of the project. This involves defining, communicating, and ensuring that the project aligns with the business vision at every stage. Their level of engagement is dynamic, blending strategic oversight with hands-on involvement in the daily progress of the project.

Dual Focus: Strategy and Implementation

Setting the Strategic Direction

The Business Visionary crafts the strategic roadmap for the project. This roadmap serves as the compass, guiding the team towards the end goals while staying true to the organization's objectives. It is an articulation of what the project aims to achieve from a business standpoint.

Addressing Business Change

Given that projects often lead to business changes, the Business Visionary is also responsible for understanding these changes in the broader context. They identify and mitigate risks related to organizational changes that stem from the project.

Ensuring Collaboration and Adoption

Stakeholder Collaboration

The Business Visionary plays a key role in ensuring effective stakeholder communication. They bridge the gap between different business units and departments, creating a unified, cross-functional approach to the project.

Business Adoption

One of the Business Visionary's crucial responsibilities is ensuring that the project's deliverables are not just technically sound but also fit for business use. They facilitate the transition from project completion to business adoption, ensuring that the team's efforts yield practical business value.

Specific Responsibilities

Requirements and Scope

The Business Visionary often participates in key sessions concerning requirements, design, and review. Their primary concern is to make sure that the technical aspects are aligned with the business vision.

Resource Allocation

Similar to the Business Sponsor, the Business Visionary also has a say in the allocation of business resources. While they may not control the purse strings, they do ensure that the necessary business resources—be it manpower or data—are available when required.

Summary

The role of the Business Visionary in a DSDM project is multifaceted, combining elements of strategic vision setting, stakeholder management, and hands-on involvement in project proceedings. Their role complements that of the Business Sponsor, providing a more granular level of business insight into the project's day-to-day operations.

The Business Visionary in Action: A Hypothetical Case Study

Scenario Overview

Imagine a large organization undertaking a transformational project to implement an advanced Customer Relationship Management (CRM) system. This project is executed using the DSDM framework. In this setting, the Business Visionary is an executive who has extensive experience in customer relationship management and is keenly aware of the organization's long-term goals.

Strategic Direction Setting

The Business Visionary initiates the project by crafting a comprehensive business vision statement, which lays out how the new CRM system aligns with the company's broader strategy of customer-centricity. They hold sessions with various stakeholders, including the Business Sponsor, Project Manager, and Technical Coordinator, to share this vision and ensure that it forms the backbone of the project.

Collaboration Across Stakeholders

Once the vision is set, the Business Visionary orchestrates a series of workshops involving multiple departments—sales, marketing, IT, and customer service. The aim is to ensure that the CRM system will address the specific needs and pain points of each department, aligning closely with the overarching vision.

Monitoring Progress and Alignment

Throughout the project, the Business Visionary maintains a vigilant eye on progress. They attend key review meetings and are regularly updated by the Project Manager. They ensure that the delivered features and functions of the CRM are in sync with the original vision, intervening when they observe a drift.

Overseeing Business Adoption

As the project nears completion, the Business Visionary shifts focus to business adoption. They work closely with the departments that will use the CRM system, helping them understand how to align their processes and teams with the new system for maximum impact.

Arbitration and Decision-making

During the course of the project, several disagreements arise within the Solution Development Team regarding feature prioritization. The Business Visionary steps in to make the final call, basing their decision on what best aligns with the established business vision.

Conclusion

This hypothetical case study illuminates how the Business Visionary serves as more than just a figurehead. They actively shape, guide, and steer the project, right from the conceptualization stage through to implementation and business adoption, thereby ensuring that the project not only completes successfully but also realizes its intended business value.

Unpacking the Role of the Technical Coordinator in the DSDM Framework

Overview

The Technical Coordinator in the DSDM framework plays an indispensable role, acting as the central hub of technical knowledge and direction for the project. While the Business Visionary is focused on aligning the project with business needs, the Technical Coordinator is the equivalent figure on the technical side. They oversee the technological health of the project, ensuring that architecture, tools, and practices are robust, scalable, and in alignment with business objectives.

Areas of Focus

Technical Architecture

The Technical Coordinator sets the framework for the technical architecture, ensuring that it aligns with the business requirements and long-term objectives. This establishes a solid foundation upon which the Solution Development Team can construct the solution.

Technical Environment

This role selects the technology stack, tools, and environment that will best meet the project's objectives. The decision-making process involves an assessment of available technologies, budget constraints, and future scalability requirements.

Best Practices

The Technical Coordinator promotes the adoption of industry-standard practices, such as code reviews, automated testing, and continuous integration, to foster a culture of quality and efficiency.

Technical Risks

Risk identification and mitigation are crucial parts of this role. The Technical Coordinator actively looks for potential bottlenecks, security vulnerabilities, and other risks, developing mitigation strategies proactively.

Quality Assurance

This role ensures that non-functional requirements like performance, security, and reliability are not only achievable but are consistently met during the solution development phase.

Responsibilities

Team Coordination and Empowerment

The Technical Coordinator not only offers technical advice but also coordinates the activities of the Solution Development Team to maintain consistency. This involves empowering team members by providing them with the necessary tools, guidance, and authority within the scope of their technical responsibilities.

Estimation and Quality Control

Accurate task estimation is vital for Agile projects. The Technical Coordinator advises on a realistic approach to task estimation that reflects technical best practices and the current state of knowledge within the team. They also engage in quality control, reviewing and validating the technical soundness of the solution before it goes live.

Transition Management

Transitioning the developed solution into a live environment is a sensitive phase that requires careful planning and execution. The Technical Coordinator manages all the technical considerations that come with this transition, ensuring that the process is smooth and devoid of setbacks.

Technical Arbitration

Finally, the Technical Coordinator is the final authority on technical disputes within the Solution Development Team. They resolve disagreements, making decisions that best align with the project's technical objectives and overarching business goals.

Case Study: The Technical Coordinator in a DSDM-Driven Software Development Project

Project Context

In this hypothetical example, a medium-sized company is developing a new customer relationship management (CRM) system. The project utilizes the DSDM framework, involving various roles such as the Business Sponsor, Business Visionary, and Project Manager. At the center of all technical aspects stands the Technical Coordinator.

Setting the Technical Architecture

From the outset, the Technical Coordinator collaborates closely with the Business Visionary to understand the business requirements. This is crucial for deciding on an appropriate technical architecture that balances scalability, security, and performance. They finalize an architecture involving microservices to allow modular and scalable development.

Tool and Environment Selection

The Technical Coordinator also selects the technology stack for the project. After careful consideration of various options and consultations with the Solution Development Team, they decide on a combination of Python for backend development, React for the frontend, and Docker for containerization. This decision ensures alignment with current team skills and future scalability.

Risk Management and Quality Assurance

During the development phase, the Technical Coordinator identifies potential bottlenecks, such as API rate limiting and data storage inefficiencies. They collaborate with the team to implement caching solutions and database optimizations to mitigate these issues. Furthermore, they establish a set of best practices for coding, testing, and deployment to ensure the quality and security of the solution.

Transition Management

As the project nears completion, the Technical Coordinator focuses on transition management. They work closely with the operations team to ensure that the deployment pipeline is robust and that rollbacks are possible in case of issues. They also coordinate the final rounds of stress testing to ensure that the system can handle anticipated user loads.

Technical Arbitration

Throughout the project, disagreements inevitably arise within the Solution Development Team—whether it's about the best approach to data storage or the implementation of specific features. The Technical Coordinator acts as the final authority in these matters, making decisions that align with both the project's technical objectives and business goals.

By actively engaging in these multiple facets, the Technical Coordinator ensures the project's technical soundness, from architecture to deployment, effectively bridging the gap between business needs and technological solutions.

The Multifaceted Role of the Business Analyst in the DSDM Framework

The Business Analyst (BA) in the DSDM framework plays a pivotal role, mediating between business needs and the technical execution of the project. Unlike traditional models where the BA might be more siloed, the DSDM Business Analyst collaborates closely with both project-level roles and the Solution Development Team. Their responsibilities extend from the conceptualization phase right through to the deployment of the project.

Core Areas of Focus

Business Vision Support

The BA is instrumental in defining and refining the business vision alongside the Business Visionary. They participate in stakeholder interviews, focus groups, and other discovery methods to understand the project's strategic goals, which helps inform the crafting of a coherent business vision.

Requirement Analysis

Gathering, analyzing, and managing requirements are among the most important duties of the Business Analyst. They ensure that all requirements are clearly documented, understandable, and actionable. This clarity is critical for the Solution Development Team to develop the solution in alignment with business goals.

Communication Management

Effective communication is a cornerstone of any successful project, and the BA serves as a communication hub. They facilitate interactions between business stakeholders and technical teams to ensure that each understands the requirements, constraints, and capabilities of the other.

Impact Analysis

Business Analysts also perform impact analysis for proposed changes, helping the team and stakeholders understand the implications of adjustments to the requirements or technical approach. This is essential for informed decision-making.

Key Responsibilities

Business Case & Benefits

While the Business Sponsor typically owns the Business Case, the BA helps in its formulation and in conducting Benefits Assessments. They ensure that the

Business Case is well-aligned with the project's requirements and strategic objectives.

Quality Assurance

The BA is charged with ensuring that the business requirements are well-defined, actionable, and quality-assured. They often use techniques like use-case modeling or user-story mapping to achieve this.

Cohesion and Implementation Support

One of the Business Analyst's final responsibilities is to ensure that the solution forms a cohesive whole that meets both business and technical requirements. They are also involved in the transition phase, working closely with the Business Visionary and other stakeholders to ensure a smooth handover to the business.

Concluding Thoughts

The role of the Business Analyst in a DSDM project is dynamic and multi-dimensional. From ensuring alignment between the business vision and technical execution to fostering communication and assessing impact, the BA is a key player in steering the project toward success.

Exploring the Multifaceted Role of the Business Analyst: A Hypothetical Case Study

Scenario Context

In a hypothetical organization aiming to modernize its customer relationship management (CRM) system, the DSDM framework is employed. The overarching goal is to develop a solution that enhances user experience while integrating seamlessly with existing systems. A Business Analyst is appointed to serve as the linchpin between the business and technical realms of the project.

Role in Vision Crafting

Right from the start, the Business Analyst collaborates closely with the Business Visionary to define the vision of the project. They hold focus group sessions and one-on-one interviews with various stakeholders, including sales, marketing, and customer service departments, to understand the functionalities and features needed in the new CRM system. Based on the gathered insights, the Business Analyst helps the Business Visionary in developing a well-articulated vision statement and aligning it with the organizational goals.

Requirement Analysis and Management

Post vision crafting, the Business Analyst begins gathering detailed requirements. They create a requirements catalogue, and using prioritization techniques like MoSCoW (Must-have, Should-have, Could-have, and Won't-have), they segregate the requirements into different categories. This helps the Solution Development Team understand which features are crucial and which can be developed in later iterations if needed.

Quality Assurance and Impact Analysis

Throughout the development process, the Business Analyst ensures that each feature being developed aligns with the defined requirements. They also continually perform impact analysis. For example, if the development team suggests a change in the database architecture for performance optimization, the BA assesses how this change would affect other systems that interact with the CRM.

Communication and Cohesion

The Business Analyst ensures that the communication lines between business stakeholders and the technical team are always open. When the Solution Development Team finishes a feature, the BA coordinates the demonstration of this feature to the stakeholders and gathers their feedback. This cycle of development, demonstration, and feedback ensures that the evolving solution remains cohesive and aligned with the business vision.

Transition Support

As the project reaches its final stages, the Business Analyst works on the transition plan. They coordinate with the IT operations team to ensure that the deployment pipelines are ready and work with the Business Visionary to prepare the business teams for the rollout.

Conclusion

In this hypothetical case study, the Business Analyst played a multi-dimensional role. From crafting the vision and managing requirements to quality assurance and transition support, their involvement was critical at every stage. The case serves as an illustration of the dynamic and central role a Business Analyst holds in a DSDM project.

The Vital Role of the Team Leader in DSDM Projects

Navigating the Dynamic Systems Development Method (DSDM) Framework

In the intricate labyrinth of a DSDM project, the Team Leader emerges as a servant-leader who guides the Solution Development Team towards successful project outcomes. While they may wear multiple hats, performing other roles such as Business Analyst or Solution Developer, their primary responsibility remains clear: to shepherd the team through the various project phases effectively.

Focal Areas

Leadership and Coordination

The Team Leader's primary task is to ensure the team's collective focus and productivity. They accomplish this by coordinating the fine details of product delivery and keeping team members aligned with project goals.

Communication Bridge

Serving as the interface between the Solution Development Team and the Project Manager, the Team Leader makes sure that communication channels are open, transparent, and efficient.

Risk and Issue Management

The Team Leader also manages risks and issues at the level of individual timeboxes within the project, ensuring they do not jeopardize the project's objectives.

Core Responsibilities

On-Time Delivery

The Team Leader ensures that the team stays committed to delivering the agreed-upon products within the pre-defined timelines. Their oversight helps keep the project on track and prevents deviations that could derail it.

Team Participation and Empowerment

The Team Leader fosters an environment that encourages full participation from each team member. By doing so, they ensure that everyone is operating within their defined roles and at their appropriate levels of empowerment.

Iterative Process Control

DSDM operates on an iterative development model, and the Team Leader makes sure that this process is properly managed and remains focused. They oversee the various iterations to make certain they are in sync with project objectives.

Testing, Reviews, and Quality Control

One of the Team Leader's key responsibilities is to schedule and oversee all testing and review activities. They ensure that the team adheres to quality standards and that products are developed according to the agreed-upon specifications.

Risk and Issue Escalation

At the Timebox level, the Team Leader actively identifies, manages, and escalates risks and issues. They communicate with higher-level roles like the Project Manager, Business Visionary, or Technical Coordinator when these risks require escalated attention.

Progress Monitoring

The Team Leader keeps a keen eye on day-to-day activities. Through consistent monitoring, they ensure that the team is making steady progress toward meeting its objectives.

Facilitated Communication

Effective communication is vital for the success of any project. The Team Leader facilitates this by ensuring that progress reports and other essential information are adequately communicated to the Project Manager.

Reviews and Continuous Improvement

Finally, the Team Leader encourages a culture of continuous improvement by leading the team in conducting reviews and retrospectives. These sessions aim to provide constructive feedback and identify areas for improvement.

Case Study: The Impact of an Effective Team Leader in a DSDM Project

Setting the Stage for Success

Imagine a medium-sized software development company embarking on a project to create a new CRM system for a client. The project is complex, with multiple stakeholders and tight deadlines. The company decides to use the

Dynamic Systems Development Method (DSDM) framework to manage the project efficiently. They appoint an experienced Team Leader to steer the Solution Development Team through the intricate phases of DSDM.

Effective Leadership and Coordination

The Team Leader quickly takes charge and sets the tone for the team, encouraging open communication and fostering a culture of collective focus. They coordinate the delivery of the first Timebox effectively, ensuring that all agreed-upon features are implemented within the set timelines.

Clear Communication Channels

The Team Leader maintains open and transparent communication with the Project Manager, regularly updating them on the project's progress. This constant flow of information helps in quick decision-making and keeps the project aligned with its goals.

Mitigating Risks and Issues

During the development phase, the team encounters a critical technical issue that threatens to delay the project. The Team Leader identifies the risk, informs the Project Manager and Technical Coordinator, and works with the team to develop a mitigation strategy. Their proactive approach helps to resolve the issue without impacting the project timeline.

Quality Assurance and Reviews

The Team Leader also plays a pivotal role in ensuring quality. They schedule and oversee regular testing and review sessions, ensuring that the developed features meet the required quality standards.

Encouraging Continuous Improvement

After the completion of each Timebox, the Team Leader leads the team in conducting a retrospective. They encourage team members to provide constructive feedback and highlight areas for improvement. These sessions become a cornerstone for the team's continuous improvement, helping them to become more efficient and productive as the project progresses.

Conclusion

The Team Leader's effective guidance, open communication, and proactive risk management play a crucial role in the successful completion of the CRM system project. Their servant-leadership approach fosters a positive work environment and ensures that the team is empowered to deliver their best.

This case study illustrates how an effective Team Leader can significantly impact a DSDM project's success, serving as the linchpin that holds the various elements of the project together.

The Integral Role of the Business Ambassador in the DSDM Framework

Overview

The Business Ambassador is a key player in the Dynamic Systems Development Method (DSDM) framework, responsible for ensuring that the project is closely aligned with business goals and expectations. With their knowledge and authority, the Business Ambassador serves as the primary liaison between the business stakeholders and the Solution Development Team. The individual in this role should be well-equipped to make important decisions that impact the business, and they often consult with Business Advisors to obtain varied perspectives.

Areas of Focus

Requirements Gathering

The Business Ambassador plays a significant role during the Foundations phase, working on the creation and prioritization of business requirements.

Decision-Making

During the Evolutionary Development phase, this role serves as the go-to person for making business-related decisions that guide the project's direction.

Communication

Effective dialogue with stakeholders, including other business users and the Solution Development Team, is a critical focus for the Business Ambassador.

Quality Assurance

Ensuring that the developed solution is in alignment with business goals and meets the requisite quality standards is another area of responsibility.

Responsibilities

Requirements Involvement

This role is deeply involved in all aspects of requirements gathering, design, and review sessions to make sure business needs are met.

Business Perspective

The Business Ambassador offers a business-centric point of view in daily decision-making processes within the Solution Development Team.

Scenario Development

They provide comprehensive business scenarios that help in defining and testing the evolving solution.

Stakeholder Communication

One of the responsibilities includes involving other users in the decision-making process and securing their agreement as necessary.

Quality Assurance

The role includes daily oversight to ensure that the evolving solution remains aligned with business objectives.

Business Acceptance Testing

Organizing and controlling the business acceptance testing of the solution is another crucial responsibility.

Documentation

While they are responsible for business documentation, the delegation to specialized roles like Technical Authors is often considered for optimum results.

Training and Support

The Business Ambassador also makes sure that the business participants involved in the deployed solution are adequately trained and supported.

Case Study: Implementing a Customer Relationship Management System with a Business Ambassador in the DSDM Framework

Project Background

A medium-sized organization decided to implement a new Customer Relationship Management (CRM) system to streamline its sales and customer service processes. A Business Ambassador was appointed, who had extensive experience in sales and a solid understanding of CRM technologies.

The Business Ambassador's Involvement

Phase 1: Foundations

During the initial Foundations phase, the Business Ambassador worked closely with the project team to outline the key requirements. They organized workshops with various business units, including sales, marketing, and customer service, to understand their specific needs.

Phase 2: Evolutionary Development

As the project moved into the Evolutionary Development phase, the Business Ambassador actively participated in making day-to-day decisions related to the CRM's features. They reviewed user stories, participated in sprint planning, and were involved in daily stand-ups with the Solution Development Team.

Communication Strategy

Throughout the project, the Business Ambassador maintained regular communication with both the business users and the Solution Development Team. Weekly update meetings were held, and critical decisions were discussed openly.

Quality Assurance

The Business Ambassador was in charge of quality assurance for the CRM implementation. They developed test scenarios based on real-world sales and customer service activities. Business Acceptance Testing was conducted, and feedback was implemented, ensuring the solution met the predefined quality standards.

Training and Deployment

Before the CRM system went live, the Business Ambassador oversaw the training of the end-users. They also worked closely with the Business Advisors to ensure that a proper support system was in place.

Outcome

Thanks to the Business Ambassador's involvement, the CRM system was implemented successfully, meeting the business objectives and quality standards. The project was delivered on time and within budget, and the organization saw a significant improvement in sales and customer service efficiencies.

This case study exemplifies the vital role a Business Ambassador can play in a DSDM project, demonstrating how they can bring invaluable business perspective and decision-making abilities to ensure the project's success.

The Integral Role of the Solution Developer in the DSDM Framework

Overview

In a project operating under the Dynamic Systems Development Method (DSDM), the Solution Developer serves as the workhorse for turning abstract business requirements into concrete solution increments. The individual in this role is a central part of the Solution Development Team and is responsible for developing the functional and non-functional aspects of the project. The Solution Developer operates within the parameters set by the Technical Coordinator and is deeply involved in iterative development alongside other key roles within the team.

Areas of Focus

Iterative Development

The Solution Developer is an active participant in the iterative cycles of development, working collaboratively with other team members to produce solution increments that align with business requirements.

Quality Assurance

While quality assurance is often a collaborative effort, the Solution Developer plays a vital role in ensuring that the solution increments are of high quality and meet the specified criteria.

Technical Adherence

This role is responsible for adhering to technical constraints and guidelines set forth by the Technical Coordinator, thereby ensuring that the solution is sustainable and maintainable.

Risk Management

Given the time-sensitive nature of DSDM projects, the Solution Developer works closely with the Project Manager to identify and manage risks, particularly those associated with timeboxing.

Responsibilities

Collaborative Development

The Solution Developer collaborates with all roles within the Solution Development Team to iteratively create the solution, including essential models and documentation.

Self-Testing

Prior to any independent testing activities, the Solution Developer conducts preliminary tests on their own deliverables to catch early issues that might affect the project.

Technical Constraints

The Solution Developer adheres to the technical constraints set by the Technical Coordinator, ensuring that the solution aligns with both business and technical needs.

Standards and Best Practices

Compliance with established technical standards and best practices is essential, and the Solution Developer is responsible for ensuring this alignment in their work.

Quality Assurance

Participation in quality assurance activities is crucial, especially when it comes to ensuring that the developed solution increments are fit for their intended purpose.

Documentation and Recording

Accurate record-keeping is vital, and the Solution Developer takes responsibility for documenting changes to requirements, interpretations, or any other factors that could affect the evolution of the solution.

Case Study: Implementing the Solution Developer Role in a DSDM Project

Setting the Stage

In a DSDM project aimed at developing a next-generation e-commerce platform, the role of the Solution Developer became pivotal for the success of the project. The project team was comprised of various roles, including a Business Visionary, Technical Coordinator, Business Analyst, and others.

Challenge Faced

The project was dealing with a high level of complexity due to the integration of machine learning algorithms for customer recommendations and various third-party payment gateways. The Solution Developer faced the dual challenge of adhering to strict technical guidelines set by the Technical

Coordinator while also meeting business requirements outlined by the Business Analyst and Business Visionary.

Actions Taken

Collaboration

The Solution Developer collaborated closely with the Business Analyst to understand the nuances of business requirements and took part in brainstorming sessions with the Technical Coordinator to decide on the architecture and tools to be used.

Iterative Development

Following the DSDM principles, the Solution Developer engaged in iterative development. Each iteration included a set of prioritized features to be implemented, and progress was reviewed at the end of each timebox.

Risk Management

The Solution Developer worked alongside the Project Manager to assess risks tied to time constraints. Through proactive risk management, they identified potential bottlenecks in the pipeline and formulated mitigation strategies.

Quality Assurance and Self-Testing

Before releasing any increments to the quality assurance team, the Solution Developer conducted rigorous self-testing to identify any early issues.

Adherence to Technical Constraints

The Solution Developer remained in constant communication with the Technical Coordinator to ensure that the solution was developed within the defined architectural and technical constraints.

Documentation

Detailed records were maintained by the Solution Developer for changes in requirements, coding interpretations, and adjustments to project scope, which were invaluable during the project retrospective and for future phases.

Outcome

Through collaborative efforts, iterative development, and effective risk management, the Solution Developer played a crucial role in successfully developing and deploying the e-commerce platform. The platform not only met but exceeded the initial business requirements while staying within the defined technical boundaries.

This case study illustrates the indispensable role of the Solution Developer in ensuring that a DSDM project aligns with both business requirements and technical constraints, thereby contributing significantly to the project's success.

The Indispensable Role of the Solution Tester in DSDM Projects

Overview

Within the framework of the Dynamic Systems Development Method (DSDM), the Solution Tester emerges as a cornerstone for ensuring project success. This role is crucial for guaranteeing that the developed solution adheres to both functional and non-functional requirements. Collaborating closely with key stakeholders like the Business Analyst, Business Ambassador, and Technical Coordinator, the Solution Tester is instrumental in driving the quality assurance process.

Areas of Focus

Test Scenario Development

The Solution Tester collaborates with business roles such as the Business Analyst and Business Ambassador to outline robust test scenarios and test cases.

Technical Testing

This involves executing comprehensive technical tests on the evolving solution to assure its quality and fit-for-purpose status.

Quality Assurance

The Solution Tester plays a vital role in reporting test results, which serves as foundational data for quality assurance activities.

Stakeholder Collaboration

In this capacity, the Solution Tester interacts with both technical and business stakeholders to fine-tune acceptance criteria and discuss test results.

Responsibilities

Test Design

One of the primary tasks involves working closely with the Business Analyst and Business Ambassador to define the test scenarios and test cases that will serve as the blueprint for the actual testing process.

Technical Testing

Performing various forms of technical tests is part and parcel of the role, ensuring that the solution conforms to pre-established standards and requirements.

Acceptance Criteria

Here, the Solution Tester collaborates with the Business Analyst and Business Ambassador to establish clear and unambiguous acceptance criteria, making sure that there is alignment between what the business needs and what the solution delivers.

Test Documentation

The role also necessitates the creation of essential test products, such as test plans, test cases, and test logs, to ensure a well-documented and transparent testing process.

Quality Assurance Reporting

Upon completing the testing cycles, the Solution Tester is responsible for submitting the test results to the Technical Coordinator. These reports are instrumental for ongoing quality assurance activities.

Team Communication

Keeping the Team Leader informed about the progress and outcomes of the testing activities is also a critical part of the role.

Stakeholder Support

Lastly, the Solution Tester assists Business Ambassadors and Business Advisors in planning and executing their own tests, making sure that all significant areas are adequately covered.

Case Study: Implementing the Role of the Solution Tester in a DSDM Project

Context

In a hypothetical DSDM project aimed at developing a cloud-based CRM solution for a mid-sized company, the Solution Tester played a pivotal role in ensuring that the final product met both functional and non-functional requirements.

Setting the Testing Grounds

Test Scenario Development

Working closely with the Business Analyst and Business Ambassador, the Solution Tester helped outline the test scenarios that would be crucial for validating the CRM's functionalities, such as data synchronization, user experience, and performance under different workloads.

Test Documentation

To avoid any ambiguities, the Solution Tester meticulously documented the test cases, acceptance criteria, and the expected outcomes in a test plan.

Execution and Reporting

Technical Testing

Once the Solution Development Team released the first usable increment, the Solution Tester executed the technical tests based on the pre-defined test scenarios. Issues like latency, data corruption, and UI responsiveness were examined.

Quality Assurance Reporting

The test results were submitted to the Technical Coordinator for quality assurance reviews. The Solution Tester used automated tools to generate comprehensive reports highlighting the performance metrics, defects, and other relevant data.

Continuous Collaboration

Team Communication

Throughout the testing phase, the Solution Tester kept the Team Leader updated with regular reports and took part in daily stand-ups to discuss any challenges faced.

Stakeholder Support

At the end of each iterative cycle, the Solution Tester collaborated with the Business Ambassadors and Business Advisors to facilitate their own acceptance tests. This ensured that the solution was on track to meet the business objectives and requirements.

Outcome

By fulfilling the responsibilities effectively, the Solution Tester ensured that the CRM solution was robust, scalable, and aligned with the business needs. The role's contribution was instrumental in identifying potential risks early, thereby aiding in the timely release of a quality product.

The Significance of the Business Advisor in the DSDM Framework

Overview

In the Dynamic Systems Development Method (DSDM) landscape, the Business Advisor holds a niche but indispensable role. Acting as the subject matter expert, the Business Advisor lends specialized insights that are critical for shaping the project, particularly during its development and testing stages. Unlike the Business Ambassador, who provides a comprehensive business viewpoint, the Business Advisor offers specific expertise in areas like regulatory compliance, domain knowledge, or other specialisms.

Areas of Focus

Specialist Input

By offering expert guidance during crucial phases such as requirements gathering and design reviews, the Business Advisor ensures the project aligns closely with specialized needs. Whether it's compliance with industry regulations or specific technological considerations, the input from this role can be invaluable.

Decision-Making

The Business Advisor also has a part to play in the decision-making process for issues requiring domain-specific insights. By doing so, they act as a safety net, ensuring that the project doesn't deviate into areas that might risk non-compliance or inefficiency.

Solution Testing

Another key area where the Business Advisor adds value is in the formulation of specialized business scenarios for solution testing. This is essential for ensuring that the solution can handle situations unique to the project's domain.

Deployment and Documentation

The Business Advisor also provides advice on how to effectively deploy solution increments and what sort of specialized documentation may be necessary for supporting the solution in a live environment.

Responsibilities

Specialist Contributions

At various stages, from requirements gathering to design reviews, the Business Advisor steps in to offer their specialized knowledge. This ensures that the project remains aligned with the intricacies related to specific industry regulations, technological constraints, or other specialized criteria.

Decision Support

For decisions that require more than a general business perspective, the Business Advisor's insights can be decisive. They assist in steering the project on the right course when it comes to specialized domains, be it regulatory compliance or otherwise.

Business Scenarios

By crafting and contributing specialized business scenarios, the Business Advisor helps in the effective testing of the evolving solution. This ensures that the final product can meet the unique challenges posed by the specialized aspects of the business environment.

Documentation and Deployment

Lastly, in areas such as user and support documentation, as well as deployment activities, the Business Advisor's advice can be instrumental. Their insights may influence how the solution is rolled out and how it is received by its end-users.

Case Study: The Business Advisor's Role in a Healthcare DSDM Project

Context

In a healthcare DSDM project aimed at developing a new Electronic Health Records (EHR) system, the Business Advisor plays a pivotal role. In this setting, the advisor is usually a healthcare compliance expert with a deep understanding of regulations such as HIPAA (Health Insurance Portability and Accountability Act) in the United States, or GDPR (General Data Protection Regulation) in the European Union.

Contribution to the Project

Specialist Input

Given the regulated nature of healthcare, the Business Advisor's input becomes critical during the requirements gathering and design phases. They ensure that the system design incorporates features necessary for compliance, such as encrypted patient data and restricted access controls.

Decision-Making

During the iterative development cycles, the Business Advisor's recommendations could affect key decisions, especially when a trade-off between functionality and compliance arises. Their advice ensures that the project stays within legal boundaries while trying to achieve operational efficiency.

Solution Testing

In the testing phase, the Business Advisor formulates specific healthcare scenarios, like a data breach or unauthorized access, to test the system's robustness. This ensures that the system can withstand real-world challenges in a healthcare environment.

Deployment and Documentation

As the system nears completion, the Business Advisor's insights on deployment come into play, particularly concerning staff training on compliance protocols. Moreover, they contribute to developing specialized documentation that outlines how the EHR system meets or exceeds regulatory standards.

Result

By playing this specialized role, the Business Advisor ensures not only that the project stays aligned with regulatory standards but also helps in averting potential future liabilities related to compliance. Their inputs enrich the project's quality and ensure a smoother transition when the solution goes live.

This case study highlights the nuanced but impactful role that a Business Advisor can play, particularly in sectors where specialized knowledge is not just beneficial but crucial.

The Multifaceted Role of the Technical Advisor in the DSDM Framework

In the labyrinthine world of software development using the Dynamic Systems Development Method (DSDM), the Technical Advisor is the harbinger of specialized technical knowledge and long-term operational viability. Unlike other roles that may concentrate on the project's immediate needs, the Technical Advisor focuses on the project's future, assessing the operational longevity and sustainability of the evolving solution. This role has an indelible impact on ensuring that the project's technical aspects align with organizational capabilities and future operational needs.

Areas of Focus

Technical Expertise

The Technical Advisor is the encyclopedia of specialized knowledge, offering insights into software architecture, data modeling, and security protocols. This expertise is crucial during requirements gathering, design, and review sessions, where decisions affecting the technical integrity of the project are made.

Operational Decision-Making

In addition to technical acumen, the Technical Advisor provides operational perspectives that are key to the project's long-term success. They weigh in on everyday decisions, ensuring the solution is not just feasible in a technical sense but is also operationally viable.

Operational Testing

One of the distinctive attributes of this role is the focus on operational or support scenarios. By doing so, the Technical Advisor guarantees that the solution will be ready for real-world challenges, extending beyond the immediacy of functional requirements.

Technical Documentation

Documentation, often considered an afterthought, gains prominence when a Technical Advisor is involved. They contribute to creating technical support documents that pave the way for the solution's long-term operational health.

Training and Deployment

Lastly, the Technical Advisor plays a crucial role in the preparation and transition phases. They offer valuable insights into training technical staff and contribute to planning the incremental deployment of solution releases.

Responsibilities in Detail

The responsibilities are manifold, encompassing technical contributions, operational decision support, and more:

Technical Contributions: Offers specialized technical advice during key project phases, thereby acting as a critical checkpoint for technical integrity.

Operational Decision Support: Aids in making operational decisions, serving as a nexus between the project's technical and operational aspects.

Operational Scenarios: Develops and tests operational scenarios, thereby becoming an arbiter of the solution's real-world readiness.

Assurance: Ensures that the solution meets both functional and non-functional requirements, particularly with an eye toward long-term sustainability.

Documentation: Assumes responsibility for the development of critical technical documentation, essential for ongoing maintenance and support.

Training and Deployment: Takes an active role in preparing technical operations and support staff, ensuring a smooth transition from development to deployment.

Delving Deeper: A Case Study on the Role of the Technical Advisor in the DSDM Framework

Setting the Scene

In a hypothetical healthcare project using the DSDM framework, the objective is to create a telemedicine platform that complies with healthcare regulations and can integrate with existing medical record systems. The project involves various roles including Team Leaders, Business Ambassadors, Solution Developers, and Solution Testers. Among them is our Technical Advisor, Alex, who specializes in healthcare IT and regulatory compliance.

Alex's Contribution: Beyond Just Technicalities

Phase 1: Requirements Gathering

When the project kicked off, Alex immediately emphasized the need for robust encryption and secure data exchange, aligning with healthcare data compliance standards such as HIPAA. His inputs were invaluable in shaping the initial set of requirements.

Phase 2: Design

During the design phase, Alex pointed out potential operational challenges like server downtime during patient consultations and advised on incorporating fail-safe mechanisms. His foresight ensured that the telemedicine platform would be resilient, adding to its operational longevity.

Phase 3: Operational Testing

Alex took the lead in crafting test scenarios that mimicked real-world operational challenges. This included high traffic loads and simultaneous access from multiple healthcare providers. The testing results were pivotal in making necessary adjustments, thereby averting potential future crises.

Phase 4: Documentation

Alex authored a comprehensive guide that outlined standard operating procedures (SOPs), technical specs, and compliance guidelines. This would become the go-to manual for future maintenance and upgrades, serving as an invaluable resource for the IT operations team.

Phase 5: Training and Deployment

During the final stages, Alex collaborated with the technical team to train them on how to manage the telemedicine platform effectively, particularly in scenarios that would require rapid troubleshooting.

The Outcome: A Project Geared for Long-Term Success

Thanks to Alex's multifaceted contributions, the project not only met its immediate functional requirements but was also operationally sound, setting it up for long-term success. His role as a Technical Advisor was instrumental in ensuring that the telemedicine platform was technically robust, compliant with healthcare regulations, and ready for the rigors of real-world operation.

The Integral Role of the Workshop Facilitator in DSDM Projects

The Lighthouse of Objectivity

In the milieu of a Dynamic Systems Development Method (DSDM) project, where the focus often oscillates between technical development and business objectives, the Workshop Facilitator serves as a linchpin for structured discussion and decision-making. Neutral and detached from the project outcomes, this role ensures that workshops are a microcosm of productivity and constructive collaboration.

Key Areas of Focus: Orchestrating Success

Pre-Workshop Planning

The Workshop Facilitator works in close coordination with the workshop owner to outline the scope and objectives. This involves a deep dive into understanding what precisely the workshop aims to achieve and how it fits into the larger project roadmap.

Participant Engagement

Prior to the workshop, the Facilitator vets the participants to ensure they are well-suited in terms of expertise and decision-making authority. The objective is to assemble a group that is equipped to address the issues on the workshop's agenda.

Workshop Facilitation

During the workshop, the Facilitator dons the hat of a moderator, ensuring that discussions are on track and that conflicts are resolved in a manner that aligns with the workshop's objectives. In essence, they shepherd the group towards a constructive outcome.

Post-Workshop Follow-Up

The role doesn't end when the workshop does. The Facilitator is responsible for measuring the workshop's effectiveness by evaluating its outcomes against the set objectives. They also ensure that the insights and decisions are disseminated to all relevant stakeholders.

Detailed Responsibilities: The Facilitator's Playbook

Before the Workshop

Scope Agreement

The Facilitator collaborates with the workshop owner to demarcate the boundaries of what the workshop should cover, thereby eliminating ambiguity.

Planning

They map out a strategic agenda that dictates the flow of the workshop, including time allocations and discussion topics.

Familiarization

If the subject matter is specialized, the Facilitator invests time in getting acquainted with it to steer the workshop effectively.

Participant Engagement

The Facilitator preps the participants to make sure they come into the workshop with a clear understanding of what to expect and what is expected of them.

During the Workshop

Facilitation

The Facilitator guides the dialogue, helping to maintain the focus of the group and intervening when deviations occur or conflicts arise.

After the Workshop

Review

The Facilitator conducts an internal assessment to gauge how well the workshop met its goals, thus providing a blueprint for future improvements.

Distribution

Finally, they are responsible for sharing the outcomes with all parties who have a stake in the workshop's subject matter, ensuring that the insights gained are utilized optimally.

Case Study: Orchestrating a Successful Workshop in a DSDM Project

Context: A Multi-Stakeholder Workshop

In a DSDM project aimed at creating an enterprise resource planning (ERP) system for a manufacturing company, a critical workshop was scheduled. The workshop involved multiple stakeholders, including Business Ambassadors, Solution Developers, and Technical Advisors. The objective was to converge on critical decisions about the system's architecture and features. Here, the Workshop Facilitator was the linchpin for ensuring a successful outcome.

Pre-Workshop Planning: Setting the Stage

Objectives and Scope

The Facilitator collaborated with the workshop owner, in this case, the Technical Coordinator, to set well-defined objectives. These ranged from finalizing the software architecture to deciding on the set of features to be included in the next iteration.

Agenda

An agenda was meticulously planned, incorporating time for introductory briefings, individual presentations, breakout sessions, and finally, a collective decision-making session.

Participant Engagement: The Right People in the Room

Suitability and Preparation

The Facilitator vetted potential participants to ensure they had the requisite knowledge and decision-making authority. Each participant received pre-workshop material to review, and their concerns were documented to be addressed during the workshop.

During the Workshop: Guiding the Process

Keeping Focus

As discussions progressed, the Facilitator intervened occasionally to steer the group back to the main objectives whenever digressions occurred.

Conflict Resolution

When differing opinions led to a conflict, the Facilitator used predefined decision-making frameworks to guide the group toward a consensus.

Post-Workshop Follow-Up: Closing the Loop

Evaluating Success

Once the workshop was concluded, the Facilitator reviewed the decisions made and actions agreed upon, evaluating them against the initial objectives to measure the workshop's success.

Sharing Outcomes

A comprehensive report capturing the workshop's outcomes and agreed-upon actions was shared with not just the participants but also with other stakeholders who would be impacted by these decisions.

Through well-planned pre-workshop activities, assertive management during the workshop, and thorough post-workshop follow-up, the Workshop Facilitator played a decisive role in steering the group towards a constructive and impactful outcome.

The Role of the DSDM Coach in Depth: Navigating the Complexities of Agile Transformation

The Quintessential Guide

In the complex and ever-evolving landscape of software development, the DSDM Coach serves as a cornerstone in organizations transitioning to or optimizing their use of the Dynamic Systems Development Method (DSDM). While most team members are absorbed in project-specific goals, the DSDM Coach provides a unique overlay of methodology expertise, helping the team to navigate the challenges of agile practices. This role is of particular importance in organizations where DSDM is newly adopted or not yet fully understood.

Areas of Focus: Spheres of Influence

Expert Knowledge: The Encyclopedia of DSDM

The DSDM Coach acts as a repository of DSDM practices, methodologies, and principles. Their in-depth understanding of the DSDM framework ensures that the development team and other stakeholders can rely on expert advice, thereby fostering an environment where DSDM principles are not just adopted but deeply ingrained.

Methodology Adaptation: Tailoring the Suit

Understanding that no two projects or organizational contexts are identical, the DSDM Coach customizes the methodology to fit the project's unique requirements. This involves a nuanced approach to scaling, modifications, and sometimes even hybridization of methodologies to suit the specific project landscape.

Team Guidance: The Human Element

The DSDM Coach works actively to promote a collaborative environment. By aiding the team in employing DSDM practices effectively, the coach ensures that agility is embedded in the fabric of the team's daily operations, from planning and execution to reviews and retrospectives.

Organizational Outreach: Beyond the Team

Another critical aspect is facilitating understanding and acceptance of DSDM practices beyond the development team. This often involves liaising with senior management, business stakeholders, and even external vendors to promote alignment and awareness of DSDM philosophies.

Capability Building: A Legacy of Expertise

The coach is committed to elevating the organizational competency in DSDM. This involves training sessions, mentorship programs, and ongoing support to build a reservoir of DSDM knowledge within the organization.

Responsibilities: The Day-to-Day

Knowledge Dissemination

A key daily task is the provision of expert advice and solutions, especially when the team encounters roadblocks that are not easily resolvable through standard DSDM practices.

Process Customization

Another critical responsibility is the alignment of DSDM practices with existing organizational processes or project-specific challenges, requiring a keen understanding of both DSDM and the project environment.

Team Support

Regular check-ins, observations, and direct involvement in meetings and decision-making processes enable the DSDM Coach to provide real-time guidance and conflict resolution, thus keeping the project on track.

External Communication

The role involves regular updates and communications with stakeholders outside the development team. This can range from formal reporting to informal conversations aimed at promoting a deeper understanding of DSDM methodologies.

Capability Enhancement

Ongoing education and training are part of this responsibility. The coach may organize regular workshops, webinars, or one-on-one training sessions to ensure that the team is continually improving its DSDM capabilities.

In summary, the DSDM Coach is not merely an observer but a proactive influencer, a disseminator of knowledge, and a catalyst for change. Their involvement can significantly elevate the chances of a project's success by ensuring that DSDM practices are implemented in the most effective manner possible.

Case Study: Transforming Project Outcomes through Effective DSDM Coaching

The Scenario: Introduction to the Complexity

In a large enterprise looking to shift from a traditional waterfall approach to an agile methodology, the project team opted for the DSDM framework. However, despite initial training and introduction to DSDM practices, the team struggled with implementation, notably in customizing the framework to fit the organizational context. Here is where the role of the DSDM Coach became critical.

The Approach: Methodology and Execution

Expert Knowledge

The DSDM Coach started by conducting a comprehensive audit of the current processes, understanding the gaps and mismatches between DSDM principles and existing practices. This served as a foundation for the subsequent training sessions, ensuring that they were tailored to address these specific gaps.

Methodology Adaptation

The DSDM Coach worked with the team to adapt the methodology to the organization's requirements. This involved aligning DSDM with existing project management practices and suggesting hybrid approaches where a full transition to DSDM wasn't feasible.

Team Guidance

To foster a collaborative environment, the DSDM Coach implemented daily stand-ups focused on DSDM principles, helping the team navigate challenges specific to this methodology. The coach also facilitated sprint planning meetings and retrospectives to ensure DSDM principles were thoroughly integrated into these critical processes.

Organizational Outreach

Concurrently, the DSDM Coach initiated a series of interactions with senior management and other stakeholders. These interactions aimed to align the understanding and expectations of DSDM throughout the organization. The coach also ensured that these stakeholders were kept in the loop about the progress and challenges, thereby securing continued support for the transformation.

Capability Building

The final layer involved developing a long-term capability building plan. The coach designed a curriculum and mentorship program focused on DSDM, aiming to cultivate in-house expertise that could sustain the DSDM practice long after the coach's engagement had ended.

The Outcome: Measurable Impact

As a result of these concentrated efforts, the project team saw a notable improvement in their agility, with sprint cycles becoming more efficient and project deliverables being more aligned with business objectives. Equally important, there was an organizational-wide shift towards accepting and understanding DSDM as a viable and beneficial approach for project management.

This case study serves to underscore the invaluable contribution that a DSDM Coach can bring to a project team and the broader organization. Through their specialized knowledge, practical implementation skills, and a focus on building long-term capabilities, they act as a cornerstone in any successful DSDM transition.

Unpacking the Synergy: Project Manager and Business Sponsor in Project Execution

A Framework for Success: The Essentials

The relationship between the Project Manager and the Business Sponsor is one of the linchpins in the successful delivery of a project. This dynamic duo has complementary roles, bridging the tactical and strategic dimensions of a project. While the Project Manager handles the operational intricacies, the Business Sponsor maintains the strategic lens, ensuring that the project aligns with organizational objectives. The efficacy of their collaboration determines not only the project's success but also its alignment with broader business goals.

Key Areas of Focus

Communication: The Lifeblood of Collaboration

Communication isn't just a responsibility; it's a necessity. Regular, informal, and direct communication channels should be established to enable both roles to keep each other updated. This ensures that the Business Sponsor is not blindsided by developments and that the Project Manager has the latest strategic inputs.

Issue Escalation: Mechanisms for Swift Resolution

The Business Sponsor should be prepared for escalations and should understand their role in resolving issues that are beyond the Project Manager's control. A well-defined escalation path ensures that urgent and critical matters are dealt with promptly, without bureaucratic delays.

Strategic Alignment: Keeping Objectives in Sight

A critical responsibility for both roles is ensuring strategic alignment. The project's objectives, timelines, and deliverables should be aligned from the onset, ideally documented in a Project Charter or equivalent. This will help avoid conflicts or misunderstandings down the line.

Key Responsibilities

Project Manager

Issue Management

The Project Manager needs to be adept at identifying, tracking, and resolving issues. Those that can be managed within the team should not unnecessarily escalate to the Business Sponsor, ensuring the latter can focus on strategic matters.

Stakeholder Communication

A vital function is to keep the Business Sponsor updated on project status. Regular reports, meetings, and ad-hoc communications serve this purpose, ensuring the sponsor is not only informed but also comfortable with the project's direction.

Guidance and Escalation

The Project Manager should also provide clarity to the Business Sponsor about their role in the project, including the types of issues that may require their intervention and how they can prepare for such scenarios.

Business Sponsor

Strategic Oversight

The Business Sponsor is responsible for ensuring that the project aligns with broader organizational objectives. They set the strategic direction and oversee its execution.

Issue Resolution

When escalated issues reach them, they must provide swift and decisive resolutions. This ensures the project remains on track and that strategic objectives are met.

Governance

While the Business Sponsor may participate in formal governance structures like Steering Committees, they should also remain accessible for direct communication with the Project Manager. This ensures that the latter is not inhibited by bureaucratic layers when seeking strategic guidance or resolving urgent issues.

Case Study: Navigating a Complex Project through Effective Collaboration

Context

In a large healthcare company, a project was initiated to implement a new Electronic Health Records (EHR) system. The Project Manager, Emily, and the Business Sponsor, Robert, were identified as the key players responsible for the project's success. The project was significant both in terms of investment and the impact on the company's operational efficiency and patient care.

Setting the Stage: Initial Alignment

Emily and Robert started with a kickoff meeting where they aligned on the project's objectives, timelines, and key deliverables. A Project Charter was collaboratively developed and approved, serving as a touchstone for strategic alignment.

The Communication Cadence

They established a bi-weekly update meeting, supplemented by weekly written status reports. Ad-hoc communications were also welcomed, facilitated through an open-door policy by Robert and quick response commitments by Emily.

Issue Escalation and Resolution

During the project, Emily's team ran into an issue related to data migration that couldn't be resolved at the operational level. Emily escalated the issue to Robert, who immediately convened a meeting with key stakeholders, including IT and legal advisors. A swift decision was made, allowing the project to proceed without substantial delays.

Governance and Oversight

Robert participated in quarterly Steering Committee meetings where Emily presented the project status. However, he remained accessible for direct communication with Emily, which was instrumental when the project faced critical decisions that couldn't wait for the next formal governance meeting.

Outcome

The collaboration between Emily and Robert ensured not just the successful implementation of the EHR system but also its alignment with broader strategic objectives like improving patient care and operational efficiency. Their effective communication, clear escalation paths, and mutual respect for each other's roles served as a blueprint for future projects within the company.

The case study demonstrates the vital role that the dynamic between the Project Manager and the Business Sponsor plays in the successful execution of a project. By establishing clear communication channels, setting mutual expectations, and respecting each other's domain expertise, they were able to navigate the complexities and challenges of the project successfully.

Unpacking the Symbiosis: The Project Manager and the Business Visionary in Context

The interaction between the Project Manager and the Business Visionary is pivotal in achieving project goals that align with overarching business objectives. While the Project Manager deals with operational concerns, the Business Visionary focuses on a high-level business vision. This relationship is key to navigating the project through its complexities and towards successful completion.

Areas of Concentration

Defining Roles Clearly

One of the primary steps for effective collaboration is the clear definition of roles. The Project Manager is responsible for day-to-day management of the project, including timelines and resource allocation. On the other hand, the Business Visionary is charged with articulating and maintaining the high-level business vision and objectives for the project.

Ensuring Effective Collaboration

For a project to succeed, it is imperative that the Project Manager and the Business Visionary collaborate effectively. This includes regular updates and checkpoints to ensure that the project remains aligned with the business vision. The Business Visionary must remain engaged throughout the project to provide needed guidance and make necessary adjustments.

Maintaining Ongoing Engagement

It's not sufficient for the Business Visionary to be involved only at the inception stage. Continuous engagement is crucial for making informed decisions throughout the project's lifecycle, including during critical phases such as Feasibility, Foundations, and Evolutionary Development.

Key Responsibilities

For the Project Manager

Project Oversight

Manages the daily logistics, ensuring that tasks are completed on schedule and within resource limitations.

Stakeholder Relationship Management

Builds and sustains a collaborative relationship with the Business Visionary, making sure they are involved and aligned throughout the project.

Cross-Functional Coordination

Synchronizes with the Business Visionary, especially during crucial phases like End of Timebox reviews, to ensure that operational and strategic visions are in harmony.

For the Business Visionary

Vision Conception and Communication

Articulates the overarching business vision, ensuring that it guides project decisions.

Influential Decision-Making

Shapes the project's business case and the prioritization of high-level requirements.

Sustained Engagement

Remains an active participant in the project from start to finish, influencing critical decision-making junctures and verifying that the project aligns with its original vision.

Case Study: Aligning the Project Manager and Business Visionary for Strategic Success

Setting the Scene

Let's consider a hypothetical scenario involving the launch of a new digital product by a technology company. The Project Manager, Alice, is an experienced professional who excels in operational details, and the Business Visionary, Bob, is a senior executive with a broad understanding of market trends and business objectives. They are both part of a larger team that includes developers, designers, and other stakeholders.

Key Challenges

Communication Gaps

Initially, Alice and Bob face communication challenges. While Alice is engrossed in the daily project activities, Bob feels disconnected, not knowing the project's ongoing status and unable to align it with his strategic vision.

Lack of Synchronicity

During the first project phase, the team realizes that the project's direction slightly diverges from the original vision. This necessitates a realignment meeting, which reveals that the roles and responsibilities weren't clearly defined from the start.

Implementing Solutions

Establishing Regular Updates

Alice initiates a bi-weekly meeting with Bob to update him on the project's progress and to solicit his high-level guidance. This helps Bob remain engaged and offer timely strategic input.

Defining Clear Roles and Responsibilities

To prevent future divergences, they decide to clarify their roles and decision-making authority. Alice will continue to manage the operational aspects, whereas Bob will take on a more active role in providing strategic direction and intervening at critical milestones.

Enabling Effective Collaboration

With these steps, Alice and Bob build a relationship based on mutual respect and understanding. Their roles now clearly defined and synchronized, the team can move more efficiently towards achieving its objectives.

Results and Takeaways

The project successfully launches and receives positive market feedback. Both Alice and Bob attribute this success to their collaborative efforts and the clear division of roles. By working closely and maintaining open lines of communication, they were able to align operational efficiency with strategic vision, creating a win-win outcome for all involved.

The lesson here is clear: a well-defined relationship between the Project Manager and the Business Visionary is crucial for project success. By understanding and respecting each other's roles, establishing effective communication channels, and collaborating effectively, they can navigate the project through its complexities and towards successful completion.

Unpacking the Synergy Between the Project Manager and Technical Coordinator

Understanding the Dynamic

The relationship between the Project Manager and the Technical Coordinator is a crucial one in balancing the project's technical quality with its managerial effectiveness. Each role brings a unique set of skills and responsibilities to the project, necessitating seamless collaboration for optimal outcomes.

Importance of Role Clarity

The Project Manager

The Project Manager is essentially the project's orchestrator, focusing on timelines, resources, and risk mitigation. They work closely with various stakeholders and team members to keep the project on track, ensuring that objectives are met within the defined scope, time, and cost constraints.

The Technical Coordinator

The Technical Coordinator, in contrast, has the duty of ensuring that the technical aspects of the project meet quality standards. This role oversees the architectural framework and verifies that the project aligns with industry standards and best practices, focusing on the technical soundness of the delivered solution.

Collaboration as the Cornerstone

For a project to succeed, the Project Manager and Technical Coordinator must actively collaborate. Open and regular communication between the two roles is vital. This dialogue often covers resource availability for technical tasks, potential risks in technology choices, or the alignment of technical objectives with the overall project goals. Their collaboration ensures that the project is not only managed effectively but also achieves the desired technical excellence.

Ongoing Engagement: A Crucial Element

The Technical Coordinator should be fully integrated into the project's life cycle. Their insights are particularly important during the Feasibility and Foundations phases, where key technical decisions are made that could have long-lasting impacts on the project.

Responsibilities in Detail

Project Manager

Project Oversight: They are the go-to person for understanding the project's status and are accountable for its overall health.

Stakeholder Engagement: Building and maintaining relationships with stakeholders, including the Technical Coordinator, is crucial.

Communication: Acts as the communication bridge between the technical and non-technical teams, thereby ensuring that everyone is aligned.

Technical Coordinator

Technical Oversight: Sets the technical tone for the project, ensuring that the architecture and technical plans are robust.

Quality Assurance: Oversees all technical activities to ensure they meet the defined quality standards.

Methodological Guidance: Works closely with the Solution Development Team to decide upon the best technical methodologies to employ.

In summary, the Project Manager and Technical Coordinator have distinct but complementary roles. Their effective collaboration ensures that the project achieves both managerial and technical success. Would you like to hear a case study or practical example to further elaborate on this topic?

Case Study: Achieving Project Success Through Cohesive Collaboration

In a large-scale software development project for a financial institution, the roles of the Project Manager and the Technical Coordinator were crucial in navigating the complexities of both management and technical domains. The project involved the development of a new customer relationship management (CRM) system that had to comply with stringent security and data integrity regulations.

The Challenge

One of the main challenges was ensuring that the CRM system was both user-friendly and compliant with financial industry standards. The Project Manager had to ensure the project stayed on schedule and within budget, while the Technical Coordinator had to ensure that the system met all technical compliance requirements. The stakes were high, as failure in either domain could result in costly delays or potential regulatory violations.

Collaboration and Decision-Making

The Project Manager

Responsible for managing resources and timelines, the Project Manager held regular update meetings with stakeholders, including the Technical Coordinator. They meticulously tracked the project's progress against milestones and coordinated with various departments to ensure that all resources were adequately allocated.

The Technical Coordinator

The Technical Coordinator was deeply involved in the technical architecture of the CRM system. They worked closely with the development team to make sure that all security protocols were flawlessly integrated into the system. Additionally, they consulted with external regulatory experts to confirm that the project was in compliance with industry standards.

Ongoing Engagement and Problem-Solving

At various points in the project, the Technical Coordinator flagged potential risks related to data encryption and user authentication. These were critical issues that required immediate attention. The Project Manager was swift in reallocating resources to address these technical concerns, even if it meant temporarily deprioritizing other features. This quick, collaborative decision-making helped avoid potential delays and ensured that the project remained compliant with regulations.

Outcome

Thanks to the effective collaboration between the Project Manager and the Technical Coordinator, the project was completed on time and within budget. The final product not only met all regulatory requirements but was also highly user-friendly, leading to quick adoption by the end-users.

Conclusion

This case study underscores the significance of the synergy between the Project Manager and Technical Coordinator. Their collaborative efforts and clear understanding of their respective roles were pivotal in steering the project towards success, achieving a balance between managerial effectiveness and technical excellence.

The Interplay Between the Project Manager and the Business Analyst in an Agile Setting

Overview

The relationship between the Project Manager and the Business Analyst in a project scenario is one of co-dependence and synergy. The Project Manager is tasked with overseeing the entire project, while the Business Analyst is pivotal in shaping the solution based on business requirements. The confluence of these roles can dramatically influence the project's success rate, particularly when Agile methodologies are involved.

Roles and Their Significance

Project Manager

The Project Manager bears the weight of the entire project, responsible for its planning, execution, and completion. This includes the management of timelines, resources, and overall project scope. Their role becomes especially crucial when issues arise that require immediate attention and resolution.

Business Analyst

The Business Analyst serves as a crucial liaison between the business stakeholders and the technical teams. Their primary focus is on understanding the business requirements in depth and ensuring that these are translated into functional specifications that the development team can work on. They must validate that the solution under development aligns with the intended business objectives.

Key Areas of Focus

Clarity of Roles

Ambiguity in roles can lead to confusion and decreased productivity. Both the Project Manager and the Business Analyst must have a distinct understanding of their roles, as well as the boundary that separates them.

Collaboration

Project success is not just the sum of individual efforts but also the product of effective collaboration. Frequent and transparent communication is vital for both the Project Manager and Business Analyst. This ensures that both parties are aligned and can make decisions that positively impact the project.

Agile Methodology

The application of Agile methodologies requires both roles to be flexible and adaptive. The Project Manager must ensure that Agile practices are followed rigorously, while the Business Analyst needs to adapt their techniques for gathering and documenting requirements in a manner compatible with Agile practices.

Key Responsibilities

Project Manager

Guidance

The Project Manager plays a critical role in guiding the Business Analyst, particularly when transitioning from traditional to Agile methodologies. They must ensure that Agile principles are not only understood but also practiced.

Communication

Open channels of communication must be maintained to discuss the status of the project, upcoming milestones, and any potential risks or issues.

Problem-Solving

An inevitable aspect of any project is encountering problems. The Project Manager must collaborate closely with the Business Analyst to identify and resolve issues that may otherwise derail the project.

Business Analyst

Requirements Gathering

The Business Analyst must work closely with business stakeholders to understand their needs and translate them into functional requirements.

Solution Assistance

The role involves more than just defining requirements; it also entails making sure that the development team is aligned with these requirements throughout the project lifecycle.

Agile Practices

In an Agile setting, the Business Analyst must adopt an iterative approach to requirement gathering and validation, thereby aligning themselves with the Agile principles that the project follows.

Case Study: Agile Project for a Retail E-commerce Platform

Context

A retail company aimed to develop an e-commerce platform to expand their market reach. The project's complexity was significant, involving numerous stakeholders, a broad scope, and tight deadlines. Agile methodologies were chosen to manage the project. The Project Manager and Business Analyst played crucial roles in driving the project to completion.

Challenge

The primary challenge was to develop a feature-rich e-commerce platform within a limited timeframe while accommodating frequent changes in business requirements.

Roles and Responsibilities

Project Manager

The Project Manager focused on planning sprints, assigning resources, and ensuring that Agile principles were adhered to. They maintained an open communication channel with the Business Analyst to keep aligned with changing business requirements.

Achievements

- Facilitated bi-weekly meetings to discuss project status and upcoming sprints.
- Created a risk mitigation strategy that was revisited and updated after each sprint.

Business Analyst

The Business Analyst worked closely with business stakeholders to gather detailed requirements. They adopted Agile techniques, such as user story mapping and prioritization techniques, to ensure the development team had clear directions.

Achievements

- Identified crucial business functionalities through stakeholder interviews and translated them into actionable user stories.
- Conducted validation checks at the end of each sprint to ensure alignment with business goals.

Results

The synergy between the Project Manager and Business Analyst was instrumental in the project's success. The platform was delivered within the projected timeline, meeting the stakeholder expectations in terms of functionality and quality. The efficient collaboration and clear division of responsibilities between the two roles ensured that the project adapted well to changes and overcame challenges effectively.

Conclusion

This case study exemplifies the importance of the relationship between the Project Manager and the Business Analyst, particularly in projects following Agile methodologies. Their coordinated efforts and shared understanding of their respective roles were key contributors to the successful delivery of a complex project.

The Symbiotic Partnership Between the Project Manager and Team Leader in Project Execution

The roles of the Project Manager and Team Leader are highly distinct but deeply interdependent in the broader context of project management. Understanding how these roles collaborate effectively is vital for the smooth flow and success of any project. Each role has unique responsibilities and areas of focus, but their coordination ensures that the project remains on course and achieves its objectives.

Areas of Critical Focus

Open Communication

An open and consistent channel of communication is essential. This keeps both parties abreast of ongoing developments, whether these relate to project progress, resource allocation, or roadblocks.

Balance of Power

The dynamic of empowerment versus control is a delicate balancing act. While the Team Leader is closer to the ground realities, the Project Manager holds the responsibility for overall project governance. Striking a balance ensures that the Team Leader can operate effectively without compromising high-level objectives.

Observation and Feedback

It is beneficial for the Project Manager to be a participant or observer in Timebox reviews and even Daily Stand-ups occasionally. This involvement provides the Project Manager with an intimate understanding of project health and identifies any needed strategic adjustments.

Key Responsibilities

Project Manager

High-Level Planning

Creating the roadmap and setting the strategic goals is the Project Manager's key role. They must ensure these align with stakeholder expectations and organizational strategy.

Stakeholder Management

The Project Manager's focus on stakeholder engagement keeps the project aligned with broader organizational goals and ensures the project has the required resources and support.

Observation

Participating in key meetings like Timebox reviews helps the Project Manager to gather direct insights into the project's health and the effectiveness of the Team Leader.

Team Leader

Day-to-Day Management

The Team Leader takes charge of the daily activities, ensuring they are aligned with the broader objectives set by the Project Manager.

Team Engagement

Facilitating the Solution Development Team's productivity is critical. The Team Leader acts as the conduit between the technical team and the high-level project strategy.

Reporting

Regular updates on project status, potential roadblocks, and opportunities should be provided to the Project Manager to ensure real-time adjustments can be made if required.

Case Study: Implementation of an Enterprise Resource Planning (ERP) System

Context

A multinational corporation decided to implement an ERP system to streamline its operations. The project was massive in scope, involving multiple departments across different geographies. Due to the scale, a seasoned Project Manager and multiple Team Leaders were designated for various modules of the ERP.

Challenges

The primary challenges were coordinating the diverse teams, managing the stakeholders' expectations, and ensuring timely delivery without compromising quality.

Roles and Responsibilities

Project Manager

The Project Manager was responsible for creating an overarching project plan and securing buy-in from the executive leadership. Their duties involved regular stakeholder meetings and setting high-level goals and deadlines.

Achievements

- Created a dynamic project plan that could accommodate scope changes without derailing the project.
- Conducted bi-monthly Steering Committee meetings to ensure alignment and buy-in from senior stakeholders.

Team Leaders

Team Leaders were allocated for different modules like Finance, Human Resources, and Supply Chain. They were responsible for daily operations, including problem-solving, team management, and coordinating with Business and Technical Advisors.

Achievements

- Used Agile methodologies to ensure flexible and adaptive planning.

- Maintained a daily communication channel with the Project Manager to report on progress, risks, and opportunities.

Results

The harmonious relationship between the Project Manager and Team Leaders proved invaluable. The ERP system was implemented successfully within the time frame and met all the quality and functionality standards.

Conclusion

This case study illustrates the indispensable relationship between a Project Manager and Team Leaders in managing a large-scale, complex project. Their roles, though distinct, were perfectly aligned, ensuring that the project was a success. The effective division of responsibilities and continuous, open communication were vital factors in the project's successful delivery.

The Relationship Between the Project Manager and the Solution Development Team

The Nuanced Dynamics

The relationship between a Project Manager and a Solution Development Team can be likened to that between a conductor and an orchestra. The Project Manager does not play an instrument but orchestrates the entire ensemble, making sure each part is in harmony with the others. In contrast, the Solution Development Team is the ensemble of skilled musicians responsible for executing the intricate parts of the performance.

Key Management Approaches

Management by Objective

This management approach sets the stage for an empowered team. By outlining specific objectives, the Project Manager provides direction without being overly prescriptive. The Solution Development Team takes these objectives and transforms them into actionable steps. This empowers the team to make their own decisions within the boundaries of the set objectives, thereby fostering creativity and innovation.

Management by Exception

Under this approach, the Project Manager steps in only when the team indicates that they are off track or unable to meet the objectives. This allows for real-time adjustments and course corrections, effectively combining the benefits of autonomy and oversight.

Responsibilities

Project Manager

Observation

In a modern Agile framework, the Project Manager assumes a less intrusive, more observational role. They act as a silent observer during critical sessions like Daily Stand-ups, absorbing information rather than steering conversations. This enables the team to focus on problem-solving rather than reporting, making the entire exercise more productive.

Facilitation

If the team hits a roadblock, the Project Manager's role is to facilitate resolution, whether that involves providing additional resources, removing impediments, or offering alternative perspectives.

Balancing Act

The most critical aspect of this relationship is the delicate balance between empowering the team and ensuring control. While the team needs the freedom to experiment and find the best solutions, the Project Manager needs to ensure that these efforts are aligned with the overall objectives.

Solution Development Team

Self-Management

In an Agile environment, teams are often encouraged to manage themselves. This requires a strong understanding of the project objectives, high-level of technical skills, and the maturity to manage time and priorities efficiently.

Communication

Open, honest, and frequent communication with the Project Manager is vital. This creates a feedback loop that helps both parties understand the current project state, any bottlenecks, and potential adjustments.

Conflict Resolution

Internal conflicts are almost inevitable in any project. The Solution Development Team should make an earnest effort to resolve such conflicts at their level, before escalating them. This minimizes disruptions and keeps the project on track.

Case Study: Implementation of a Customer Relationship Management (CRM) System

Context

A technology firm aimed to implement a new Customer Relationship Management (CRM) system to improve their sales process and customer service. The Project Manager and the Solution Development Team had to work closely together to ensure the successful rollout of this intricate system.

Challenge

The primary challenge was integrating the new CRM system with existing platforms while adhering to a tight schedule. There were numerous technical and business-specific requirements that had to be met.

Roles and Responsibilities

Project Manager

The Project Manager focused on high-level planning, stakeholder engagement, and alignment of the Solution Development Team with the broader project objectives. They adopted the "Management by Objective" approach, setting clear goals for each Timebox.

Achievements

- Conducted Timebox review meetings that facilitated the timely resolution of impediments.
- Managed to keep stakeholders informed and aligned, resulting in fewer last-minute changes to requirements.

Solution Development Team

The team consisted of software developers, quality analysts, and business analysts. They were primarily responsible for the actual implementation of the CRM system. The team adopted a "Self-Management" approach, empowered by the clear objectives set by the Project Manager.

Achievements

- Efficiently self-organized, leading to the successful integration of the CRM system with existing platforms.
- Adopted effective communication strategies, which enabled them to keep the Project Manager informed and to escalate issues promptly.

Results

The harmonious and balanced relationship between the Project Manager and the Solution Development Team proved to be a key factor in the project's success. The CRM system was implemented on time and met all the business-specific and technical requirements.

Conclusion

This case study illustrates the potency of a well-balanced relationship between a Project Manager and a Solution Development Team. Through clear role definitions, management by objectives, and a keen focus on responsibilities, both parties were able to synergize their efforts for successful project completion.

Deepening the Understanding of Project Manager-Stakeholder Relationship Dynamics

The relationship between the Project Manager and stakeholders is not merely transactional but is deeply interwoven into the fabric of project success. This complex relationship extends beyond status reports and milestone checks; it is central to effective risk management, stakeholder buy-in, and the overall health of the project. The quality of this relationship can often make or break a project. Therefore, understanding the dynamics, responsibilities, and principles that underpin this crucial relationship is imperative.

Core Principles Revisited

Transparency as a Trust Catalyst

Transparency is not just about disclosing facts but creating an environment where stakeholders feel comfortable questioning, clarifying, and contributing. This openness can significantly influence stakeholder trust and can make collaborative problem-solving more efficient.

The Nuances of Frequency and Formality

While adhering to pre-agreed communication intervals is important, being attuned to the need for 'just-in-time' communications is also essential. Moreover, the level of formality should be adaptable to the stakeholder's comfort and the situation at hand. Rigidity in these aspects can hamper effective communication.

The Importance of Unbiased Reporting

Fact-based reporting serves as the backbone of stakeholder communications. Project Managers should ensure that the data is both comprehensive and presented without an angle that serves a particular agenda. An unbiased narrative allows stakeholders to make informed decisions.

Expanded Responsibilities

Project Manager's Role

Facilitator, Not a Gatekeeper

The Project Manager should act as a conduit for communication, ensuring that the correct information reaches the right stakeholders. However, it's critical to note that the Project Manager should not become a gatekeeper, controlling all information flow. Such a bottleneck can lead to inefficiencies and mistrust.

Proactive Issue Identification

Besides managing issues that have been brought up, the Project Manager should proactively identify potential future issues and bring these to the attention of relevant stakeholders.

Stakeholders' Role

Constructive Engagement

Engagement is not just about attending meetings or reading reports; it involves critically evaluating information, asking questions, and providing inputs. Stakeholders should adopt a constructive engagement model to facilitate better project outcomes.

Agile Feedback Mechanisms

Instead of waiting for formal intervals to provide feedback, stakeholders should adopt a more agile approach, giving timely inputs as and when needed. This agility can often prevent minor issues from ballooning into major obstacles.

Conclusion

The relationship between the Project Manager and stakeholders is multi-faceted, governed by principles of transparency, frequency, and unbiased reporting. While the Project Manager has a pivotal role in managing this relationship, the stakeholders too have significant responsibilities. The aim is to foster a dynamic and symbiotic relationship, promoting better decision-making, effective risk management, and ultimately, successful project outcomes.

Case Study: Strengthening Project Manager-Stakeholder Relationships in an AI Implementation Project

Introduction

This case study explores an AI implementation project at a multinational corporation. The focus is on how the Project Manager, Sarah, navigated complex stakeholder relationships, facilitated effective communication, and ultimately drove the project to success.

Stakeholder Landscape

The stakeholder matrix was diverse, ranging from C-level executives to mid-level management and technical teams. Sarah identified early on that varying levels of AI understanding across stakeholders would require differentiated communication strategies.

Challenges Faced

Lack of Transparency

Sarah noticed a culture of withholding bad news, with stakeholders often providing optimistic yet misleading status updates.

Infrequent and Ineffective Communication

Although the organization had a standard monthly update cycle, crucial information often arrived too late for preventive action.

Uninformed Decisions

Due to biased reporting and lack of full disclosure, several stakeholders were making decisions based on incomplete information.

Strategies Employed

Building a Culture of Transparency

Sarah initiated open 'no-blame' forums where team members could openly discuss challenges without fear of repercussions. This shift led to quicker problem identification and resolution, thus building stakeholder trust.

Adaptive Communication Protocols

Sarah implemented a more adaptive communication plan, including bi-weekly updates and emergency 'red-flag' briefs. This plan accommodated the diverse needs of the stakeholder group, making information flow more timely and actionable.

Data-Driven Reporting

Sarah insisted on using metrics and KPIs to support all project updates. By eliminating subjective biases from reporting, stakeholders received an unambiguous picture of project status, enabling better decision-making.

Outcomes

Improved Stakeholder Engagement

The initiatives led to a more engaged and informed stakeholder community.

Faster Issue Resolution

The new communication protocols and open forums expedited the issue resolution process significantly.

Successful Project Outcome

The AI implementation was completed ahead of schedule and below budget, validating the efforts put into managing stakeholder relationships effectively.

Conclusion

The case study exemplifies that effective stakeholder management is not a 'nice-to-have' but a critical success factor. By fostering transparency, adapting communication strategies, and insisting on data-driven reporting, Project Managers can significantly improve project outcomes and stakeholder satisfaction.

Agile Project Manager's Guide to Mastering Roles and Responsibilities

Overview

The intricacies of roles and responsibilities in Agile projects are often the linchpin for the project's success or failure. Effective role definition and collaboration among team members can make the difference between a smoothly running project and one riddled with issues. Below are key tips an Agile Project Manager should consider to manage roles and responsibilities optimally.

Business Ambassador

Selection Criteria: Choose an individual who not only has the skills but also the domain knowledge to impact the quality of the solution.

Stakeholder Confidence: Ensure that the selected Business Ambassador enjoys the full confidence of the business stakeholders, especially for making crucial decisions in the Evolutionary Development phase.

Handling Multiple Roles

Dual Hatting: While it's possible for one person to serve dual roles like Visionary and Ambassador, it's not advisable for one person to be both the Business Ambassador and Business Advisor due to the distinctiveness of each role.

Single Points of Contact

Business Sponsor: Aim for one, but if multiple sponsors exist, ensure a clear escalation mechanism.

Business Visionary: Multiple visionaries often dilute the project's focus. If unavoidable due to politics, use a Steering Group to consolidate various viewpoints.

Navigating Political Complexities

Steering Group: If organizational politics necessitate multiple Visionaries, aim to designate a key Visionary and use a Steering Group to represent various interests effectively.

Utilizing DSDM Team Model

Diagrammatic Representation: Use the DSDM Team Model to clarify roles visually. Make this information transparent to all stakeholders.

Role Discussions

Alignment: Frequently discuss and realign role responsibilities to ensure everyone is on the same page about expectations.

Dual Roles for Project Managers

Role Awareness: If serving as both the Project Manager and Team Leader, remain keenly aware of which hat you're wearing at any given moment to avoid conflicts.

Solution Testers

Integration: Incorporate Solution Testers into the main team rather than isolating them into a distinct Quality Assurance unit.

Technical Coordination Team

Cross-Functional Expertise: Particularly beneficial in large, multi-team projects. Assign team members to specialize in overseeing one or more roles across all teams.

Resource Constraints

Role Combination: In resource-scarce situations, consider combining the Business Analyst and Team Leader roles, as both are essential to determining the solution's feasibility.

Case Study: Agile Role Management in a Healthcare Software Project

Context

A healthcare company embarked on an Agile project to develop a new patient management system. The project's complexity was considerable, involving multiple stakeholders, a blend of technical and healthcare expertise, and aggressive timelines. For this case, let's focus on how roles and responsibilities were managed effectively.

Challenge

The principal challenge lay in aligning the diverse stakeholders and team members to ensure efficient and quality development within the stipulated timeframe.

Roles and Responsibilities

Project Manager

The Project Manager worked tirelessly to keep everyone aligned and served as the interface between the project team and external stakeholders.

Achievements

- Conducted frequent role discussions to realign responsibilities.
- Established a Steering Group to consolidate the viewpoints of multiple Business Visionaries.

Business Ambassador

A senior healthcare consultant was chosen as the Business Ambassador due to their extensive domain knowledge and stakeholder confidence.

Achievements

- Acted as the primary point of decision-making during the Evolutionary Development phase.
- Successfully communicated healthcare regulations and best practices to the Solution Development Team.

Solution Testers

Rather than forming a separate QA team, Solution Testers were integrated into the main development team.

Achievements

- Provided immediate feedback, enabling swift iterations.
- Ensured that the solution met healthcare compliance standards.

Results

The concerted efforts and clear demarcation of roles and responsibilities led to the successful completion of the project within the designated timeline. The software met all quality and compliance requirements, winning praise from stakeholders.

Conclusion

This case study serves as a strong example of how precise management of roles and responsibilities can be a catalyst for the successful delivery of a complex Agile project. The Project Manager's proactive approach in realigning roles, setting up governance structures like the Steering Group, and encouraging team integration were key to this success.

Chapter Thirteen

Decoding the Lifecycle: A Blueprint for Project Success

Delving Deeper into DSDM Project Management Across Lifecycle Phases

A Comprehensive Guide for DSDM Project Managers

Key Takeaways

Navigating through a project lifecycle is no walk in the park, especially when employing the Dynamic Systems Development Method (DSDM). The nuances in each phase require specialized attention to deliver value and meet objectives effectively. Below are some practical considerations that a DSDM Project Manager should keep top of mind during each phase for optimized project delivery.

Pre-Project Phase

Objective

This phase sets the tone for the entire project. The primary goal is to establish the viability of the project idea and identify potential sponsorship.

Practical Consideration

Think beyond the basic introduction of the project. At this stage, you need to ensure alignment with the organization's strategic business goals. Whether you are working in an informal setting or within a larger organization, the focus should be on demonstrating the potential return on investment (ROI) and securing commitment from sponsors.

Feasibility Phase

Objective

The Feasibility Phase is your first reality check. Here, the aim is to assess the technical and business feasibility of the project.

Practical Consideration

Engage stakeholders and technical experts for high-level assessments. Cost-benefit analysis and risk evaluations should be thorough to decide whether to proceed or terminate the project early, thus avoiding resource wastage.

Foundations Phase

Objective

This phase is designed to build a strong foundation for your project, touching on business, technical, and management aspects.

Practical Consideration

You'll need to create a robust business case and clearly outline the project's scope. If feasibility is uncertain, it may be prudent to precede this phase with a formal Feasibility Phase. This step will ensure that all aspects are rigorously examined before committing to full-scale development.

Evolutionary Development Phase

Objective

The crux of your project lies in this phase, where the solution undergoes iterative development and constant improvement.

Practical Consideration

Effective timeboxing is crucial. You must align the iterations with the business case and meet the expectations of your sponsors. This phase may include multiple iterations (timeboxes), and each should bring you closer to a workable solution that aligns with your defined objectives.

Deployment Phase

Objective

Here, the developed solution is prepared for a live environment, making it crucial to focus on meticulous planning.

Practical Consideration

Your deployment plan needs to be highly detailed and must align with your overall project scope and objectives. Coordination with IT, business units, and other stakeholders is essential for a smooth transition.

Post-Project Phase

Objective

In this phase, the emphasis is on measuring the business benefits realized as compared to what was anticipated.

Practical Consideration

Metrics and Key Performance Indicators (KPIs) come into play here. You need to compare the actual impact of the solution against the projected benefits outlined in the business case. This assessment is not just for accountability but also for learning and improving future projects.

Incremental Delivery Strategies

The choice between a single increment and multiple increments usually becomes clear during the Foundations Phase. It is crucial to align this choice with the project's complexity, timelines, and stakeholder expectations.

Case Study: Implementing DSDM in a Financial Services Firm

Context

A mid-sized financial services firm aimed to overhaul its legacy customer relationship management (CRM) system. The project was complex, involving multiple departments, strict compliance requirements, and high stakeholder expectations. The DSDM framework was chosen for this agile transformation, with the Project Manager playing a pivotal role across all phases.

Pre-Project Phase

Objective

To validate the project idea and garner organizational support.

Achievement

The Project Manager initiated discussions with C-suite executives and aligned the project's goals with the firm's strategic objectives. A compelling project proposal secured sponsorship from the board.

Feasibility Phase

Objective

To assess the technical and business feasibility of replacing the legacy CRM system.

Achievement

Conducted a cost-benefit analysis and consulted with technical experts to confirm the feasibility. A 'go' decision was taken based on the risk assessment and potential ROI.

Foundations Phase

Objective

To set the groundwork for the project by developing a robust business case, scope delineation, and timelines.

Achievement

A comprehensive business case was developed, incorporating input from stakeholders across the firm. Established project scope and gained alignment from all departments.

Evolutionary Development Phase

Objective

Iterative development and improvement of the new CRM system.

Achievement

Implemented timeboxes effectively to align with the business case and meet stakeholder expectations. Each timebox concluded with a functional component that was either ready for deployment or for further iteration.

Deployment Phase

Objective

To roll out the developed CRM system into the production environment.

Achievement

A well-structured deployment plan was executed, involving coordination between IT, compliance, and business units. Successful launch with minimal disruptions.

Post-Project Phase

Objective

To measure the realized business benefits.

Achievement

Employed metrics and KPIs to evaluate the new CRM system's performance. The benefits were closely aligned with what was projected, justifying the investment and showcasing the project as a model for future endeavors.

Conclusion

This case study underlines the practical considerations a DSDM Project Manager should focus on during each lifecycle phase. Adhering to these principles contributed to the project's success, meeting both its objectives and stakeholder expectations.

Unpacking the Project Manager's Role in the DSDM Feasibility Phase

The Feasibility phase in the DSDM framework represents a critical juncture that largely dictates the future trajectory of the project. The Project Manager, often in collaboration with the Business Analyst and other key roles, focuses on several key foundation products during this phase. Understanding the nuances of these products and how they interrelate is essential for informed decision-making and effective governance.

Roles and Responsibilities of the Project Manager

Business Case Development

The Project Manager works alongside the Business Analyst and Business Sponsor to draft the preliminary business case. Here, the focus is on articulating high-level objectives, expected ROI, and alignment with organizational goals.

Scope Definition through PRL

The Project Manager assists in formulating a Prioritised Requirements List (PRL), which becomes an early indicator of the project's scope. The Business Analyst and Business Visionary are primarily involved, but the Project Manager ensures that the PRL aligns with the broader project goals and strategy.

Solution Architecture Outlining

In collaboration with the Business Analyst, Technical Coordinator, and Business Visionary, the Project Manager contributes to shaping the Solution Architecture Definition (SAD). This involves sketching out the technical aspects of the solution and its alignment with business needs.

Development Approach and Standards

The Development Approach Definition (DAD) outlines the methodological framework that will guide the development team. Here, the Project Manager and Technical Coordinator collaborate to provide a high-level overview of the working standards and approaches.

Crafting the Delivery Plan

The Project Manager takes the lead in crafting the initial delivery plan, ensuring alignment with the project's business case and stakeholder expectations. This plan outlines the project structure and is crucial for setting the stage for the Foundations phase.

Management Approach

The Management Approach Definition (MAD) is vital for setting up the governance framework for the project. The Project Manager collaborates with the Business Sponsor to decide on key management practices, ensuring they are compatible with the DSDM approach.

Feasibility Assessment and Governance

The Feasibility Assessment document becomes a key deliverable that summarizes all the above elements. It serves as the basis for decision-making by higher-ups, such as investment committees, who will decide whether the project moves to the Foundations phase.

Practical Considerations for Project Managers

Product Consideration

A discerning evaluation of which foundation products are critical for the project is vital. The Project Manager must ensure alignment with both organizational standards and project-specific demands.

Collaboration

Building a collaborative atmosphere, especially with the Business Analyst, helps in more effective scope definition, project justification, and foundational planning for the next phases.

Governance

Creating a robust Feasibility Assessment is paramount. This document is often the cornerstone for project continuation and serves as a preliminary blueprint that guides decision-makers.

Case Study: Implementing the Feasibility Phase in a DSDM Project for a Healthcare Application

Introduction

This case study outlines the roles, responsibilities, and considerations for a Project Manager during the Feasibility phase of developing a healthcare application. The project aims to provide healthcare providers with a tool to manage patient records and facilitate telehealth consultations.

Business Case Development

The Project Manager collaborated with the Business Analyst and Business Sponsor to establish the initial business case. The primary objective was to improve healthcare delivery by enabling secure and efficient management of patient records. The expected ROI included cost-savings due to reduced administrative time and increased patient satisfaction.

Scope Definition Through PRL

A Prioritized Requirements List (PRL) was established with less than 10 high-level requirements such as secure data storage, ease of use, and HIPAA compliance. The Project Manager ensured that these requirements aligned with the strategic objectives stated in the business case.

Solution Architecture Outlining

The Solution Architecture Definition (SAD) was outlined with significant contributions from the Project Manager. Given the sensitive nature of healthcare data, the architecture prioritized security and scalability.

Development Approach and Standards

The Development Approach Definition (DAD) was put together to guide the development team. It was decided that a hybrid of Scrum and DSDM would be followed. The Project Manager and Technical Coordinator collaborated to outline the development standards to ensure that they complied with healthcare regulations.

Crafting the Delivery Plan

The Project Manager drafted an initial delivery plan that broke down the project into a series of Timeboxes. This plan outlined the primary objectives for each Timebox and allocated resources accordingly.

Management Approach

A Management Approach Definition (MAD) was compiled, focusing on key issues such as data privacy, scalability, and project governance. The Project Manager and Business Sponsor reached a consensus on these fundamental considerations to ensure compatibility with DSDM principles.

Feasibility Assessment and Governance

The Feasibility Assessment document synthesized all the elements from the Business Case to the MAD. This document was then presented to the healthcare provider's investment committee, who found the project to be feasible and approved its transition to the Foundations phase.

Conclusion

Through effective collaboration, meticulous planning, and a focus on both strategic alignment and technical feasibility, the Project Manager played a pivotal role in steering the Feasibility phase towards successful completion and subsequent transition to the Foundations phase.

The Foundations Phase in Project Management

The Foundations phase in project management is a cornerstone for the entire lifecycle of the project. It is a crucial phase where the vision, scope, and operational blueprint of the project are established. It sets the stage for the smooth running of the subsequent phases and serves as a reference point for decision-making.

Key Roles and Responsibilities

Project Manager

- Leadership: Guides the team through the development of foundational documents and plans.
- Coordination: Orchestrates collaborations between various stakeholders to ensure clarity and alignment.

Business Analyst

- Requirement Gathering: Identifies and documents high-level project requirements.
- Collaboration: Works with the Business Visionary and Ambassador to refine and prioritize these requirements.

Business Sponsor

- Funding: Allocates necessary resources and funds for the project.
- Alignment: Ensures that the project aligns with broader organizational goals.

Business Visionary

- Strategy: Develops the project's overarching business vision.
- Direction: Helps set priorities based on the project's strategic importance.

Business Ambassador

- Liaison: Acts as the bridge between the business and the Solution Development Team.
- Clarification: Provides day-to-day business perspective to the team.

Technical Coordinator

- Technical Expertise: Offers guidance on the technical aspects of the project.
- Facilitation: Aids in the development of the Solution Architecture Definition and Development Approach Definition.

Solution Development Team

- Execution: Responsible for developing the solution in alignment with the Foundations phase documents.
- Feedback: Communicates any technical hurdles or changes needed to the Project Manager and Technical Coordinator.

Key Products and Their Purposes

Business Case (Recommended)

Purpose: To articulate the rationale behind the project, including the anticipated benefits and estimated development costs. It serves as an executive summary for why the project should proceed.

Prioritised Requirements List (PRL) (Mandatory)

Purpose: Provides a prioritized list of high-level requirements, offering a blueprint for what the project aims to achieve. The list follows the MoSCoW guidelines for prioritization.

Solution Architecture Definition (SAD)

Purpose: To outline the technical framework within which the solution will be developed, ensuring that both the technical and business sides understand the architecture's boundaries and possibilities.

Development Approach Definition (DAD)

Purpose: Lays down the ground rules for how the Solution Development Team will operate, including development methodologies, coding standards, and review processes.

Delivery Plan (Mandatory)

Purpose: Sketches out the timeline for the project, taking into account the resources available and the project's scope. It breaks down what will be achieved and by when.

Management Approach Definition (MAD)

Purpose: Outlines the management strategy, focusing on elements like governance structure, risk management, and communication plans.

Foundations Summary

Purpose: Serves as an executive summary of the Foundations phase, encapsulating all the key documents, decisions, and plans into a cohesive overview for quick reference.

Conclusion

The Foundations phase is instrumental in setting the tone and direction for the entire project. It demands collaborative effort from all key stakeholders and requires the Project Manager to exhibit excellent leadership, coordination, and communication skills.

Case Study: Foundations Phase in a Software Development Project

Background

In a mid-sized software company, a new project was initiated to develop a Customer Relationship Management (CRM) system. The Foundations phase was led by a seasoned Project Manager, Sarah, who had successfully managed multiple projects within the organization.

Key Roles and Their Contributions

Project Manager: Sarah

- Created a comprehensive Delivery Plan and aligned it with the business goals.
- Collaborated with Business Analysts to form the Prioritised Requirements List.

Business Analyst: Mark

- Conducted stakeholder interviews and gathered high-level requirements.
- Worked on drafting the Business Case alongside Sarah.

Business Sponsor: Emily

- Approved initial funding for the Feasibility phase and committed to future allocations based on the Business Case.

Business Visionary: Raj

- Provided strategic direction for the CRM system, ensuring it aligned with the company's long-term growth plan.

Technical Coordinator: Alan

- Contributed to the Solution Architecture Definition (SAD), outlining the technical components needed for the CRM system.

Key Products Developed

Business Case

- Highlighted the expected ROI and impact on customer engagement.

Prioritised Requirements List (PRL)

- Utilized MoSCoW guidelines to prioritize features like data analytics, user interface design, and integration with existing systems.

Solution Architecture Definition (SAD)

- Described the technical architecture, specifying that the project would be developed on a microservices architecture.

Delivery Plan

- Laid out a 12-month timeline, divided into four quarters, each with specific deliverables and milestones.

Management Approach Definition (MAD)

- Included a risk management strategy and defined key performance indicators for project assessment.

Outcomes

Upon completion of the Foundations phase, the project had a well-defined roadmap, clear objectives, and full buy-in from key stakeholders. The team proceeded to the next phases with clarity and a shared understanding of the project's purpose and scope.

Lessons Learned

- Early collaboration among key roles is crucial for aligning different perspectives.
- A well-articulated Business Case can significantly ease the process of securing funds and resources.
- Prioritized requirements serve as a vital guide in later stages, ensuring the project remains focused and aligned with the business needs.

The Foundations phase was instrumental in aligning the project team and key stakeholders, setting the stage for a successful project.

Foundations and Evolutionary Development Phases in Agile Project Management

Foundations Phase: A Closer Look

The Foundations Phase serves as the critical groundwork for agile projects, ensuring that the project is planned, resourced, and prepared effectively for upcoming phases. The primary objective of this phase is to provide a comprehensive understanding of the project's requirements, limitations, and potential.

Functions and Objectives

Alignment with Business Goals: Ensuring that the project is in sync with organizational objectives is paramount. It not only validates the project's importance but also helps in obtaining executive buy-in.

Resource Planning: This phase allows the Project Manager to outline required resources, thus ensuring that manpower and materials are optimally utilized.

Risk Assessment: Identifying potential risks early in the project enables better planning and preventive measures.

Key Products: Importance and Application

Business Case: This document offers a snapshot of the expected benefits, costs, and risks, providing a baseline for measuring the project's performance and value.

Prioritised Requirements List (PRL): Using MoSCoW guidelines ensures that essential features are prioritized, creating a focused pathway for development.

Solution Architecture Definition (SAD): This outlines the technical environment, systems, and architecture, providing a roadmap for the development team.

Delivery Plan: It serves as a high-level timetable that guides the project team throughout the timeline, specifying what needs to be accomplished during each stage.

Evolutionary Development Phase: What to Expect

The Evolutionary Development Phase is where the solution or product comes to life through iterative cycles. It's the backbone of Agile methodology and is guided by the principle of incremental progress, allowing for regular assessment and adaptation.

Key Aspects

Iterative Development: This phase adopts an iterative approach, allowing for frequent modifications and refinements.

User Feedback: Active user participation is encouraged to ensure that the solution aligns with real-world requirements.

Quality Assurance: Continuous testing is integrated into the development process to maintain high quality and reliability of the product.

Role of the Project Manager

The Project Manager's role in the Evolutionary Development Phase is to ensure that the team remains focused on delivering value. They achieve this by:

Monitoring Progress: Tracking key performance indicators to ensure alignment with project goals.

Resource Allocation: Distributing tasks and responsibilities according to the team's skills and project requirements.

Risk Management: Identifying and addressing any potential setbacks or obstacles in real-time.

By understanding the distinct characteristics and requirements of the Foundations and Evolutionary Development phases, Project Managers can better navigate the complexities of agile projects, leading to more effective and efficient outcomes.

Case Study: Implementing Foundations and Evolutionary Development Phases in a Fintech Project

Context and Background

A fintech company aimed to launch a new mobile payment system. To ensure the project's success, they decided to adopt Agile methodology, focusing on the Foundations and Evolutionary Development phases.

Foundations Phase: Approach and Outcomes

Key Products Created

Business Case: Crafted to gain executive buy-in, it outlined the benefits of capturing a growing market for mobile payments.

Prioritised Requirements List (PRL): Developed collaboratively with business analysts, it focused on essential features like security, user experience, and speed.

Solution Architecture Definition (SAD): Provided a clear roadmap for the development team, detailing the tech stack to be used.

Challenges and Solutions

Resource Allocation: Initially, there was a struggle to secure adequate resources. The comprehensive Business Case helped garner the necessary support.

High-Priority Requirements: The PRL underwent several iterations as stakeholders contributed feedback, but a finalized version was agreed upon within the timeline.

Evolutionary Development Phase: Approach and Outcomes

Iterative Development

Cycle Length: Each development cycle lasted two weeks, culminating in a viable product increment.

Feedback Loops: After each cycle, user testing was conducted, and feedback was integrated into the next cycle.

Role of the Project Manager

Ensuring Alignment: The Project Manager kept the team aligned with the project goals through regular stand-up meetings.

Risk Mitigation: Proactively addressed risks such as security concerns and potential delays.

Results and Lessons Learned

The fintech project was successfully launched, receiving positive user feedback, particularly regarding its user-friendly design and secure transactions. Some key takeaways included the importance of thorough planning in the Foundations Phase and the need for flexibility and adaptability during the Evolutionary Development Phase.

The case study exemplifies how effective management of the Foundations and Evolutionary Development phases can lead to a successful Agile project. It also highlights the pivotal role played by the Project Manager in steering the project through its various phases.

The Significance of the Deployment Phase in Agile Project Management

The Deployment Phase is not merely a concluding act in Agile project management, but a vital stage that determines how well the solution integrates with the business and delivers its intended benefits. A meticulously planned and executed Deployment Phase can be the difference between a project that delivers value and one that falls short of expectations.

Key Activities and Their Importance

Coordination of Deployment Activities

A seamless transition into the live environment is critical for project success. Ensuring proper coordination involves numerous tasks such as final testing, documentation, and ensuring that the deployment plan is compatible with the existing IT environment.

Increment Retrospective

Reflecting on what worked well and what didn't is crucial for continuous improvement. This activity provides a platform for the team to discuss the challenges faced and the opportunities for improvement, which could be implemented in future phases or projects.

Project Review Report

This document encapsulates the key achievements and challenges of the project increment. It serves as a record for stakeholders and can be used for auditing purposes or as a point of reference for future projects.

Review and Governance Checkpoint

This activity allows the team to make critical decisions about the next steps. Based on the project review and the delivered value, the team can decide whether to move forward with a new increment, go back to revise the Foundations Phase, or close the project.

Key Products in Deployment Phase and Their Components

Project Review Report

First Element: Project Increment Assessment

This part of the report focuses on evaluating what was achieved compared to what was planned. It's a factual analysis that serves as a performance review for the project increment.

Second Element: Business Value Assessment

Measuring the business value realized is critical in judging the project's overall success. This section should explicitly link the achieved benefits with the initial objectives outlined in the Business Case, providing a clear view of the return on investment.

Conclusion

The Deployment Phase in Agile project management plays an instrumental role in determining the project's overall success and its alignment with business objectives. Adhering to well-structured activities and producing key deliverables during this phase ensures that the project concludes on a positive note, delivering tangible value to the business.

Delving Deeper: A Case Study Illustrating the Deployment Phase in Agile Project Management

Case Study Context

A leading e-commerce company decided to upgrade its customer recommendation algorithm. The project followed an Agile methodology and reached the Deployment Phase after several iterations in the Evolutionary Development Phase. The focus here is to explore how key activities and products in the Deployment Phase contributed to the project's success.

Key Activities Undertaken

Coordination of Deployment Activities

The project manager collaborated with the DevOps team to ensure the new algorithm was smoothly integrated into the existing system. A deployment schedule was shared with stakeholders to avoid any downtime during peak business hours.

Increment Retrospective

A meeting was organized involving the Project Manager, Business Visionary, Technical Coordinator, and the Solution Development Team. The discussion revolved around the effectiveness of the new algorithm, the challenges encountered during its development and deployment, and the potential areas for improvement.

Project Review Report

A comprehensive Project Review Report was prepared, capturing both the accomplishments and setbacks.

Review and Governance Checkpoint

The Project Manager presented the Project Review Report to senior management. After a thorough discussion, it was agreed that the algorithm had significantly improved customer engagement metrics and that the project would proceed to the Post-Project Phase for benefit realization tracking.

Key Products Generated

Project Review Report

First Element: Project Increment Assessment

The report included an in-depth analysis of development speed, defect rates, and stakeholder satisfaction, demonstrating a favorable outcome on all counts.

Second Element: Business Value Assessment

The report explicitly linked the rise in customer engagement metrics to the objectives outlined in the Business Case, thereby showcasing a positive return on investment.

Lessons Learned

- Early engagement with operational teams can significantly ease the deployment process.
- Conducting a retrospective helps in identifying invaluable insights for future projects.
- The Project Review Report serves as both a performance metric and a tool for internal communication.

Conclusion

The Deployment Phase was executed meticulously, aligning the technical aspects perfectly with business objectives. The key activities and products were pivotal in ensuring that the project was not only completed successfully but also brought measurable business value.

Chapter Fourteen

MoSCoW and Timeboxing: Twin Pillars of Agile Project Management

The Synergistic Relationship of MoSCoW Prioritization and Timeboxing in DSDM

Understanding the inherent relationship between MoSCoW Prioritization and Timeboxing is key to leveraging the full potential of the Dynamic Systems Development Method (DSDM) Agile framework. These practices offer a structured yet flexible approach to project management, addressing some of the most common pitfalls, such as scope creep and missed deadlines.

MoSCoW Prioritization: Setting the Course

Objective

The MoSCoW method serves as a critical tool for priority setting. It categorizes tasks into four groups: Must-Have, Should-Have, Could-Have, and Won't-Have This Time. By assigning each task to one of these categories, stakeholders can establish a common understanding of what is non-negotiable versus what can be deferred or omitted.

Essential Benefits

Streamlined Communication: It aids in setting clear, universally understood expectations among all stakeholders.

Risk Mitigation: This method provides a cushion against unpredictability by designating which tasks can be dropped if necessary.

Focused Resource Allocation: By highlighting the Must-Have tasks, MoSCoW ensures that the most critical aspects of a project receive the necessary attention and resources.

Timeboxing: Driving the Pace

Objective

Timeboxing serves as a catalyst for productivity by allocating specific timeframes to tasks or groups of tasks. This method acts as a countermeasure to scope creep and procrastination, ensuring that the project maintains its pace.

Essential Benefits

Deadline Commitment: It instills a discipline that keeps the team accountable for timelines.

Resource Optimization: Timeboxing restricts the time allocated to each task, pushing for more efficient work without the need for endless fine-tuning.

Incremental Progress: The use of timeboxes encourages consistent, incremental progress toward project completion.

Synergistic Application

When MoSCoW and Timeboxing are combined, they form a powerful synergy that enhances project management in the following ways:

Aligning Priorities and Time: Must-Have tasks become the focus of each timebox, creating a sense of urgency and ensuring critical project elements are completed as planned.

Adaptive Resource Allocation: Timeboxing offers the flexibility to reallocate resources effectively when priorities change.

Strategic Execution: Both methods offer a structured approach that keeps the project aligned with overarching business goals and timelines.

Conclusion

The DSDM framework gains robustness through the integration of MoSCoW prioritization and Timeboxing. Their symbiotic relationship helps to guide projects with a balanced combination of discipline and flexibility, setting the stage for timely delivery without compromising on the quality or scope of deliverables.

A Case Study Illustration: MoSCoW Prioritization and Timeboxing in a Digital Transformation Project

Introduction

In a hypothetical Digital Transformation project for a retail business, the objective is to upgrade the existing point-of-sale (POS) system across 100 stores within a fixed three-month timeline. This project exemplifies the strategic employment of MoSCoW Prioritization and Timeboxing within the DSDM framework.

Utilizing MoSCoW Prioritization

Objective

To segregate tasks into clear priority categories, ensuring that core functionalities and features are not compromised.

Implementation

Must-Have: Complete integration with existing inventory system, basic sales transaction features.

Should-Have: Features like discounts and loyalty points, high-speed processing.

Could-Have: Interface customization, multi-language support.

Won't-Have This Time: Advanced analytics reporting, mobile application support.

Employing Timeboxing

Objective

To split the three-month period into bi-weekly timeboxes that can accommodate the segregated tasks.

Implementation

- Timebox 1: Complete the system design and begin coding for Must-Have features.
- Timebox 2: Finish coding for Must-Have and Should-Have features.
- Timebox 3: Testing and debugging.
- Timebox 4: User training and Could-Have features.
- Timebox 5: Rollout to pilot stores.
- Timebox 6: Full deployment and final reviews.

Synergistic Application: MoSCoW Meets Timeboxing

Timebox Re-evaluation: After Timebox 2, the team realized that the loyalty points feature (a Should-Have) would need more time. It was moved to Timebox 4, while one of the Could-Have features (multi-language support) was deferred to a later project phase.

Adaptive Planning: Timebox 3 revealed that debugging took less time than expected, allowing the team to integrate interface customization, a Could-Have feature initially planned for Timebox 4.

Outcome

The project was completed within the stipulated three-month period, delivering all Must-Have and Should-Have features. Two of the Could-Have features were also integrated thanks to efficient resource allocation and effective use of time. The team managed to adhere to the project timeline while ensuring that all critical functionalities were in place, validating the efficacy of using MoSCoW Prioritization and Timeboxing in tandem.

Conclusion

The case study demonstrates how MoSCoW Prioritization and Timeboxing can be synergistically applied within the DSDM framework to navigate the complexities and constraints of a real-world project effectively. This strategic amalgamation contributes to optimal resource utilization, timeline adherence, and ultimately, project success.

Advanced Strategies for Priority Management in DSDM: Risk, Effort, and Contingency Factors

Managing priorities is a crucial component of the DSDM (Dynamic Systems Development Method) Agile Framework. When utilizing the MoSCoW prioritization model, the challenge goes beyond merely categorizing tasks. The objective extends to wisely allocating effort across these categories in a manner that optimally balances risk and contingency, while ensuring maximum value delivery.

DSDM's Guiding Principles for Priority Management

Must-Have Effort Allocation

DSDM advocates dedicating no more than 60% of the total project effort to 'Must-Have' tasks. This allows organizations to set boundaries around their core requirements, leaving room for adjustments, unforeseen challenges, and potential value-added elements.

Could-Have Effort Allocation

DSDM recommends setting aside approximately 20% of the project effort for 'Could-Have' tasks. This bucket acts as a contingency reserve, enabling project teams to flexibly address issues while keeping the spotlight on essential objectives.

Critical Aspects for Efficient Priority Balancing

Context-Specific Risk Assessment

The balance between priority categories can be influenced by each project's unique risk profile. For high-risk projects or those characterized by significant uncertainty, a more conservative approach may be appropriate, potentially devoting less than the standard 60% of effort to 'Must-Have' items.

Team Expertise and Project Environment

The experience level of the team, along with a well-understood work environment, can allow for deviations from DSDM's standard recommendations. If the team's past performance indicates reliable estimating practices, it may be viable to allocate a slightly higher percentage of effort to 'Must-Have' tasks without incurring significant risk.

Commitment to Transparency

One of the intrinsic virtues of Agile methodologies is their transparency. Keeping all stakeholders abreast of planned work, associated efforts, and progress ensures that there is minimal risk of veering off course after the 'Must-Have' tasks are completed.

Opportunities for Value Enhancement

In certain scenarios, the effort needed for 'Must-Have' tasks might substantially fall below the 60% mark. This excess capacity could be capitalized on by the organization to increase the scope of 'Should-Have' tasks, thereby amplifying the value delivered by the project.

Conclusion

Balancing priorities within the DSDM framework entails more than simply categorizing tasks into different buckets. It requires a nuanced approach to allocate effort effectively across these categories while mitigating risk and enabling contingencies. These practices ultimately contribute to a project's success by ensuring a more strategic focus and better utilization of resources.

Case Study: Effective Priority Management in a Software Development Project Using DSDM

Background

A software development company embarks on a mission-critical project to build an application for a financial institution. Given the complexity of the project and the need for rapid delivery, the team chooses to employ the DSDM framework. They adopt MoSCoW prioritization to manage tasks and decide on a 6-month timeframe for the project.

Initial Task Breakdown

Must-Have Tasks

- Core functionalities such as user authentication, transaction processing, and data security.
- Compliance with financial regulations.

Should-Have Tasks

- Additional features like financial analytics and reporting.

Could-Have Tasks

- User interface enhancements and additional customization options.

Priority Balancing Strategy

Risk Evaluation

The team recognizes that they are entering a highly regulated space where mistakes can have significant consequences. Therefore, they opt for a more conservative approach and allocate only 55% of the project effort to 'Must-Have' tasks.

Team Skillsets

The project team is a seasoned group of professionals with extensive experience in financial software development. Due to this, they are comfortable allowing for a slightly higher percentage of effort—25%—to 'Should-Have' tasks.

Transparency Mechanism

The team utilizes Agile project management tools to keep stakeholders updated on task progress and effort allocation, thereby ensuring clarity and reducing the risk of scope creep.

Opportunity for Value Add-Ons

After completing 50% of the project timeline, the team finds that the 'Must-Have' tasks are well ahead of schedule. They utilize the extra capacity to add more 'Should-Have' features, significantly increasing the project's value without affecting the initial timeline.

Outcomes

- All 'Must-Have' and 'Should-Have' tasks were successfully completed.
- 15% of 'Could-Have' tasks were also achieved, owing to efficient priority management.

- The project was delivered on time and within budget, and it met all compliance standards.

Lessons Learned

- A conservative approach in allocating effort to 'Must-Have' tasks provided the leeway needed to manage uncertainties and add more features.
- The experienced team was able to manage their time effectively, thereby allowing for an expanded scope without additional risk.
- Transparency played a pivotal role in maintaining stakeholder trust and keeping the project on track.

This case study demonstrates how a nuanced approach to priority management within the DSDM framework can lead to successful project outcomes. It underscores the importance of balancing risk, effort, and contingency factors while maintaining focus on delivering maximum value.

MoSCoW in DSDM: A Dynamic Process of Planning, Execution, and Review

The Role of Collaboration in the Planning Phase

Planning within the DSDM framework isn't a solitary endeavor but a collaborative process, requiring the input of a variety of stakeholders. Each role has specific contributions:

Business Roles: Focus on ensuring that priorities are in line with actual business needs.

Solution/Technical Roles: Validate the technical feasibility and efficiency of the plans.

Business Analyst: Acts as the bridge between the technical and business aspects of the project.

Project Manager: Takes into account risk factors to ascertain that the priorities are balanced appropriately.

Priority Agreement: A Crucial Stage-Setter

One of the fundamental steps in MoSCoW prioritization within DSDM is to reach a consensus on the classification of tasks, especially concerning 'Should-Have' and 'Could-Have' priorities. Having a clearly defined set of criteria helps in this regard. The criteria should be objective and should be a collective decision involving all stakeholders to prevent future disagreements.

Timebox Execution: Ground-Level Priority Management

When it comes to the actual implementation during Timeboxes, the reins primarily lie with the Solution Development Team. They are responsible for formulating realistic plans and estimates for each Timebox. The Project Manager plays a more observational role, scrutinizing the plans to ensure that:

- Priorities are well-balanced.
- All significant risks have been factored in.
- Team members take ownership of their estimates.

The Importance of Continuous Review

Static plans are anathema to Agile methodologies like DSDM. Priorities should be reviewed and adapted as the project progresses. Any change in requirements, whether an addition or an unexpected complication in existing requirements, should trigger a re-evaluation of priorities. The essence is to keep the 'Must-Have' effort within the limits agreed upon at the project outset.

Case Study: Implementing MoSCoW in DSDM for a Software Upgrade Project

Context and Objectives

Consider a hypothetical scenario where a financial institution is planning to upgrade its core banking software. The project is run under the DSDM framework, aiming to enhance speed, efficiency, and user experience. With a strict deadline, the project leans heavily on MoSCoW prioritization to identify and deliver the most critical features within the allotted time.

Collaborative Planning: Assembling the Team

The Business Roles in this scenario include C-suite executives, who define high-level business needs. Technical Roles involve the IT department and external consultants, who ensure technical feasibility. A Business Analyst connects both realms, and a Project Manager oversees risk and ensures that priorities align with the project's goals.

Setting Priority Criteria: Agreeing on What Matters

The criteria for 'Should-Have' and 'Could-Have' are set collaboratively. For instance, it's agreed that features affecting transaction speed are 'Should-Have,' while UI enhancements are categorized as 'Could-Have.'

Timebox Execution: Sprint-Level Prioritization

During the sprint planning, the Solution Development Team identifies that they can implement two 'Should-Have' features and four 'Could-Have' features within the next sprint. The Project Manager reviews these allocations, ensuring risks are well-distributed and the sprint's priorities align with the overarching project goals.

Continuous Re-Prioritization: Addressing the Unexpected

Midway through the project, a security vulnerability is discovered that requires immediate attention. The team collectively agrees to move this to 'Must-Have.' To accommodate this new priority, a 'Could-Have' feature aimed at UI enhancements is moved to a future sprint.

Conclusion

By adhering to MoSCoW principles in a disciplined yet flexible manner, the financial institution can focus on the most vital aspects of the software upgrade, while also leaving room for unexpected changes and improvements. The clear framework of MoSCoW ensures that despite challenges, the project stays aligned with its initial objectives and time constraints.

MoSCoW in DSDM: A Framework for Managing Business Expectations

The Role of Minimum Usable SubseT (MUST) in Setting Expectations

The concept of Minimum Usable SubseT plays a pivotal role in DSDM projects. By allocating around 60% of the project's effort to the "Must-Have" tasks, DSDM establishes a robust foundation for project delivery. This methodology ensures the delivery of core functionalities while providing a buffer zone for "Should-Have" and "Could-Have" tasks. This strategy provides a level of comfort and reliability among stakeholders.

Strategic Benefits of Aligned Business Expectations

The MoSCoW method allows for a more strategic and predictable alignment with business objectives. When stakeholders know that the Must-Haves are securely within reach, and that the Should-Haves and Could-Haves are also likely to be accomplished, it creates a harmonious relationship between the project team and the business stakeholders.

Safeguard Mechanisms for Priority Requirements

By dedicating approximately 20% of the project's effort to Could-Have tasks, DSDM inherently builds in a safeguard against undermining the Must-Have and Should-Have tasks. This cushion allows for more secure planning and delivery, ensuring that resources aren't overextended.

The Downfall of Over-Promising

A common pitfall in project management is the tendency to over-promise. Promising the delivery of all Must-Have, Should-Have, and Could-Have tasks often leads to inflated estimates and ultimately, disappointment. A reasonable approach to estimates is crucial for maintaining credibility and fulfilling stakeholder expectations.

Impact on Project Quality and Predictability

The well-calibrated balance of task prioritization in conjunction with timeboxing contributes to the overall predictability and quality of the project. This disciplined approach avoids the pitfalls of rushed development or scope creep, leading to a more consistent and high-quality output.

Utilizing Metrics for Continuous Improvement

Employing metrics that track the completion rates of Should-Have and Could-Have tasks across timeboxes or Project Increments can serve as a diagnostic tool. These metrics offer real-time insights into the project's health, either reaffirming that the project is on track or signaling potential risks that may need to be addressed.

Case Study: Implementing MoSCoW for Business Expectation Management in a DSDM Project

Setting the Scene: The Project at Hand

An organization was struggling with the delivery of its flagship software product. Deadlines were missed, stakeholders were frustrated, and the quality was not up to par. The decision was made to switch to the DSDM framework, with a strong emphasis on using the MoSCoW method for prioritization.

Implementation of Minimum Usable SubseT (MUST)

The first step was to clearly define what constituted the Minimum Usable SubseT of features that the project must deliver. These were agreed upon with stakeholders and constituted about 60% of the total project effort. This immediately relieved some pressure from the development team and set clear expectations with stakeholders.

Stakeholder Alignment and Business Expectations

Once the Must-Haves were agreed upon and locked in, stakeholders had a much clearer idea of what to expect. This fostered an environment of trust and aligned the team's efforts with business objectives. It also provided room to negotiate Should-Haves and Could-Haves, making the most out of the remaining 40% of the project effort.

Safeguarding Critical Features

The Could-Have tasks were carefully chosen to serve as a buffer. This strategic reserve ensured that any unexpected delays or problems would not affect the delivery of Must-Have and Should-Have features.

The Importance of Realistic Estimates

The team was careful not to over-promise. This was crucial for maintaining the integrity of the project plan and for avoiding stakeholder disappointment down the line. Estimates were regularly reviewed and adjusted as needed, maintaining a dynamic and adaptive planning process.

Quality and Predictability

The disciplined approach of MoSCoW prioritization, coupled with timeboxing, led to more predictable deliveries and higher quality. Stakeholders were pleasantly surprised by the consistency and began to have renewed faith in the development team.

Utilizing Metrics for Insight

Metrics were employed to monitor the proportion of Should-Have and Could-Have tasks being completed. This not only provided a constant pulse check on the project's health but also offered early warning signs when things were not going as planned, allowing for timely corrective actions.

This case study illustrates the powerful impact of using MoSCoW for business expectation management within the DSDM framework. The methodology provided a structured, disciplined approach that significantly improved project outcomes and stakeholder satisfaction.

Aligning MoSCoW Prioritization with Business Vision: A Deep Dive

Understanding the Congruence Between MoSCoW and Business Vision

The Business Visionary is often situated at the intersection of business strategy and project execution. The MoSCoW prioritization method serves as an invaluable tool to bring these two worlds into harmony. When used skillfully, MoSCoW aligns each task or feature's relative importance with the overarching business goals outlined in the vision and Business Case. This ensures a high level of congruence between the day-to-day work of the project team and the strategic imperatives of the organization.

The Multi-Faceted Role of the Business Visionary

Expert Prioritization

The Business Visionary, commonly the Business Sponsor, assumes the critical role of aligning the project's scope and objectives with the business vision. This involves a thorough application of the MoSCoW method to determine which tasks or features are essential ('Must Haves'), beneficial ('Should Haves'), optional ('Could Haves'), or out of scope ('Won't Haves') for the current project cycle.

Impactful Evaluation

The prioritization exercise extends beyond merely ranking tasks; it also entails assessing the business value and potential ROI of each requirement. The Business Visionary employs various metrics and qualitative assessments to ensure that the 'Must Haves' directly contribute to the ROI expected from the project.

Rigorous Delivery Oversight

The Business Visionary is not merely a spectator after the planning phase but is deeply involved in the project's execution. They work closely with the project manager and other key stakeholders to track progress. This oversight is facilitated by metrics and Key Performance Indicators (KPIs), which serve as quantifiable measures of how well the project is fulfilling the business vision. The Business Visionary uses these KPIs to make informed decisions about resource allocation and to identify any required course corrections.

The Synergy between MoSCoW and Business Vision

The strategic use of the MoSCoW method ensures that the project delivers not just a product but a product that is closely aligned with the business vision.

The Business Visionary uses MoSCoW as a dynamic tool, not a one-time checklist. It's a living part of the project, revisited and adjusted as necessary to adapt to any changes in organizational objectives or market conditions. This dynamic approach ensures that the project remains agile and responsive, delivering maximum business value at every stage.

Case Study: Leveraging MoSCoW Prioritization to Drive Business Vision

Context and Challenge

A global technology company embarks on a project to develop a next-generation customer relationship management (CRM) system. The Business Visionary is faced with numerous competing demands: features that sales teams want, functionalities that the marketing department has requested, and essential compliance features that are non-negotiable. The challenge is to reconcile these disparate needs while keeping an eye on the overall business vision and expected ROI.

MoSCoW Prioritization in Action

Initial Planning

The Business Visionary collaborates with various stakeholders to list out all possible features and requirements for the CRM system. Each feature is categorized using the MoSCoW method:

- Must Haves: Core CRM functionalities without which the system would be unusable.
- Should Haves: Additional features that would make the system much more efficient but aren't absolutely essential.
- Could Haves: Nice-to-have features that can enhance user satisfaction.
- Won't Haves: Features that are out of scope for the current project timeline.

Business Impact Assessment

After the initial categorization, the Business Visionary works with financial analysts to attach a potential ROI to each feature. For example, a 'Should Have' feature that significantly increases user efficiency might have a high ROI and could be bumped up to a 'Must Have' if it aligns with the business vision.

Continuous Monitoring

Throughout the project, the Business Visionary keeps tabs on the development process. KPIs and metrics are scrutinized to ensure that the project stays in line with both the business vision and the Business Case. If the 'Must Haves' are developed faster than anticipated, some 'Should Haves' or even 'Could Haves' are escalated to take advantage of the available resources.

Outcome

By adhering strictly to MoSCoW prioritization and continuously aligning it with the business vision, the project not only delivers a robust CRM system but also exceeds initial ROI expectations. This methodical approach ensures that the most crucial functionalities are developed and deployed first, contributing directly to the business vision of becoming a market leader in customer relationship management solutions.

Deepening the Understanding: Guiding Principles for Agile Project Managers in MoSCoW Prioritization

The Subtleties of Requirements Decomposition

Decomposing high-level requirements into more detailed and actionable sub-requirements is more than just a procedural necessity; it's an art form. The objective is to reach a level of detail that allows for tangible work to be carried out, without causing "analysis paralysis." This is crucial because Agile methodologies like DSDM prioritize rapid delivery and iterative refinement over upfront specification. The granularity achieved through this decomposition process enables flexibility, allows for more accurate prioritization, and can help avoid the common pitfall of misinterpreting requirements.

Addressing the "Everything is a Must-Have" Conundrum

The notion that all requirements are Must-Haves represents a form of tunnel vision, often perpetuated by an incomplete understanding of the project's true business needs or a lack of stakeholder alignment. This viewpoint not only stifles flexibility but also undermines the concept of Agile itself, which is built on the principle of adaptability. Solving this conundrum requires a blend of stakeholder education, ongoing dialogue, and sometimes even conflict resolution skills to negotiate what is genuinely essential for the project's success.

The Agile Project Manager as a Facilitator and Moderator

The Agile Project Manager wears many hats, from facilitator to moderator to risk assessor. While they may not assign priorities, their role is indispensable in ensuring that the MoSCoW method is applied effectively and sensibly. They are responsible for ensuring stakeholder alignment, which often involves navigating differing opinions and interests. Furthermore, they must remain vigilant in maintaining a balanced portfolio of tasks within each timebox, to ensure that the project neither under-delivers nor stretches itself too thin.

Continuous Alignment with Evolving Business Goals

Business objectives are not static; they evolve as markets change, technologies advance, and organizational priorities shift. It's crucial for the Agile Project Manager to maintain a dynamic perspective on project priorities, ready to adjust and realign them in response to any shifts in business goals or stakeholder expectations. This adaptability ensures that the project stays relevant and continues to deliver value, rather than becoming a rigid entity that gradually loses alignment with the organization's evolving needs.

Case Study: Navigating MoSCoW Prioritization in a Complex Agile Project

Scenario Overview

Let's consider an Agile Project Manager overseeing a software development project aimed at building a customer relationship management (CRM) system. The project initially has an extensive list of features, including contact management, sales tracking, and customer service modules. Stakeholders across different departments have strong opinions about what should be designated as 'Must-Have' features.

Requirements Decomposition: The Fine Line

The Project Manager decides to host workshops where high-level requirements are decomposed into granular, actionable items. The use of techniques like user stories helps the team identify the essential building blocks for each module. This granularity allows the team to differentiate between the 'Must-Have' features necessary for a minimum viable product (MVP) and 'Should-Have' or 'Could-Have' features that can add incremental value.

Addressing the "Must-Have" Predicament

During these workshops, the sales department insists that the sales tracking module is a 'Must-Have,' while the customer service team argues that the customer service module is non-negotiable. The Project Manager steps in to guide the conversation, asking probing questions to help stakeholders distinguish between essential needs and desirable features. Through careful negotiation, it is agreed that contact management is the true 'Must-Have,' while sales tracking and customer service modules are 'Should-Haves.'

The Agile Project Manager: A Balancing Act

Throughout the project, the Project Manager keeps a vigilant eye on the balance of effort across these priorities. They also monitor the project's alignment with evolving business objectives. A quarterly business review indicates a rising need for better customer service, prompting a re-evaluation of priorities. The customer service module is upgraded to a 'Must-Have,' and the team adjusts its efforts accordingly.

Ongoing Alignment and Adaptability

Regular stakeholder check-ins, facilitated by the Project Manager, ensure that the project remains aligned with business objectives. Metrics tracking the completion of 'Should-Have' and 'Could-Have' items serve as early indicators of the project's health, allowing for timely adjustments.

The role of the Agile Project Manager in effectively applying the MoSCoW method cannot be understated. Their ability to facilitate requirements decomposition, resolve conflicts over priorities, and adapt to changing business needs is crucial for the project's success.

Streamlining Project Delivery with MoSCoW and Timeboxing: How Both Practices Complement Each Other

Uniting Two Agile Giants: MoSCoW and Timeboxing

Combining MoSCoW for requirement prioritization with Timeboxing for disciplined delivery provides a comprehensive framework for Agile Project Management. Together, these methods create a synergistic effect, significantly enhancing the probability of delivering projects within time constraints while achieving vital business goals.

Foundations of Effective Timeboxing

Establishing Parameters for Timeboxing

Before entering the Evolutionary Development phase, the Agile Project Manager should collaborate with the team to settle on crucial aspects of Timeboxing, such as:

Default Timebox Length: A standard length for Timeboxes must be chosen wisely. Shorter Timeboxes yield quicker feedback, while longer ones allow for the completion of more complex tasks.

Formality Level: It's essential to determine the strictness level for adhering to Timeboxing. The decision should account for the project's unique constraints and objectives.

Variables Impacting Timebox Length

Although maintaining uniform Timebox lengths is generally beneficial, exceptional circumstances may necessitate alterations:

Alignment with External Milestones: Projects with external dependencies may require tweaking Timebox durations to synchronize with outside deadlines.

Resource Availability: Factors like team member availability during holidays or temporary resource shortages can make a case for adjusting Timebox lengths.

Benefits of Short, Focused Timeboxes

Enabling Continuous Assessment and Adaptability

Short Timeboxes offer multiple advantages in an Agile setup:

Regular Progress Reviews: Frequent checkpoints enable timely interventions if the project begins to deviate from its path.

Swift Course Correction: The agility afforded by shorter cycles allows for rapid adjustments in response to newly emerged requirements or unforeseen challenges.

MoSCoW: The Fine Tuner of Timeboxes

Initial Prioritization

In the planning phase for each Timebox, MoSCoW prioritization provides an effective way to set the immediate agenda. It helps in delineating which tasks are indispensable and which can potentially be postponed.

Facilitating Ongoing Adjustments

As the Timebox progresses, real-world developments often necessitate re-evaluating initial priorities. MoSCoW's inherent flexibility provides a structured method for carrying out such adjustments, ensuring that the most critical tasks receive due attention while less vital tasks can be deferred or reprioritized.

Conclusion: The Complementary Nature of MoSCoW and Timeboxing

By synergistically integrating MoSCoW and Timeboxing, Agile Project Managers can significantly enhance both the quality and timeliness of project deliveries. While Timeboxing offers a structured approach to manage time effectively, MoSCoW ensures that this time is spent most productively by focusing on the highest-priority requirements. This strategic amalgamation thus delivers a potent mix of agility and discipline that is crucial for successful project execution.

The Real-World Application of MoSCoW and Timeboxing: Unpacking a Hypothetical Scenario

Setting the Scene: A New Software Development Project

Imagine an Agile team embarking on a new software development project aimed at creating a mobile application for eCommerce. The timeline is tight, with only three months to complete the project, and stakeholder expectations are high. In this setting, the team decides to implement MoSCoW for requirement prioritization and Timeboxing for sprint planning.

The Role of MoSCoW: Initial Requirement Prioritization

Listing Must-Haves, Should-Haves, and Could-Haves

At the project's outset, the team collaborates to identify and categorize the feature set. For example:

Must-Haves: Secure payment gateway, user registration and login, basic search functionality.

Should-Haves: Product reviews, recommendation engine.

Could-Haves: Social media sharing, multi-language support.

Aligning with Business Objectives

The priorities are then matched against the business objectives to ensure alignment. For instance, the secure payment gateway is a Must-Have not just because it is crucial for the app's functionality, but also because it aligns with the business goal of providing a secure and reliable shopping experience.

Incorporating Timeboxing: Sprint Planning and Execution

Deciding Timebox Length

The team opts for two-week Timeboxes (sprints) after assessing the nature of the work and their estimated velocities.

Planning the First Sprint

Using MoSCoW, they decide that the Must-Have features should be tackled in the first two sprints, followed by Should-Haves in the subsequent sprints.

The Synergy: Adapting to Real-World Challenges

Unforeseen Challenges

During the second sprint, the team encounters a bottleneck: the secure payment gateway integration is proving more complex than estimated.

Utilizing MoSCoW within the Timebox

They reevaluate the priority list for the ongoing sprint using MoSCoW, deciding to defer some of the Could-Haves in favor of allocating more resources to the payment gateway.

Resulting Outcomes

The bottleneck is resolved without impacting the Must-Have features. Additionally, frequent Timebox assessments enabled the team to realize the issue promptly, allowing for quick course correction.

Summary: The Interplay of MoSCoW and Timeboxing

This hypothetical scenario illustrates how MoSCoW and Timeboxing can work in tandem to navigate challenges and keep a project on track. MoSCoW provided the structure for setting and reevaluating priorities as the project progressed, while Timeboxing offered the discipline needed to make those priorities a reality within a constrained timeline. This dual application not only helped meet business objectives but also offered the adaptability to deal with unplanned challenges effectively.

The integration of MoSCoW and Timeboxing serves as a powerful toolkit for Agile Project Managers, offering a balanced approach that marries prioritization with disciplined time management.

Exploring the Two Timebox Styles in DSDM: Structured and Free Format

DSDM Timeboxing: A Dual Approach

Dynamic Systems Development Method (DSDM) integrates the practice of timeboxing as a fundamental component in its Agile project management framework. According to DSDM, there are two main styles of timeboxing:

1. DSDM Structured Timebox
2. Free Format Timebox

DSDM Structured Timebox: A Methodical Approach

Key Features

The DSDM Structured Timebox follows a precise and planned structure, which allows for meticulous forward planning and resource allocation. This type of Timebox is particularly beneficial when engaging with stakeholders like Business Ambassadors, who might have constrained schedules.

Structured Steps

The DSDM Structured Timebox comprises several key stages, each with its distinct purpose:

Timebox Kick-Off: Establishes a common understanding of objectives, resources, and known dependencies among the team members.

Investigation: Engages in initial modeling, detailing of requirements, and understanding their acceptance criteria and dependencies.

Refinement: Focuses on the iterative development and testing processes, aiming to meet the acceptance criteria set out in the Investigation stage.

Consolidation: Conducts final quality control checks, implementing any actions that arose from the Refinement review.

Close-Out: Achieves formal acceptance of all deliverables produced within the Timebox.

Free Format Timebox: Flexibility at Its Core

Core Principles

The Free Format Timebox offers more flexibility, with fewer structural demands than its DSDM Structured counterpart. This style is akin to the approach seen in other Agile frameworks like Scrum.

Structure and Flow

While it starts with a Kick-Off and ends with a Close-Out, similar to the DSDM Structured Timebox, the middle phase is less prescriptive. It allows for various formal or informal review points, which can be arranged as needed.

Stakeholder Engagement

This style of timeboxing leans heavily on the consistent availability of the Business Ambassador to provide real-time feedback and adjustments, making it ideal for projects where stakeholder engagement can be more fluid.

Deciding Between Structured and Free Format Timeboxes

The choice between the two styles often depends on the nature of the project and the specific requirements of stakeholders involved. A DSDM Structured Timebox is more suitable for projects where stakeholder time is limited and must be planned meticulously, whereas a Free Format Timebox fits well with projects that allow for a more flexible, dynamic mode of stakeholder engagement.

Case Study: Implementing Structured and Free Format Timeboxes in a Software Development Project

Scenario Overview

Imagine a software development project aimed at creating a mobile application. The project involves multiple stakeholders, including a Business Ambassador with a tight schedule and developers who work in different time zones. Here, both DSDM Structured and Free Format Timeboxes are employed to balance the rigidity needed for stakeholder schedules with the flexibility required for development work.

Utilizing DSDM Structured Timebox for Business Ambassador Engagement

Planning Phase

The project starts with a DSDM Structured Timebox to align with the Business Ambassador's schedule. All key steps, including the Timebox Kick-Off and Close-Out, are carefully planned and agreed upon in advance.

Stakeholder Participation

The Business Ambassador participates in the Timebox Kick-Off to help define the objectives and outline the acceptance criteria for this phase. Scheduled review sessions during the Investigation and Consolidation stages ensure that the Ambassador's input is integrated.

Implementing Free Format Timebox in Development Phases

Agile Environment

The development team opts for a Free Format Timebox to better accommodate varying time zones and work schedules. This setup allows for greater flexibility in development sprints and accommodates for unplanned adjustments or iterations.

Ongoing Reviews

Informal review sessions can be inserted wherever needed, permitting real-time feedback from the Business Ambassador. This keeps the project agile and adaptable.

Bringing It All Together: A Synergistic Blend

Structured for Business, Flexible for Development

By using DSDM Structured Timeboxes for the more rigid schedules and Free Format Timeboxes for the agile development stages, the project achieves a harmonious balance. It meets the requirements of the constrained schedules of business stakeholders while providing the development team with the agility they need.

Resulting Benefits

The project successfully navigates the complex requirements and schedules involved, ensuring stakeholder satisfaction and project delivery within the defined timeframes.

The case study illustrates the value of being able to switch between different Timebox styles depending on the project's specific needs and stakeholder involvement. Choosing the right approach can significantly influence the project's success, offering a blend of both structure and flexibility.

The Role of Daily Stand-Up in Agile Project Management: A Deep Dive into Best Practices and Agile Project Manager Responsibilities

Setting the Stage: The Daily Stand-Up as a Crucial Agile Mechanism

The Daily Stand-Up is more than just a meeting; it serves as a lynchpin for Agile project management methodologies. Conducted daily, it provides an effective platform for clear communication, issue identification, and quick decision-making, which are all pivotal for the success of an Agile project. This article delves into the specific roles and responsibilities of an Agile Project Manager during these stand-ups and outlines some best practices to make these meetings efficient and productive.

The Triple Objectives of Daily Stand-Ups

Information Sharing: Each team member provides an update on what they've achieved, what's on the agenda for the day, and any obstacles they're facing. This transparent communication helps everyone get on the same page quickly.

Replanning: The Stand-Up is an opportunity for the team to identify impediments and challenges. Although these are not typically resolved within the stand-up itself, they become focal points for discussions that follow.

Alignment: Perhaps one of the less tangible but equally important aspects of the stand-up is its role in keeping everyone aligned toward common project objectives. A well-run stand-up ensures that everyone knows how their work fits into the larger mission.

Roles and Responsibilities of the Agile Project Manager

Passive Observer or Active Participant?

Primarily, the Agile Project Manager serves as an observer in the Daily Stand-Up, but their role extends beyond passive attendance. Here's a breakdown:

Issue Escalation: The Project Manager is alert for issues that could require escalation or intervention from above. This is crucial for preempting problems that could derail a project if not promptly addressed.

Progress Tracking: The Daily Stand-Up provides the Project Manager with insights into the team's actual state and pace, which aids in more accurate planning and resource allocation.

Communication: If there are updates from higher up that could impact the current Timebox or project stage, the Agile Project Manager is responsible for communicating these to the team.

Best Practices for Running Efficient Stand-Ups

Structuring the Conversation

Three Questions Format: This framework helps keep the meeting focused. Each team member succinctly answers three key questions, offering everyone a snapshot of the project's status.

Time Management: Discipline in timing is essential. A 15-minute cap ensures that the meeting remains a quick sync-up rather than turning into a lengthy discussion.

Off-line Discussions: Not all issues can or should be resolved within the stand-up. Identifying such topics and moving them to a different setting is essential for maintaining focus.

Observer Interaction: It's good practice to give observers a moment at the end to share any pertinent updates or observations. This keeps the channel of communication open between the team and stakeholders.

Remote Team Management: Managing remote stand-ups adds another layer of complexity and requires additional structure, like an electronic team board for tracking status.

Attendance Monitoring: Absenteeism can be a red flag. Consistent absence from stand-ups should trigger an investigation into potential underlying issues.

Retrospective Inputs: Observations made during stand-ups can serve as valuable data points for future retrospectives, aiding in continuous improvement.

Case Study: Implementing Effective Daily Stand-Ups in a Multi-Team Agile Project

The Context: Complexity and Coordination

In a large-scale Agile project involving multiple teams across different time zones, the Daily Stand-Up presented unique challenges. Each team had its own set of priorities and timelines, and coordination became increasingly difficult. The Agile Project Manager was tasked with ensuring that these stand-ups were productive and facilitated cross-team communication.

The Intervention: Streamlining the Daily Stand-Up

Introducing a Global Stand-Up

To tackle the issue of multi-team coordination, a global stand-up was introduced. This was a short, focused meeting following each team's individual stand-up, where representatives from each team would update the Project Manager and other stakeholders.

Utilizing Technology for Remote Teams

Due to the geographically dispersed teams, technology played a pivotal role. A digital team board was used, and video conferencing tools were optimized to ensure seamless communication.

Real-time Issue Escalation

The Project Manager used a real-time tracking tool that allowed for immediate issue flagging and escalation. This ensured that any major blockers were addressed promptly, even if they arose in a different time zone.

The Outcomes: Enhanced Productivity and Alignment

Improved Information Flow

With the global stand-up in place and the utilization of technology, information flowed more freely between teams. This led to a more coherent and unified approach to problem-solving.

Effective Issue Resolution

The real-time tracking and issue escalation led to faster resolution of problems, ensuring that no single issue would delay the entire project.

Better Resource Allocation

The Project Manager gained a bird's-eye view of the entire project landscape. This allowed for more effective resource allocation, as it was easier to identify which teams needed additional support.

Lessons Learned: The Agile Project Manager's Role Redefined

This experience demonstrated that the role of the Agile Project Manager in facilitating effective Daily Stand-Ups goes beyond mere observation. Active intervention, planning, and technology utilization were key in transforming the stand-up from a routine meeting to a strategic tool for project success.

In-depth Examination of Empowered Teams and Change Management in Timeboxed Agile Development

The Intricacies of Decision-Making: Speed vs. Accuracy

Quick decision-making is a necessity in an Agile environment, but it should not come at the cost of making erroneous choices that deviate from the project's objectives. Speed and accuracy in decision-making are both vital, yet they require a fine balance. Fast decisions that lack accuracy can lead to resource wastage and could potentially put the project off track. On the other hand, indecision or overly cautious decision-making can cause delays, impacting the timelines set within the Timebox.

The Scope of Team Empowerment: Defined yet Flexible

In Agile, the notion of empowerment is not an open carte blanche for teams to make any decisions they deem fit. Rather, it is bounded empowerment within the limits of the Timebox. Teams are generally granted the latitude to make decisions on details or on aspects that do not fundamentally shift the Timebox's defined scope. For decisions that could potentially disrupt the Timebox, a more formal escalation procedure is needed to ensure alignment with the larger project objectives.

The Types of Changes and Their Management

Changes within a Timebox can be broadly classified into two categories:

Internal Changes

These are changes that stay within the boundaries of the Timebox. They might involve minor tweaks to features or adjusting the sequence of tasks. Teams should be empowered to make these changes without requiring external approvals.

External Changes

These are more drastic changes that affect the scope or alter the high-level requirements. For example, upgrading a 'Could Have' requirement to a 'Must Have' status is a change that needs to be escalated to project-level authorities.

The Agile Project Manager's Role in Boundary Setting and Review

One of the key responsibilities of an Agile Project Manager is to establish the limits within which the team is empowered to operate. These boundaries should be clearly defined, usually at the end of the 'Foundations' phase of the project. Regular reviews of these boundaries are advisable, particularly at the end of each Timebox, to ascertain their effectiveness and make any necessary adjustments.

Case Study: Navigating Empowerment and Change in a Timeboxed Agile Project

Context and Project Objectives

Let's consider a hypothetical project where a software development team is tasked with creating an e-commerce platform within a six-month timeframe. The project employs the Agile methodology and has decided to use two-week Timeboxes.

Initial Empowerment Boundaries Set by the Agile Project Manager

At the onset of the project, during the Foundations phase, the Agile Project Manager defines clear boundaries for decision-making. The team is empowered to make choices concerning feature implementation details, as long as these choices do not alter the predefined high-level requirements.

Encountering Scope Changes Mid-Timebox

During the third Timebox, the team identifies an opportunity to integrate a machine learning-based recommendation engine. This feature was initially categorized under 'Could Have.' The team believes that elevating this feature to 'Must Have' status could significantly improve user experience and sales.

The Escalation Process

Given the potential shift in high-level requirements, this change is escalated to the project-level roles, including the Product Owner, Stakeholders, and the Agile Project Manager. After a quick but thorough assessment, the change is approved and the Timebox scope is adjusted.

Reviewing Empowerment Boundaries

At the end of the Timebox, a review indicates that the empowerment boundaries were effective but need slight adjustments to accommodate changes like the one encountered. The Agile Project Manager takes the opportunity to clarify the types of changes that would require escalation in future Timeboxes.

Lessons Learned

The case illustrates the need for clearly defined, yet flexible, empowerment boundaries within Timeboxes. It also showcases the importance of having an effective escalation process for changes that may significantly alter the project's scope or objectives.

This case study demonstrates how empowered teams, operating within well-defined boundaries and equipped with a clear escalation process, can dynamically adapt to challenges and opportunities while maintaining alignment with broader project objectives.

Deepening the Understanding of MoSCoW Prioritization in Agile Projects

Critical Aspects of MoSCoW Methodology

The MoSCoW prioritization method has been time-tested in various Agile frameworks, especially in the Dynamic Systems Development Method (DSDM). It provides a structured way to approach requirements prioritization but can be misapplied if not understood deeply. The best practices for employing this method require keen attention to numerous subtleties.

Interplay of Business Roles and Requirements

It's crucial that key business roles, like the Business Visionary and Business Analyst, are not just familiar but deeply ingrained in the MoSCoW method. Their decisions often carry significant weight and are usually the cornerstone upon which prioritization is done. Therefore, their accurate understanding of what constitutes a 'Must-Have' versus a 'Could-Have' is essential for the method to be effective.

Reversing the Prioritization Mentality

Starting with 'Won't-Haves' as a default is not just a contrarian approach; it serves as a forcing function for stakeholders to defend why a requirement should be elevated to a higher category. This mental gymnastics can often expose weaker justifications and ensure that only truly critical requirements get categorized as 'Must-Haves.'

Workarounds and Cost-Benefit Analysis

Evaluating potential workarounds is an often-overlooked aspect of prioritization. Sometimes a 'Must-Have' might not be so indispensable if there is an alternative that can be implemented at a fraction of the cost or time. Here, a nuanced understanding of the business case and context becomes indispensable.

Dependencies and Cascading Risks

A nuanced understanding of dependencies can be the difference between a successful project and a failed one. If a 'Must-Have' is dependent on a 'Could-Have,' then the project is set up for potential failure unless the 'Could-Have' is elevated in priority. Therefore, meticulous examination of dependencies is non-negotiable.

Alignment with Objectives and Scope Control

Every requirement needs to have a clear line of sight to a project objective. This is not just a box-ticking exercise but a key strategy to guard against scope creep. If a requirement does not align with a 'Must-Have' project objective, its priority needs reevaluation. Scope control becomes a byproduct of this alignment, ensuring that team members do not wander into fulfilling interesting but unessential requirements.

By paying attention to these aspects, Agile Project Managers and teams can utilize the MoSCoW method to its fullest potential, ensuring a structured yet flexible way to manage project requirements.

Case Study: Implementing MoSCoW Prioritization in a FinTech Agile Project

Background

In the fast-paced world of financial technology (FinTech), a leading company aimed to develop a robust, user-friendly mobile banking application. The project was conducted under an Agile framework, specifically using DSDM. Given the complex nature of the project, with multiple stakeholders and tight deadlines, effective prioritization was critical. The MoSCoW methodology was adopted to align the development process with business goals.

Initial Requirements Collection

At the onset of the project, a broad set of requirements was gathered, involving the Business Visionary, Business Ambassadors, and Business Analysts. Requirements ranged from fundamental features like secure login and fund transfer to advanced features like currency exchange rates and investment portfolio management.

MoSCoW Prioritization Session

Stakeholder Education

Before diving into prioritization, the project manager ensured that all involved business roles understood the MoSCoW method's principles. An informational session was held to brief stakeholders on the significance of proper requirement categorization.

Initial Categorization

The team began by initially designating all items as 'Won't-Have,' which helped in emphasizing the necessity to justify moving any requirement up in priority.

Indispensability Test

To filter out 'Must-Haves,' stakeholders were prompted to consider if the absence of each requirement would lead to project failure. For instance, secure login was deemed indispensable, thus a 'Must-Have,' while features like displaying currency exchange rates were categorized as 'Could-Have.'

Workaround Assessment

For certain features, the team assessed if workarounds existed. For example, although multi-factor authentication was highly desirable, an alternative of one-time passwords (OTP) via email was available. This relegated multi-factor authentication to a 'Should-Have.'

Alignment with Business Objectives

All requirements were scrutinized for alignment with overarching business objectives. For instance, the investment portfolio management feature directly aligned with the goal of becoming a comprehensive financial management platform, thus pushing it to a 'Should-Have' status.

Outcome

The MoSCoW methodology aided in defining a clear scope, thereby controlling scope creep effectively. 'Must-Have' requirements were successfully implemented in the initial iterations, followed by a majority of 'Should-Have' and 'Could-Have' features, depending on time and resources. The result was a well-prioritized, feature-rich mobile banking application that not only met but exceeded stakeholder expectations.

Timeboxing in Agile Project Management: An In-Depth Guide to Success

Timeboxing is an essential feature of Agile methodologies such as Scrum and Dynamic Systems Development Method (DSDM). It serves as a powerful tool for managing time and scope by assigning specific durations, known as Timeboxes, to various tasks and objectives. To maximize the benefits of Timeboxing, Agile Project Managers can adopt several best practices. Below are key strategies and tips to help you achieve Timeboxing success.

Effective Strategies for Timeboxing in Agile Environments

Assess Early Completion as a Benchmark

The effectiveness of your Timebox planning can often be gauged by how early tasks can be completed. For instance, if a Solution Tester can begin testing well before the Timebox end date, or if User Stories are completed ahead of schedule, it's a positive indicator of well-executed planning. Early completion allows for greater flexibility in accommodating unplanned work or challenges.

Prioritize Faithfully

Adhering to the Timebox duration is crucial. Encourage team members to prioritize their tasks efficiently, focusing initially on 'Must-Have' requirements. Trust in the Timebox allows the team to channel their efforts more effectively.

Strict Adherence to Time Limits

Resist the temptation to extend the Timebox duration. If tasks remain incomplete, take this as an opportunity to assess what was achieved and where the gaps are. Use this learning to refine the planning of future Timeboxes.

Account for Varied Skill Sets

A well-rounded Timebox should include a mix of Must-Haves, Should-Haves, and Could-Haves. However, individual team members' skills may still affect the feasibility of meeting objectives. It's important to readjust plans in light of these skill-based considerations.

Daily Stand-Up Checks for Real-Time Insight

Utilize daily stand-up meetings to monitor the progress of the current Timebox. This will help identify issues in real-time, allowing for quick course corrections.

Foster a Blame-Free Environment

Cultivating an atmosphere of trust and accountability is vital. Teams that are comfortable reporting their progress and challenges are generally more effective in meeting Timebox objectives.

Include All Key Stakeholders in the Kick-Off

A well-executed Timebox kick-off meeting sets the stage for the entire Timebox. Ensure that all essential stakeholders are included, so that expectations and objectives are uniformly understood.

Clarify Acceptance Criteria Early

The acceptance criteria should be explicitly stated during the kick-off meeting and further refined during the Investigation phase. This avoids ambiguities that could otherwise delay tasks.

Proactively Identify and Monitor Risks

During the kick-off meeting, outline any potential risks that could impact the Timebox and make plans to mitigate them. Continue to monitor these risks throughout the Timebox duration.

Use Retrospectives for Continuous Improvement

Post-Timebox retrospectives offer invaluable insights into what went well and what needs improvement. Take the time to dissect these findings and apply them to future Timeboxes for better results.

Case Study: Timeboxing Strategies in Action for an Agile Software Development Team

Background

A mid-sized software development company was transitioning from a traditional Waterfall approach to Agile methodologies. The Agile Project Manager adopted Timeboxing as a core feature in their new Scrum framework. The team consisted of eight members, including developers, testers, and a business analyst.

Objectives

1. Complete development and testing of five key User Stories within a two-week Timebox.

2. Involve all key stakeholders in the Timebox kick-off.
3. Maintain a blame-free environment to foster better communication and accountability.

Strategies Implemented

Kick-Off Inclusion

The Agile Project Manager ensured that all key stakeholders, including customer representatives and senior management, were part of the kick-off meeting. The meeting served to align everyone on the Timebox objectives and acceptance criteria.

Prioritization and Task Allocation

Based on the MoSCoW methodology, tasks were categorized as Must-Haves, Should-Haves, and Could-Haves. Team members were then assigned tasks according to their skill sets, ensuring an efficient use of resources.

Daily Stand-Up Monitoring

Daily stand-ups were used as a real-time checkpoint for progress within the Timebox. On Day 3, it was noted that one of the Must-Have tasks was falling behind schedule. Immediate adjustments were made to the team's workload to bring the task back on track.

Risk Mitigation

Potential risks identified during the kick-off were reviewed daily. When a key software library update risked delaying the project, a mitigation plan was enacted swiftly, avoiding Timebox disruption.

Post-Timebox Retrospective

After the Timebox concluded, a retrospective meeting was held. While four of the five key User Stories were completed successfully, one Could-Have task had to be moved to the next Timebox. Lessons were drawn from this, especially concerning the estimation accuracy for such tasks.

Outcomes

1. 80% of the User Stories were completed successfully within the Timebox.
2. Stakeholder satisfaction was high due to transparent communication and the blame-free environment.
3. The retrospective led to improved task estimation strategies for future Timeboxes.

The case study clearly demonstrates the effectiveness of implementing robust Timeboxing strategies in Agile environments. Adopting such practices can substantially enhance project outcomes and stakeholder satisfaction.

Chapter Fifteen

INTERACTIONS: BUILDING A COLLABORATIVE PROJECT ENVIRONMENT

Expanding the Understanding of Collaboration and Communication in Agile Project Management with DSDM

Why Communication and Collaboration are Critical

In Agile methodologies, particularly the Dynamic Systems Development Method (DSDM), effective communication and collaboration are not just beneficial, they are imperative. Poor communication has long been cited as a key factor in the failure of projects, leading to misunderstandings, delays, and missed opportunities. Similarly, lack of collaboration can break down team dynamics and compromise the ability to solve complex problems efficiently.

Delving into Common Communication Pitfalls

Ambiguity in Language

The use of inconsistent terminology or ambiguous phrases can be detrimental. When team members are not aligned in their understanding of project terms, misunderstandings can escalate into major issues.

Inaccessible Stakeholders

Not having access to key decision-makers or experts can grind project progress to a halt. These bottlenecks are particularly problematic in Agile frameworks where quick decisions are often required.

Confirmation Bias

Ignoring or disregarding information that contrad't align with pre-existing beliefs or expectations can result in flawed decision-making. It's essential that teams remain open to new information, even when it contradicts their current understanding.

Overlooking Key Stakeholders

Neglecting to involve all key stakeholders can lead to a lack of alignment and agreement, posing a risk to project success.

Inefficient Communication Channels

Selecting the wrong medium for a message can result in misinterpretation or non-receipt of essential information.

Overemphasis on Written Communication

While written formats like emails and documentation are necessary, they lack the nuances conveyed through verbal or face-to-face interactions.

Guidance for Agile Project Managers

Fostering a Collaborative Culture

The cultural aspect of teamwork should not be underestimated. Building a culture that encourages open dialogue and collaborative problem-solving is foundational.

Structured Communication Plans

Having a defined plan for who should communicate what, when, and how can make a noticeable difference in a project's trajectory.

Prioritizing Active Listening

Active listening skills should be encouraged across the team to foster an environment where different viewpoints are considered and evaluated before making any decisions.

Stakeholder Mapping

An often-underutilized tool, a stakeholder map can serve as a visual representation of who needs what information and when.

Diversified Communication

Relying solely on one form of communication can be limiting. Incorporating a mix of written, verbal, and even visual mediums can often communicate complex ideas more effectively.

Establishing Feedback Mechanisms

Feedback loops, especially in Agile environments, allow for the rapid identification of issues or opportunities for improvement. This iterative process can be invaluable for continuous improvement and alignment.

Effective communication and collaboration are more than just good practices; they're prerequisites for Agile project success. The strategies outlined above offer a structured approach for Agile Project Managers to foster these vital skills.

Case Study: Enhancing Collaboration and Communication in a DSDM Project

Background

In a software development firm employing the Dynamic Systems Development Method (DSDM), the project team faced challenges in communication and collaboration. Despite initial enthusiasm, progress lagged, misunderstandings were rampant, and stakeholder engagement was minimal. The Agile Project Manager decided to implement several of the best practices discussed earlier to address these issues.

Interventions

Creating a Shared Language Glossary

The Project Manager initiated the creation of a project-specific glossary, ensuring all team members and stakeholders had a common understanding of terminology.

Regular Access to Stakeholders

Weekly stakeholder meetings were instituted to facilitate faster decision-making, provide updates, and align objectives.

Openness to Contradictory Information

The team was encouraged to actively seek out and consider contradictory information or viewpoints, breaking down pre-existing confirmation biases.

Comprehensive Stakeholder Mapping

A detailed stakeholder map was created and updated regularly, ensuring that all relevant parties were included in communications and decision-making processes.

Utilizing Varied Communication Channels

A combination of daily stand-up meetings, regular emails, and an internal project portal was implemented to ensure multi-faceted communication.

Implementation of Feedback Loops

Regular retrospectives were initiated after each Timebox, and the outcomes were shared not just with the team but also with the stakeholders to foster a culture of continuous improvement.

Results

After implementing these strategies, the team saw a marked improvement in several key performance indicators:

Alignment and Engagement: Stakeholder engagement improved, as evidenced by their more active participation in meetings.

Speed of Decision-Making: With the new feedback loops and stakeholder involvement, decisions were made more rapidly and were better aligned with project objectives.

Team Satisfaction: The improved clarity and openness led to higher job satisfaction levels among team members.

Project Velocity: Improved communication and collaboration resulted in a faster pace of development, effectively improving the project's velocity.

This case study demonstrates the tangible benefits of prioritizing effective communication and collaboration in an Agile (DSDM) project. While challenges are inevitable, applying structured best practices can significantly mitigate risks and improve project outcomes.

Expanding on Communication Skills and Terminology in Agile DSDM Projects

The Critical Nature of Soft Skills in DSDM Environments

The Limitations of Technical Skills

In Agile projects based on the Dynamic Systems Development Method (DSDM), possessing technical skills is a given but not a guarantee for project success. The complex and often rapidly-changing nature of these projects requires more than just technical know-how. It demands a set of soft skills that can adapt to change, foster collaboration, and facilitate effective communication within the team and with stakeholders.

The Need for Soft Skills

In a DSDM project, soft skills serve as the glue that holds the technical aspects and human elements together. Skills like active listening, negotiation, and empathy don't just add value; they are often pivotal in navigating the challenges that arise during a project's life cycle.

Assessment and Improvement of Soft Skills

Evaluation Metrics

Assessing soft skills is inherently subjective but crucial. Project Managers should employ both qualitative and quantitative metrics, such as 360-degree feedback, one-on-one interviews, and team retrospectives, to evaluate the efficacy of communication within the team.

Development Programs

Upon identification of gaps, Project Managers should introduce training programs and coaching sessions to build these skills. Moreover, assessments should be ongoing, allowing for iterative improvement and timely intervention when deficiencies are detected.

The Integral Role of Clear Terminology

The Pitfalls of Jargon

Complex terminology and jargon can alienate team members who may not share the same specialized knowledge. Such language barriers can lead to misunderstandings, incorrect implementations, and, ultimately, project delays.

Standardizing Terminology

Creating a project glossary can serve as a "universal translator," providing all team members and stakeholders with a common understanding of terms and abbreviations. This tool is particularly useful in multidisciplinary teams where the lexicon can differ significantly between departments.

Inclusion in Project Documentation

Inclusion of this glossary in the project documentation and its frequent update can serve as an evergreen reference, reducing friction in communication and enhancing project execution.

In summary, both soft skills and clear, standardized terminology play indispensable roles in the success of a DSDM project. While each serves a different need, they are complementary and, when effectively managed, contribute to a more coherent, efficient, and successful project. Would you like this elaborated through a case study or practical example?

Case Study: Enhancing Communication Skills and Terminology in a DSDM Project

Project Overview

Background

A mid-sized technology company was undergoing a transformation project using the Dynamic Systems Development Method (DSDM). The aim was to overhaul its legacy systems and implement a new customer relationship management (CRM) system. While the technical team was highly skilled, the project faced significant delays and misalignment issues.

Identifying the Challenges

Soft Skills Gap

Upon initial assessments, it was evident that the team lacked key soft skills such as active listening and effective negotiation. The team members often talked past each other, leading to misunderstandings and incorrect implementations.

Terminological Confusion

There were also issues with terminology. Different departments used the same terms to refer to different processes, causing confusion and delays. For example, the term "customer profile" had different meanings for the sales and tech departments.

Implementing Solutions

Soft Skills Training

A two-day workshop focused on active listening, negotiation, and empathy was organized for the team. Role-playing exercises allowed team members to practice these skills in scenarios mimicking real project challenges.

Creation of a Project Glossary

A project glossary was developed, clearly defining all terms and abbreviations pertinent to the project. Each term was provided with a description, along with the department that commonly uses it. This glossary was distributed to all stakeholders and integrated into the project's documentation.

Measuring Impact

Improved Team Collaboration

Post-implementation of these measures, there was a notable improvement in team collaboration. Team members began to understand each other better and were more willing to compromise, resulting in faster decision-making and issue resolution.

Alignment and Efficiency

The introduction of a standardized project glossary eradicated the misunderstandings that had been plaguing the project. Team members spent less time clarifying terms, leading to a more streamlined workflow.

Concluding Remarks

This case study underlines the importance of soft skills and clear terminology in the success of a DSDM project. By addressing these often-overlooked aspects, the project was brought back on track, highlighting that effective communication is as crucial as technical competence in Agile project management.

Further Exploration of Communication Planning in Agile Projects: Unpacking Principles and Roles

Addressing the Limitations of Technology in Communication

Importance of Being Mindful

While technology, particularly email, serves as a powerful tool for communication, it can be a double-edged sword. Its misuse can lead to critical issues such as information overload, as pointed out. Being mindful of how and when to use technology in communication is a nuanced task that requires careful planning.

Core Principles for Effective Communication Planning

The Necessity of Context-Sensitive Choices

The principles outlined, such as choosing the right medium, knowing your audience, and deciding the frequency and type of communication, are foundational. What these principles offer is a roadmap to making informed, context-sensitive choices that are aligned with the project's goals and stakeholder needs.

Flexibility in Implementation

While these principles serve as a guide, it's crucial to maintain a degree of flexibility. Agile environments are dynamic, and communication plans may need to be adapted as projects evolve. For example, if a critical stakeholder's role changes, your communication strategy must also adapt to maintain effective engagement.

The Central Role of the Project Manager in Communication Planning

An Orchestrator of Dialogues

The Project Manager serves as an orchestrator of dialogues both within the project team and with external stakeholders. By identifying stakeholder roles and assessing internal team communication needs, the Project Manager can tailor strategies that foster open, transparent, and effective communication.

Importance of Tool Evaluation

Deciding on the best technical options is not just a logistical decision but also a strategic one. Tools should facilitate rather than hinder communication. By meticulously evaluating available options based on utility, ease of use, and how well they integrate with existing systems, Project Managers can make informed decisions that contribute to the project's overall effectiveness.

Case Study: Communication Planning in an Agile Project for a Financial Institution

Overview

A mid-sized financial institution decided to adopt the Agile methodology for its new customer relationship management (CRM) system development. The project team consisted of internal IT staff, a few business analysts, and external contractors specializing in CRM implementations. While everyone had experience in their respective fields, the team had limited exposure to Agile practices and Dynamic Systems Development Method (DSDM).

The Challenge

Despite the varied expertise, the project faced multiple challenges primarily related to ineffective communication. The team struggled with information overload due to excessive email threads, misalignment of expectations among stakeholders, and the absence of a unified communication platform.

Implementing Effective Communication Principles

Role of the Project Manager

The Project Manager recognized the communication issues early in the project. He took the initiative to re-evaluate and redesign the communication plan, keeping the following points in focus:

Medium and Frequency

The team agreed to minimize the use of emails for internal communications, instead opting for a project management tool that integrated a chat function. This move substantially reduced information overload and kept all project-related communications in one place.

Two-Way Communication

Regular stand-up meetings were instituted to allow for two-way communication. These meetings helped in capturing immediate feedback and acted as a platform for clarifying any ambiguities.

Stakeholder Engagement

The Project Manager created a stakeholder map and identified the primary influencers and decision-makers. Quarterly in-person meetings were set up with these stakeholders to keep them informed and engaged.

Results

Implementing these changes led to a noticeable improvement in team collaboration and stakeholder engagement. Miscommunications were reduced, and team members reported feeling more aligned with project objectives. Consequently, the project was delivered on time and within budget.

This case study serves as an example of how vital proper communication planning is in Agile projects and how Dynamic Systems Development Method (DSDM) can be effectively employed to meet these challenges.

Detailed Exploration of Communication Choices in Agile Project Management

The matter of selecting the appropriate communication channels in Agile project management, especially under frameworks like Dynamic Systems Development Method (DSDM), is of critical importance. Effective communication functions as the linchpin that holds the complexities of a project together, and poor choices in communication methods can lead to misunderstandings, delays, or even failure. In this article, we shall delve into the merits and demerits of different communication channels, and identify best practices for making astute communication choices.

Advantages and Limitations of Various Channels

Face-to-Face Interaction

Advantages: This form allows for the richest form of communication, covering verbal cues, body language, and immediate feedback.
Limitations: Geographical constraints can make this impractical for distributed teams. Also, it may not always provide a record of the discussion unless documented.

Conferencing Tools (Video & Tele)

Advantages: Provides a near face-to-face experience and can be recorded for future reference.
Limitations: Technology issues such as poor connectivity can hamper communication.

Chat Platforms

Advantages: Effective for quick discussions and immediate clarifications, with a record of the conversation.
Limitations: May not be suitable for complex discussions requiring nuanced understanding.

Email

Advantages: Provides a formal record and is excellent for asynchronous communication.
Limitations: Risk of being overlooked in an overloaded inbox and lacks the nuance of verbal communication.

Collaborative Workspaces

Advantages: Enables real-time collaboration and is excellent for project tracking.
Limitations: May require training and can be less intuitive compared to other tools.

Documents

Advantages: Necessary for maintaining formal records and compliance.
Limitations: Tend to be static and may not reflect real-time changes.

Guiding Principles for Communication Choices

Synergy Across Channels

Opt for a mix of communication channels, each complementing the other, to ensure that the limitations of one method are balanced by the strengths of another.

Context Sensitivity

The nature of the information, urgency, and the audience's preferences must be considered when choosing a communication channel.

Consider User Preferences

Remember that not all team members may be comfortable or proficient with certain types of communication tools. Make choices that are inclusive.

Address Constraints

Especially in the case of remote or distributed teams, ensure that all members have equal access to the chosen communication tools.

Ensure Dynamic and Engaging Interactions

The medium is just a vehicle; the quality of communication also depends on how interactive and engaging the conversation is.

Conclusion

Communication choices in Agile Project Management should be strategic, thoughtful, and tailored to the project's specific needs and challenges. By weighing the advantages and limitations of each method and adhering to the guiding principles, project managers can pave the way for more effective and efficient communication.

Case Study: Streamlining Communication in a Global Agile Team

Introduction

A multinational company was facing significant communication challenges in their software development department that employed the DSDM framework. The team was distributed across three continents, and a plethora of communication tools were in use. There was a noticeable lack of consistency in the way information was shared and stored, leading to delays and misunderstandings.

Problem Statement

Geographical Disparity: Team members were distributed across different time zones, making synchronous communication difficult.

Tool Overload: Multiple tools were in use, including email, chat platforms, and a couple of project management tools. Information was fragmented.

Lack of Engagement: Remote team members often reported feeling left out or uninformed about critical decisions.

Strategy Implemented

Assessment and Tool Rationalization

An initial audit was conducted to evaluate the effectiveness of existing communication channels. Based on the findings, the team decided to narrow down the tools to:

- Video Conferencing for weekly meetups
- A single chat platform for quick communication
- A unified project management tool that included a feature for document storage

Setting Guidelines

Clear guidelines were set for what type of information should be shared through which channel. Urgent and important messages, for example, would be conveyed through direct video calls, whereas day-to-day updates were handled through the chat platform.

Training and Onboarding

All team members received training on how to use the selected project management tool effectively, ensuring everyone was on the same page.

Regular Check-ins

To ensure ongoing improvement, the team instituted monthly communication audits as part of their retrospectives to gather feedback and make necessary adjustments.

Results

Improved Collaboration: Streamlining the tools and methods of communication made it easier for team members to collaborate.

Reduced Misunderstandings: Having clear guidelines reduced the risk of messages being lost or misunderstood.

Increased Engagement: Remote team members reported feeling more integrated into the team, attributing it to the enhanced communication strategies.

Lessons Learned

- Simplifying and streamlining communication tools can greatly improve the effectiveness of team interactions.
- Guidelines for communication should be well-defined and adhered to rigorously.
- Continuous evaluation is key to adapting and refining communication strategies over time.

The case underscores the critical role of judicious communication choices in Agile project management, especially in complex, distributed environments.

Addressing the Communication Challenge: An In-depth Analysis

The Importance of Choosing Between Visual and Verbal Communication

Strategic Implications

The decision to employ visual or verbal communication methods has far-reaching implications for a project's trajectory. It influences the speed of information transfer, clarity of instructions, and level of stakeholder engagement, among other factors.

Efficiency and Speed

Visual communication methods, such as Kanban boards or graphical dashboards, provide quick snapshots of project status and can swiftly communicate a lot of information. On the other hand, written reports, while thorough, may require significant time to compose and read.

Precision and Clarity

Visual tools like flowcharts or diagrams can simplify complex processes or structures, offering a clearer understanding than verbose descriptions. In contrast, verbal or written formats can be more precise in detailing the nuances and conditions that are critical for a project.

Stakeholder Engagement

Different stakeholders may have different preferences or requirements for how they receive information. For example, senior executives might prefer dashboards for quick insights, whereas developers may require detailed written specifications.

Tactics for Implementing the Right Communication Strategy

Assessment Phase

Begin by assessing the existing communication methods in terms of their effectiveness, audience, and context. Are they contributing to project success, or are they a source of confusion and delay?

The Balance Approach

Ideally, a mix of both visual and verbal communication should be employed. Each has its own set of strengths and weaknesses, and using them in tandem can fill the gaps left by the other.

Flexibility and Adaptability

It's essential to remain flexible in your communication strategy. What works at one project stage may not be effective at another. Be prepared to adapt your methods according to the project's evolving needs.

Continuous Feedback and Iteration

Incorporate feedback mechanisms to continuously assess the effectiveness of your communication channels. Whether it's through project retrospectives or direct stakeholder feedback, this data is invaluable for making ongoing improvements.

Summary

Choosing between visual and verbal communication methods is a complex, strategic decision that can have a lasting impact on your Agile project. By considering the efficiency, precision, and stakeholder needs, and by being flexible in your approach, you can significantly enhance your project's chances for success.

Case Study: Visual vs. Verbal Communication in Agile Project Management

Background

In an Agile project following the DSDM framework, the team was faced with the task of implementing a complex data migration. The initial approach relied heavily on written documents, including technical specifications, to guide the development process.

Challenges

The team soon encountered difficulties, including:

- Misinterpretation of written instructions
- Delayed decision-making due to the time-consuming nature of digesting lengthy documents
- A lack of a holistic view of the migration process

Implementation of a Mixed Communication Strategy

Visual Communication Tools

The project manager introduced a series of visual tools to supplement the written documents:

- Flowcharts to outline the migration path
- A Kanban board for task tracking
- Dashboards to monitor real-time progress and bottlenecks

Verbal Communication Channels

Scheduled stand-ups and review meetings were used to discuss progress, issues, and to clarify any points of confusion. The team also started leveraging chat tools for quick, real-time problem-solving.

Results

This dual approach resulted in:

- Faster decision-making: Visual tools allowed the team to grasp complex scenarios more quickly.
- Improved clarity: Verbal discussions helped to clarify ambiguities.
- Increased stakeholder engagement: The mixed strategy accommodated the different informational needs of various stakeholders, including non-technical management who were more comfortable with visual representations.

Lessons Learned

- One communication method doesn't fit all scenarios or stakeholders.
- The efficiency of communication methods is context-dependent and can significantly influence project outcomes.

- Continuous iteration and feedback are essential for refining a communication strategy.

Ongoing Day-to-Day Communication in Agile Projects: Unlocking the Full Potential of Team Boards

The use of Team Boards in Agile frameworks like DSDM offers a robust medium for ongoing, effective communication. These boards serve as a "single source of truth" for all project stakeholders, thereby centralizing project metrics, statuses, and key action items. This elaboration digs deeper into the constituents, importance, and best practices for using Team Boards effectively in Agile communication.

The Multi-Faceted Importance of Team Boards

A Hub for Transparent Communication

Team Boards provide a central platform for transparent and real-time communication. With statuses, progress markers, and other key metrics displayed clearly, team members can better align their activities with the overarching project goals.

A Catalyst for Accountability

By visually representing who is responsible for what, Team Boards instill a sense of accountability. Team members are more likely to take ownership of tasks, timelines, and problem-solving when information is laid out transparently for all to see.

Facilitating Quick Decision-Making

A well-organized Team Board presents complex project data in a simplified manner. This accessibility allows stakeholders to make informed decisions rapidly, a crucial factor in Agile's fast-paced environment.

Navigating Key Elements for Maximum Effectiveness

Timebox Objectives: The North Star

The Timebox Objective serves as the guiding light for what the team seeks to achieve in a given iteration. Ensuring this is prominent on the board helps keep the team aligned and focused.

Story Tracking: The Pulse of Progress

In Agile frameworks, the user story or requirement is the basic unit of work. Effective tracking shows, at a glance, what has been accomplished, what is in progress, and what awaits attention.

Visual Cues: The Language of Urgency

Blocked Work Indicators, often in bold or contrasting colors, quickly draw attention to bottlenecks or impediments, allowing for quicker resolution.

The Clock is Ticking: Time Countdown

An ever-present countdown of time left in the Timebox keeps the team's focus sharp. It serves as a subtle but constant reminder of the urgency inherent in Agile methodologies.

Ensuring Best Practices for Optimal Outcomes

Maintain Simplicity

While the impulse to capture every piece of data may be strong, over-cluttering the board can dilute its effectiveness. A balance between comprehensiveness and simplicity is essential.

Routine Refresh

Regular updates, ideally daily, keep the board's data current and its utility high. Stale information undermines the board's purpose and credibility.

High Visibility, High Impact

The board's location should be in a space frequently accessed by the team to ensure its contents are consistently reviewed. For distributed teams, a digital equivalent should mirror the physical board for consistent information sharing across geographies.

Case Study: Implementing Team Boards in an Agile Software Development Project

Introduction

In an Agile software development project at a mid-sized tech company, the project management team faced challenges with ongoing communication and accountability. Stakeholders found it difficult to keep track of the rapidly changing statuses of work items, leading to delays and bottlenecks.

The Situation Before Team Boards

Prior to implementing Team Boards, the team relied on multiple disparate sources for project updates, including emails, meetings, and disparate tracking tools. This led to information gaps, misinterpretations, and ultimately, delays in project milestones.

Implementation Strategy

The project management team decided to adopt Team Boards as a primary communication tool. After initial brainstorming, they identified key elements that needed to be on the board, such as Timebox Objectives, Story Tracking, Blocked Work Indicators, and a Time Countdown.

Phase 1: Design and Placement

A physical board was designed with easy-to-read fonts and visually arresting colors, particularly for Blocked Work Indicators. The board was placed in a common area where team members often gathered.

Phase 2: Roll-out and Training

A brief training session was conducted to familiarize team members with the new system. Each member was shown how to update their work statuses on the board.

Phase 3: Digital Adoption

For remote stakeholders and team members, an electronic version of the board was developed. This mirrored the physical board and was updated in real-time.

Outcomes

Improved Transparency

Post-implementation, stakeholders reported a significant improvement in their understanding of work statuses and overall project progression.

Enhanced Accountability

The visual nature of the board made it easier for team members to understand their responsibilities, leading to better ownership of tasks and timelines.

Faster Decision-Making

With real-time, visually organized information readily available, both team members and stakeholders were able to make quicker and more informed decisions.

Conclusion

The implementation of Team Boards vastly improved the project's communication landscape. It successfully addressed the initial challenges, adding value not just in terms of better information flow, but also in fostering a culture of accountability and rapid decision-making.

This case study serves as a real-world example of how implementing Team Boards can significantly enhance communication effectiveness in Agile projects.

Deep Dive into the Significance and Dynamics of Daily Stand-ups in Agile Project Management

Daily Stand-ups are a quintessential practice in Agile methodologies, notably the Dynamic Systems Development Method (DSDM). They act as a pulse check, ensuring that teams remain aligned with their objectives, understand their responsibilities, and have an avenue to address immediate concerns. This article elaborates on the objectives, structure, facilitation, and best practices for conducting effective Daily Stand-ups in an Agile setting.

Objectives of the Daily Stand-up

Quick Updates

The primary objective is to provide quick, focused updates from each team member regarding their progress and upcoming tasks.

Fine Adjustments

Beyond mere updates, the Daily Stand-up serves as a platform for making minor tweaks to the work planned for the next 24 hours.

Flagging Issues

If team members encounter roadblocks or foresee potential bottlenecks, the stand-up is the venue to flag these issues promptly.

Alignment and Reaffirmation

The meeting also acts as a forum for the team to realign its focus toward the overarching Timebox objectives.

Who Should Facilitate?

While the Team Leader often assumes the role of facilitator, the ideal scenario is for the team members to facilitate themselves, embodying the self-organizing principles of the Solution Development Team.

Project Manager's Involvement

Though present, the Project Manager typically assumes a passive role as an observer. Their input, however, becomes crucial when discussing project-level issues that might impact the team's activities in the immediate future.

Scope of the Daily Stand-up

Not a Reporting Session

Contrary to some misconceptions, the Daily Stand-up is not a status reporting session for the Project Manager's benefit.

Task Swapping

If necessary, the team may choose to reallocate tasks based on the updates and discussions during the stand-up.

Adjustments to the Delivery Plan

Only in exceptional cases where significant changes or challenges have emerged should adjustments be made to the broader Delivery Plan.

Best Practices for Daily Stand-ups

Time Management

The essence of the Daily Stand-up is brevity. The stand-up should not exceed 15 minutes to maintain focus and efficiency.

Task Focus

Discussion should be task-centric, revolving around what has been accomplished, what is on the day's agenda, and any obstacles hindering progress.

Location

Ideally, the stand-up should be conducted around the Team Board, as this visual tool can aid in discussion and decision-making.

Active Participation

Every member should come prepared to discuss their tasks succinctly, enabling a more productive and efficient meeting.

Case Study: Optimizing Daily Stand-ups in an Agile Development Team

Background

The Software Development team at XYZ Corp adopted the Agile framework, specifically DSDM, to improve their project delivery. However, they observed that their Daily Stand-ups were often running over time, lacked focus, and sometimes descended into prolonged discussions that should have been reserved for separate meetings.

Identifying Issues

Upon reviewing the format and execution of their Daily Stand-ups, the team identified the following issues:

- Lack of preparation from team members.
- Veering off-topic from the day's agenda.
- Prolonged discussions on intricate problems.

Implementing Solutions

Time Management

A timer was introduced, limiting each team member's update to two minutes, ensuring the meeting concluded within 15 minutes.

Task Focus

Team members started sending pre-stand-up summaries via a shared channel, allowing everyone to stay updated before the meeting, focusing the discussion on tasks and obstacles only.

Location

They moved their stand-ups to be conducted around the Team Board, effectively utilizing it as a visual aid to keep discussions aligned and focused.

Active Participation

To foster a culture of active participation, team members were encouraged to come to the stand-up prepared to talk about their work succinctly. Focused questions were posed to help guide the conversation and ensure everyone had a chance to speak.

Outcomes

With these changes in place, the team observed a noticeable improvement in the efficiency and focus of their Daily Stand-ups. Meetings ended on time, and there was a significant reduction in off-topic discussions. Team members reported feeling more aligned and aware of each team member's responsibilities and challenges.

Implementing these best practices significantly optimized the effectiveness of the Daily Stand-ups, making them a more powerful tool in Agile Project Management for XYZ Corp.

Exploring the Agile Project Manager's Role in Facilitating Communication for Co-located Teams

Co-location often heralds a fertile ground for communication in Agile frameworks like Dynamic Systems Development Method (DSDM). However, the Agile Project Manager plays a pivotal role in optimizing this setting to its fullest potential. From space allocation to managing resources and establishing communication norms, the Agile Project Manager's responsibilities are manifold and critical.

Agile Project Manager's Role in Space Allocation

Ensuring Proximity for Enhanced Communication

One of the Agile Project Manager's primary tasks is to organize the workspace such that team members are in close proximity to one another. This closeness allows for spontaneous and informal communication, which is the bedrock of Agile methodologies.

Incorporating Stakeholder Desks

Having a couple of extra desks for stakeholders and business roles can be beneficial. These individuals can participate in the development process, providing real-time feedback and facilitating a more holistic development cycle.

Dedicated Stand-up Space

The Agile Project Manager should designate an area solely for the Daily Stand-ups. This space should be set away from workstations to minimize distractions and foster focused discussions.

Role in Resource Management

Hardware and Software

Whether it's fast computers, dual monitors, or specialized software, the Agile Project Manager needs to ensure that the team has the right tools to accomplish their tasks efficiently.

Team Board Maintenance

The Project Manager should also ensure that the physical Team Board is well-maintained and updated. For distributed members, an electronic board should mirror the physical one to keep everyone on the same page.

Ensuring Effective Communication Channels

Bridging the Gap for Multi-Site Teams

If the team is distributed across multiple locations, the Agile Project Manager should establish robust video conferencing facilities to mimic the benefits of a co-located environment as closely as possible.

Time Zone Management

When team members operate in different time zones, the Project Manager needs to identify overlapping hours where synchronous communication can occur, thereby minimizing the challenges associated with time differences.

Conclusion

The Agile Project Manager is not merely a supervisory role but an enabler who sets the stage for effective communication and collaboration. By focusing on space allocation, resource management, and communication channel optimization, the Project Manager can significantly contribute to the efficacy of a co-located Agile team.

Case Study: Agile Project Manager's Role in Facilitating a Co-located Environment

Background

In a software development firm implementing the Dynamic Systems Development Method (DSDM), the Agile Project Manager faced challenges with a newly formed team. Despite being co-located, the team was not communicating effectively, leading to misunderstandings and delays.

Agile Project Manager's Intervention

Initial Assessment

The Agile Project Manager started by conducting an assessment of the current workspace, team dynamics, and communication patterns. This helped identify the areas that needed immediate attention.

Space Reorganization

The Project Manager restructured the workstations, creating a more open environment that encouraged face-to-face interactions. Dedicated spaces for Stand-up meetings and extra desks for stakeholders were also introduced.

Hardware and Software Upgrades

Old computers were replaced, and essential software tools were installed. The team board was moved to a more central location and updated daily.

Communication Norms

The Agile Project Manager established new communication norms, such as mandatory attendance at Daily Stand-ups and a set protocol for using video conferencing tools for interacting with remote stakeholders.

Results

Improved Communication

Post-intervention, the team reported that communication had significantly improved. Daily Stand-ups were more focused, and collaboration between team members and stakeholders increased.

Enhanced Productivity

With the right tools at their disposal, the team was more productive. The new layout and hardware facilitated quicker problem-solving and efficient task management.

Stakeholder Satisfaction

The inclusion of stakeholders in the new workspace arrangement led to more timely feedback, resulting in a product that better met business requirements.

Lessons Learned

The role of the Agile Project Manager extends beyond mere supervision to actively shaping the environment and culture. Effective space management, resource allocation, and communication channels are vital for the success of a co-located Agile team.

This case study underscores the pivotal role an Agile Project Manager plays in setting up an optimal co-located environment, effectively turning a struggling team into a more cohesive and productive unit.

Mastering Communication Challenges in Distributed Agile Teams: A Deeper Look

Managing communication effectively in distributed Agile teams is no small feat. While Agile methodologies like the Dynamic Systems Development Method (DSDM) were originally designed with co-located teams in mind, the modern workplace often requires adapting these principles for distributed teams. Let's delve deeper into the nuances that make communication in distributed teams uniquely challenging, the strategies to overcome these obstacles, and the pivotal role of an Agile Project Manager in orchestrating this complex dance.

In-Depth Analysis of Communication Challenges

Time Zones

Time zones are a glaring challenge. Not only do they make scheduling meetings difficult, but they also limit the window of opportunity for real-time collaboration. This can lead to delays in decision-making and problem-solving, slowing down the project's momentum.

Language and Cultural Barriers

Language differences can lead to misunderstandings, while cultural variations can influence work styles, attitudes towards hierarchy, and communication preferences. This adds a layer of complexity to the simple act of conveying a message or understanding a task requirement.

Lack of Physical Interaction

Physical cues like body language and facial expressions play a vital role in effective communication. In a distributed setting, the absence of these non-verbal cues can make interactions seem less personal, impacting the level of trust and cohesion within the team.

Strategies for Effective Communication

Structured Communication

Scheduled, regular meetings using video conferencing technology can create a semblance of structure and predictability, helping to offset some challenges of distance.

Technology Leverage

Cloud-based tools and platforms can facilitate seamless document sharing and real-time communication. Incorporating tools that allow for asynchronous updates, like a virtual Team Board, can also be invaluable.

Cultural Sensitivity

A preliminary session on cultural sensitivity can go a long way in minimizing misunderstandings. This creates an environment where everyone feels respected and valued, thereby enhancing communication.

Working Hour Overlaps

Identifying a window of time where all team members are available for synchronous activities can significantly improve real-time collaboration. This can be particularly crucial for problem-solving sessions or critical decision-making meetings.

Role of the Agile Project Manager

Comprehensive Communication Planning

The Agile Project Manager should create a robust communication plan that outlines the frequency, mode, and participants for each type of communication event, from daily stand-ups to sprint reviews.

Technology Enablement

Selecting the right communication platforms and possibly customizing them for team-specific needs is critical. The Agile Project Manager should also ensure everyone is trained to use these tools efficiently.

Continuous Monitoring

Periodic reviews should be conducted to assess the effectiveness of the chosen communication strategies. If something is not working as planned, the Agile Project Manager should be agile enough to adapt and pivot, ensuring that communication remains streamlined and effective.

Case Study: Implementing Effective Communication Strategies in a Globally Distributed Agile Team

Background

Imagine an Agile Project Manager named Alex who is responsible for overseeing a globally distributed team working on a complex software development project. The team has members in North America, Europe, and Asia, making it a truly 24/7 operation. However, this also creates a range of communication challenges, including time zone differences, cultural variations, and limited face-to-face interactions. Alex recognizes the need for a comprehensive strategy to ensure seamless communication across the team.

Strategies Employed

Time Zone Management

Alex starts by identifying a two-hour window where all team members are generally available. This window is designated for essential synchronous activities like stand-ups and decision-making sessions. For other asynchronous activities, the team uses an electronic Team Board where updates can be made and reviewed in any time zone.

Overcoming Language and Cultural Barriers

To ensure everyone is on the same page, Alex arranges for a cultural sensitivity training session. Additionally, team members are encouraged to be explicit about their communication, avoiding jargon or idioms that might not be universally understood.

Technology Utilization

Alex selects a suite of cloud-based tools designed for Agile teams. This includes a video conferencing tool for virtual meetings, a project management tool that mimics a physical Team Board, and a shared document repository. Training sessions are conducted to make sure everyone is comfortable using these platforms.

Results

After implementing these strategies, the team experiences a notable improvement in communication efficacy. The stand-up meetings are more focused, the Team Board is always up-to-date, and team members express feeling more connected and aligned with each other. Alex continues to monitor the situation and is prepared to make further adjustments as needed.

By applying a comprehensive set of strategies tailored to the unique challenges of a distributed environment, Alex is able to foster effective communication, keeping the project on track and the team engaged.

The Multifaceted Nature of Collaboration within Agile and DSDM Frameworks

Collaboration is an integral part of Agile methodologies, including the Dynamic Systems Development Method (DSDM). It goes beyond mere teamwork and emerges as a vital component that can make or break a project. This article elaborates on the facets and significance of collaboration in Agile and DSDM frameworks, shedding light on its key elements and how to foster a collaborative environment effectively.

Why Collaboration is Fundamental in Agile and DSDM

The Role of Interpersonal Relationships

Collaboration is inherently people-centric. The quality of interpersonal relationships within the team significantly impacts the effectiveness of collaborative efforts. Without a foundation of mutual respect and trust, it becomes exceedingly difficult to achieve true collaboration.

The Influence of Cultural Factors

Shared values and beliefs can serve as a catalyst for enhancing collaboration. On the flip side, mismatched values or conflicting assumptions can become roadblocks. Therefore, alignment on the team's values, mission, and goals is indispensable for successful collaboration.

Key Ingredients for Effective Collaboration

Personal Behavioral Traits

The individual styles and behavioral traits of team members play a decisive role in the collaboration process. While some team members might be naturally inclined to collaborate, others may need structured guidance or training to improve their collaborative skills.

The Power of Diverse Thinking

A collaborative environment that encourages diversity of thought is likely to produce more robust solutions. It is not about unanimous agreement but about the constructive utilization of diverse perspectives to solve complex problems.

The Balance of Give and Take

Effective collaboration is a two-way street. It involves an element of compromise and a willingness to adapt based on team input. Active listening and open dialogue are vital for the give-and-take that a collaborative environment requires.

Strategies for Enhancing Collaboration in DSDM Projects

The Role of Leadership

The Agile Project Manager or Team Leader plays a pivotal role in setting the tone for collaboration. Their behavior and attitudes toward teamwork can significantly influence the rest of the team.

Importance of Training and Coaching

Focused coaching sessions can be invaluable for team members who struggle with collaboration. These training sessions can equip individuals with the tools and techniques they need to improve.

Recognition as a Motivator

Recognizing and rewarding collaborative efforts can reinforce the importance of teamwork. Celebrating these successes can serve as a potent motivator for sustained collaboration.

Utilization of Collaborative Tools

Shared workspaces, Agile boards, and specialized communication platforms can act as facilitators for collaboration, breaking down barriers and making it easier for team members to work together effectively.

The Need for Regular Check-ins

Periodic meetings to assess the level of collaboration can provide insights into what's working and what needs adjustment. These check-ins act as a mechanism to proactively address any emerging issues that could hamper collaboration.

Case Study: Enhancing Collaboration in a DSDM Project

Background

In a mid-sized software development company, a project was initiated using the Dynamic Systems Development Method (DSDM) framework. While the project had a promising start, it soon became evident that the level of collaboration among team members was not up to the mark. This lack of effective collaboration was affecting project milestones and overall team morale.

Problem Identification

Upon review, it was found that the team faced issues related to misaligned values and cultural differences. Additionally, there was a clear lack of effective communication tools that could facilitate collaboration.

Solutions Implemented

Leadership Intervention

The Agile Project Manager took the initiative to address these concerns. A series of team-building exercises were organized, aimed at fostering trust and understanding among team members.

Focused Training Sessions

Training sessions were conducted to educate team members on the importance of collaboration and how to use specific techniques to improve collaborative efforts. Role-playing exercises were used to simulate real-world scenarios, helping team members understand the practical implications of effective collaboration.

Technology Overhaul

The existing communication tools were evaluated, and a new suite of collaboration-friendly software was introduced. This included project management tools with built-in chat functionalities, video conferencing tools, and a cloud-based team board accessible to all team members.

Recognition and Rewards

A recognition program was initiated to celebrate successful collaborative efforts. Teams that demonstrated exceptional collaboration were publicly acknowledged in company meetings, reinforcing the importance of teamwork.

Periodic Reviews

Bi-weekly meetings were instituted to assess the state of collaboration among team members. These meetings served as a platform for open discussion and helped identify any new challenges that needed to be addressed.

Results

Within a few months, the team saw significant improvements in collaboration. Milestones were being met more consistently, and team morale saw a considerable boost. The project eventually concluded successfully, thanks in large part to the newly fostered collaborative environment.

This case study illustrates how a multi-pronged approach, including leadership intervention, training, technological support, and periodic reviews, can significantly improve collaboration in a DSDM project.

Building Effective Collaboration in Agile Teams: A Deeper Dive into Challenges and Strategies

Essential Ingredients for Effective Collaboration: Further Insights

Mutual Trust and Respect

Trust is not merely an emotional comfort but a functional necessity in an Agile team. The absence of trust can lead to defensive postures, hidden agendas, and resistance to collaboration. Trust becomes even more vital in a dynamic Agile environment, where team members often have to rely on each other's competencies without a rigid hierarchical structure.

Open-Mindedness and Approachability

The willingness to consider new ideas is not just a "nice-to-have," but essential for innovation. It allows a team to explore uncharted territories in problem-solving. Approachability, on the other hand, ensures that team members feel comfortable sharing those new ideas without fear of criticism.

Availability

Being available does not only mean physical presence but also psychological availability. Team members should be prepared to contribute constructively to discussions and problem-solving sessions. They should also be open to unplanned interactions, which are often where the most innovative solutions are born.

Common Barriers to Collaboration: Extending the Conversation

Organizational Silos

These silos can restrict information flow, lead to duplicated efforts, and create an environment where collective problem-solving is difficult. Breaking down these silos often involves organizational change that goes beyond the scope of a single project.

Resource Scarcity

Limited resources can lead to a zero-sum mindset where sharing becomes a perceived risk. Such a mindset is counterproductive in an Agile environment, which thrives on collaboration and collective problem-solving.

Culture of Competition

While a certain level of competition can be motivating, an excess can promote toxic behaviors like knowledge hoarding and can be detrimental to a collaborative culture.

Strategies for Overcoming Barriers: Expanded View

Organizational Restructuring

Simply reshuffling departments or reporting lines may not suffice. The organizational restructuring should be aimed at promoting functional relationships and effective communication pathways that support collaboration.

Incentive Realignment

Rewards and recognition should not solely focus on individual achievements. An ideal incentive system would reward collective performance and collaborative behaviors, subtly promoting a shift from "I" to "We."

Leadership Training

Leadership in an Agile environment is not just about managing tasks but also about cultivating an ecosystem that is conducive for collaboration. Leaders should be equipped with the skills to balance both competitive and collaborative forces within the team.

Case Study: Implementing Effective Collaboration in a Fictive Agile Team

Background

Let's consider a hypothetical software development team that has transitioned to using the Dynamic Systems Development Method (DSDM). Despite adopting Agile practices like Daily Stand-ups and Sprint Planning, the team struggles with collaboration. Team members are talented but isolated, hindered by organizational silos and a reward system that emphasizes individual performance.

Challenges Faced

Organizational Silos

The development team and Quality Assurance (QA) operate as separate entities, leading to bottlenecks and lapses in communication.

Resource Scarcity

The company has limited licenses for specialized software, causing reluctance among team members to share resources.

Individualistic Goals

The existing reward system promotes individual achievements, creating a culture that discourages collaboration.

Strategies Implemented

Organizational Restructuring

The first move was to form cross-functional teams comprising both developers and QA professionals. This change facilitated better communication and quicker decision-making, breaking down previous silos.

Incentive Realignment

The management team overhauled the existing reward system. The new framework included parameters like "Best Collaborative Effort" and "Team of the Month" to promote collective achievement.

Leadership Training

Team leads underwent specific training modules on fostering a collaborative environment, which included courses on effective communication, conflict resolution, and the promotion of a growth mindset.

Outcome

Post-implementation of these strategies, the team displayed a significant improvement in collaboration. The cross-functional approach eliminated bottlenecks, and the new incentive scheme led to a noticeable shift in team dynamics. While not all challenges were completely eradicated, the leadership training equipped team leads with the skills required to maintain a balance between competition and collaboration.

By adopting a structured approach to encourage collaboration, the team was able to better align with Agile and DSDM principles, ultimately leading to more efficient and effective project delivery.

Deepening the Understanding of T-Shaped Skills in Collaborative Agile Teams

Defining T-Shaped Skills Further

T-shaped skills are more than just a blend of specialized and general skills; they represent a mindset that values the integrative approach to problem-solving. Such individuals possess not only the technical depth in their field (the vertical bar of the "T") but also the curiosity and capacity to engage across a variety of disciplines (the horizontal bar).

The Multi-Faceted Advantages of T-Shaped Skills

Multi-Dimensional Problem-Solving

Individuals with T-shaped skills have a balanced approach to problem-solving. Their specialized skills provide the depth needed for intricate challenges, while their general skills contribute a breadth of understanding that often results in more comprehensive solutions.

Collaboration and Synergy

T-shaped individuals serve as 'bridges' between different specialized roles within a team. By understanding multiple perspectives, they facilitate smoother communication and contribute to a more synergistic work environment.

Resilience and Flexibility

The adaptable nature of T-shaped individuals makes them better equipped to handle project pivots or role adjustments, which is vital in Agile frameworks that are inherently dynamic.

Innovation at the Intersection

The ability to see a problem from both a specialized and a generalized viewpoint often sparks innovative solutions, setting T-shaped individuals apart in their ability to contribute creatively to projects.

Assembling a T-Shaped Team: A Blueprint for Success

Strategic Recruitment

Selecting candidates with T-shaped skills is the first step in building a high-performance team. Recruitment strategies should focus on identifying not just technical competence but also a demonstrable aptitude for cross-disciplinary collaboration.

Continuous Training and Skill Enhancement

Organizations should invest in training programs that nurture both the vertical and horizontal aspects of T-shaped skills. This could involve specialized workshops, general soft skills training, and cross-disciplinary exposure.

Dynamic Project Assignments

Project roles should be assigned in a manner that enables team members to exercise their T-shaped skills. This could mean involving a software developer in customer interviews or inviting a product manager to code reviews, for example.

Culture of Knowledge Sharing

Promote an organizational culture that values and encourages knowledge sharing. Implementing knowledge-sharing platforms, organizing inter-departmental meetups, or even informal "lunch-and-learn" sessions can be effective ways to foster this.

Case Study: Implementing T-Shaped Skills in an Agile Team for Enhanced Performance

Context

A software development company using the Agile framework noticed that while their teams were high-performing in their specialized roles, there was a lack of cohesiveness and inter-disciplinary understanding. Project deliverables were technically excellent but often lacked an integrative approach that considered multiple aspects of the product.

Intervention

Skill Auditing and Identification

The first step involved a comprehensive skills audit to identify the existing T-shaped skills within teams and to pinpoint gaps that needed to be filled.

Targeted Training Programs

Based on the audit, a series of training programs were designed, focusing on enhancing the 'horizontal bar' skills like effective communication, basics of UI/UX design, and even rudimentary coding for non-developers.

Re-structuring Project Teams

Teams were restructured to include a mix of T-shaped individuals and those who were in the process of broadening their skill sets. The idea was to blend specialized knowledge with generalized understanding.

Iterative Feedback Loop

The Agile Project Manager established an iterative feedback loop involving all team members, aimed at continually assessing the impact of T-shaped skills on project outcomes.

Results

Improved Communication

The newly formed teams displayed improved communication, with fewer instances of tasks falling through the cracks due to misunderstandings.

Accelerated Problem-Solving

The ability to understand problems from multiple viewpoints led to quicker identification of issues and more efficient problem-solving processes.

Enhanced Product Quality

The end products started reflecting a well-rounded approach, effectively merging technical prowess with user-centric design and other crucial elements.

Increased Job Satisfaction

Team members reported a greater sense of fulfillment as they felt more engaged and valuable due to their expanded roles and capabilities.

Key Takeaways

The implementation of T-shaped skills into Agile teams brought about significant improvements in both project outcomes and team dynamics. This case study serves as a testament to the multi-faceted advantages of fostering T-shaped skills in collaborative environments.

DSDM Teams: From Structure to Strategy

Further Insights into DSDM's Inclusive Team Composition

DSDM goes beyond the traditional, development-centric view of Agile teams. It enriches the team structure by integrating roles that focus on governance, such as Business Sponsors and Business Visionaries, along with roles that provide critical support to the development process, such as Business Analysts and Technical Architects. This layered approach helps in balancing both the business and technical aspects of a project.

Why a Holistic Approach to "Team" Matters

DSDM's definition of a "team" extends beyond the walls of the development room. By recognizing the impact of external stakeholders—such as suppliers, regulatory bodies, or even customers—the framework ensures that a project is not developed in a vacuum. This alignment with a broader set of interests and requirements makes the end product more robust and fit-for-purpose.

The Significance of Stakeholder Management in DSDM

Effective stakeholder management is not just a checkbox in DSDM; it's an integral part of the methodology. From the initial Feasibility stage to the Foundations stage, there is a conscious effort to identify, analyze, and engage stakeholders. This proactive engagement serves to ensure that stakeholder needs and constraints are factored into the project from the outset, reducing the likelihood of later-stage adjustments or disagreements.

Benefits Derived from DSDM's Team Structure

Risk Mitigation

The comprehensive stakeholder engagement strategy reduces the possibility of project failure due to unforeseen challenges or disagreements arising late in the project.

Amplified Collaboration

The inclusion of diverse roles facilitates cross-discipline understanding and cooperation, making the team more responsive and adaptive to changes.

Fostering Transparency

DSDM's approach makes sure everyone is on the same page, thereby enhancing project transparency. This is vital for timely decision-making and for building trust among stakeholders.

Key Steps for Implementing DSDM Team Structures

Comprehensive Stakeholder Identification

The first step is to identify everyone who has a stake in the project, which is broader in scope when compared to other Agile methodologies.

Clarifying Roles and Responsibilities

Once stakeholders are identified, roles must be clearly defined and documented. This is often an iterative process, continually refined as the project progresses.

Early Stakeholder Engagement

The early inclusion of stakeholders, especially during the Feasibility and Foundations stages, sets the stage for a collaborative project environment.

Maintaining Open Communication Channels

It's imperative to keep lines of communication open, structured, and frequent to ensure that the project stays aligned with stakeholder needs and expectations.

Case Study: Implementing DSDM Team Structures in a Financial Services Project

Background and Challenges

A leading financial services firm decided to adopt the DSDM framework for a high-stakes project involving the development of a new transaction processing system. The project posed several challenges, including a complex stakeholder landscape that involved regulatory bodies, multiple departments within the firm, external technology vendors, and end-users. Traditional Agile frameworks had been less successful in earlier projects due to insufficient stakeholder engagement.

Structuring the DSDM Team

Comprehensive Stakeholder Identification

The project began with a thorough process of stakeholder identification, recognizing not only the internal development and business teams but also external entities like vendors and regulators.

Assigning Roles and Responsibilities

Roles such as Business Sponsor, Business Visionary, and Technical Coordinator were explicitly defined. A stakeholder matrix was created to outline the responsibilities and decision-making powers of each role.

Early Stakeholder Engagement

Key stakeholders were engaged early during the Feasibility and Foundations stages. This ensured alignment on critical issues such as compliance requirements, system features, and project milestones.

Communication Strategy

Frequency and Modes

The Agile Project Manager developed a comprehensive communication plan, which outlined the frequency and modes of communication with different stakeholders. Regular steering committee meetings were held with high-level stakeholders, while daily stand-ups were organized for the Solution Development Team.

Feedback Loops

Feedback mechanisms were put in place to capture stakeholder input continuously. This allowed for agile course corrections throughout the project lifecycle.

Outcomes

Risk Mitigation

The inclusive approach to stakeholder engagement paid off, with the project successfully navigating several potential roadblocks, such as regulatory hurdles and technical challenges.

Enhanced Collaboration

The diverse team structure led to effective cross-disciplinary collaboration, ensuring a balanced approach to problem-solving.

Increased Transparency

The open communication channels and defined roles led to a transparent environment. This fostered trust and empowered the team to make informed decisions quickly.

Lessons Learned

The success of this project validated the efficacy of DSDM's comprehensive approach to team structure and stakeholder engagement. It demonstrated the importance of initial planning, continuous communication, and inclusive stakeholder management for reducing risks and enhancing project outcomes.

Shared Team Goals and Ways of Working: A Fundamental Basis for Collaboration in DSDM Projects

Importance of Shared Goals and Norms

Unified Objective

A single, shared objective is not merely a lofty ideal but a necessity in a DSDM project environment. It serves as the guiding light for all collaborative efforts, ensuring that each member is aligned with the overarching vision of the project.

Establishing Norms

The importance of setting behavioral norms cannot be overstated. These norms act as the governing rules for interaction and decision-making within the team. They provide the framework within which collaboration happens, thereby minimizing conflicts and streamlining workflows.

Role of Early Phases and Products in DSDM

Early Phases for Alignment

The Feasibility and Foundations phases in a DSDM project are pivotal. These initial stages serve to align all stakeholders around the shared objectives and agreed-upon norms. Such alignment is not a one-off activity but a continual process that often starts with these early phases.

Significance of Business Case

In the DSDM framework, the Business Case is more than just a mandatory document; it's a unifying artifact. By clearly articulating the project's business vision and expected outcomes, it removes ambiguities and serves as a continual point of reference for the team, thereby strengthening collaborative efforts.

Implementation Steps for Establishing Shared Goals and Norms

Identify Shared Goal

The very first step in any DSDM project should be to establish a shared goal that resonates with all team members. This sets the stage for a focused and unified approach throughout the project lifecycle.

Create a Business Case

The Business Case serves a dual purpose. Firstly, it provides the detailed reasoning behind the project, offering a solid base upon which all subsequent decisions can be made. Secondly, it acts as a shared reference point that keeps everyone on the same page.

Set Behavioral Norms

In a collaborative environment, especially one as dynamic as a DSDM project, a set of agreed-upon behavioral norms or guidelines should be established. This sets the ground rules for interaction and cooperation among team members.

Regular Review and Reiteration

Having established the shared goals and norms, it's essential to revisit them at various project milestones. This ensures that the team remains aligned and adapts to any changes in project scope or objectives.

In-Depth Exploration of the Role of Early Phases and Products in DSDM

The Function of Early Phases in Aligning Team Goals

Priming the Team for Success

The initial phases of a DSDM project, specifically the Feasibility and Foundations stages, are designed to prime the team for successful collaboration. During these phases, stakeholders, team members, and executives converge to evaluate the project's viability and outline its foundational elements.

Pre-emptive Identification of Challenges

One of the less obvious but critical aspects of these early stages is the pre-emptive identification of potential challenges or roadblocks. Knowing these in advance allows for the development of strategies to mitigate them, hence reducing risk and fostering a more collaborative atmosphere.

The Power of Artifacts: Business Case and Beyond

Clarity Through Documentation

While Agile methodologies often emphasize adaptability and responsiveness over detailed upfront planning, the Business Case in a DSDM project is a notable exception. This document serves to crystallize the project's objectives and expected outcomes, providing a clear roadmap that facilitates better decision-making and collaboration.

Continuous Reference and Alignment

The Business Case isn't a document to be filed away and forgotten; rather, it is to be continuously referenced throughout the project. This ongoing utilization ensures that even as individual tasks and short-term objectives evolve, the overarching goal remains constant, keeping the team aligned.

Synchronizing Early Phases and Artifacts for Optimal Collaboration

Holistic Planning

The Feasibility and Foundations phases should be closely integrated with the development of the Business Case. This alignment serves to ensure that the project's goals, as articulated in the Business Case, are viable and in complete harmony with what is planned in these early phases.

Multi-Dimensional Review

Incorporating regular reviews that take into account both the early-phase outputs and the Business Case ensures that the project remains on course. These reviews serve as recalibration points, helping to realign the team and adapt to any changes in project scope or objectives.

Cultivating a Collaborative Culture in DSDM Projects: A Multi-Faceted Approach

Core Features of a Collaboration-Friendly Culture

Fostering Transparency

Openness and honesty are not merely good-to-have virtues in a team; they are essential for nurturing a culture that supports collaboration. When team members are encouraged to be forthright about challenges, mistakes, and ambiguities, it allows for timely problem-solving and adjustment.

Counteracting the Blame Game

In organizations where a culture of blame prevails, collaboration suffers. It becomes imperative to dismantle such a culture and replace it with one that fosters collective responsibility and constructive dialogue.

Learning as a Collective Enterprise

When mistakes are considered opportunities for collective learning rather than individual failure, it cultivates an environment where team members feel secure enough to take calculated risks, ask questions, and propose new ideas.

The Pivotal Role of the Agile Project Manager

Championing Cultural Values

The Agile Project Manager is not just a task overseer but also a cultural steward of the team. They have a pivotal role in nurturing a supportive and open environment conducive to collaboration.

Team Protection and Nurturance

The Agile Project Manager can act as a protective buffer if the surrounding organizational culture is not conducive to collaboration. By shielding the team from external pressures and distractions, the manager enables them to focus on constructive teamwork.

Striking a Balance Between Top-Down and Bottom-Up Culture Building

While it's ideal for a supportive culture to be a top-down initiative from organizational leadership, the reality is often different. The Agile Project Manager can instigate a micro-culture within the team that eventually influences the broader organizational culture.

DSDM-Specific Practices that Augment Collaboration

Workshop-Driven Collaboration

Structured workshops provide a formalized setting for open dialogue, idea sharing, and collective problem-solving. These events serve as catalysts for better teamwork and collaboration.

Iterative Learning through Development Cycles

DSDM's emphasis on iterative development is not just a project management tactic but also a cultural strategy. Iterative cycles allow for regular checkpoints for self-assessment, collective learning, and continuous improvement, thereby enriching the collaborative ethos of the team.

Expanding on the Role of Workshops and Iterative Development in Cultivating Collaborative Culture

The Facets of Workshop-Driven Collaboration

Alignment and Consensus

One of the primary advantages of conducting workshops in a DSDM environment is the alignment of team members around core project goals and responsibilities. Workshops serve as platforms for open dialogue where consensus can be achieved.

Skill Development

Workshops often serve as training grounds for enhancing various soft and hard skills among team members. This can include anything from conflict resolution to technical problem-solving methods.

Relationship Building

In addition to skill development and alignment, workshops also facilitate interpersonal relationship building, which is a cornerstone of effective collaboration.

The Cultural Benefits of Iterative Development

Regular Self-Assessment

Each iteration or development cycle concludes with a retrospective, a form of self-assessment that allows the team to reflect on what worked well and what didn't. This kind of reflection is essential for creating a learning culture.

Adaptability and Resilience

With each iterative cycle, teams become more adaptable as they learn to course-correct based on the retrospective outcomes and stakeholder feedback. This builds resilience, which is a vital attribute in a collaborative culture.

Collective Responsibility

Iterative development fosters a sense of collective responsibility. When the team is collectively involved in assessing the work after each iteration, it naturally leads to a more cohesive and accountable team environment.

The use of workshops and iterative development in DSDM projects go beyond merely being tools for project execution. They are instrumental in shaping a team culture that places a premium on collaboration and continuous improvement.

Leadership in a Collaborative Culture within DSDM Frameworks

Characteristics of Facilitative and Collaborative Leadership

Servant-Leader Approach

This approach emphasizes the leader's role as a servant to the team, prioritizing the needs of team members and facilitating their work. The goal is to build a supportive environment where everyone feels empowered to contribute.

Active Participation

Though the servant-leader approach is non-authoritarian, it's not synonymous with passive leadership. The leader is an active participant in the project, offering insights, asking questions, and engaging with the team in a meaningful way.

Encouragement of Self-Organizing Teams

A facilitative leader supports the idea of self-organization. By relinquishing micromanagement tendencies, the leader encourages the team to take responsibility for their tasks and decision-making, leading to greater autonomy and, subsequently, better performance.

Role of Agile Project Manager and Team Leader in DSDM

No-Blame Culture

In line with the servant-leader approach, both the Agile Project Manager and Team Leader should cultivate a no-blame culture. This involves creating an environment where mistakes are seen as opportunities for growth and collective learning.

Shielding the Team

Leadership in DSDM extends to protecting the team from external disruptions. Whether it's scope changes from stakeholders or undue pressure from senior management, the leaders act as shields, allowing the team to maintain focus and morale.

Shared Responsibility

While the Agile Project Manager and Team Leader are instrumental in setting the leadership style and cultural tone, maintaining this culture is a shared responsibility. Each team member has a role to play in sustaining an environment conducive to collaboration and high performance.

By embracing facilitative and collaborative leadership styles and strategically integrating them within the DSDM framework, organizations can markedly improve project outcomes, team satisfaction, and overall productivity.

Case Study: Implementing Facilitative Leadership in a DSDM Project

Background

In a mid-sized technology company, a DSDM project was initiated to develop a new customer relationship management (CRM) system. The project faced challenges such as fluctuating stakeholder requirements and demoralized team members due to a previously failed project. Leadership was identified as a pivotal factor to turn the situation around.

Introducing the Servant-Leader Approach

The Agile Project Manager adopted a servant-leader approach, focusing on meeting the team's needs and removing obstacles. Simple changes like setting up a more ergonomic workspace and re-negotiating deadlines had an immediate positive impact on team morale.

Active Participation and Open Communication

The Project Manager and Team Leader were actively involved in all phases of the project, not merely as overseers but as engaged participants. Daily stand-ups and bi-weekly sprint reviews became platforms for open dialogue rather than status reporting.

Encouragement of Self-Organizing Teams

With the support from leadership, the team transitioned from being task-driven to becoming a self-organizing entity. They took ownership of tasks and made collective decisions about how to address challenges, reinforcing the sense of shared responsibility and commitment.

Cultivating a No-Blame Culture

The leaders took extra efforts to establish a no-blame culture. Instead of reprimanding a team member for a coding error, they organized a "lessons learned" session where everyone could discuss what went wrong and how to avoid similar mistakes in the future.

Shielding the Team

The Agile Project Manager actively shielded the team from external pressures. When stakeholders attempted to introduce scope changes mid-sprint, the Project Manager successfully negotiated to include those changes in the next sprint, thereby safeguarding the team's focus and work rhythm.

Outcomes

The project was completed on time and within budget, but more importantly, the team reported significantly higher levels of satisfaction and morale. The servant-leader approach combined with the collaborative principles inherent in DSDM led to a synergistic effect, yielding higher productivity and a far more positive work environment.

By understanding and implementing facilitative and collaborative leadership within the DSDM framework, organizations can foster a culture that not only improves project outcomes but also contributes to the overall well-being and development of team members.

Agile Project Manager's Guide to Nurturing Human Factors: People, Teams, and Interactions

Focusing on Effective Communication Strategies

The Imperative for Clear and Timely Communication

A harmonious team environment thrives on effective communication. Agile Project Managers need to lay the groundwork for open, transparent dialogue.

Implementation Guidelines

Schedule frequent team gatherings and one-on-one sessions. Facilitate environments where open dialogue is not just encouraged but expected.

Assessing Team Communication Capabilities

Why Assessment Matters

People come from diverse communication backgrounds. Recognizing these nuances enables more effective interactions.

Implementation Guidelines

Carry out assessments or workshops to gauge communication strengths and weaknesses within the team. Utilize this data for communication optimization strategies.

Leveraging Communication Technologies

The Role of Modern Tools

Today's technology landscape offers a plethora of tools to aid in project communication.

Implementation Guidelines

Use modern collaboration tools judiciously. While platforms like Slack or Microsoft Teams facilitate ongoing dialogue, remember that complex or sensitive matters are often best handled face-to-face.

Advocating for Co-Location of Team Members

The Benefits of Physical Proximity

Co-location often leads to improved communication, primarily through non-planned, spontaneous interactions.

Implementation Guidelines

When feasible, secure a dedicated workspace for the team. This encourages natural interactions and fosters a cohesive team environment.

Understanding Team Development Stages

Navigating Forming, Storming, Norming, and Performing

Recognizing the stages of team development can offer valuable insights into team dynamics.

Implementation Guidelines

Design activities or discussions aimed at shepherding the team through these stages. Consider the needs and conflicts that typically arise at each stage.

Celebrating Team Diversity

The Advantage of Varied Perspectives

Diversity enriches team dynamics and leads to more innovative problem-solving.

Implementation Guidelines

Promote an atmosphere where diversity is valued. Encourage team members to share their unique perspectives and skills.

Extending the Communication Net

Broadening the Communication Scope

The team's communication strategies must also include stakeholders and other entities within the organization for the project to truly succeed.

Implementation Guidelines

Ensure regular, structured communication with all stakeholders. Make them a part of critical decisions and keep them informed of project developments.

Case Study: The Role of an Agile Project Manager in Enhancing Communication and Team Dynamics

Project Overview

In a mid-sized software development company, an Agile Project Manager was tasked with overseeing a critical project. The team had a mix of experienced and junior developers, along with remote and in-house team members. Challenges around effective communication and team cohesion were immediately evident.

Challenges Faced

Uneven Communication Skills: The team was diverse in terms of experience and communication skills.

Remote Work Complications: Working remotely added layers of complexity to the communication process.

Varying Team Dynamics: The team was newly formed and was navigating through the 'forming' and 'storming' stages.

Strategies Employed by the Agile Project Manager

Focused Assessment of Communication Skills

A workshop was conducted to evaluate the communication styles of individual team members. The findings were then used to tailor communication protocols suited to the team's diverse needs.

Technology as an Enabler

To bridge the gap between remote and in-house team members, collaboration tools like Slack and Zoom were effectively utilized for daily stand-ups and ad-hoc meetings. However, critical discussions were reserved for face-to-face meetings or video calls involving all team members.

Facilitating Co-location

A dedicated project room was set up for in-house team members, and remote members were flown in quarterly for week-long co-located work sessions.

Team Dynamics Workshop

A two-day workshop was designed to address the various stages of team development. This helped team members understand the natural progression of team dynamics, reducing conflicts and accelerating the 'norming' phase.

Celebrating Diversity

Team-building activities were used to highlight the benefits of diverse perspectives within the team, building a culture of inclusion and mutual respect.

Inclusive Stakeholder Communication

A monthly newsletter was introduced, featuring project updates and key milestones, to keep all stakeholders in the loop.

Outcomes

Improved Team Cohesion: The team rapidly moved through the 'storming' phase into 'norming' and 'performing'.

Enhanced Communication: Open, honest communication became the norm rather than the exception.

Stakeholder Satisfaction: Transparent communication with stakeholders led to increased confidence in the project' s progress.

The Agile Project Manager's strategic approach to nurturing communication and team dynamics led to a highly successful project outcome.

Chapter Sixteen

Requirements and User Stories: The Building Blocks of Agile Projects

The Agile Approach to Requirements Management in DSDM Projects: Balancing Flexibility and Precision

The Significance of Agile Requirements Management in DSDM

The DSDM (Dynamic Systems Development Method) framework advocates for an Agile approach to requirements management. This approach acknowledges that business needs are not static; they evolve as the project progresses and as the team gains a deeper understanding of the project scope and objectives. The Agile mindset, therefore, recommends capturing requirements at a high level initially, providing the flexibility to refine them as you move along. This is consistent with the Agile principle that values "responding to change over following a plan."

What Constitutes a Requirement?

In its simplest form, a requirement is an articulated need for a particular function, service, or feature. The specificity of these needs can vary widely based on the type of project or industry involved. Whether it is a training company that requires solutions for scheduling and room reservation, or a custom-built car needing mobility and steering capabilities, the core idea is the same: capture what is needed.

Distinguishing Between Functional and Non-Functional Requirements

Functional Requirements (FRs)

These requirements focus on the specific functionality or features that the end product should have. The critical point here is to specify what needs to be achieved without dictating how it should be achieved. This approach leaves room for innovation and adaptability, two tenets of Agile methodologies.

Non-Functional Requirements (NFRs)

Contrary to functional requirements, non-functional requirements are concerned with how well the system performs specific tasks. These could range from system responsiveness to availability metrics. Non-functional requirements set the performance standards that the solution must meet.

The Importance of Requirement Categorization

Accurately categorizing requirements into functional and non-functional types has multiple benefits. First, it lends clarity to the project scope and ensures that all stakeholder needs are considered. Second, it leaves the 'how' open-ended, thereby encouraging creative problem-solving methods to achieve the 'what.' This flexibility is particularly valuable in Agile environments like DSDM, where adaptability and responsiveness to change are highly prized.

Case Study: Agile Requirements Management in a DSDM Project for a Healthcare Platform

Project Overview

The project in focus aimed to develop a healthcare platform that would provide telehealth services, allowing patients to consult with healthcare professionals online. Due to the volatile nature of healthcare regulations and the rapid advancement in telehealth technology, the project was undertaken using the DSDM framework.

Initial Requirements Definition

In the early stages, high-level requirements were gathered. These included functional requirements like secure video conferencing, prescription management, and appointment scheduling. Non-functional requirements were also identified, such as ensuring data security and a user-friendly interface with a response time of under two seconds.

Flexibility in Requirements

As the project advanced, telehealth regulations underwent several changes, necessitating adjustments in the platform's features. The DSDM approach provided the flexibility to adapt to these changes without derailing the project. New functional and non-functional requirements were incorporated, and some of the initially identified requirements were refined.

Role of Agile Principles

Consistent with Agile principles, the team was able to respond effectively to changes in the regulatory environment and technology landscape. The high-level definition of requirements allowed them to pivot without wasting resources or time.

Outcomes

The project was completed successfully, meeting all the functional and non-functional requirements. More importantly, the platform was agile enough to adapt to new healthcare regulations that were enacted shortly after its launch.

Lessons Learned

The case study exemplifies how an Agile approach to requirements management, particularly within the DSDM framework, can offer the flexibility needed to adapt to change while maintaining project integrity. The initial high-level capture of requirements, followed by incremental refinement, proved to be an effective strategy in a dynamic and uncertain environment.

This case study illustrates the tangible benefits of adopting an Agile approach to requirements management in DSDM projects. It underlines the importance of flexibility, adaptability, and a keen understanding of both functional and non-functional requirements.

The Agile Approach to User Stories in DSDM Frameworks: An In-Depth Understanding

Why User Stories Matter in Agile and DSDM

User Stories serve as the linchpin for aligning development work with user needs and business value. They are instrumental in breaking down complex functionalities into smaller, more manageable pieces that are easily understandable. Their user-centric nature ensures that development remains focused on delivering real value to end-users and stakeholders.

Anatomy of a User Story

The 3 "C's" in Detail

Card: This is the documented user story that usually fits on a physical card or a digital equivalent. The aim is to keep it short and simple, focusing only on what is essential.

Conversation: This is the explanatory dialogue that takes place among team members to further clarify the details, remove ambiguities, and understand the scope and constraints. Conversations could be formal or informal but are aimed at achieving a common understanding.

Confirmation: This refers to the acceptance criteria that are necessary to consider the story 'done.' These criteria are established beforehand and serve as the benchmarks against which the implementation is measured.

Understanding the Card Components

Front of the Card: Contains basic identifiers and the formatted user story statement that serves as an initial summary.

Back of the Card: Houses the acceptance criteria that are crucial for Quality Assurance (QA) teams and developers alike. These criteria usually take the form of questions that expect a "Yes" or "No" answer and serve to validate whether the development work meets the stated requirement.

Navigating Complexity Through User Stories

User Stories are not just tools for simplicity; they are also frameworks for navigating complex project landscapes. By focusing on individual user roles and their specific needs, User Stories enable the project team to dissect complex functionalities into smaller components that are easier to manage, develop, and test.

Balancing Detail and Flexibility

While User Stories provide necessary structure, they are intentionally left incomplete to some extent. The details are filled in progressively, usually through conversations among team members as the project evolves. This adaptive approach aligns well with the DSDM philosophy of being responsive to change.

Case Study: Implementing User Stories in a DSDM Project for a Financial Services Firm

Overview

A large financial services company embarked on a digital transformation journey with the aim of overhauling its customer service experience. A cross-functional team was assembled to work within the DSDM framework. The team opted for User Stories as a way to capture requirements for the new customer service platform.

Approach Taken

User Story Creation

- During the initial Feasibility and Foundations phases, the team collaborated with stakeholders to draft high-level User Stories.
- The stories were captured on physical cards and displayed on a project board for visibility.

The 3 "C's" in Action

Card: Each card contained a simple, concise description focusing on a specific user need.

Conversation: The team held regular sessions to delve into each story's details, ensuring that developers, designers, and business analysts were on the same page.

Confirmation: Acceptance criteria were set, discussed, and agreed upon before any development began, mitigating the risk of feature creep or misunderstandings later on.

Adaptive Detailing

- As the project advanced through its iterative cycles, the stories were refined, and additional details were added based on feedback from interim releases.

Outcomes

Clarity and Focus: The use of User Stories helped maintain a clear focus on user needs and business value throughout the project lifecycle.

Efficient Communication: The 3 "C's" model facilitated seamless communication among team members, allowing for rapid adjustments and iterations.

Quality Assurance: The predefined acceptance criteria ensured that the delivered features met the project's goals and user needs.

Lessons Learned

- The importance of keeping User Stories concise yet flexible was validated.
- The value of early and continuous stakeholder involvement was underscored.
- The approach reinforced the importance of having explicit acceptance criteria to serve as a robust measure of a feature's completeness and quality.

By meticulously adhering to the structure and philosophy of User Stories, the project not only delivered a robust customer service platform but also ensured that the end product was closely aligned with user needs and business objectives.

The INVEST Model: An Indispensable Guide for High-Quality User Stories

The INVEST model encapsulates the best practices for crafting effective User Stories, a core technique in Agile and DSDM methodologies. This model emphasizes six fundamental characteristics that every User Story should possess: Independent, Negotiable, Valuable, Estimable, Small, and Testable. Each of these attributes contributes to the efficacy and workability of User Stories, ensuring they are well-suited for Agile development environments.

Key Components of the INVEST Model

Independent

Stories should be self-contained, allowing for a more flexible planning process and minimizing interdependencies among them. When stories exhibit too many dependencies, it is often advisable to consider combining them to alleviate the complexities arising from intertwined requirements.

Negotiable

User Stories serve as conversation starters rather than fixed contracts. This leaves room for negotiation, particularly concerning the details, which are worked out closer to the development phase. This attribute supports the Agile principle of embracing change, allowing for course corrections as new information emerges.

Valuable

Each User Story should be crafted to deliver discernible business value to the stakeholders. It is critical that the language employed in describing the story resonates with the stakeholders, ensuring that the business value is not only clear but also compelling.

Estimable

The story should carry sufficient details to enable estimation without overwhelming the team with minutiae. Striking this balance is crucial for effective sprint planning and resource allocation.

Small

The 'Small' criterion stipulates that User Stories should be compact enough to be developed within a single iteration. When stories grow too large, known as 'Epics,' they need to be decomposed into smaller, more manageable stories that still adhere to the other INVEST principles.

Testable

A User Story should be concrete enough to be testable, ensuring that it meets its acceptance criteria. Specificity is key here, as vague or ambiguous stories hinder the ability to validate whether the requirements have been successfully met.

Checks for Well-Written User Stories

No Overlap or Conflict: Ensure that the stories do not duplicate or contradict one another, which could lead to wasted effort or inconsistencies.

Conformance to Standards: All User Stories should comply with organizational and project-specific standards to ensure cohesion and maintainability.

Traceability: Each User Story should be traceable back to the Business Case and overarching project objectives, reinforcing its relevance and value.

Cross-Referencing: Where appropriate, stories should be cross-referenced with related stories, especially when they pertain to the same feature but involve different user roles.

Case Study: Implementing the INVEST Model in a FinTech Project

Overview

A FinTech startup aimed to develop a new mobile banking application. The project team decided to employ the Agile methodology, specifically the DSDM framework, for its development process. The Product Owner, together with Business Analysts and key stakeholders, employed the INVEST model to craft User Stories for the application's features, such as account management, fund transfers, and real-time alerts.

Application of the INVEST Model

Independent

The team ensured that each User Story was independent to allow for changes in priority. For example, the story for 'real-time account balance updates' was designed to be independent of the story for 'fund transfers,' allowing either to be developed first depending on business needs.

Negotiable

During the grooming sessions, the team refrained from locking into specific solutions, leaving room for negotiation and adaptation. This approach paid off when they found a more efficient third-party service for notifications, which required altering the initially thought-out details for the 'real-time alerts' story.

Valuable

Each User Story was clearly aligned with business objectives and customer needs. The story for enabling 'biometric authentication,' for instance, was linked directly to the goal of enhancing user security, a key selling point for the app.

Estimable

The stories were formulated in a way that allowed for straightforward effort estimation. For example, the story for 'transaction history search' provided enough information for the developers to estimate its complexity, yet was not bogged down with unnecessary detail.

Small

The 'Fund Transfers' User Story was initially quite large and complex, so the team broke it down into smaller stories, such as 'domestic transfers,' 'international transfers,' and 'transfer to a phone number.'

Testable

The team included acceptance criteria for each story, ensuring they were testable. For the 'real-time account balance updates' story, criteria included performance metrics like 'update latency should not exceed 2 seconds.'

Results

By adhering to the INVEST model, the team was able to maintain a high level of agility and responsiveness to change. Their well-crafted User Stories facilitated smoother sprints, clearer communications, and a more targeted focus on delivering business value. The mobile banking application was successfully rolled out, meeting critical stakeholder expectations and achieving a high user adoption rate.

This case study exemplifies how the INVEST model can guide the creation of high-quality User Stories, ultimately contributing to the success of Agile projects.

A Closer Examination: Anchoring Agile Projects

Foundational Elements: Objectives, Vision, and Business Case

Why They Matter

An Agile project's success significantly depends on its foundational elements: Objectives, Business Vision, and Business Case. These elements act as an anchor, providing stability and direction in an environment known for its iterative and flexible nature.

Interconnectedness

Each foundational element serves as a filter through which more detailed requirements, such as User Stories, must pass. This ensures alignment with the overall strategic goals, enabling more effective prioritization and decision-making.

The Role of the Feasibility Phase

Setting Clear Objectives

The Feasibility phase is where the Business Analyst transforms an ambiguous Terms of Reference into a focused project objective. The objective manifests itself as the highest-level Epic User Story, guiding subsequent requirements gathering and validation activities.

Business Vision

The Business Vision document articulates the strategic direction and the long-term goals of the project. This helps in tailoring the development and prioritization of User Stories, thereby ensuring they resonate with the project's overarching aims.

The Business Case

Creating a robust Business Case is crucial for gaining stakeholder buy-in. It outlines the project's benefits, costs, and potential impact, offering a roadmap that aligns the project's direction with the organizational strategy.

Relevance of User Stories During Feasibility

Stakeholder Identification

User Stories, particularly Epics and Themes, are excellent tools for pinpointing key stakeholders. Their format inherently specifies a 'role,' making it easier to identify who should be involved in discussions and decision-making.

Articulating Business Value

The 'So that' clause in a User Story succinctly captures the underlying business value or problem to be solved. This makes it simpler to align project activities with strategic goals.

High-Level Acceptance Criteria

Crafting high-level acceptance criteria during the Feasibility phase provides an early view into what must be true for the project to be considered successful. These criteria can be instrumental in shaping the project's trajectory.

Scoping the Project

The presence of high-level User Stories serves as an initial framework for scoping the project. This is particularly useful for feasibility studies, early cost-benefit analyses, and for providing stakeholders with a tangible sense of the project's scale and complexity.

Case Study: Implementing Foundational Elements in an Agile Software Development Project

Project Background

Imagine a medium-sized software company undertaking a project to develop a new content management system. The project team operates within an Agile framework and uses Dynamic Systems Development Method (DSDM) for guidance.

Setting the Stage: Feasibility Phase

Objective

The Business Analyst collaborates with stakeholders to convert the project's initial Terms of Reference into a clear objective: "Develop a content management system that facilitates content creation, approval, and publishing workflows for mid-sized organizations."

Business Vision

The long-term vision is to position this new content management system as an industry standard for mid-sized businesses, offering robust features, user-friendly interfaces, and scalability.

Business Case

The Business Case outlines the expected ROI, including increased revenue streams from software licenses and subscription fees, decreased development costs via reusing components, and alignment with the company's strategic focus on developing software solutions for mid-sized businesses.

Utilizing User Stories

Stakeholder Identification

The Epic User Story for the project objective helps identify the key stakeholders: Content Creators, Approvers, Publishers, and IT Admins.

Articulating Business Value

A User Story like "As a Content Creator, I need an intuitive interface so that I can focus on content creation without technical distractions" captures the specific business value of user-friendliness, aligning with the broader business vision.

High-Level Acceptance Criteria

Acceptance criteria for this Epic User Story might include:

- "Is the system's user interface intuitive enough for a new user to navigate without prior training?"
- "Can a content creator initiate a new content submission within three clicks?"

Project Scoping

The initial set of high-level User Stories helps define the project scope, aiding the team in conducting a preliminary cost-benefit analysis and in narrowing down the list of features for the first few iterations.

This case study exemplifies how foundational elements and User Stories interplay to anchor an Agile project effectively, ensuring alignment with organizational strategies and stakeholder expectations.

The Role of the Foundations Phase in DSDM for Requirements Management

Foundations: A Nexus for Structuring, Prioritizing, and Planning Requirements

In the Foundations phase of a DSDM Agile project, the nebulous concepts and high-level requirements that surfaced during the Feasibility phase are molded into a structured format. The Foundations phase is a pivotal point for the meticulous planning of how the project's requirements will be addressed.

Collaborative Requirements Elaboration: The Power of Workshops

Workshops play an indispensable role in bringing together the right stakeholders for collaborative requirements elaboration. The key activities during these workshops are:

Defining Requirements: Stakeholders like the Business Visionary, Ambassador, and Advisors come together to fine-tune the requirement details.

Estimating and Planning: The Solution Development Team and Project Manager convert the requirements into actionable tasks, estimating effort and scheduling them in the Delivery Plan.

Transitioning from Epics to User Stories: Focused Specificity

This phase is crucial for decomposing Epics into actionable User Stories. These User Stories must meet specific criteria:

Specificity and Sizing: By the end of this phase, User Stories should be sufficiently detailed and scoped to fit into a Development Timebox.

Volume Limitation: DSDM recommends limiting the number of Requirements/User Stories to fewer than 100 for the sake of manageability.

Prioritised Requirements List (PRL): The Baseline for Project Execution

The Prioritised Requirements List becomes the governing document for the upcoming phases. It serves two primary functions:

Inventory of Requirements: It houses all agreed-upon User Stories that will guide the planning and execution of the project's first Increment.

Governance Mechanism: The PRL acts as a benchmark, allowing the team to evaluate any new requirements against the established baseline.

The Vital Role of Non-Functional Requirements

Special emphasis must be laid on identifying non-functional requirements like performance metrics, security considerations, and usability factors. These are crucial as they can introduce constraints that, if not identified early, may become substantial impediments later in the project.

Case Study: Implementing Foundations Phase in a FinTech Startup's DSDM Project

Setting the Context

Imagine a FinTech startup is launching a new personal finance management application. After navigating the Feasibility phase, the team moves on to the Foundations phase to solidify their requirements. The focus is on building a highly secure, user-friendly, and responsive app.

Workshop Dynamics: Where Stakeholders Converge

The startup organizes multiple workshops attended by different stakeholders: the Product Owner representing the business vision, developers, designers, and even potential users. The objective is to refine the requirements and agree on a structured plan for development.

Defining Requirements: During these workshops, detailed User Stories emerge, such as "As a user, I need to categorize my expenses so that I can track my monthly budget."

Estimating and Planning: The development team then breaks down these User Stories into tasks, estimates the required effort, and slots them into their Delivery Plan.

Breaking Down Epics and Volume Control

Initially, the team had an Epic like "Comprehensive Expense Management." Now, it gets decomposed into smaller User Stories like "Expense Categorization," "Monthly Budget Setting," and "Spending Analysis."

Specificity and Sizing: Each User Story is then broken down to the point where it can be developed and tested within a two-week Sprint.

Volume Limitation: Given that the project is complex, the team is conscious about not exceeding 100 User Stories, ensuring they maintain a manageable workload.

Prioritised Requirements List as a Guiding Light

After the workshops and several iterations, a Prioritised Requirements List (PRL) is created. This list serves:

As an Inventory: It includes all User Stories, ranked by priority, to be addressed in the first development Increment.

For Governance: Any new requirements that come up in later phases are evaluated against this PRL to assess their impact on the project scope and timeline.

Addressing Non-Functional Requirements

Being a FinTech application, security is a critical non-functional requirement. User Stories related to data encryption, two-factor authentication, and GDPR compliance are identified and added to the PRL.

By diligently adhering to the Foundations phase's best practices, the startup successfully aligns its project execution strategy with its business objectives, setting the stage for a well-managed Agile project.

The Heartbeat of Agile: Navigating the Evolutionary Development Phase in DSDM Projects

The Essence of Evolutionary Development

In the DSDM framework, the Evolutionary Development phase serves as the dynamic core of Agile projects. It is where requirements are not just elaborated but are brought to life through incremental development and frequent iterations.

Fine-Tuning Requirements: Initial Decomposition and Analysis

At the onset of each Development Timebox, the team turns its focus to specific User Stories drawn from the Prioritised Requirements List (PRL).

Granularity: By decomposing these User Stories into smaller tasks or sub-stories, the team ensures that the requirements are more manageable and actionable.

Just-in-Time Analysis: Detailing is intentionally restricted to the User Stories that are slated for the current Timebox, an approach that avoids unnecessary complexity and keeps the project aligned with current objectives.

Continual Refinement: Iterative Emergence of Requirements

As the team dives into development, they concurrently refine the initial requirements, honing them into more precise definitions.

Updating the PRL: The Business Analyst captures any emergent details in the PRL, ensuring it remains a living document that reflects the project's evolving nature.

Focus on Value: With every iterative cycle, the project stays aligned with its strategic objectives by concentrating on the delivery of the most valuable features first.

Navigating New Terrains: Handling Emerging Requirements

It is a given in Agile projects that new requirements will surface during the Evolutionary Development phase.

Facilitation and Analysis: The Business Analyst leads discussions to assess the feasibility and impact of integrating new requirements.

Stakeholder Involvement: Decisions about incorporating new requirements are not made in isolation. The Business Ambassador and Business Visionary are consulted to weigh the implications of such changes on the project scope.

Quality Assurance through Testing: The Solution Tester is instrumental in defining the acceptance criteria for these new requirements, ensuring they meet quality standards before integration.

By adopting these activities and roles during the Evolutionary Development phase, Agile teams employing DSDM can master the art of balancing stability with adaptability, ensuring the project remains aligned with both its initial goals and emerging realities.

Navigating Real-World Complexities: A Practical Exploration of the Evolutionary Development Phase in DSDM

The Scenario: Development in a Financial Software Project

Imagine an Agile team working on a project to create a new financial tracking software. The Feasibility and Foundations phases have concluded, and the team has entered the Evolutionary Development phase, with well-defined Epics and a Prioritized Requirements List (PRL).

Unpacking User Stories: The First Development Timebox

The team kicks off the first Development Timebox by examining selected User Stories from the PRL. They decompose each story, breaking down features like "Transaction Tracking" and "Budget Analysis" into smaller tasks such as "Create Transaction Entry Form" and "Design Budget Summary Dashboard."

Just-In-Time Analysis

As the team only focuses on stories slated for the current Timebox, they avoid spending resources on future, uncertain elements of the project. This streamlines the development process and aligns closely with real-time business objectives.

Adapting to Change: Mid-Project Requirement Emergence

Two weeks into the Timebox, a key stakeholder suggests the inclusion of "Cryptocurrency Transaction Tracking" as a new feature, seeing its potential value.

Facilitation and Analysis

The Business Analyst initiates a discussion about this new feature, assessing its feasibility and the potential impact on the existing scope and timeline.

Stakeholder Input

Both the Business Ambassador and Business Visionary are consulted. They agree that while this feature would extend the scope, it aligns with the market needs and thus should be included.

Solution Testing

The Solution Tester drafts the acceptance criteria for this new feature. These criteria include metrics for transaction speed and data accuracy.

Keeping the PRL Dynamic

As the team integrates this new feature, they update the PRL, adding the new User Story and adjusting priorities where necessary. They also incorporate the newly defined acceptance criteria and additional tasks for development and testing.

By keeping these real-world complexities in mind and following the DSDM's structured approach to Evolutionary Development, the team successfully adapts to new requirements while keeping the project aligned with both its initial goals and emerging business needs. Would you like to explore another practical example or topic?

Navigating the Sea of Requirements: An Agile Project Manager's Guide to DSDM

Sourcing Requirements: Knowing Who to Ask

The first critical step in effectively managing requirements is ensuring they are sourced from the appropriate individuals.

High-Level vs Detailed Requirements

High-Level Requirements: Should come from the Business Visionary, who brings the big-picture view and is crucial for shaping the initial scope.

Detailed Requirements: These must be elicited from Business Ambassadors and Advisors, as they are the closest to the end-users and understand the day-to-day functionalities needed.

Striking the Balance: Detailing Requirements

Maintaining an appropriate level of detail is vital to prevent analysis paralysis and ensure that the project remains manageable.

Adhering to DSDM Guidelines

Keep the number of requirements constrained, particularly at early phases, to maintain a sharp focus and avoid over-complication.

Prioritizing with a Purpose

Requirement prioritization should be in lockstep with project objectives to ensure that what is developed first and foremost brings the most value to the business.

Alignment with Objectives

The Prioritised Requirements List (PRL) must reflect the project's strategic goals to keep the team and the project on course.

Workshop Wonders: Consensus Building

Workshops serve as an excellent mechanism to involve all stakeholders in agreeing upon requirements and their respective priorities.

Stakeholder Engagement

A workshop is an invaluable tool for direct negotiation and helps build a collective understanding and agreement among team members.

Establishing a Baseline: The Cornerstone of Scope Control

An agreed-upon baseline of requirements is vital for successful scope management. Without this, managing changes becomes a Herculean task.

The Importance of a Solid Baseline

This sets the stage for what is to be delivered and provides a reference point against which changes can be managed.

Adapting to Change: Managing Emerging Requirements

DSDM's iterative nature means that new requirements will inevitably arise. It's essential to know how to manage these effectively.

Iterative Management

New requirements can either broaden the project's scope or deepen the existing requirements. Knowing how to handle these is key to maintaining a balanced project scope and schedule.

Monitoring Progress: The Role of the PRL

Your PRL isn't just a static document; it's a dynamic tool that can be used for tracking progress.

Utilizing Burn-down Charts

Some PRL templates offer the functionality of capturing progress via Burn-down charts, providing a visual cue for project health and any necessary corrective action.

Agile Project Management in Action: A Case Study on Managing Requirements in a DSDM Project

Setting the Scene: The Company and Its Objectives

XYZ Corp, a rapidly growing e-commerce business, sought to overhaul its outdated inventory management system. With a Business Visionary at the helm and a diverse stakeholder group, the project's primary objectives were to enhance inventory tracking, streamline the ordering process, and improve vendor management.

Phase 1: Feasibility and Foundations

During the Feasibility phase, high-level requirements were gathered primarily from the Business Visionary. By the end of the Foundations phase, the team had an agreed-upon baseline, comprised of fewer than 100 User Stories, outlining the project's core functionalities and constraints.

Workshops for Consensus

Several workshops were held during the Foundations phase to elaborate on the high-level Epics and decompose them into actionable User Stories. These sessions were crucial in aligning the stakeholder group and avoiding any misunderstandings that could lead to scope creep.

Phase 2: Evolutionary Development

As the project moved into the Evolutionary Development phase, new User Stories started to emerge due to the iterative nature of DSDM. The Prioritised Requirements List (PRL) became the central document, continually updated to reflect these changes.

Adaptation and Course Correction

During this phase, new requirements arose that initially seemed to widen the project scope. However, the Business Visionary and Business Ambassadors were consulted to evaluate the real impact, and it was determined that these could be accommodated without a scope change but rather as a deepening of existing requirements.

Phase 3: Monitoring and Closure

Burn-down charts extracted from the PRL were instrumental in tracking progress. These charts highlighted some slippage midway through the project, prompting a reassessment of priorities and resources, allowing the project to be delivered successfully within its initial scope and timelines.

Lessons Learned

- The stakeholder workshops were vital for achieving consensus and ensuring everyone was on the same page.
- The flexible nature of DSDM allowed for the inclusion of emerging requirements without derailing the project, thanks to the well-managed PRL.
- Active monitoring through the Burn-down charts provided timely insights, enabling corrective action.

This case study serves as a practical demonstration of how adhering to DSDM guidelines and best practices in Agile Project Management can lead to successful outcomes even in complex, evolving scenarios.

Chapter Seventeen

Estimating in Agile: Navigating Uncertainty with Confidence

Agile Estimating in DSDM: A Comprehensive Guide to Mastering the Art

Importance of Agile Estimating in DSDM

Estimating in an Agile environment, specifically using the Dynamic Systems Development Method (DSDM), is an evolving process. As Agile is about adapting to change, estimates too must evolve to ensure that they remain aligned with ever-changing project requirements. Several key considerations and best practices are involved in Agile estimating within DSDM projects.

Leveraging MoSCoW Prioritization for Contingency

In DSDM, estimating is deeply tied to the MoSCoW prioritization method, which classifies project requirements into four categories: Must-have, Should-have, Could-have, and Won't-have. This prioritization method serves as a built-in mechanism for risk mitigation by providing a level of contingency. It helps in setting the scope of the project in a way that accounts for potential unknowns or changes down the line.

Striking a Balance Between Precision and Accuracy

The quest for precision and accuracy in estimating is a balancing act. Too much detail early on may lead to inefficiencies and limit flexibility. Conversely, overly broad estimates could result in a lack of focus and resource allocation challenges. The key is to have estimates that are as precise and accurate as they need to be at different stages of the project lifecycle.

Empowering the Team: Ownership of Estimates

In line with Agile principles, those who are responsible for a deliverable should ideally be the ones estimating the effort for it. This ownership not only contributes to more realistic estimates but also empowers team members, thereby increasing accountability and enhancing project outcomes.

The Need for Periodic Re-validation

Estimates are not static; they are living, breathing parts of the project that need to be revisited and revised as new information becomes available. Re-validation is particularly crucial for aligning with the team's actual velocity and making any necessary adjustments in project planning.

Diverse Applications of Estimates

Estimates serve various functions during the lifecycle of a DSDM project. They are vital for:

- Evaluating the Business Case
- Conducting Feasibility Studies
- Planning and Resource Allocation
- Communicating with Stakeholders
- Prioritizing Features

Understanding Assumptions and Risks

Estimates are often based on a set of assumptions, be it about resource availability, technology, or external dependencies. Clearly defining these assumptions and understanding the associated risks enables dynamic project management that can swiftly respond to changes.

Conclusion

Estimating in DSDM projects is a nuanced activity that requires a deep understanding of Agile principles, a focus on team empowerment, and an ability to adapt and refine as the project evolves. By adhering to these key considerations and best practices, Agile Project Managers can navigate the complexities of DSDM projects more effectively.

Case Study: Agile Estimating in a DSDM Project for E-Commerce Platform Development

Project Overview

An organization decided to undertake the development of a new e-commerce platform using the Dynamic Systems Development Method (DSDM). The primary project objectives included providing a user-friendly interface, ensuring robust security features, and enabling smooth integration with existing inventory management systems.

MoSCoW Prioritization and Contingency Planning

The project team used MoSCoW prioritization to separate the critical features from the less essential ones. Must-haves included fundamental security measures and basic user interface elements. This allowed the team to set aside a contingency for unexpected issues while ensuring that the most crucial elements would be completed.

Ownership and Realistic Estimation

Team members responsible for specific deliverables, such as payment gateway integration or user interface design, took ownership of the estimating process for those parts. This led to more realistic estimates because those who would actually perform the tasks had a say in the time and resources needed.

Iterative Re-validation and Adjustments

As the project progressed through various Development Timeboxes, the team found that some initial estimates were off the mark. By taking into account the actual velocity and other metrics, they revised future estimates. This iterative re-validation helped in aligning the project better with its objectives and available resources.

Assumptions and Risks

The project assumed a specific level of availability for key resources, including third-party APIs for payment processing. When one of the APIs experienced unexpected downtime, the project's risk management strategy, which was built on clearly defined assumptions, allowed for quick adjustments to be made.

Stakeholder Communication and Prioritization

Estimates were not just an internal project management tool; they were also used for stakeholder communication. The Business Case was updated based on the initial estimates, and as the project progressed, further refinements were communicated transparently to stakeholders, ensuring alignment and setting realistic expectations.

Results and Insights

The project was completed successfully, meeting all of its Must-have requirements and most of its Should-have and Could-have features. This case study highlights the pivotal role of agile estimating in successfully managing and completing a DSDM project. The key takeaways include the importance of ownership in estimates, the necessity for iterative re-validation, and the utility of having a robust risk management strategy built on well-defined assumptions.

By applying these considerations and best practices in Agile estimating, you can significantly increase the likelihood of your DSDM project's success.

Managing Uncertainties in Agile Estimating: A Comprehensive Guide

The Nature of Uncertainty in Agile Methodologies

Uncertainties are inherent aspects of any project and especially pronounced in Agile environments. Agile methodologies like DSDM not only acknowledge these uncertainties but also build strategies to manage them. As the project progresses, uncertainties reduce, and the reliability of estimates consequently improves.

Delineation of Risks and Assumptions

In Agile estimating, risks and assumptions serve as two pillars that hold up the edifice of estimates.

Risks

Risks are the potential stumbling blocks that might or might not materialize but could affect the project if they do.

Assumptions

Assumptions are the educated guesses or premises upon which estimates are built. They are subject to scrutiny and change.

Making both these elements explicit before presenting numerical estimates adds a layer of transparency and scrutiny, enabling the team to dissect and understand the estimates better.

Types of Uncertainties and Their Sources

Uncertainties in an Agile project can stem from several factors:

Volatility of Business Needs

Changing high-level requirements can shake the project's foundation.

Team Dynamics

The uncertainty originating from unknown or inexperienced team members can be a project risk.

Communication Barriers

Differences in geographical location, time zones, and organizational hierarchy can pose challenges to seamless communication.

Other Commitments

The team members' other responsibilities can dilute focus and affect productivity.

Technological Unknowns

Integrating or adapting new technologies introduces its own set of uncertainties.

Strategies for Effectively Managing Uncertainties

Mitigation Plans

Initial estimates should factor in the time and effort needed to create mitigation plans for each significant area of uncertainty.

Validation Activities

Where assumptions carry substantial risk, allocate time for validation activities early in the project to confirm their accuracy or make necessary adjustments.

Documentation

Always keep a written record of the assumptions and risks identified. This documentation can be revisited and revised as the project progresses and as more information becomes available, allowing for dynamic adjustments to the estimates.

By acknowledging, scrutinizing, and strategically planning for uncertainties, Agile teams can effectively navigate the complex terrain of project development, steering their projects towards successful outcomes.

Case Study: Applying Strategies for Managing Uncertainties in an Agile Project

Project Background

In a software development project utilizing the DSDM framework, uncertainties were identified in several areas, such as adopting a new technology stack, team dynamics due to remote working conditions, and rapidly changing business requirements.

Uncertainty Mitigation Strategies Implemented

Establishing a 'Risk and Assumption Log'

The Project Manager instituted a 'Risk and Assumption Log' that was regularly updated and reviewed during Sprint planning sessions. This log was used to scrutinize each risk and assumption and to develop specific mitigation or validation strategies.

Inclusion of 'Risk Time' in Estimates

Time was specifically allocated within the project estimates for addressing risks. For example, when adopting a new technology, a 'spike' was introduced into the Sprint to allow team members to explore and understand it, thereby reducing uncertainty.

Early Validation of Major Assumptions

Where assumptions involved considerable risk, such as a new authentication protocol meeting security standards, targeted validation activities were included early in the project lifecycle to either validate or revise those assumptions.

Buffer for High-Impact Unknowns

A time and resource buffer was set aside to deal with high-impact unknowns, such as unexpected changes in business requirements or unforeseen technological hurdles. This buffer was drawn upon only when absolutely necessary, thereby maintaining the integrity of the initial project estimates.

Outcome

As a result of these strategies, the project team was better prepared to handle uncertainties, thereby resulting in fewer disruptions and a smoother project flow. The mitigation activities led to early discovery and resolution of issues, while the validation activities ensured that the project remained aligned with the business objectives.

By systematically managing uncertainties through well-defined strategies, Agile teams can greatly enhance project predictability and success.

Exploring Top-Down Estimating: Unpacking Its Methodology, Strengths, and Weaknesses

Definition: Understanding the Essence of Top-Down Estimating

Top-down estimating is a forecasting approach that derives a high-level approximation of project scope, cost, or duration based on the visible or overarching features of the project. It primarily leans on the estimator's expertise and historical data from similar projects.

Methodological Steps in Top-Down Estimating

Step 1: Identify High-Level Features

The first task is to spot the principal components or features that characterize the project. These are generally the most visible aspects that stakeholder interest centers around.

Step 2: Cluster Similar Elements

Grouping analogous items streamlines the estimating process by allowing a more uniform assessment of time, resources, or cost associated with each cluster.

Step 3: Analogical Time Assessment

Leveraging past experience with comparable projects, estimators deduce the time allocation for each group of elements.

Step 4: Validation

The provisional estimates undergo a validation process to ensure alignment with project objectives, budget constraints, or timeframes.

Step 5: Two-pronged Perspective

The generated estimate can be analyzed through two different lenses:

1. Ascertaining what can be achieved within a stipulated timeframe.
2. Evaluating the duration necessary to complete a pre-defined set of deliverables.

Advantages and Disadvantages: A Balanced View

Advantages

Speedy High-Level Planning

Top-down estimates are quick to produce, making them useful for preliminary planning stages or for projects with tight deadlines.

Adaptability to Data Scarcity

This method is especially beneficial when in-depth specifics are elusive or yet to be defined.

Experience-Driven Reliability

The method relies on the real-world experience of the estimator, which often imparts a level of reliability to the estimate.

Disadvantages

Lower Accuracy

Top-down estimates often lack the granular detail found in bottom-up estimates, leading to less precision.

Subjectivity Risks

The heavy reliance on individual expertise makes the process more prone to personal bias and potentially inconsistent outcomes.

Case Study: Utilizing Top-Down Estimating in a Software Development Project

Context: The Project Scenario

Imagine a medium-sized software company that has just secured a contract for developing a comprehensive Customer Relationship Management (CRM) system for a client. The project manager, well-versed in software development projects, is tasked with providing a high-level estimate of project duration and cost to senior management.

Step-by-Step Application of Top-Down Estimating

Step 1: High-Level Features Identification

The project manager identifies the main components of the CRM system, such as the user interface, database management, reporting features, and integration with existing systems.

Step 2: Grouping Similar Elements

Given the complex nature of the CRM system, components like user interface and database management are further grouped under "Core Development," while reporting features and system integration are categorized as "Additional Features."

Step 3: Analogical Time Assessment

Drawing upon previous experience with similar projects, the project manager estimates that "Core Development" will take around six months, and "Additional Features" will require an additional two months.

Step 4: Validation

The project manager consults with the development team and other project stakeholders to validate the estimates. After some adjustments, the final high-level estimate is agreed upon.

Step 5: Perspective

The project manager presents the estimate in two ways to the senior management:

1. What features can be delivered in eight months?
2. How long will it take to complete the full CRM system, including additional features?

Learnings: Reflecting on the Advantages and Disadvantages

Advantages Realized

1. Quick Estimation: The project manager was able to provide a high-level estimate in a short time frame, aiding in rapid decision-making.
2. Experience-based: The use of historical data and prior project experience resulted in a realistic and practical estimate.

Disadvantages Encountered

1. Lack of Detail: The high-level nature of the estimate lacked granular details, necessitating further refinement as the project progressed.
2. Subjectivity: The estimate was highly dependent on the project manager's experience, which could be a limitation if their past projects were not closely aligned with the current project's specifics.

The use of top-down estimating provided the project manager with a quick, albeit high-level, project estimate that was valuable for initial planning and stakeholder discussions. However, it was clear that more detailed, bottom-up estimates would be needed in the project's later stages for precise planning and execution.

T-Shirt Estimating: Advantages, Disadvantages, and Suitability

Further Insights into Methodology

The T-shirt estimating technique is often employed in Agile environments where teams prefer a lightweight, conversational method to traditional estimation techniques. It serves as a springboard for dialogue among team members, creating a platform where they can align their perceptions of effort, complexity, and inter-dependencies among various tasks.

Advantages Explored

Quick and Easy to Use

One of the primary benefits of T-shirt sizing is its ease and speed. Teams can quickly arrive at a rough estimate, enabling swift decision-making processes. This speed is especially beneficial in dynamic environments where the focus is on rapid delivery.

Facilitates Team Discussions and Consensus

T-shirt estimating fosters a collaborative culture. By discussing varying opinions on the size of a task, team members contribute their expertise and perspective. This not only aids in achieving a more accurate estimate but also helps in identifying potential challenges early.

Disadvantages Unveiled

Lack of Granularity

While T-shirt estimating is quick and collaborative, it lacks the detail needed for long-term planning or for projects requiring high precision. There is no numerical value attached, and this lack of granularity can lead to issues in tasks that demand meticulous planning.

Subjectivity and Experience

The method depends significantly on the individual experiences and perceptions of team members, making it a rather subjective approach. If the team lacks experience or if members have significantly different skill sets, the estimates may not be reliable.

Suitability and Context

Best Use-Cases

T-shirt estimating is ideally suited for projects that are in their initial phases and for teams that are relatively new to working together. It's also useful for smaller tasks or projects where the risk associated with an inaccurate estimate is low.

When to Avoid

T-shirt estimating is not advisable for projects requiring highly accurate or detailed estimates. In cases where financial or operational risks are high, more rigorous estimating methods should be considered.

T-Shirt Estimating: A Practical Example for Deeper Understanding

Scenario Overview

Let's consider a software development project that involves building a mobile application with multiple features like user authentication, social media integration, real-time notifications, and so on. The team decides to use T-shirt estimating in the initial stages to quickly gauge the overall effort and complexity of the project.

Steps Taken for T-Shirt Estimating

Requirement Identification

The team identifies four main features that need to be developed:

1. User Authentication
2. Social Media Integration
3. Real-Time Notifications
4. Dashboard Analytics

Initial Assessment

Team members independently evaluate the complexity of each feature and assign initial T-shirt sizes as follows:

1. User Authentication: Medium (M)
2. Social Media Integration: Small (S)
3. Real-Time Notifications: Large (L)
4. Dashboard Analytics: Extra Large (XL)

Collaboration and Consensus Building

The team comes together to discuss their estimates. There's a disagreement on "User Authentication"—some members think it should be Large (L) because of the complexity involved in implementing advanced security features. After a thorough discussion, they agree to revise it to Large (L).

Final Sizing

The final T-shirt sizes are:

1. User Authentication: Large (L)
2. Social Media Integration: Small (S)

3. Real-Time Notifications: Large (L)
4. Dashboard Analytics: Extra Large (XL)

Lessons Learned and Considerations

Advantages Realized

- The team quickly arrived at a rough estimate, aiding immediate planning.
- Team discussions clarified the requirements and identified potential challenges, like the complexity of implementing security features in user authentication.

Disadvantages Faced

- The team realized that T-shirt sizes were not granular enough for financial planning and later adopted more detailed estimating methods.
- Inexperience with real-time notification systems made the initial estimate for that feature less reliable.

Adaptation and Future Strategy

The team decided to use T-shirt estimating for initial scoping and sprint planning but agreed to switch to more precise methods like Story Points for detailed planning and financial allocations.

The example above illustrates how T-shirt estimating can serve as a quick and collaborative tool for initial project scoping, while also highlighting its limitations in providing granular, reliable estimates for detailed planning.

Story Point Estimating: Advantages, Disadvantages, and Nuances

In-Depth Understanding of Story Point Estimating

Definition Unpacked

Story Point Estimating goes beyond merely categorizing requirements into broad levels of effort or complexity. Instead, it quantifies this effort using story points, which are numerical values arrived at through a team consensus. This gives a more detailed view of the work ahead, providing data that is invaluable for planning, tracking, and adjustments.

Methodology Explained

The methodology for Story Point Estimating is more complex than that of T-shirt sizing but offers greater precision. It typically involves multiple rounds of estimation to reach a consensus, and the values are often based on the Fibonacci sequence to reflect the inherent uncertainty in increasingly complex tasks. This iterative approach helps to unearth nuances in understanding and to reconcile different viewpoints, making the final estimate more reliable.

Advantages and Disadvantages

Why Choose Story Point Estimating

Precision: Story points provide a granular understanding of the effort required, enabling more accurate planning and allocation of resources.

Team Understanding: The consensus-based approach fosters team discussions, which can lead to uncovering hidden complexities or dependencies.

Effective Sprint Planning: With more precise estimates, the planning of sprints becomes more accurate, improving the likelihood of meeting deadlines without compromising quality.

Possible Drawbacks

Initial Time Investment: The process can be time-consuming, especially when team members have widely differing views on effort or complexity.

Learning Curve: It requires a reasonable level of familiarity with the tasks at hand, making it less suitable for teams new to the domain.

Lack of Universality: Story points are not standardized across teams or organizations, making them less useful for cross-team comparisons.

Closing Thoughts

Story Point Estimating provides an agile team with the tools needed for detailed planning and nuanced understanding of project requirements. While it does require a more substantial initial investment of time and a deeper understanding of the tasks, the payoff comes in the form of more accurate sprint planning and better resource allocation.

Story Point Estimating: A Practical Example

Context Setting

Consider a software development team working on an e-commerce application. The team is experienced and has been using Agile methodologies for a while. They are about to start a new sprint and have a backlog of user stories to consider.

Pre-Estimation Preparation

The team prepares for the estimation meeting by ensuring that all team members have access to a set of cards with Fibonacci numbers (1, 2, 3, 5, 8, 13, etc.).

Estimation Process

First User Story: "Implementing a Shopping Cart"

Requirement Presentation: The Product Owner presents the user story: "As a user, I want to add items to a shopping cart so that I can review them before purchasing."

Individual Estimation: Each team member privately selects a card; the choices range from 3 to 8.

Reveal and Discuss: The cards are revealed. Because of the variance, the team discusses why they chose their respective numbers.

Consensus Building: After the discussion, a second round of estimation is done. This time, all team members select '5'.

Final Estimation: '5' story points are assigned to this user story.

Second User Story: "Implementing a Payment Gateway"

Requirement Presentation: The next user story is: "As a user, I want to pay for the items in my cart using a credit card."

Individual Estimation: Choices range from 8 to 13 this time.

Reveal and Discuss: The team discusses their estimates, considering factors like security and third-party integrations.

Consensus Building: A consensus is reached at '13' after the discussion.

Final Estimation: '13' story points are assigned to this user story.

Advantages and Insights

Deep Understanding: The team now has a better understanding of the complexities involved in each user story.

Effective Planning: Knowing that the first user story is '5' and the second is '13' allows for more precise sprint planning.

Disadvantages and Considerations

Time-Consuming: This process took a significant amount of time but provided valuable insights.

Expertise Required: The discussion revealed that not everyone was aware of the complexities of payment gateway integration, underlining the need for expertise in the estimation process.

Conclusion

The team concluded the estimation meeting with a nuanced understanding of the efforts required for the upcoming sprint. They are now better prepared to tackle the challenges, having allocated '5' story points to the shopping cart implementation and '13' to the payment gateway.

This practical example demonstrates how Story Point Estimating can provide a detailed, nuanced view of project requirements, facilitating more effective sprint planning.

Top-Down Estimating in Agile Environments: An In-Depth Analysis

Defining Top-Down Estimating

Top-down estimating is a form of high-level estimation used primarily in the initial stages of a project when concrete, detailed information may not be available. This technique is not confined to but is frequently applied in Agile settings. It allows for a macroscopic view of the project, breaking it down into sizable chunks or categories that can be more readily estimated.

Methodological Approaches

Estimating by Velocity

When employing this method, the team's historical "velocity" serves as the basis for future projections. Velocity is defined as the number of story points a team can deliver within a fixed time frame, usually a sprint or another time-boxed iteration.

This method is particularly effective when there's an existing dataset that reflects the team's past performance. It's a relatively straightforward way to make informed judgments about what the team can achieve in future iterations.

Estimating by Example

This technique is useful when there isn't sufficient historical data, especially in the context of Agile teams that may be newly formed or undergoing transformation. Here, a small subset of tasks, often denoted in story points or even T-shirt sizes, is meticulously estimated. These "example estimates" serve as a yardstick for the larger work packages or user stories.

Advantages and Disadvantages

Advantages

Quick Implementation: The process is expedient, allowing for immediate planning and decision-making.

Early-Phase Relevance: Top-down estimating is particularly useful in the preliminary stages of a project when detailed granularity is not yet available.

Standardization: It works well for projects where features and tasks are consistent in size and complexity, providing a semblance of uniformity in estimates.

Disadvantages

Precision Trade-off: The method tends to be less accurate compared to more granular, bottom-up methods.

Law of Averages Assumption: This method often assumes that any overestimates will balance out underestimates, which may not always be the case.

Need for Continuous Adjustment: As the project progresses and more information becomes available, there might be a need to revise the estimates, adding a layer of ongoing management overhead.

Applicability in Agile Environments

In Agile methodologies, where change is frequent and expected, top-down estimating can serve as an effective initial planning tool. It aligns well with Agile's preference for 'just enough' planning and can be adapted as iterations proceed and more data becomes available.

Practical Example: Applying Top-Down Estimating in Agile Environments

Scenario: Agile Software Development Project

Let's consider a hypothetical Agile software development project to create a mobile application for a retail store. The project consists of three main components: User Interface (UI), Backend, and Database Integration.

Steps Involved in Top-Down Estimating

Phase 1: High-Level Breakdown

At the start of the project, the Agile team breaks down the project into these three high-level components. Given that detailed requirements are not yet available, top-down estimating becomes an appropriate choice.

Phase 2: Using Historical Velocity

Assume that the team has a historical velocity of 25 story points per sprint. The product backlog has been estimated to be roughly 200 story points, which means the team anticipates approximately eight sprints for completion.

Phase 3: Velocity-Based Allocation

The team then allocates these story points across the three major components:

- UI: 75 Story Points (3 Sprints)
- Backend: 100 Story Points (4 Sprints)
- Database Integration: 25 Story Points (1 Sprint)

Phase 4: Validation and Refinement

As each sprint progresses, more granular tasks are identified, and the initial estimates are refined. After Sprint 1, the team may discover that the UI is more complex than initially thought, leading to a revised estimate and a reallocation of story points.

Implications and Adjustments

The initial top-down estimate serves as a framework for planning and is refined iteratively as the project progresses. As the team gains more information, the top-down estimates are adjusted, providing a flexible, adaptive approach to project management that aligns well with Agile principles.

Benefits Realized

- Quick initial planning enabled immediate start of sprints.

- Iterative refinement ensured estimates remained relevant and accurate.

Challenges Encountered

- Initial estimates for the UI were off, requiring mid-course corrections.
- Some level of subjectivity in initial estimates led to minor variances down the line.

Summary

In this example, top-down estimating provided an effective, Agile-friendly approach to project estimation and planning. While not without its limitations, the method offered enough flexibility for ongoing refinement, allowing the team to adapt to emerging insights and changes.

Bottom-Up Estimating: A Deep Dive into Methodology and Applications

Intricacies of Bottom-Up Estimating

Bottom-Up Estimating stands as a bastion of detail-oriented planning in project management. The technique is built on the premise that a high level of granularity in estimating tasks not only improves the accuracy of the overall project estimate but also facilitates efficient resource allocation and risk assessment.

Critical Elements in Bottom-Up Estimating

Task Decomposition

One of the first steps is to break down larger tasks into their constituent sub-tasks. This creates a granular view that allows for more precise estimation. Unlike top-down estimating, where broad strokes are applied to large categories of work, bottom-up estimating drills down into the specifics.

Inclusion of All Stakeholders

It's imperative that all stakeholders, from developers and testers to business analysts, are involved in this estimation process. Their expertise contributes to the granularity and the accuracy of the estimates.

Validation and Cross-Reference

Each individual estimate should ideally be validated by more than one source. This could mean having multiple experts weigh in on an estimate or cross-referencing with historical data. The aim is to build an estimate that is not only detailed but also validated across multiple perspectives.

The Dynamic Nature of Estimates

Bottom-up estimates are often considered 'fixed' due to their detailed nature. However, they can and should be adjusted as new information becomes available. This means that bottom-up estimating, although detailed, is not rigid. It allows for adaptability and should be revised as necessary to reflect project realities.

Benefits and Drawbacks

Benefits

High Accuracy: Because of the detailed nature of these estimates, they tend to be more accurate compared to other methods.

Resource Allocation: Detailed estimates make it easier to allocate resources efficiently, thereby potentially saving time and costs in the long run.

Accountability: With each task meticulously estimated, it's easier to hold team members accountable for delays or discrepancies.

Drawbacks

Time-Consuming: The method requires a lot of upfront time investment, which may not be feasible for all projects.

False Sense of Precision: Detailed does not necessarily mean accurate. If the underlying assumptions are wrong, the detailed nature of the estimate may provide a misleading sense of security.

Case Study: Bottom-Up Estimating in Software Development

Project Overview

In a hypothetical software development project aimed at building a content management system, a team of developers, business analysts, quality assurance testers, and project managers decided to utilize the bottom-up estimating technique. The project comprised multiple modules like User Management, Content Creation, and Analytics Dashboard, among others.

Step-by-Step Implementation of Bottom-Up Estimating

Task Decomposition

Each module was broken down into several components, which were further decomposed into individual tasks. For example, the User Management module included tasks such as 'Design Database Schema,' 'Develop User Registration API,' 'Create User Dashboard,' etc.

Individual Task Estimation

Each of these tasks was then meticulously estimated. The developer responsible for 'Design Database Schema' estimated it would take 12 hours, whereas the 'Develop User Registration API' was estimated to take 20 hours by another developer.

Involvement of Stakeholders

Quality assurance testers, database administrators, and front-end developers were all included in this estimation process, adding their specialized perspective.

Validation

Each task's estimate was cross-verified by another expert or compared against past project data, adding a layer of validation to the estimates.

Resulting Benefits and Drawbacks

Benefits

High Accuracy: The project was completed within 5% of the initial time estimate, which was deemed a significant achievement.

Resource Allocation: The detailed estimates allowed the project manager to allocate resources with high efficiency.

Enhanced Accountability: The team members were very much aware of their responsibilities and deadlines, making the process smoother.

Drawbacks

Time Investment: It took the team almost two weeks just to complete the estimation process, delaying the project start.

Overconfidence: In some areas, the estimates were too optimistic, giving a false sense of security. This was remedied during the project, but it did introduce some delays.

The bottom-up estimating approach proved to be beneficial for this software development project, even with the associated drawbacks. The high accuracy of the estimates and the efficiency in resource allocation made it a worthwhile investment.

Estimation Styles Across the Project Lifecycle in DSDM

Analytical Context: Estimation within DSDM

Dynamic Systems Development Method (DSDM) inherently calls for a blend of both top-down and bottom-up estimation styles. The flexibility of DSDM allows it to adapt to varying levels of requirement clarity and project complexities, making the integration of these two estimation styles particularly effective.

Phases and Suitable Estimation Styles

Early Lifecycle Phases: Feasibility and Foundations

At the onset, DSDM projects usually contend with ambiguous requirements and a volatile scope, characteristics that are well-suited for top-down estimating.

Reasons for Suitability:

Speed: Quick estimations can facilitate immediate strategic decisions, which is crucial when stakeholders are gauging the project's viability.

Flexibility: Top-down estimating can easily be refined or adjusted as new information surfaces or if the scope changes.

Evolutionary Development: Timebox Planning

Once the project transitions into the Evolutionary Development phase, a shift towards bottom-up estimating becomes more apt.

Reasons for Suitability:

Accuracy: At this juncture, the clarity of scope and well-defined requirements allows for detailed task-level estimations, which contribute to precise resource allocation and scheduling.

Validation: The bottom-up estimates can serve to validate or recalibrate the initial top-down estimates, increasing the reliability of the overall project timeline and resource allocation.

The DSDM Way: Bridging the Estimation Gap

Bottom-Up Estimating in the First Timebox

A common practice in DSDM is to employ bottom-up estimating for the initial Timebox during the tail end of the Foundations phase. This serves multiple objectives:

Early Validation: The close scrutiny of the first Timebox allows the project team to assess the feasibility of their top-down estimates made earlier. Any significant discrepancies can be flagged and adjustments made.

Smooth Transition: Employing bottom-up estimating at this point serves as a gradual transition from broad to detailed estimating, allowing for the operational nuances to be incorporated seamlessly into the planning stage.

Strategic Insights

In a DSDM environment, effective estimation is not just about choosing one method over the other. It's about understanding the phase-specific requirements and intricacies of the project, and then judiciously applying the most fitting estimation technique. This adaptive approach enhances the accuracy and reliability of the project outcomes, while allowing sufficient flexibility to accommodate inevitable changes and uncertainties.

Case Study: Implementing Estimation Styles in a DSDM Project for a Digital Transformation Initiative

Project Context

A large enterprise embarks on a digital transformation journey with the aim of modernizing its legacy systems. The company adopts the DSDM framework for its flexibility and robustness. The project has a broad scope, encompassing various departments and functionalities, making it an ideal candidate for a mixed-method approach to estimation.

Early Lifecycle Phases: Top-Down Approach

In the Feasibility and Foundations phases, the project team opts for a top-down estimating method. This allows them to quickly gauge the scale of the project and provide stakeholders with a high-level view of the required resources and timelines.

Key Actions:

Scoping: Broad features and components like "Backend Modernization," "UI/UX Overhaul," and "Data Migration" are identified.

Estimation: Using past projects and expert opinion, the project manager assigns high-level estimates to these categories.

Outcome: The stakeholders receive a preliminary estimate that informs their decision to greenlight the project, with the understanding that these numbers will be refined.

Evolutionary Development Phase: Bottom-Up Approach

As the project moves into the Evolutionary Development phase, the team employs a bottom-up estimating approach for more granular planning.

Key Actions:

Task Decomposition: Each feature is broken down into smaller tasks. For example, "Backend Modernization" is split into tasks like "API Development," "Database Optimization," etc.

Detailed Estimation: Each task is meticulously estimated, involving the developers, testers, and analysts in the process.

Outcome: The project manager now has a detailed roadmap, allowing for optimized resource allocation and precise milestone tracking.

Bridging the Gap: Validation and Transition

As a best practice within DSDM, the first Timebox of the Evolutionary Development phase is estimated using a bottom-up approach.

Key Actions:

Bottom-Up Estimation: A detailed bottom-up estimate is made for the tasks involved in the first Timebox.

Validation: This detailed estimate serves to validate or adjust the initial top-down estimates.

Outcome: The process results in higher confidence levels among the stakeholders and aligns the project for a successful outcome.

Concluding Thoughts

This case study demonstrates the practical application of both top-down and bottom-up estimating methods in a DSDM project. By employing a strategy tailored to the phase and the nature of tasks, the project was better positioned for success, balancing both speed and accuracy in its estimates.

Estimation Strategies in the Feasibility Phase: Exploring the Nuances

The Feasibility phase stands as the gateway to any project, setting the tone for subsequent planning and execution. It's a stage primarily geared towards scoping out the general contours of a project—its viability, cost, and duration. The estimation methods used here often veer towards the high-level and generalized, designed more to provide a 'sense' of the project rather than a blueprint. Among various methods, top-down estimating often takes center stage. This article aims to delve into the critical aspects of employing top-down estimating in the Feasibility phase.

Key Objectives

Establish a Project Outline Business Case: The overarching goal is to define the problem or opportunity, identify potential solutions, and provide initial financial justifications.

Generate High-Level Estimates: Here, the aim is not pin-point accuracy but a range within which the project is expected to fall in terms of cost and time.

Estimation Approach: Spotlight on Top-Down Estimating

Time Basis

The estimates at this stage are often made in terms of weeks or months rather than hours or days. This broad timeframe suits the higher-level nature of feasibility analysis.

Rough Estimates

At this juncture, we are not looking for an exact number but a reasonable range. The queries that need addressing are essentially, "What is the ballpark cost?" and "How much time are we roughly looking at?"

Range Estimates

Given that the feasibility stage is rife with uncertainties, it's prudent to present estimates as ranges—establishing both lower and upper bounds to cater for eventualities.

Key Considerations

Small Number of Overarching Requirements

Typically, the Feasibility phase is populated with fewer, albeit substantial, requirements—often less than 10. The estimation approach here should match this brevity; a detailed breakdown into sub-tasks is generally premature.

Dealing with Uncertainty

The Feasibility phase is often a labyrinth of unknowns. Accordingly, it's common practice to categorize all requirements as 'Must-Haves' to ensure that the core objectives of the project are non-negotiable.

Defining the Range Estimates

Lower Bound: This estimate must be conservative enough to ensure that at least the 'Must-Have' requirements can be realistically met within this range.

Upper Bound: This should encapsulate a worst-case scenario, considering all the associated risks and uncertainties.

Conclusion

Estimation in the Feasibility phase is a challenging but vital endeavor. It requires a blend of art and science, where the skill lies in creating a balance between providing enough detail to inform decision-making while acknowledging the inherent uncertainties. Employing top-down estimating techniques can offer the right level of abstraction and speed, ensuring that the project starts on a solid foundation.

Estimation Strategies in the Feasibility Phase: A Real-World Application

Introduction

Having laid down the theoretical groundwork for employing top-down estimating in the Feasibility phase, let's transition to its application in a real-world scenario. We will focus on how a hypothetical software development company used this approach to navigate the complexities of this initial phase.

Project Background

The software development company was presented with an opportunity to develop an extensive Customer Relationship Management (CRM) system for a large enterprise client. The Feasibility phase was crucial in assessing whether to move ahead with the project.

Employing Top-Down Estimating

Establishing the Business Case

The company initially laid out the key objectives and high-level requirements, which included data migration, interface design, and third-party integrations. A Project Outline Business Case was created to define the problem space, the proposed solution, and the preliminary financial metrics.

Time-Based Estimates

In line with top-down estimating practices, they initially estimated the project would require somewhere between 12 and 18 months, avoiding the trap of overly specific day-based or week-based estimates at this early stage.

Rough Estimates

The company's project management team calculated a rough cost range based on previous similar projects and industry standards. The range was presented to the stakeholders as between $1.2 million and $1.8 million.

Key Considerations

Small Pool of Requirements

Since the project was in the Feasibility phase, only a handful of overarching requirements were considered for the initial estimate, thus avoiding the intricacies of a detailed breakdown.

Accounting for Uncertainties

All high-level requirements were classified as 'Must-Haves' to counter the inherent uncertainties. This strategy also served to set clear expectations with the client about the fundamental deliverables.

Range Estimates

Lower Bound: The project management team made sure that at least the core functionalities, like data migration and basic interface design, could be completed within the lower bound of 12 months and $1.2 million.

Upper Bound: Additional features and potential risks were included in the upper bound, accounting for a duration of 18 months and a cost of $1.8 million.

Conclusion

The software development company successfully navigated the Feasibility phase using top-down estimating techniques. This enabled them to present a convincing business case to the stakeholders, thereby setting the stage for a well-planned and realistic project lifecycle.

The real-world application illustrates how the principles and techniques of top-down estimating in the Feasibility phase can be implemented to lay a robust foundation for a project. It demonstrates the balance between abstraction and detail, providing valuable insights for making informed decisions.

Estimation Strategies in the Foundations Phase: Practical Applications

After examining the theoretical elements of the estimation process in the Foundations phase, we'll explore its practical applications. Let's consider a hypothetical construction company tasked with building a large residential complex. The Foundations phase is especially crucial in this industry to generate an actionable Delivery Plan and to reevaluate the Business Case with more refined estimates.

Project Context

The construction company has finished the Feasibility phase and has received approval to move into the Foundations phase. The project involves multiple residential towers, parking facilities, and amenities like a gym and swimming pool.

Utilizing Top-Down Estimating

Revisiting the Business Case

The project management team goes back to the original Business Case, incorporating changes based on newly gathered information, such as updated construction material costs and revised labor estimates.

Detailed Delivery Plan

Given the increased detail available in the Foundations phase, the company now develops a more comprehensive Delivery Plan, factoring in the estimates for each building component and auxiliary features.

Key Considerations

Enhanced Requirements Detail

The number of requirements has ballooned from just a handful during the Feasibility phase to nearly a hundred, ranging from structural engineering specifications to environmental compliance.

Diminished Uncertainty

With the more detailed requirements, the estimated project completion time is narrowed down to a 16-20 month window, as opposed to the more broad 12-24 month estimate made during the Feasibility phase.

Decision-Making

The estimates are now robust enough for a 'go or no-go' decision. The refined cost and time estimates instill confidence in stakeholders and pave the way for resource allocation in accordance with the Delivery Plan.

Conclusion

In a construction setting, or any complex project environment, the Foundations phase serves as a bridge between the preliminary Feasibility phase and the more defined Development phases. The increased detail and reduced uncertainty are skillfully managed through top-down estimating, which continues to serve as a versatile and speedy method for making key decisions. It sets the stage for the next phases, ensuring that the project continues on a trajectory that is both feasible and aligned with stakeholder expectations.

Real-World Application of Foundations Phase Estimating: A Construction Case Study

Introduction

Let's delve into a real-world case where top-down estimating was employed successfully during the Foundations phase of a construction project. The project in question was a residential high-rise development in a major metropolitan area.

Revisiting the Business Case

Upon entering the Foundations phase, the project management team revisited the initial Business Case. They updated it based on more current market research and refined estimates for construction materials and labor costs. These refinements allowed the team to secure additional funding from investors.

Detailed Delivery Plan

With the aid of top-down estimating, the team was able to break down the high-rise project into various components such as structural engineering, plumbing, electrical systems, and interior design. Each component was given a top-down estimate, which was then compiled into a comprehensive Delivery

Plan. This plan was then scrutinized by senior management and external stakeholders to ensure it met expectations for scope, timeline, and budget.

Key Considerations

Enhanced Detail

The greater detail provided during the Foundations phase made it easier to assign specific tasks to different departments, ensuring that each component was accounted for in the overall estimate.

Decision-Making

The Delivery Plan, backed by more precise estimates, gave senior management the confidence to proceed with the project. Moreover, the plan served as a crucial tool for resource allocation and informed negotiations with subcontractors and suppliers.

Outcomes

Due to effective top-down estimating in the Foundations phase, the project was completed within a margin of 5% of the estimated cost and timeline, which is considered highly successful in the construction industry. It also allowed for timely adjustments when unexpected complications arose, owing to the robustness of the initial estimates and planning.

Conclusion

This real-world example illustrates how top-down estimating during the Foundations phase can provide a firm basis for complex projects, allowing them to proceed with a high degree of confidence and increasing the likelihood of successful outcomes. It demonstrates the practical utility of top-down estimating as a strategic tool for both planning and decision-making.

Advanced Insights into Estimation Strategies in the Evolutionary Development Phase

The Evolutionary Development phase plays a pivotal role in the project lifecycle, serving as the implementation stage where all the planning starts to manifest into tangible outcomes. Given the limited time frame of Development Timeboxes, accurate estimation becomes even more crucial. The shift towards bottom-up estimating, therefore, marks a significant transition in the estimation approach as the team leverages greater detail and confidence to generate highly precise estimates.

Detailed Overview of Key Objectives

Precision in Timebox Deliverables

The primary objective at this stage is to precisely outline what each Development Timebox will yield. Unlike earlier phases, the scope here is not only well-defined but is also limited to what can be accomplished within a Timebox. Bottom-up estimating plays a key role in dissecting each requirement into individual tasks to allocate effort and resources meticulously.

Validation through Experience

Another cornerstone objective is to continuously review and update estimates. This iterative validation is based on the actual performance metrics and learnings from previous Development Timeboxes, thereby fine-tuning the overall project estimates for future Timeboxes.

In-depth on Estimation Approach: Bottom-Up Estimating

With a higher degree of detail and constrained scope, bottom-up estimating is not only advisable but is also highly effective. At the onset of each Development Timebox, the Solution Development Team dives deep into each requirement to assess the individual tasks involved, thereby generating a cumulative effort estimate that informs both scheduling and resource allocation.

Key Considerations During Estimation

Increased Confidence and Domain Knowledge

By the Evolutionary Development phase, team members are well-versed with the project's nuances. This familiarity significantly enhances the reliability of bottom-up estimates as the team can draw from past experiences and performance metrics.

The Significance of Focused Scope

Given the short duration of Development Timeboxes, usually ranging from 2 to 4 weeks, the scope is inherently limited. This focused scope complements the detailed nature of bottom-up estimating, making it possible to generate highly accurate, task-level estimates without overwhelming the team.

The Role of MoSCoW Prioritization

Prioritizing tasks using the MoSCoW method (Must-Have, Should-Have, Could-Have, and Won't-Have) is an integral part of the estimation process in this phase. This technique not only helps in identifying the essential deliverables but also serves as a contingency mechanism to adapt to any unforeseen changes or challenges.

Case Study: Application of Estimation Strategies in the Evolutionary Development Phase

Context and Scenario

In this hypothetical case study, let's consider a software development project to build a customer relationship management (CRM) system. The project has progressed to the Evolutionary Development phase, where several Development Timeboxes are planned to implement various features like lead tracking, email automation, and analytics dashboards.

Application of Bottom-Up Estimating

Step-by-Step Estimation for a Timebox

At the start of a Development Timebox focused on implementing the lead tracking feature, the Solution Development Team carries out a bottom-up estimation exercise. Each requirement is decomposed into smaller tasks, like designing the UI, developing the backend logic, and integrating with existing databases. The team estimates the effort required for each task, and these are summed up to get the total Timebox estimate.

Role of Experience in Validation

Iterative Learning

As the team completes each Timebox, the actual efforts and outcomes are meticulously recorded. These are compared against the initial estimates to understand any deviations. Lessons from this comparative analysis are then applied to improve the estimates for subsequent Timeboxes, making them increasingly accurate.

Use of MoSCoW Prioritization

Adaptability and Contingency

The MoSCoW technique is applied to categorize the requirements of the lead tracking feature. For instance, basic data entry and display functionalities are tagged as 'Must-Have,' while advanced features like auto-tagging leads based on behavior are classified as 'Could-Have.' This helps the team to know where to focus their efforts and provides a fallback plan in case any delays or issues arise.

Summary

By applying bottom-up estimating in tandem with experience-based validation and MoSCoW prioritization, the team is able to not only create accurate estimates but also adapt to changing circumstances effectively. This multi-faceted approach significantly increases the chances of project success, ensuring that both time and resources are optimally utilized.

Estimating in Agile Projects: A Comprehensive Toolkit for Agile Project Managers

Agile Project Managers hold the essential responsibility of steering teams through the labyrinthine terrain of Agile methodologies. A critical dimension of this role is the ability to conduct precise and reliable project estimations. This comprehensive guide outlines key tips that Agile Project Managers can implement to master the art and science of Agile estimation techniques.

Tips for Agile Estimation

Challenge Assumptions, Not Final Figures

Critical evaluation is vital during the estimation process. However, it is more constructive to examine the underlying assumptions rather than contesting the final numerical estimates. Challenging the assumptions can lead to more refined estimates without compromising team morale.

Smaller Work, More Precision

Estimations tend to be more accurate when dealing with smaller, more defined pieces of work. The limited scope and reduced complexity contribute to an improved degree of precision, making it easier to commit to deadlines.

Provide Estimates as a Range

A range offers a more nuanced representation of the uncertainty and risk associated with a project or task. Encourage the team to provide estimates as a range rather than as a fixed number, as this approach is generally less misleading and more adaptive to evolving project dynamics.

Team-Generated Estimates

To ensure that estimates are as realistic as possible, the team responsible for executing the tasks should generate them. This process increases the team's ownership of and commitment to the estimated time frames and outcomes.

Continuous Comparison

A routine assessment of estimated versus actual time and resource utilization is advisable. Agile Project Managers can facilitate this ongoing validation, assisting in identifying and resolving any discrepancies that arise.

Collective Estimation

Involving the whole Solution Development Team in the estimation process capitalizes on diverse skill sets and perspectives. This collective approach enhances the quality of the estimate by revealing overlooked factors or potential misunderstandings.

Ongoing Re-Estimation

Agile methodologies call for constant adaptability and refinement. Encourage a culture of continuous re-estimation, underpinned by techniques such as MoSCoW prioritization, to maintain alignment between project goals and realities.

Embrace Changes and Learnings

The Agile framework is designed for flexibility and adaptability. Do not let early estimates constrain the ability to incorporate new insights, pivots, or changes that arise during the project lifecycle.

Protect Against External Pressures

External demands for increased certainty in the early phases can compromise the Agile approach. Be wary of such pressures and advocate for a realistic level of ambiguity in estimates, especially in the early stages of a project.

Account for Non-Productive Time

Factor in the time likely to be spent on non-project activities, like email communication or organizational meetings. A typical guideline suggests assuming approximately 4/5th of a working day as productive time for project work.

Conclusion

Estimation in Agile projects is not merely a quantitative exercise but a nuanced interplay of team dynamics, project realities, and strategic foresight. By employing these tips, Agile Project Managers can navigate the complexities of estimation more adeptly, setting the stage for project success.

Case Study: Agile Estimation in a Mid-Sized Software Development Project

Introduction

In a mid-sized software development project, the Agile Project Manager faces unique challenges, ranging from team dynamics to complex technical requirements. The project has a span of approximately six months and involves multiple cross-functional teams.

Scenario

For the sake of this case study, assume the project aims to develop a new feature set for an existing enterprise-level software solution. The feature set is extensive and requires significant back-end and front-end development.

Implementing the Tips for Agile Estimation

Challenge Assumptions, Not Final Figures

During the initial estimation sessions, one team provided a rather optimistic estimate. The Agile Project Manager encouraged the team to revisit the assumptions behind this figure, resulting in a more realistic timeframe.

Smaller Work, More Precision

The tasks were divided into smaller user stories and sub-tasks, making it easier for the team to estimate them. This action improved the precision and reliability of the overall project estimates.

Provide Estimates as a Range

Given the innovative nature of the project, several uncertainties remained. The teams were thus instructed to provide their estimates as a range. This practice helped manage stakeholder expectations more effectively.

Team-Generated Estimates

The Solution Development Team themselves generated all the estimates, which were then reviewed during sprint planning meetings. This approach increased the team's commitment to meeting the set deadlines.

Continuous Comparison

At the end of each sprint, the Agile Project Manager facilitated a retrospective, where the team compared their initial estimates to the actual time spent on tasks. This exercise led to improved estimation in subsequent sprints.

Collective Estimation

Each sprint planning meeting involved the collective participation of developers, designers, and QA engineers. This diversity of perspectives led to well-rounded estimates that accounted for various aspects of the project.

Ongoing Re-Estimation

After the completion of each sprint, the remaining work was re-estimated, incorporating learnings and adjustments from completed sprints. This re-estimation used the MoSCoW prioritization technique to reassess 'Must-Have' and 'Could-Have' features.

Embrace Changes and Learnings

During the project, new insights from user feedback required changes in the planned feature set. The estimates were revised accordingly, without causing disruption or affecting team morale.

Protect Against External Pressures

The Agile Project Manager made it clear to the stakeholders that while the team would strive for accuracy, estimates would always have a degree of uncertainty, especially in the initial stages.

Account for Non-Productive Time

Estimates included a buffer for meetings, email communications, and other non-productive activities, setting more realistic expectations and schedules.

Conclusion

By applying these tips for Agile estimation, the Agile Project Manager successfully navigated the complexities of a mid-sized software development project. The project was completed on time and within budget, thanks in part to the rigorous and thoughtful approach to estimation.

Chapter Eighteen

Lifecycle Planning: A Strategic Approach

Planning in Pre-Project Phase: A Deep Dive into Programme/Portfolio-Level Considerations

The Pre-Project phase serves as an integral precursor to the actual project work, bridging the gap between mere ideas and actionable plans. The importance of this stage cannot be overstated, as it sets the strategic tone for the entire project lifecycle. At this juncture, planning activities ascend from the specificities of individual projects to encompass broader programme or portfolio considerations. The ultimate objective is twofold: to ascertain whether the project aligns with larger organizational goals and to determine if a Feasibility assessment is warranted.

Objectives of Planning in the Pre-Project Phase

Assessing Strategic Alignment

One of the primary objectives of planning during this phase is to assess the strategic alignment of the proposed project. Here, considerations extend beyond the tactical elements of a single project to include the coherence and integration with the existing project portfolio and broader organizational goals.

Resource Allocation

Resource allocation takes center stage as another vital objective. This involves identifying and earmarking both human and capital resources that are essential for a comprehensive Feasibility assessment. It's not just a matter of what is required, but also what is available and at what cost.

Timing

The final key objective is timing, which involves determining when the Feasibility assessment should commence and how long it should take. This is a crucial aspect, as timing influences resource availability, cost implications, and the alignment with other organizational activities.

Roles and Responsibilities

Programme/Portfolio Managers

These individuals are typically at the helm of Pre-Project planning, where their focus lies predominantly in ensuring strategic alignment and assessing the overall health of the project portfolio. They perform a pivotal role in deciding whether a project progresses to the Feasibility phase.

Project Sponsors

Project sponsors, often senior management or stakeholders, provide invaluable insights into the business case for the project. They play an integral part in assessing the potential value and risks of the proposed project, thereby influencing the decision to proceed to a full Feasibility study.

Resource Managers

Resource managers are entrusted with the critical task of confirming the availability and allocation of resources required for the Feasibility assessment. Their role encompasses a broad range of resources, from human capital to software and infrastructure, thus playing a significant role in the ultimate decision to proceed with a project.

Case Study: Pre-Project Planning for a Large-Scale Software Upgrade

Background

In a multinational corporation planning a major software upgrade, the Pre-Project phase was initiated to determine whether the upgrade was both feasible and aligned with broader organizational objectives. A cross-functional team was assembled, consisting of Programme/Portfolio Managers, Project Sponsors, and Resource Managers.

How Objectives Were Addressed

Assessing Strategic Alignment

Programme/Portfolio Managers undertook a comprehensive analysis of the proposed upgrade in relation to other ongoing projects and organizational goals. They evaluated the long-term benefits, the alignment with corporate strategy, and the potential return on investment. A risk assessment was also conducted to consider the implications of not proceeding with the upgrade.

Resource Allocation

Resource Managers compiled a detailed inventory of necessary resources—ranging from software engineers to server capacities and licenses needed for a full Feasibility study. The budgetary implications of these resources were assessed and compared against the projected value of the upgrade.

Timing

The team collectively decided on a three-month window for carrying out the Feasibility study. This decision factored in the availability of key personnel, budget cycles, and other organizational activities, ensuring that there were no conflicts that could impede the project.

Roles and Responsibilities in Action

Programme/Portfolio Managers

They presented their findings to the executive board, articulating how the software upgrade would enhance operational efficiency and offer a competitive edge. The board was also apprised of the associated risks and alternative options.

Project Sponsors

The sponsors, in this case, executives from the IT and Operations departments, provided crucial insights into the operational benefits and validated the business case. Their involvement was pivotal in securing the executive board's approval.

Resource Managers

Having confirmed resource availability, the Resource Managers developed a tentative schedule and allocated resources for the Feasibility study, which was approved along with the project's progression to the Feasibility phase.

This case study exemplifies how meticulous planning in the Pre-Project phase, addressing each of the key objectives and roles, can influence the decision to proceed to the Feasibility phase, thereby setting the stage for a potentially successful project.

Planning During the Feasibility Phase: Guiding Principles and Best Practices

The Feasibility phase in Agile Project Management is an essential inflection point where high-level planning lays the groundwork for more detailed future phases. Given its significance, this guide elaborates on the best practices and guiding principles for planning during the Feasibility phase, aiming to set the stage for a successful project.

Objectives of Planning in the Feasibility Phase

Preliminary Scope Definition

This involves the initial capture of high-level requirements, providing a bird's-eye view of what the project aims to achieve. While not detailed, this outline is vital for aligning the project with organizational goals and laying the foundation for subsequent planning.

Foundations Phase Planning

This entails a more granular level of planning aimed at the next phase, including timelines, deliverables, and resources required. The objective is to transition smoothly into the Foundations phase with a clear roadmap.

High-Level Project Outline

Here, a broad-stroke view of the project's size, duration, and expected deliverables is established, offering stakeholders an approximate idea of what to expect in the project's full lifecycle.

Components of the Feasibility Phase Plan

Delivery Plan for Foundations

The plan serves as a detailed guide for the Foundations phase. It outlines the expected timelines, milestones, and resource allocations. At this juncture, key roles and responsibilities may also be formalized.

Facilitated Workshops

For ensuring that all stakeholders are on the same page, facilitated workshops may be planned. These workshops typically cover requirement elicitation, scope refinement, and initial risk assessments, among other essential topics.

Evolutionary Development & Deployment

Given that detailed information is still limited, planning for these subsequent phases is kept at a high level. Duration ranges and resource profiles are estimated to provide a general sense of the scale and complexity.

Strategic Alignment

Aligning the project with strategic business objectives is crucial. Hard deadlines, milestones, and expectations for each Project Increment are laid out to ensure that the project contributes to achieving these objectives.

Risk Management

With high uncertainty levels at this stage, risk management is indispensable. Risk buffers should be incorporated into both cost and time estimates to account for unforeseen complications.

Tailoring the Approach

Often, the Project Approach Questionnaire (PAQ) might indicate specific areas where the default project management framework might not be fully applicable. Any such deviations should be adequately documented, either in the Management Approach Definition or Development Approach Definition, to ensure alignment with the unique aspects of the project.

Case Study: Implementing Feasibility Phase Planning in an Agile Software Development Project

Overview

In this case study, we'll explore how a hypothetical software development company, XYZ Tech, navigated the Feasibility phase for a customer relationship management (CRM) software project. The project had to align with both XYZ Tech's broader business goals and the specific needs of its client.

Objectives Met During the Feasibility Phase

Preliminary Scope Definition

The project team conducted initial workshops with stakeholders to capture high-level requirements, such as basic functionalities and expected performance metrics. This exercise helped in laying down an approximate scope for the project, serving as a starting point for more detailed discussions.

Foundations Phase Planning

A roadmap was developed for transitioning into the Foundations phase. This included identification of key milestones, assignment of roles and responsibilities, and planning of the resources required for the Foundations phase. A timeline was agreed upon, with clearly defined deliverables for the next phase.

High-Level Project Outline

An approximate size and duration for the CRM project were also outlined during this phase. This gave the stakeholders an idea of the scale of the project, facilitating better decision-making.

Key Components Developed

Delivery Plan for Foundations

The detailed plan for the Foundations phase was created, including the timeline, milestones, and resources. The document was approved by the Steering Committee and distributed to all stakeholders.

Facilitated Workshops

Workshops were planned for various aspects like requirement refinement and risk assessment. The dates were set, and the participants were identified, ensuring a multi-disciplinary approach.

Evolutionary Development & Deployment

While detailed information was still limited, a high-level plan was created for the subsequent phases. Estimates of durations and resource needs were outlined, providing a rough sketch for future planning.

Strategic Alignment

The project was aligned with the strategic goals of both XYZ Tech and its client. Hard deadlines were set, and milestones were identified to ensure that the project contributes to achieving these strategic objectives.

Risk Management

A risk register was developed to identify potential risks and prepare contingency plans. Given the high level of uncertainty, a risk buffer was built into the estimates for both cost and time.

Tailoring the Approach

After completing the Project Approach Questionnaire (PAQ), some minor deviations from the standard agile framework were identified. These were documented in the Development Approach Definition, and approvals were obtained for these changes.

This case study showcases the importance of thorough planning during the Feasibility phase, even when detailed information is limited. The groundwork laid during this phase significantly impacts the success of subsequent phases and ultimately the entire project.

Mastering Project Foundations: A Blueprint for Agile Success

The Foundations phase acts as a keystone in Agile Project Management, seamlessly bridging the gap between the abstract frameworks of the Feasibility phase and the actionable directives of the subsequent phases. It serves as the linchpin for laying down granular details for project scope, timelines, and resources. This guide offers a comprehensive look at key objectives, plan components, and essential considerations for effective planning during the Foundations phase.

Objectives of Planning in the Foundations Phase

Detailed Requirement Understanding

Building on the rough sketches of the Feasibility phase, this objective aims to dig deeper into the project requirements. It allows for fine-tuning specifications, which provides a clear path for both the development team and stakeholders.

Timeboxing and Resource Allocation

The Foundations phase is essential for laying down a preliminary schedule of Development Timeboxes for the first Project Increment. This also includes the identification and allocation of resources necessary to meet these Timeboxes.

Development and Control Approaches

Here, the project defines how it will approach software development and management controls. Whether the team will use Scrum, Kanban, or another agile framework, this is the stage where that decision is finalized.

Deployment Strategy

Planning for the eventual deployment of the project's deliverables into a live environment takes place here, laying the groundwork for smooth business transition and user adoption.

Components of the Foundations Phase Plan

Refined Delivery Plan

The Delivery Plan undergoes a transformation to become more accurate and detailed, offering committed timelines for the first Project Increment.

Timebox Schedule

The schedule outlines the sequence, focus, and resource commitments for each Development Timebox within the first Project Increment.

Methodological Approaches

This component provides a detailed roadmap for development and control practices, fine-tuned to meet the unique requirements of the project.

Deployment Strategy

The Deployment Strategy takes a preliminary shape at this stage, outlining the business changes, organizational impacts, and training needs that the new solution will necessitate.

Planning Areas

Timebox Schedule

The schedule should elaborate on the number of Timeboxes, their duration, and focus areas. This helps in resource planning and sets the pace for the project.

Development Approach

It's imperative to formalize the methodologies and practices that the Solution Development Team will adhere to. This ensures a cohesive and streamlined development process.

Deployment Strategy

The team should agree on a high-level strategy for solution deployment, taking into account facets like organizational change management and requisite training.

Risk Management

While the Foundations phase reduces the level of uncertainty seen in the Feasibility phase, risk management still plays a significant role. Estimates may range from optimistic to pessimistic, particularly if a fixed-price commitment is not in the equation. Being transparent about the confidence level in these estimates can aid in managing stakeholder expectations.

Navigating Complexity: A Case Study on Foundations Phase Planning

Introduction

This case study illuminates the planning intricacies of the Foundations phase through the lens of an actual Agile Project. Project "Elevate" aimed to build a new customer relationship management (CRM) system for a mid-size tech company. The case study focuses on how the project management team successfully navigated the various components and objectives of the Foundations phase.

Objectives Realization

Detailed Requirement Understanding

The project began with a series of workshops where key stakeholders refined the high-level requirements into specific user stories and epics. The involvement of cross-functional team members ensured that the requirements were not only business-focused but also technically feasible.

Timeboxing and Resource Allocation

Using the refined requirements, the team set forth a preliminary schedule for the first Project Increment. They allocated specific resources to Development Timeboxes based on skillset alignment and availability.

Development and Control Approaches

After evaluating multiple methodologies, the team decided on a hybrid approach that integrated aspects of both Scrum and Kanban. This allowed for iterative development while also maintaining a continuous workflow.

Deployment Strategy

The deployment plan took into account not just the technical aspects but also change management initiatives like training sessions and stakeholder communications to ensure smooth user adoption.

Plan Components Execution

Refined Delivery Plan

The Delivery Plan was updated with more exact deadlines based on the refined scope and resource availability. A roadmap was shared with all stakeholders to set clear expectations.

Timebox Schedule

A detailed schedule outlining the first Project Increment was circulated among the team. Each Timebox had specific objectives and resource allocations.

Methodological Approaches

The project's hybrid development methodology was well-documented and shared within the team. This allowed team members to understand their roles and responsibilities clearly.

Deployment Strategy

A draft deployment strategy was created, which included timelines for internal testing, staged deployment, and full release.

Planning Areas and Risk Management

Timebox Scheduling

The Timebox schedule was revisited periodically to make adjustments based on the project's pace and resource availability.

Development Approach

Though the development methodology was decided upfront, it was open for revisits and refinements based on regular retrospectives.

Deployment Strategy and Risks

Risk assessment was conducted to identify potential pitfalls during deployment. Strategies like phased rollout and rollback plans were put in place as risk mitigants.

By meticulously planning during the Foundations phase, Project "Elevate" managed to set a strong baseline, eventually leading to its successful execution.

A Deep Dive into Timebox Planning During the Evolutionary Development Phase

Timebox planning within the Evolutionary Development phase is a cornerstone of project management under the Dynamic Systems Development Method (DSDM) framework. This specific phase mandates a rigorous level of planning to ensure that the Solution Development Team effectively realizes the predetermined objectives within a given Timebox, or a defined time period.

Objectives of Timebox Planning

Task-Level Planning

In the Evolutionary Development phase, objectives are meticulously dissected into executable tasks. This demands a high level of precision, facilitated by a thorough investigation of the project's requirements.

Resource Allocation

Allocating the right resources to the right tasks is pivotal. Resource allocation not only involves human capital but also other assets like tools, facilities, and information.

Monitoring and Control

The importance of closely tracking progress and flagging potential issues cannot be overstated. Proactive monitoring and control mechanisms are essential to achieving the agreed-upon outcomes within the Timebox.

Key Components of Timebox Plans

Task-Level Estimates

The planning stage involves a detailed task breakdown, which allows for more accurate time and resource estimates.

Ownership and Responsibility

Clearly defined roles and accountabilities for each task eliminate ambiguities and streamline execution.

Timebox Objectives

Setting clear and achievable objectives for each Timebox ensures that the team knows what success looks like.

Resource Commitment

Resource commitment is defined upfront to minimize future conflicts and resource crunches.

Planning Procedures

Kick-off Meeting

The Timebox planning starts with a Kick-off meeting where high-level objectives and the Timebox duration are set.

MoSCoW Prioritization

The Must-Have, Should-Have, and Could-Have requirements are sorted to clarify what is non-negotiable and what can be deferred if needed.

Detailed Planning

Post Kick-off meeting, the team delves into detailed task-level planning, using the high-level objectives as a guide.

Team Board

Transparency is achieved through capturing the plan on a Team Board, which could be a physical board or an electronic version for remote teams.

Roles and Responsibilities

Team Leader

The Team Leader shoulders the responsibility for comprehensive planning, resource allocation, and issue communication to the Project Manager.

Solution Development Team

The Solution Development Team is intrinsically involved in both the detailed planning and the execution phases of the Timebox.

Risk Management and Contingencies

Given the fixed nature of a Timebox's duration, it is critical to have a contingency plan. The 'Could Have' requirements serve this purpose, acting as a buffer that can be deferred without jeopardizing the coherence of the Solution Increment.

Case Study: Timebox Planning in a Software Development Project

Context

In a recent software development project, the company opted for the Dynamic Systems Development Method (DSDM) framework. The Evolutionary Development phase was initiated, and it was crucial to ensure meticulous Timebox planning to meet the stringent deadlines and deliver a high-quality product.

Objective Setting

Before diving into the planning, the project manager and the team agreed upon clear objectives for each Timebox. The objectives ranged from completing user interface modules to backend API integrations.

MoSCoW Prioritization

The MoSCoW method was diligently applied to prioritize features and functionalities. For example, the 'Must-Have' features included critical user authentication components, while the 'Could-Have' list included less vital elements like social media sharing capabilities.

Detailed Task-level Planning

The team broke down each objective into detailed tasks. Tasks like "Design Login Screen" were further divided into sub-tasks like "Create Wireframe," "Code HTML/CSS," and "Integrate Backend."

Resource Allocation

The team leader was responsible for assigning tasks to individual team members based on their expertise and workload. For instance, frontend development tasks were assigned to frontend engineers, while database tasks were allocated to backend developers.

Team Board and Monitoring

A digital Team Board was used to track progress. The board had columns like "To-Do," "In Progress," and "Completed." Team members moved tasks across these columns as they progressed, offering real-time tracking.

Risk Management

In the Timebox dedicated to user authentication, a critical bug was identified, putting the 'Should-Have' and 'Could-Have' tasks at risk. The team decided to defer some 'Could-Have' features to focus on fixing the bug, thereby ensuring the Timebox still delivered a coherent Solution Increment.

Conclusion

Through meticulous planning and adaptability, the team successfully navigated the Evolutionary Development phase, delivering each Timebox's objectives while maintaining quality and timelines.

The case study demonstrates how effective Timebox planning during the Evolutionary Development phase can lead to successful project outcomes, even when unforeseen risks arise.

Amplifying the Tenets of Deployment Planning: A Comprehensive Guide for Project Managers

Deployment planning serves as the culminating phase of a project, focusing on the seamless migration of a developed solution into a live operational environment. This phase, activated usually in the latter stages of the Evolutionary Development phase, can be daunting in its complexity and scope. Given the potential impacts on stakeholders, resources, and the organization at large, the planning for this phase requires a meticulous approach.

Key Objectives in Deployment Planning

Ensuring a Seamless Transition

The paramount objective is to transition the new or updated system into the production environment without causing disruptions or downtimes.

Efficient Resource Allocation

From reserving conference rooms for training to coordinating with IT for environment setups, resources should be earmarked well in advance.

Risk Mitigation Strategies

Deployment planning must incorporate contingency measures to address any unplanned disruptions or system failures.

Preparing Stakeholders

In preparation for the 'go-live' date, stakeholders should be educated and informed to ensure a smooth transition.

Critical Components of Deployment Planning

Scheduling and Milestones

The plan should outline a series of key activities, categorized by crucial milestones leading up to the deployment.

Identification of Necessary Resources

A comprehensive list of all required resources should be prepared, covering everything from hardware and software needs to human resource requirements.

Role Assignments

Clearly specified roles and responsibilities will help streamline the deployment activities and ensure accountability.

Contingency and Rollback Plans

Anticipating possible deployment hitches is vital. The plan must include rollback options and alternative pathways in case of unexpected challenges.

Key Considerations

Resource Availability Constraints

The plan must account for various constraints like room availability for training sessions or dedicated time slots from key personnel.

Impact Analysis

A detailed analysis should be conducted to evaluate how the deployment will affect different organizational units, internal processes, and stakeholders.

Update of the Overall Delivery Plan

As the specifics of the deployment become clearer, this information needs to be integrated into the overall project's Delivery Plan to maintain alignment.

Roles and Responsibilities

Project Manager

Responsible for the oversight of the entire deployment plan, aligning it with the broader project objectives.

Deployment Team

Tasked with the actual execution of the plan, transforming the developed solution into a live application.

IT and Operations Staff

Focused on the technical aspects, they ensure that all hardware and software components are ready and tested before deployment.

Risk Management and Contingency Measures

Given the vital nature of this phase, risk management is not just an option but a necessity. This involves rigorous planning to tackle any unforeseen difficulties, ensuring that there are predefined solutions for a variety of scenarios.

Case Study: Deployment Planning for a Major Software Upgrade

Context

A large financial institution was gearing up for a significant software upgrade across its multiple locations. The project management team recognized the intricacies involved in deploying this upgrade without disrupting the ongoing operations.

Objectives

- Achieve a seamless transition to the new software platform.
- Ensure all necessary resources, both human and technical, are available for the deployment.
- Develop risk mitigation strategies for any unplanned disruptions.
- Educate and prepare stakeholders, including employees and upper management.

Deployment Plan Components

Milestone Schedule

A Gantt chart was created, delineating the various stages of the deployment, each associated with specific milestones such as testing, staging, and final deployment.

Resource Allocation

Comprehensive documentation outlined the required resources, including servers, databases, and IT staff.

Role Assignments

A RACI chart (Responsible, Accountable, Consulted, Informed) was developed, outlining the roles and responsibilities for each aspect of the deployment.

Contingency Planning

A detailed contingency plan was in place, covering scenarios like failed deployment, data loss, and downtimes.

Key Outcomes

- The deployment was completed ahead of schedule, owing to meticulous planning and resource allocation.
- The rollback plan was not needed but provided the team with the confidence to proceed.
- Stakeholders were well-prepared, thanks to a comprehensive communication plan that kept them informed at every step.

Lessons Learned

- Early involvement of all relevant departments is crucial.
- Contingency plans are invaluable, even if they are not utilized.
- Effective communication with stakeholders can make or break the deployment phase.

The case study illustrates the importance of thorough planning in the deployment phase, which can significantly contribute to a project's overall success.

Planning Benefits Assessment Activity: Comprehensive Framework for Post-Project Analysis

Benefits assessment in the post-project phase stands as a capstone to the entire project management process. It is here that the theoretical value propositions made during project initiation are put to the empirical test. Such an assessment not only helps gauge the project's overall success but also contributes to organizational learning.

Key Objectives

Measure Effectiveness
The primary objective is to evaluate the degree to which the project has achieved its stated goals and how effectively the solution is performing in the live environment.

Process Improvement
The secondary objective revolves around learning; it's about understanding what worked well and what didn't, with a view to refine processes for future projects.

Cost-Benefit Analysis
Undertake a thorough ROI analysis to evaluate whether the project has provided value for the investment made.

Planning Components

Metrics Definition
Defining clear KPIs is a foundational step. These indicators should be directly related to the project's goals and offer quantifiable means of assessment.

Timing and Schedule

Plan a timeline for when the benefits will be assessed. This might include immediate post-deployment reviews as well as longer-term assessments to capture sustained benefits or issues.

Data Collection

Choose methodologies for gathering data, be it through automated tracking systems, user surveys, or another source that fits the project type.

Stakeholder Communication

Decide how to package and present the findings. Will there be a formal report, a presentation, or a dashboard that updates in real-time?

Key Considerations

Ownership and Delegation

While the Business Visionary typically owns this process, various aspects like data collection and analysis might be delegated to a Business Analyst or another qualified individual.

Timeline Constraints

Benefits often manifest over varying periods. Your plan should allow enough time to capture both immediate and long-term impacts.

Resource Availability

Be clear on what resources are required for this assessment, which could range from analytical tools to personnel time.

Roles and Responsibilities

Business Visionary

Maintains overall ownership of the benefits assessment, ensuring that it remains aligned with organizational goals.

Business Analyst

Handles the nuances of the benefits assessment, such as metrics tracking, data analysis, and compiling reports.

Other Stakeholders

May include project sponsors, department heads, or external partners who have a vested interest in the project's success.

Conclusion

Planning for post-project benefits assessment is a robust process that requires thoughtful consideration of various elements. Such assessments are not mere formalities but critical tools that feed into the organization's strategic planning and continuous improvement efforts.

Case Study: Benefits Assessment for an ERP Implementation Project

Context

Company XYZ recently completed the implementation of an Enterprise Resource Planning (ERP) system aimed at streamlining operations and reducing administrative costs. As the Business Visionary, you are responsible for evaluating whether the project achieved its goals.

Objective Setting

Measuring Effectiveness

The primary objective is to assess operational efficiencies gained through the ERP system. Key Performance Indicators (KPIs) include the time taken for order-to-shipment and rate of order errors.

Process Improvement

By tracking pain points or glitches during the initial months of ERP operation, the goal is to identify areas for future process improvements.

Cost-Benefit Analysis

The ROI calculation will include savings on labor costs due to automation and gains in operational efficiency against the project's overall expenditure.

Metrics Definition and Data Collection

KPIs

- Time taken for order-to-shipment
- Rate of order errors
- Labor cost savings

Data Sources

- ERP system's built-in analytics
- Employee surveys

- Financial records

Timing and Stakeholder Communication

A benefits assessment schedule is established, covering immediate post-deployment metrics as well as six and twelve-month reviews. A dashboard is also created to share real-time information with key stakeholders.

Roles and Responsibilities

Business Visionary

You oversee the entire benefits assessment, from KPI selection to stakeholder communication.

Business Analyst

Involved in the actual collection and analysis of data, translating numbers into actionable insights.

IT Department

Ensures that all data collection tools are functioning correctly and supports the Business Analyst in data extraction and interpretation.

Outcomes

After the first six months, the ERP system shows a 20% reduction in order-to-shipment times and a 15% reduction in order errors. The ROI analysis indicates that the savings in labor costs alone have covered 40% of the project costs.

Conclusion

The benefits assessment validates the ERP implementation as a success, both in terms of operational efficiencies and financial savings. These findings will not only contribute to ROI justification but also provide valuable insights for any future projects requiring significant change management and technology adoption.

By meticulously planning and executing the benefits assessment, you ensure a thorough, fact-based evaluation, fortifying the organization's decision-making and strategic planning.

Incremental Planning: The Imperative of Revisiting Foundations Between Project Increments

Within the framework of Dynamic Systems Development Method (DSDM), revisiting the Foundations phase after each Project Increment isn't an ad-hoc practice but a prescribed one. The activity provides an opportunity to recalibrate the project and realign it with its overarching objectives, thus ensuring continual relevancy and focus.

Objectives for Revisiting the Foundations Phase

Viability Assessment

After the conclusion of each Project Increment, the viability of the entire project needs to be re-assessed in terms of its Business Case. This process provides an informed decision-making platform for either proceeding to the next Increment or making pivotal changes.

Plan Refinement

As part of recalibration, the Foundations phase serves as a cornerstone for refining subsequent plans. This includes revisiting requirements, re-prioritizing objectives, and fine-tuning the schedule for the next Increment.

Key Steps in the Process

Business Case Revalidation

Utilizing updated metrics like actual expenses, manpower effort, and benefits realization so far, the Business Case undergoes a thorough revalidation process.

Requirements Review

Requirements slated for the upcoming Increment should be rigorously assessed. The goal is to ensure their relevance, urgency, and viability in the evolving project landscape.

Timebox Scheduling

Updated project information and revalidated requirements will feed into the scheduling of Timeboxes for the subsequent Increment.

Review of Approaches

A succinct but important step is to reassess the Management and Development Approaches to confirm that they still align with the evolving project needs and objectives.

Roles and Responsibilities

Project Manager
The onus of oversight for this recalibration process rests with the Project Manager, who ensures that the activities and outcomes are in sync with high-level project objectives.

Business Analyst
A critical role in this phase is played by the Business Analyst. They are instrumental in revisiting and revising the requirements and helping the Project Manager in recalibration.

Team Leaders and Members
Their input in fine-tuning the plan for the next Increment is invaluable. They bring in the ground-level data and insights that can greatly affect plan refinement.

Case Study: Revisiting the Foundations Phase in a Large-Scale Software Development Project

Context
In a large-scale software development project aimed at creating an enterprise resource planning (ERP) system, the project was broken down into multiple Project Increments. Each Increment was focused on developing specific modules like Inventory Management, Human Resources, and Financial Planning. After the completion of the first Increment—Inventory Management—the team found it necessary to revisit the Foundations phase.

Objective
The primary objective was to reassess the project's alignment with its Business Case and to fine-tune the plans for developing the next module—Human Resources.

Steps Taken

Business Case Revalidation

After the successful deployment of the Inventory Management module, the project costs, and the benefits were re-evaluated. This revalidation proved that the project was still on track in terms of ROI and provided the confidence to proceed to the next Increment.

Requirement Revisitation

The Human Resources module had initially been scoped with a set list of features. However, due to changes in labor laws and internal company policies, some new requirements emerged. These were added to the priority list for the upcoming Increment.

Timebox Replanning

Based on the new set of requirements and the lessons learned from the first Increment, Timeboxes for the Human Resources module were rescheduled. Some were shortened, and others were extended to provide a balanced workload and to meet the newly introduced legal deadlines.

Reassessing Approaches

The Development Approach, which had emphasized a Waterfall model in the first Increment, was reassessed. A decision was made to incorporate more Agile practices in the subsequent Increments, given the volatile nature of the requirements.

Roles and Responsibilities

Project Manager

Led the entire recalibration exercise and was pivotal in making the decisions for requirement changes and approach adjustments.

Business Analyst

Provided crucial insights into the changing landscape of labor laws affecting the Human Resources module, thus influencing the priority of new features.

Team Members

Offered ground-level feedback on the challenges and successes of the first Increment, which was instrumental in the replanning effort.

Conclusion

Revisiting the Foundations phase proved to be a highly beneficial exercise. It not only confirmed the project's ongoing viability but also provided the team with an opportunity to update and refine their approach, thus setting the stage for a more efficient and relevant next Increment.

Maximizing Success: Expert Strategies for Planning in DSDM Projects

The role of an Agile Project Manager in a Dynamic Systems Development Method (DSDM) framework is pivotal to ensuring that planning aligns with agile principles. This ensures an effective balance between flexibility and discipline, thereby driving project success.

Collaborative Planning: A Deeper Look

Importance
In the DSDM framework, the collective intelligence of the team is a resource that must be capitalized upon during the planning phase. Collaborative planning introduces a wealth of diverse perspectives and specialized expertise into the decision-making process.

Tip Elaborated
While the Delivery Plan forms the backbone of the project, involving team members like Solution Developers, Business Analysts, and Business Ambassadors in the planning process can significantly improve its quality. Not only does this approach enrich the plan itself, but it also fosters a sense of collective ownership and commitment, thereby enhancing team morale and productivity.

Timebox Planning Ownership: Further Insights

Importance
Timebox planning is an integral part of DSDM and serves to enhance focus and efficiency. By assigning the primary responsibility of this to the Solution Development Team, you allow those who will execute the plan to have a say in its formation.

Tip Elaborated
While the Project Manager is not tasked with creating the Timebox Plan, a review of this plan is crucial to ensure its alignment with broader project objectives and the Timebox's predefined goals. This ensures that while the team has ownership, the work is in sync with strategic objectives.

Tool Selection: Why it Matters

Importance

The tools utilized for planning should be agile-friendly. They should offer the team the flexibility to adapt to changes quickly, which is a cornerstone of any agile project.

Tip Elaborated

Choosing planning tools that resonate with agile principles provides a strong foundation for project execution. Such tools should allow easy adjustments to the plan and offer features that facilitate real-time collaboration among team members.

Value-Driven Work: Key Points

Importance

In a DSDM project, every task should contribute directly to the realization of project objectives. Non-value-adding activities are essentially resource drains and should be eliminated.

Tip Elaborated

Regularly scrutinizing the work items listed in the plan to ensure their alignment with the Business Case is an effective way to keep the project on track. This is particularly important for avoiding scope creep and for maintaining a keen focus on delivering real value.

Case Study: Implementing Agile Planning Tips in a DSDM Project

Overview

In a recent DSDM project aimed at developing a Customer Relationship Management (CRM) system for a medium-sized organization, the Agile Project Manager implemented several best practices discussed in the previous section. Here is how the application of these tips played a crucial role in steering the project towards success.

Collaborative Planning

During the formulation of the Delivery Plan, the Project Manager ensured that not just Business Analysts, but also Business Ambassadors and Solution Developers were involved. This move had an immediate impact: the plan became more practical and accepted by the team, and it was easier to get stakeholder buy-in as well.

Timebox Planning Ownership

The Solution Development Team was empowered to own Timebox planning. Each Timebox plan was reviewed by the Project Manager to make sure it was in alignment with project objectives. This dual ownership model served to enhance both accountability and alignment, thereby streamlining the execution phase.

Tool Selection

The Project Manager chose agile-friendly planning tools that allowed real-time collaboration and quick adaptability to change. Such a tool was especially useful in a remote work setup, helping to maintain team cohesion and ensure that everyone was updated on any planning changes.

Value-Driven Work

Regularly scheduled review meetings were held to examine the work items in the plan. During these meetings, each task was scrutinized to ensure it aligned with the Business Case and project objectives. Non-value-adding activities were promptly identified and eliminated, allowing the team to focus solely on tasks that would offer genuine business value.

Lessons Learned

The project was a success, primarily because planning was closely aligned with agile principles. Collaborative planning and tool selection fostered teamwork and adaptability, while Timebox ownership and value-driven work kept the project aligned with business objectives.

This case study illustrates the efficacy of implementing the tips discussed, showcasing their real-world applicability and impact.

Chapter Nineteen

Quality: Ensuring Excellence in Agile Projects

Delving Deeper into Understanding Quality in DSDM Projects

The concept of quality in Dynamic Systems Development Method (DSDM) is indeed an expansive one, weaving through every aspect of a project from the technical to the human. While it's easy to pin down quality as simply "meeting specifications," the DSDM framework calls for a more nuanced approach. Let's dissect the layers and intricacies involved in achieving optimal quality in DSDM projects.

Components of Quality

Solution Quality

Business Needs: This is the cornerstone of quality, gauging the success of a project by how well the solution addresses business challenges or enhances capabilities. It's the starting point for any discussion on quality.

Technical Robustness: An often-overlooked component, technical robustness is about reducing future costs related to support and maintenance. It aims to ensure that the system can adapt and evolve, without leading to an escalation in costs.

Usability: Usability is a user-centric quality measure that takes into account how efficiently and comfortably the end-users can accomplish their tasks using the solution. Elements like intuitive design and accessibility fall under this category.

Maintainability: Ensuring that a solution is maintainable goes hand-in-hand with its technical robustness. This considers the ease with which the system can be updated, including the presence and quality of documentation.

Process Quality (Quality Management)

Best Practices: These are predetermined methods or guidelines, often codified at organizational or industry levels. Adhering to these not only enhances the quality of the end-product but also improves the development process itself.

Governance: This entails having a structure for oversight, from regular check-ins to an established hierarchy of responsibility. It assures that the project is proceeding along the right paths.

Importance in DSDM

Alignment with Principles

The DSDM principle "Never compromise on quality" resonates perfectly with the multi-dimensional nature of quality. It helps to create a robust framework for maintaining quality across both the solution and the process.

Flexibility for Compliance

DSDM's adaptability allows it to conform to a variety of quality standards, be it ISO, CMMI, or internally developed frameworks, without hindering its agile nature.

People Over Process

DSDM acknowledges that while processes set the stage, it's the people who bring a project to life. As such, human skills and professionalism become focal points in maintaining quality.

Practical Guidance

Solution Quality: Employ strategies like automated testing and code reviews to continually validate the quality of the solution as it evolves.

Process Quality: A meticulously crafted quality assurance checklist and regular audits can serve as powerful tools for upholding quality standards throughout the project lifecycle.

Case Study: Implementing Quality Management in a DSDM Project

Overview

In a large-scale DSDM project undertaken by a financial institution, the challenge was to migrate existing customer data to a new, more robust platform. The project had high stakes, involving sensitive data and requiring strict compliance with financial regulations and internal governance frameworks.

Quality Components Addressed

Solution Quality

Business Needs: The primary objective was to ensure a secure and efficient data migration that would enhance the customer experience. This was regularly reviewed through stakeholder meetings and updates.

Technical Robustness: Security measures were paramount, given the sensitivity of the data. Encryption techniques and multiple layers of firewall were implemented.

Usability: The new platform underwent rigorous user acceptance testing (UAT) to ensure that it would be user-friendly for both employees and customers.

Maintainability: A complete documentation package was prepared, allowing for straightforward future updates to the platform.

Process Quality

Best Practices: The project strictly followed ISO 27001 standards for information security management, along with industry best practices for data migration.

Governance: A governance board was established, consisting of representatives from IT, legal, and business departments, ensuring multidisciplinary oversight.

Implementation Techniques

Automated Testing

An automated testing suite was developed to test various quality criteria, including security vulnerabilities and system performance, thereby ensuring that each code change met predefined quality benchmarks.

Regular Audits

Compliance officers conducted regular audits using a comprehensive quality checklist based on ISO standards and internal guidelines. These were used to rectify any deviations promptly.

Skill Development

Continuous skill development programs were organized for the team members, aligning them with the DSDM principle of 'People Over Process,' thereby emphasizing the role of skilled professionals in achieving quality.

Outcome

By adhering to these comprehensive quality measures, the project was not only delivered on time but also exceeded stakeholder expectations in terms of data integrity, security, and usability. It set a precedent within the organization for how to manage quality effectively in DSDM projects.

This case study offers insights into how multi-faceted quality measures, right from technical to human aspects, can collectively contribute to a project's success. Would you like to know more about any specific aspect?

MoSCoW Prioritization and Quality in DSDM Projects

Revisiting the MoSCoW Prioritization Framework

The MoSCoW prioritization framework is intrinsic to DSDM, allowing for a nuanced understanding of feature scope and its impact on project quality. This classification system ensures that the project stakeholders are well-aligned on which features are essential for project success and what can be considered 'above and beyond'. This agreement is particularly crucial in agile environments where changes are frequent and adaptability is key.

Why MoSCoW Matters in Quality Perception

The perception of quality in a DSDM project is often directly linked to how well the MoSCoW prioritization is executed. In a well-managed DSDM project, failure to deliver a 'Must-Have' feature would be an unequivocal compromise on quality. On the other hand, the inclusion of 'Could-Have' or even some 'Should-Have' features can elevate the perceived quality of the project by adding extra value.

Integrating MoSCoW with Other Quality Dimensions

Project Viability and Business Alignment

Delivering only the 'Must-Have' features may meet the minimum viable product criteria but could fail to fully align with the larger business objectives. In contrast, achieving 'Must-Have' and 'Should-Have' features generally indicates a project that is not just viable but also adds significant business value, thereby improving quality perception.

Flexibility in Planning

The MoSCoW method provides the flexibility needed in agile environments to adapt the project scope without jeopardizing quality. If unforeseen challenges arise, 'Could-Have' and some 'Should-Have' features can be deferred, allowing the project to still meet the 'Must-Have' requirements, thereby delivering a quality product.

Customer Satisfaction

Fulfilling 'Should-Have' and 'Could-Have' requirements often leads to increased customer satisfaction, another metric of quality. These features, while not critical, offer additional value and can distinguish the product in a competitive market.

Final Thoughts

The balanced application of MoSCoW prioritization enables DSDM projects to manage feature scope effectively while maintaining a high-quality output. It allows for the clear setting of quality benchmarks that are aligned with the project's objectives, the client's expectations, and the team's capabilities.

Case Study: Implementing MoSCoW Prioritization to Enhance Quality in a DSDM Project

Background

The project involved developing an enterprise resource planning (ERP) software for a manufacturing company. The team decided to follow the DSDM methodology and began by defining the feature scope using MoSCoW prioritization.

Initial MoSCoW Prioritization

Must-Have: Core modules for inventory management, production planning, and financial accounting.

Should-Have: Additional features like report generation, user-access controls, and a dashboard interface.

Could-Have: Integrations with existing CRM software, mobile accessibility, and machine learning-based predictive analytics.

Won't-Have: Social media integration, chatbots, and other non-essential features.

Planning for Quality

The team aligned the MoSCoW categories with their quality objectives. They acknowledged that failing to deliver any 'Must-Have' features would be unacceptable and would compromise the project's quality. They also understood that including 'Should-Have' and 'Could-Have' features would significantly enhance the perceived quality of the project.

Mid-Project Reassessment

Halfway through the project, the team faced several challenges, including resource constraints and changes in external compliance regulations. They revisited the MoSCoW prioritization and made the following adjustments:

- Moved some 'Could-Have' features to the 'Won't-Have' category.
- Elevated the importance of compliance-related changes to 'Must-Have'.

Outcome and Quality Perception

By the end of the project, the team successfully delivered all 'Must-Have' and most 'Should-Have' features. They also managed to include a couple of 'Could-Have' features that were not initially planned but became feasible due to some resource-saving measures.

Quality Assessment

Project Viability: All 'Must-Have' features were successfully implemented, making the software viable for deployment.

Business Value: Most 'Should-Have' features were incorporated, aligning the software with broader business objectives.

Extra Value: The inclusion of some 'Could-Have' features added extra value, exceeding the client's initial quality expectations.

Lessons Learned

The project demonstrated the effectiveness of using MoSCoW prioritization as a tool for defining quality objectives. The flexibility to adapt to changes without compromising on essential features showcased the strength of the DSDM methodology in maintaining high-quality standards.

The case study illuminates the importance of MoSCoW prioritization in managing both scope and quality effectively in a DSDM project.

Integrating Technical Quality into DSDM Projects

The Nuanced Role of Acceptance Criteria in Defining 'Fitness for Purpose'

In DSDM, the "fit for purpose" concept is operationalized through a well-crafted set of acceptance criteria, which act as an essential set of constraints and guidelines. This set of criteria effectively functions as a contract between the stakeholders and the development team. Its role goes beyond mere feature specification to encapsulate various dimensions of quality, including usability, performance, security, and maintainability.

Parameters Shaping 'Fit for Purpose'

Usability: This considers user experience, accessibility, and other factors that affect the ease with which the solution can be employed.

Performance: Metrics related to speed, responsiveness, and scalability.

Security: Includes various protocols and practices aimed at protecting the integrity and confidentiality of data.

Maintainability: This entails ease of updating the software, implementing patches, and general system upkeep.

The Downside of Neglecting Acceptance Criteria

Ignoring or inadequately defining acceptance criteria is a recipe for failure in multiple ways. Not only does it create a vagueness around what 'quality' means in the context of the project, but it can also lead to scope creep, reduced stakeholder satisfaction, and, in the worst case, a failed project.

Consequences

Wrong Functionality: Teams may spend resources developing features that don't align with actual business needs.

Flaws and Errors: Lack of a quality benchmark may result in a buggy or unstable solution.

Increased Support Costs: Poor quality necessitates ongoing, costly maintenance.

Complexity and Risk: Unclear quality standards can induce unnecessary complexity, affecting both timelines and budgets.

The Importance of Collaboration

The multifaceted nature of 'fit for purpose' necessitates a comprehensive discussion among all stakeholders, including the project manager, business analyst, and development team. This collaborative discussion ensures that the acceptance criteria are neither too lax nor overly stringent, but just right for achieving the project's business objectives while maintaining stakeholder satisfaction.

Case Study: Implementing 'Fit for Purpose' Acceptance Criteria in a DSDM Project

Context

In a recent DSDM project aimed at developing a customer relationship management (CRM) system for a medium-sized enterprise, the concept of 'fit for purpose' played a pivotal role. The business required a system capable of handling thousands of customer interactions daily while providing real-time analytics.

Setting the Acceptance Criteria

After numerous stakeholder interviews and collaborative discussions, the project team established a comprehensive set of acceptance criteria that included:

Usability

- Easy-to-navigate user interface
- Role-based access control

Performance

- Capability to handle 2,000 concurrent users
- Response time under 2 seconds for key operations

Security

- Multi-factor authentication
- Compliance with GDPR and other relevant data protection laws

Maintainability

- Modular architecture for easy updates
- Comprehensive documentation for support teams

Project Execution

The project was broken down into multiple increments. Each increment underwent rigorous testing against the agreed acceptance criteria. This strategy ensured that any deviations were detected early and corrected before they could snowball into larger issues.

Outcome

The CRM system was delivered on time and within budget, meeting all the defined acceptance criteria. Post-implementation reviews confirmed that the solution was indeed 'fit for purpose,' fulfilling both the technical requirements and business needs.

Key Takeaways

- Early and clear definition of acceptance criteria can act as a North Star, guiding a project to successful completion.
- A collaborative approach to defining quality ensures a balanced and realistic set of acceptance criteria.
- Rigorous adherence to these criteria during the project execution phase can mitigate risks and ensure that the solution is truly 'fit for purpose.'

By closely adhering to a well-defined set of acceptance criteria, the project was able to deliver a solution that was not just feature-complete but also robust, secure, and easy to maintain—truly 'fit for purpose.'

Maintainability in DSDM Projects: A Comprehensive Exploration

Maintainability in the context of Dynamic Systems Development Method (DSDM) is a pivotal attribute that should not be relegated to afterthoughts or be considered merely as an operational checkbox to be ticked. This attribute directly influences not just the technical robustness of the project but also its economic sustainability. It dictates how easily modifications can be made post-deployment, affecting the Total Cost of Ownership (TCO) and, by extension, the Return on Investment (ROI).

Strategic Importance of Decision-Making in Maintainability

Significance of Aligning with Business Goals

The DSDM framework recognizes that decisions concerning maintainability are intrinsically strategic. They need to align with long-term business objectives, whether those objectives are quick market penetration, long-term user engagement, or modular scalability. This strategic alignment ensures that the project does not create downstream issues that erode its initial success.

DSDM Approaches to Maintainability

DSDM suggests three core approaches for maintainability, each catering to different strategic needs:

Maintainability as a Required Attribute: This approach prioritizes maintainability from the outset. It is apt for projects that foresee a long lifecycle and multiple future iterations.

Deliver First, Re-engineer Later: This approach allows for rapid market entry, with a built-in plan to improve maintainability in subsequent versions.

Short-term, Tactical Solution: This is generally a stop-gap arrangement where the solution is designed for immediate needs with no intention of long-term maintenance.

Risks and Their Management

Identifying Potential Risks

Understanding and agreeing upon maintainability objectives bring forth the need for comprehensive risk assessment. Potential risks include, but are not limited to, increased costs, technical debt, and system obsolescence.

Risk Management Strategies

It's essential to develop a risk management strategy that offers solutions or mitigations for identified risks. This could involve contingency planning, budgeting for future re-engineering, or designing a phased approach to incorporate maintainability features in future iterations.

Conclusion

DSDM provides the flexibility to approach maintainability in different ways to align with project and organizational objectives. However, the choice of approach has implications that can affect not just project deliverables but the broader economic viability of the project. Therefore, maintainability in DSDM projects is not just an operational concern but a strategic one that requires proactive planning and continuous risk assessment.

Case Study: Implementing Maintainability in a DSDM Project for a Financial Services Platform

Introduction

For the purpose of elaboration, let's consider a hypothetical DSDM project undertaken by a financial services company. The project's objective was to develop a secure and robust online banking platform. Given the sensitive nature of the financial transactions and the long-term implications of the platform, maintainability was a crucial concern.

Strategic Decision-Making

Business Objectives and Maintainability

The organization had clear long-term objectives of customer retention, compliance with evolving regulations, and modular introduction of additional features. These objectives made it imperative to focus on maintainability as a 'Required Attribute' from the project's inception.

Aligning with DSDM's Maintainability Approach

The project team and stakeholders unanimously agreed to prioritize maintainability. The technical architecture was designed to be modular, making it easier to update individual components without affecting the entire system.

Risk Assessment and Management

Identification of Risks

Risks identified included potential bottlenecks in system performance, escalating costs for future compliance updates, and the possibility of security vulnerabilities emerging over time.

Risk Mitigation Plans

Performance Bottlenecks: A proactive monitoring system was set up to identify and address bottlenecks before they could impact the system.

Compliance Updates: A reserved budget was set aside specifically for compliance-related updates.

Security Concerns: Regular security audits were planned, and a contingency strategy was prepared for immediate patches if vulnerabilities were discovered.

Implementation and Review

Periodic Reviews

Maintainability objectives and risks were revisited at the end of each Project Increment. This allowed for real-time adjustments and ensured that the project stayed aligned with its long-term goals.

Feedback Loops

Customer feedback and system performance metrics were continuously monitored. Any issues that could potentially impact maintainability were immediately escalated and addressed.

Conclusion

The project was a success, not just in terms of delivering a high-quality banking platform but also in ensuring its long-term maintainability. The strategic approach to maintainability and rigorous risk management contributed significantly to this outcome.

This case study serves to illustrate the strategic importance of maintainability in DSDM projects, and how a well-planned approach can lead to sustainable project success.

Expanding the Synergistic Approach: Business and IT Collaboration in DSDM for Quality Solutions

Understanding Business Ownership and Roles

The Principle of Business Ownership

DSDM posits that projects are fundamentally business endeavors and hence, the business should actively 'own' the solution. This ownership is not merely symbolic but encompasses a tangible set of responsibilities and accountabilities to ensure the project's success.

Multiplicity of Business Perspectives

The inclusion of various business roles, each with specific focus areas, creates a rich tapestry of perspectives. This mitigates the risk of the project getting skewed towards a single viewpoint, thus aligning it more closely with the multifaceted needs of the business.

DSDM Practices: Facilitating Quality through Collaboration

Defined Roles and Responsibilities

The emphasis on early and consistent role definition ensures that stakeholders are cognizant of their roles and responsibilities throughout the project's lifecycle. This keeps everyone engaged and invested in the project, increasing the likelihood of its success.

Facilitated Workshops

Facilitated Workshops serve as crucibles for intensive discussion and consensus building among various project stakeholders. They are particularly useful for reconciling divergent viewpoints and aligning the team's understanding of MoSCoW priorities, requirements, and estimates.

Communication Mechanisms

The use of modelling, daily stand-ups, and team boards fosters an environment that prizes open and direct communication. These mechanisms serve as safeguards against misunderstandings or misalignments that could negatively impact the project's quality.

Timeboxing and Iterative Development

These methodologies imbue the project with the agility to adapt to shifting business needs. The iterative cycles provide regular checkpoints for reassessment and realignment, thus acting as corrective measures that can steer the project back on course, should it start to deviate from business objectives.

Conclusion

In a DSDM project, the collaboration between business and IT is not merely a procedural formality but a strategic necessity. By ingraining the business perspective into the project's DNA through well-defined roles and employing collaborative practices, DSDM creates a framework that is conducive to delivering high-quality solutions that are tightly aligned with business needs.

Case Study: Implementing a DSDM Project for Business-IT Synergy

Background

A leading retail company embarked on a DSDM project to revamp its inventory management system. Given the project's magnitude and importance, there was an acute need to ensure high-quality deliverables that aligned closely with the company's business objectives.

Business Ownership and Roles

Setting the Stage

The project was firmly grounded in the principle of business ownership. The CTO served as the Business Sponsor, overseeing budgetary alignment and financial feasibility. The Head of Retail Operations, a domain expert, took on the role of the Business Visionary, defining the overarching objectives for the project.

Establishing Team Synergy

Additional roles such as Business Ambassadors and Business Advisors were meticulously chosen to represent a full spectrum of perspectives, from procurement to sales, ensuring a well-rounded approach to the project's execution.

DSDM Practices Employed

Role Clarity through Onboarding Workshops

At the onset, workshops were conducted to elaborate on the roles and responsibilities of each stakeholder. This initiative removed any ambiguity, fostering better cooperation among team members.

Decision-making through Facilitated Workshops

Critical decisions on feature priorities and requirement specifications were made in Facilitated Workshops, involving both business and IT team members. These workshops proved crucial for aligning the project with the actual needs of various departments, thereby enhancing its business relevance.

Transparent Communication

The project used daily stand-ups, team boards, and modelling tools to facilitate ongoing communication. This suite of tools ensured that everyone stayed on the same page throughout the project, fostering an atmosphere of collective ownership.

Adaptive Development

Iterative development cycles and timeboxing allowed the project to remain flexible. When unforeseen challenges arose, like supply chain disruptions, the project was able to realign swiftly, ensuring that the most crucial business needs were still met.

Outcome

The project was not only completed on time and within budget but also exceeded quality expectations. The resultant inventory management system was robust, user-friendly, and fully aligned with the company's business strategy, thereby validating the efficacy of DSDM's approach to business-IT collaboration for quality solutions.

This case study exemplifies how DSDM's synergistic approach between business and IT can lead to high-quality solutions that are closely aligned with organizational objectives.

Embedding Quality Across the Lifecycle in DSDM Projects

Quality Assurance as a Continuous Process

Quality assurance in DSDM isn't an isolated event but rather a continuous cycle that operates throughout the project's life. This ensures that the project remains focused on delivering a solution that is not only functional but also maintainable, reliable, and scalable.

Strategic Placement of Quality Decisions Across Phases

Feasibility Phase: Setting the Foundation for Quality

The feasibility phase in DSDM serves as the initial stage for making pivotal decisions around quality. During this phase, project stakeholders agree upon high-level acceptance criteria that will act as a north star throughout the project lifecycle. The considerations around Total Cost of Ownership (TCO) are also initiated here, aiming to set early expectations around the quality of maintainability.

Foundations Phase: Crystalizing Quality Criteria

In the Foundations phase, the high-level quality criteria agreed upon during the Feasibility phase are further refined and documented in the Prioritised Requirements List. Decisions regarding architectural frameworks that are conducive to these quality criteria are also made. The Review and Testing Strategy is laid out in the Development Approach Definition, solidifying the means by which quality will be assessed.

Evolutionary Development Phase: The Crucible of Quality

Quality assurance continues to be an ongoing process through the Evolutionary Development phase. Acceptance criteria are aligned with Timebox objectives, ensuring that each Timebox aims to meet specific quality benchmarks. Testing isn't a separate phase but an integrated part of the development process. The aim is to catch issues early during the development of individual requirements, thereby ensuring that any defects can be rectified in a timely manner.

The Essence of Process Quality

Ensuring Best Practices

DSDM emphasizes the consistent application of best practices across projects, tailored to their unique needs. This level of standardization helps in delivering consistently high-quality solutions.

Safeguarding Against Omissions

Quality in DSDM is also about what you don't do. Systematic quality considerations work as preventive measures, helping to avoid costly mistakes and omissions that can compromise the project's integrity.

Learning as a Pillar of Quality

One of the cornerstones of maintaining a high standard of quality in DSDM projects is the integration of lessons learned from past projects. This culture of continuous improvement helps in refining the quality processes over time.

Case Study: Embedding Quality in a DSDM Project - A Hypothetical Example

Context and Background

Imagine a DSDM project undertaken by a healthcare provider aiming to develop an Electronic Health Record (EHR) system. The stakes are high due to the sensitive nature of the data and the project's direct impact on patient care.

Feasibility Phase: Establishing the Groundwork

At the onset, key stakeholders including medical staff, IT professionals, and hospital administrators collaborate to define high-level acceptance criteria. One of the primary considerations is the secure and compliant storage of patient data, aligning with the Health Insurance Portability and Accountability Act (HIPAA) standards. The Total Cost of Ownership (TCO) is also considered, factoring in the costs of long-term data storage and system maintenance.

Foundations Phase: Deep Dive into Quality Criteria

In this phase, the high-level acceptance criteria are further refined. For example, the team decides that any data exchange between different departments must be encrypted. Architecture choices are also made during this phase, opting for a cloud-based solution to offer scalability and reliability. The Development Approach Definition document details how regular audits and compliance checks will be conducted to assess quality.

Evolutionary Development Phase: Iterative Quality Checks

Each Timebox is designed with specific objectives that align with the quality criteria. For instance, one Timebox may focus on developing the feature for secure message transmission between medical professionals. Automated and manual tests are integrated into the development process to ensure that each feature or module meets the predefined quality criteria.

Process Quality: Ensuring Uniformity

To ensure that best practices are followed, the project employs a checklist based on both HIPAA guidelines and in-house compliance metrics. Lessons learned from previous projects, like effective methods for data encryption or user authentication, are applied.

Outcomes

The project successfully delivers an EHR system that not only meets the functional requirements but also excels in maintainability, scalability, and compliance. The strategic embedding of quality decisions across the project lifecycle ensures that the system is robust and 'fit-for-purpose,' aligning well with the business needs and regulatory requirements.

This hypothetical example illustrates how DSDM's approach to quality assurance can be adapted to suit the unique needs and constraints of a given project while ensuring high-quality results.

Unpacking Process Quality in Dynamic Systems Development Method (DSDM)

Understanding the nuances of Process Quality in DSDM involves recognizing its role in guiding effective project execution, preventing omissions, and ensuring consistent high-quality output. This involves several key facets.

Why Process Quality Matters in DSDM (Section 22.3.1)

Guidance Across the Project Lifecycle

A structured project process aligned with best practices serves as a roadmap, guiding the team on when to take specific actions and make critical decisions.

Prevention of Oversights

A well-crafted process serves as a safety net, minimizing the risk of missing out on essential project components, thereby enhancing the overall quality of the solution delivered.

Learning from the Past

The incorporation of lessons from previous projects into the existing process contributes to a more informed and effective approach, elevating the quality of both current and future projects.

The Cornerstones of Process Quality (Section 22.3.2)

Planning for Quality: Say What You Do

The project process should be meticulously outlined, capturing everything from governance procedures to performance metrics. This forms the foundation upon which the entire project rests.

Execution: Do What You Say

Rigorous adherence to the pre-defined plan ensures the delivery of a project that meets quality benchmarks. Deviation from this plan can compromise the quality of the final product.

Verification: Prove It

The utility and efficiency of the established process should be validated through measurable outcomes. This confirms that the process is effective and offers value.

Iterative Improvement: Improve It

Process quality is not static. Continuous refinement based on empirical feedback and lessons learned ensures that future projects benefit from an ever-improving framework.

How DSDM Ensures Process Quality

Foundational Governance

During the Foundations phase, Management Approach Definition and Development Approach Definition documents are often created, laying the groundwork for project governance and quality assurance strategies.

Professional Integrity and Empowerment

The DSDM framework presupposes a level of professionalism and self-organization among team members, enabling them to make decisions that are aligned with project objectives.

Transparency Mechanisms

Tools such as Team Boards and methods like Daily Stand-ups and Timebox Reviews offer clarity in terms of project plans and progress, thereby ensuring that nothing falls through the cracks.

Documentation for Accountability and Learning

Timebox Review Records and Project Retrospectives act as formal documents that can be audited. They offer a comprehensive review of what went right or wrong during the project, laying the foundation for organizational learning.

Case Study: Implementing Process Quality in a DSDM Project

In a hypothetical project to develop a cloud-based Customer Relationship Management (CRM) system, the DSDM methodology was employed with a keen focus on Process Quality. Here's how it unfolded:

Laying the Foundation for Process Quality (Section 22.3.1)

Governance and Best Practices

The team began by outlining the Management Approach Definition and Development Approach Definition. This laid down the rules for governance and indicated how best practices would be employed.

Avoiding Omission

The process definition was critically reviewed by an external auditor to ensure it was comprehensive and that no crucial steps would be missed.

Incorporation of Past Lessons

The team took insights from a previously unsuccessful project within the organization. They incorporated lessons learned about cloud security and agile development into the current project.

Four Pillars in Action (Section 22.3.2)

Planning for Quality

The project process, complete with governance protocols and performance metrics, was detailed and circulated to all team members.

Execution

A rigorous series of Timeboxes were followed, ensuring that all elements in the plan were executed accurately.

Verification

After each Timebox, a review was conducted to measure the outcomes against predefined metrics to ascertain the efficacy of the process.

Iterative Improvement

Based on Timebox Reviews, several minor adjustments were made to the process, refining the approaches to testing and integration.

Ensuring Process Quality Through DSDM Practices

Professional Integrity

The project team followed the DSDM principle of 'Build incrementally from firm foundations,' ensuring professionalism and quality work from the start.

Transparency

Daily Stand-ups and Team Boards were used to maintain an open line of communication among team members, leading to quick identification and resolution of issues.

Record-Keeping

All Timebox Reviews and Project Retrospectives were documented diligently, providing a repository for lessons learned, which could be consulted for future projects.

The cloud-based CRM project was delivered on time and within budget, fulfilling all defined quality criteria. The success was attributed to the robust Process Quality framework laid down and followed meticulously as part of the DSDM methodology.

Predictability in Process Quality within DSDM

The Symbiosis of Predictability and Quality

Predictability and quality are mutually reinforcing within DSDM. Ensuring predictability in the delivery schedule, cost, and scope improves quality by conforming to the predetermined benchmarks. Conversely, a focus on quality often leads to more predictable outcomes as the project follows a structured approach, rooted in best practices and informed by historical data.

Expanding on Key Aspects of Predictability in DSDM

Time Management and Quality Control

The Timebox approach within DSDM doesn't merely work to prevent delays but is a tool for ongoing quality assessment. Adherence to the schedule is a direct indicator of the process's effectiveness and, by extension, its quality. This systematic approach to time management offers a predictable pattern that stakeholders can rely on, thereby reducing uncertainty and fostering confidence.

Financial Stewardship and Quality Indicators

Budget adherence serves as another critical marker for project quality. Meeting financial commitments in the face of unpredictable variables—such as market conditions, supply chain issues, or human resource constraints—speaks to the robustness of the project process. Financial predictability not only safeguards the project's viability but also serves as a metric for evaluating the quality of decision-making and governance within the project.

Feature Management and Strategic Alignment

The Prioritised Requirements List is an essential tool for achieving predictability in what will be delivered. While the list is flexible, it helps to ensure that what is delivered is consistent with business objectives and stakeholder expectations. The ability to adjust this list based on project performance also adds a layer of predictability, as it helps project teams adapt to unforeseen challenges without compromising quality.

Ensuring Predictability: Tools and Strategies

To ensure predictability within DSDM, various tools and techniques are employed:

1. MoSCoW Prioritization: This helps in determining which features are essential and which can be deferred, lending predictability to the feature scope.
2. Risk Logs: These logs provide early warning systems for possible disruptions to the schedule, budget, or scope.
3. KPI Monitoring: Regular tracking of Key Performance Indicators offers real-time insights into the project's adherence to its quality and predictability objectives.

Case Study: Implementing Predictability in a DSDM Project for Quality Outcomes

Overview

In this hypothetical case study, a leading e-commerce company decided to upgrade its payment gateway system to better handle increased customer traffic and enhance security features. Using the DSDM framework, the company sought to implement predictability measures to assure quality throughout the project lifecycle.

Key Strategies Adopted

Timebox Planning

A meticulous timebox planning was undertaken, including multiple cycles of evolutionary development. The project team committed to delivering a functional module at the end of each timebox, ensuring incremental value and constant evaluation.

Budgeting and Contingency Planning

The project was carefully budgeted, including a contingency fund to deal with unpredicted costs like third-party service fees, sudden price surges, and other variables. This approach provided the financial predictability required to maintain quality.

Prioritised Requirements List

From the outset, a Prioritised Requirements List was drawn, in collaboration with stakeholders, to decide which features were 'Must-have,' 'Should-have,' or 'Could-have.' This list helped in keeping the project's scope predictable and aligned with business objectives.

Outcomes

On-time Delivery: All major milestones were met on time, thanks to rigorous adherence to the Timebox plans.

Budget Adherence: The project was completed within the budget, with the contingency fund barely touched. This was considered a significant success indicator for process quality.

Stakeholder Satisfaction: The features delivered in each Increment were precisely what had been prioritized, resulting in high stakeholder satisfaction levels.

This case study exemplifies how the DSDM framework's focus on predictability can lead to high-quality outcomes by integrating time, cost, and scope management into the project's fabric.

The Nexus of Formality and Agility in DSDM Process Quality

The Complex Landscape of Formality

In an era of increasing regulations and stringent quality expectations, the concept of formality in Process Quality within DSDM projects comes to the forefront. However, formality doesn't have to equate to rigidity. The correct level of formality is often contingent upon an amalgamation of various factors such as governance requirements, project complexity, and organizational culture.

The Balancing Act: Flexible Yet Structured

When it comes to balancing the level of formality, the end goal is to achieve a harmonious integration of agility and governance. In DSDM, the focus is on the trifecta of being:

Flexible: To seamlessly adapt to changes and modify plans as the project evolves.

Robust: To ensure compliance with organizational and external standards.

Efficient: To yield maximum output within constraints of time and resources.

Excessive formality can potentially introduce an element of inertia, at odds with the inherent dynamism of Agile methodologies.

Formality Benchmarks within DSDM

Project Approach Questionnaire (PAQ)

One of the key tools in gauging the required formality in DSDM is the PAQ. This comprehensive questionnaire serves as a preliminary assessment mechanism to determine the project's compatibility with DSDM and to tailor the project approach to align with organizational demands.

Risk Assessment

Another crucial step is risk assessment, which aims to pinpoint and prioritize risks that could impact the project. This risk-oriented approach feeds into the level of formality required for quality assurance.

Advantages of Contextual Formality in DSDM

Business Alignment: The DSDM framework involves business stakeholders throughout, ensuring that business objectives guide the quality processes.

Fitness for Purpose: A less formalized, more iterative approach to reviews allows for a solution that is fit for its intended purpose.

Dynamic Adaptation: Agility in formal procedures allows for an adaptive approach, minimizing the administrative burden of formal changes.

By embedding the right level of formality in Process Quality procedures, DSDM projects can be well-positioned to meet both business and quality objectives efficiently.

The Advantageous Interplay of Formality and Agility in DSDM Process Quality

Formality Meets Agility: The Balancing Act

In DSDM projects, formal procedures and Agile methodologies need not be mutually exclusive. Striking the right balance ensures that projects are agile enough to adapt to changing circumstances while being sufficiently structured to meet governance and quality standards. Too much formality can stifle agility, while insufficient structure can lead to quality and compliance issues.

Formality Benchmarks in DSDM

Project Approach Questionnaire

This questionnaire is instrumental in setting the stage for how formal the processes within a DSDM project need to be. It gauges the compatibility between the project's needs and the DSDM approach, enabling teams to make data-driven decisions on formality levels.

Risk Assessment

Risk assessment complements the PAQ by identifying risks that could impact project outcomes. This assessment helps tailor the formality level needed for quality assurance, allowing teams to prioritize resources and actions accordingly.

Advantages of Striking the Right Formality Balance in DSDM

Business Alignment: The DSDM framework's inherent structure ensures alignment with business goals without sacrificing agility.

Fitness for Purpose: Tailored levels of formality enable ongoing reviews and adjustments, leading to solutions that precisely meet their intended purpose.

Dynamic Adaptation: Being agile in formal processes allows projects to adapt as business needs evolve, without the red tape commonly associated with formal change procedures.

In essence, embedding the correct level of formality in your DSDM project's Process Quality can be a strategic enabler, contributing to both project success and organizational compliance. Would you like to hear more about a case study or practical example to elaborate on this topic?

Navigating the Terrain of Quality Reviews in DSDM Projects

The Essence and Scope of Quality Reviews in DSDM

Purpose and Intent

Quality Reviews in DSDM projects act as dual-purpose instruments:

Compliance Check: These reviews validate if the project adheres to established organizational standards and procedures.

Health Assessment: They evaluate whether the project is optimally leveraging DSDM methodologies for a successful outcome.

The goal here isn't to add layers of bureaucracy but to offer valuable insights into how well the project aligns with quality benchmarks and organizational objectives.

Forms and Structures

Quality Reviews can manifest in various forms, ranging from casual evaluations to more formal structures like Gateway Reviews. The type of review often correlates with the organizational culture as well as the scale and intricacy of the project. In more formal settings, these reviews may even result in decisive Go/No-Go outcomes based on predefined metrics and Key Performance Indicators (KPIs).

Steering Questions for a DSDM Project Quality Review

Foundational Queries

A robust Quality Review process in a DSDM context should pivot around the following key questions:

Business Involvement: Is business stakeholder engagement at an adequate level to warrant the chosen methodology?

Team Empowerment: Are team members granted sufficient authority to make and act upon decisions?

Lifecycle Conformity: Does the project follow the predetermined phases of the DSDM lifecycle?

Product Realization: Are the deliverables, whether aligned with the original or adjusted scope, being realized as planned?

Feedback Utilization: Is feedback from various review stages and testing adequately informing project adjustments?

Task Prioritization: Is the project in sync with the priority structure for tasks and deliverables?

Timebox Observance: Are Timeboxes being efficiently used and strictly followed?

Configuration Management: Is this aspect being managed in a manner that aligns with both DSDM principles and organizational needs?

By systematically addressing these questions, Quality Reviews can serve as an effective tool for risk management, enabling projects to course-correct in real-time, thus improving the likelihood of a successful outcome.

Quality Reviews in DSDM: A Case Study Synopsis

Context and Challenges

Consider a healthcare software development project that aims to digitize patient records. The project is complex, involving multiple stakeholders from doctors to government health departments, and follows the DSDM framework. Due to the sensitive nature of healthcare data, there are stringent compliance requirements. The project, therefore, needed an effective Quality Review process to ensure all objectives and standards were met.

Approach to Quality Reviews

Types of Reviews Employed

Given the complexity and sensitivity of the project, the team opted for both informal check-ins and formal Gateway Reviews. Informal reviews focused on day-to-day tasks and incremental developments, whereas Gateway Reviews were conducted at the end of significant milestones.

Key Questions Addressed

Business Involvement: Stakeholder interviews and surveys were conducted to assess the level of business involvement.

Team Empowerment: Team performance and decision-making were monitored to ensure members were sufficiently empowered.

Lifecycle Conformity: The project was audited against DSDM lifecycle phases, including Feasibility and Foundations.

Product Realization: Checks were made to ensure that the digital records system being developed was in line with initial and evolving requirements.

Feedback Utilization: Post-review action items were tracked to see if feedback was effectively used for course corrections.

Task Prioritization: Periodic reviews of the Prioritised Requirements List were conducted.

Timebox Observance: Timebox adherence was strictly monitored, especially since healthcare is a time-sensitive industry.

Configuration Management: Due to compliance needs, rigorous configuration management checks were put in place.

Outcomes

The Quality Reviews proved invaluable. They highlighted gaps in stakeholder involvement early on, which were then addressed. They also caught potential compliance issues, enabling preemptive action. Most importantly, they ensured that the project stayed true to its DSDM roots while adapting to real-world challenges, thus ensuring a successful project delivery.

The case study underscores the vital role that Quality Reviews play in DSDM projects, serving as an indispensable tool for risk management and project success.

Elevating Quality in DSDM Projects: A Guide for Agile Project Managers

For Agile Project Managers overseeing DSDM projects, the quest for quality is not just an added bonus but a fundamental requirement. Quality in this context extends beyond the deliverables; it permeates every facet of project management. Here are some actionable tips to ensure top-notch quality in your DSDM projects.

Nine Crucial Tips for Quality Assurance

1. Uphold Quality as a Non-Negotiable Standard

The first rule of thumb is simple: quality should never be compromised. Regardless of pressures like time constraints or resource limitations, inferior quality is never an acceptable outcome.

2. Incorporate Quality from the Inception

Begin with the end in mind by embedding quality criteria into your project from the get-go. Doing so sets the tone and expectations for the entire team and the stakeholders involved.

3. Foster Continuous Stakeholder Engagement

Regular interaction with stakeholders not only boosts their confidence in the project but also provides invaluable feedback that can help elevate quality. This approach aligns perfectly with DSDM's philosophy of continuous stakeholder collaboration.

4. Understand the Relativity of Quality

Every project has unique requirements and stakeholder expectations. Quality, in this context, is relative and should be defined and measured against the specific objectives and expectations for each project.

5. Equip and Empower Your Teams

In an Agile environment, an empowered team is a high-performing team. Ensure your teams have the tools, knowledge, and autonomy to contribute meaningfully to the project's quality.

6. Decentralize Control and Responsibility

Quality control should not be the exclusive domain of the project manager. Instead, foster a culture where everyone owns the quality of their deliverables. This collective ownership enhances the quality of the project as a whole.

7. Define Roles and Responsibilities

Be explicit about what is expected from each role within your DSDM project. A clearly defined set of roles and responsibilities ensures that every team member knows how they contribute to the project's quality.

8. Leverage DSDM's Built-In Quality Tools

DSDM provides several products, like Management Approach Definitions and Timebox Review Records, designed to facilitate quality planning and monitoring. Make the most of these tools to keep your project on the path to high quality.

9. Keep a Real-Time Record for Auditing

An effective quality assurance mechanism necessitates real-time record-keeping. Accurate, concurrent documentation helps in ongoing audits and can prove invaluable in stakeholder reporting and post-project reviews.

Conclusion

Ensuring quality in a DSDM project is a multifaceted endeavor that demands attention, preparation, and continuous improvement. By incorporating these quality-focused principles and practices, Agile Project Managers can significantly elevate the quality of their DSDM projects.

Case Study: Implementing Quality Assurance in a DSDM Project for Financial Services

Background

In a hypothetical scenario, a financial services company initiated a DSDM project aimed at creating a new customer relationship management (CRM) system. The organization faced regulatory pressures and a highly competitive market, making the need for quality assurance paramount. The Agile Project Manager took charge of ensuring that quality was maintained across all aspects of the project.

Actions Taken

Upholding Quality Standards

From the project's initiation, the Project Manager emphasized the non-negotiable nature of quality, aligning the team and stakeholders around this central tenet. Regular quality audits were scheduled to ensure compliance with both organizational and industry standards.

Embedding Quality from the Start

The team incorporated quality metrics and acceptance criteria in the project's foundational documents. This step ensured that every team member was aligned on what 'quality' meant in the context of this particular project.

Engaging Stakeholders

Regular sprint reviews were held with business stakeholders to solicit feedback. These sessions proved instrumental in refining system features and functionalities, keeping the focus on delivering quality outcomes.

Assessing Quality Relatively

The Project Manager recognized that the quality standards for this project were distinct due to the specific regulatory requirements of the financial sector.

This understanding helped in tailoring the project's quality metrics to match its unique demands.

Team Empowerment

To foster a sense of ownership, team members were empowered to flag any potential quality issues they identified. This led to a more proactive approach to problem-solving and quality assurance.

Decentralizing Control

Quality was not solely the responsibility of any single entity; instead, everyone from developers to testers and business analysts had a role to play in maintaining it.

Clearly Defined Roles

Role definitions were communicated explicitly at the project's onset. This clarity helped in the seamless collaboration between various departments such as IT, compliance, and customer service.

Utilization of DSDM Tools

DSDM-specific products like Timebox Review Records were used to document quality-related decisions, making it easier to monitor and audit the quality assurance process.

Real-Time Audit Trails

All quality metrics were tracked in real-time, enabling a comprehensive and concurrent view of how the project was performing in terms of quality. This real-time tracking proved invaluable during internal and regulatory audits.

Outcomes

The project was completed on time and within budget, with high-quality deliverables that exceeded stakeholder expectations. Furthermore, the CRM system successfully passed all compliance checks, thanks to the robust quality assurance processes in place.

By implementing these principles and strategies, the Agile Project Manager was able to oversee a successful, high-quality DSDM project. It illustrates how adherence to quality-focused practices can yield superior results, even in complex, regulated environments like financial services.

Chapter Twenty

Risk Management in Agile Projects: A Comprehensive Guide

The Intricacies of Implementing Effective Risk Management in DSDM Projects

Emphasizing the Role of Risk Management

Risk management in DSDM projects is not an auxiliary function but a core aspect that influences virtually every facet of project implementation. It aligns closely with DSDM's focus on delivering business value and accommodating change within a structured framework.

Classification of Project Risks

In DSDM projects, risks often fall into two primary categories:

Operational Risks: These are the risks associated with the logistics, resource allocation, and general operational aspects of the project.

Strategic Risks: These pertain to higher-level concerns like alignment with business goals, stakeholder engagement, and market dynamics.

Understanding the type of risk faced is crucial for its effective management.

Interplay of Culture and Risk Appetite

The culture of the organization and the individual risk appetites of the project team members significantly influence risk management strategies. These elements determine how aggressively or conservatively the team will act in response to potential risks.

DSDM-Specific Risk Management Practices

Identification and Assessment

DSDM recommends a systematic approach to identify and assess risks. Key documentation, such as the Project Approach Questionnaire (PAQ) and Instrumental Success Factors (ISFs), should be consulted for this purpose.

Countermeasure Planning

Planning for risk mitigation or avoidance strategies in DSDM is often an iterative process, refined at the end of each Timebox.

Monitoring and Management

The risk log, maintained by the Project Manager, is a critical tool in this step. It provides real-time insights into the status of various risks and the effectiveness of countermeasures.

Shared Responsibility

Though the Project Manager plays a vital role, risk management in DSDM is considered a shared responsibility. Each team member, including business stakeholders, has a role to play in identifying, assessing, and mitigating risks.

Lessons for Future Projects

The systematic approach to risk management in DSDM provides a rich repository of lessons learned. These can be invaluable for future projects and can even be escalated to program or portfolio levels for broader organizational learning.

Concluding Thoughts

A robust approach to risk management is vital for the success of DSDM projects. It provides a structured yet flexible framework that aligns closely with DSDM principles. By making risk management a continuous, shared responsibility, DSDM projects can more effectively navigate uncertainties and deliver value to the business.

Case Study: Implementing Risk Management in a DSDM Project for a Financial Services Firm

Background

A leading financial services firm decided to adopt DSDM for a mission-critical project aimed at improving its customer experience platforms. Given the project's scale and the heavily regulated nature of the financial services industry, effective risk management was a high priority.

Identifying Risks

The first step was to identify the potential risks. The team consulted various DSDM-specific documents like the Project Approach Questionnaire (PAQ) and Instrumental Success Factors (ISFs). They identified a variety of operational and strategic risks, ranging from compliance issues to potential shortfalls in user adoption.

Risk Assessment

The team categorized the risks based on their impact and likelihood. Regulatory compliance risks, for instance, were deemed high-impact and high-likelihood, given the industry's stringent regulatory environment.

Countermeasure Planning

Proactive and reactive risk mitigation strategies were formulated. For compliance risks, a proactive strategy included regular consultation with legal experts. Reactive strategies involved contingency plans for possible scenarios of non-compliance.

Continuous Monitoring

The Project Manager maintained an updated risk log accessible to all team members. This helped in tracking the risk statuses and allowed for timely interventions.

Shared Responsibility

Each identified risk was assigned an owner among the team members. The Business Sponsor took ownership of the strategic risks related to market alignment and regulatory compliance.

Business Ownership of Risks

Considering the high stakes, the Business Visionary and Business Sponsor were actively involved in risk management activities. Their engagement was particularly high when dealing with risks related to business objectives and regulatory compliance.

Lessons Learned

After the project's successful completion, a detailed review was conducted to document the lessons learned in risk management. This documentation formed part of a knowledge base for future projects, not just in the financial services department but also for other initiatives across the organization.

Conclusion

The case exemplifies how risk management, when done systematically and in alignment with DSDM principles, can contribute to the successful delivery of complex projects in challenging industries.

Practical Strategies for Managing Risks in Agile Projects

Agile methodologies prioritize flexibility and adaptability, but these features also introduce various types of risks. Effective risk management is crucial for the successful implementation of Agile projects. This article outlines the major risk sources in Agile projects and provides strategies for their mitigation.

Major Risk Categories and Their Management Strategies

Working Environment

Risk

Poor collaboration and lack of alignment within the team can lead to misunderstandings and inefficiencies.

Mitigation

Cultivate an organizational culture that emphasizes collaboration and open communication. Utilize tools and practices that foster teamwork, such as daily stand-ups and pair programming.

Competence and Professionalism

Risk

Insufficient skills or a lack of commitment among team members can jeopardize project outcomes.

Mitigation

Conduct thorough vetting during team formation and provide ongoing training and professional development opportunities.

Project Management Style

Risk

The management style may not align with the needs and capabilities of the Agile team, creating conflicts and reducing performance.

Mitigation

Tailor the management approach to match the team's maturity level. For less experienced teams, a more directive style may be appropriate, while mature teams may benefit from a coaching or facilitating style.

Describing Business Needs

Risk

Miscommunication or late communication of business requirements can result in unsatisfactory deliverables.

Mitigation

Adopt practices like User Stories or Business-Driven Development (BDD) to clearly and timely communicate requirements. Make sure that business representatives are actively engaged throughout the project.

Lack of Clarity in Business Vision

Risk

Ambiguous or shifting business goals can lead to ineffective iterations and resource wastage.

Mitigation

Ensure the presence and active participation of a Business Visionary who can offer direction and make real-time adjustments to align with strategic objectives.

Requirements Validation

Risk

Requirements may be misunderstood or misimplemented, leading to wasted effort and potential rework.

Mitigation

Integrate continuous validation steps into the development cycle, such as automated testing and regular stakeholder reviews.

Lack of Contingency

Risk

Lack of preparedness for unforeseen disruptions can lead to delays or compromised quality.

Mitigation

Build some buffer into the project's scope, schedule, and budget to allow for adjustments in response to unexpected events.

Inflexible Requirements

Risk

Requirements that are too rigid can make the project less responsive to change, leading to failure in meeting customer expectations.

Mitigation

Develop a prioritized and flexible feature set that allows for adjustments as new insights and requirements emerge.

Change - Other Types

Risk

Other unforeseen changes in business environment, personnel, or technology can impact the project.

Mitigation

Adopt a resilient project structure that can absorb and adapt to changes without significant disruption.

Project Approach

Risk

Choosing an unsuitable Agile approach can lead to friction and inefficiencies.

Mitigation

Leverage coaching and mentoring to ensure that team members understand and align with the chosen Agile methodology.

Ineffective Monitoring and Governance

Risk

Poor monitoring practices can lead to a lack of transparent and accurate information for governance.

Mitigation

Implement robust reporting and KPI tracking, ensuring both transparency and reliability of information for effective governance.

Conclusion

Managing risks effectively is crucial for the success of Agile projects. By understanding the major sources of risk and implementing targeted mitigation strategies, project managers can significantly enhance the likelihood of project success.

In-Depth Analysis of Select Risk Categories and Mitigation Strategies in Agile Projects

Working Environment: Risk and Mitigation

Risk

In Agile projects, a poorly coordinated team that lacks alignment can become a significant source of risk. When team members don't collaborate efficiently, misunderstandings can escalate, leading to faulty deliverables and delayed timelines.

Mitigation

To tackle this, establish a culture that prizes collaboration and open communication. Methods such as daily stand-up meetings or scrum sessions can be employed to ensure everyone is on the same page. Additionally, tools that facilitate communication and task tracking, like Slack or Jira, can enhance teamwork.

Competence and Professionalism: Risk and Mitigation

Risk

A less competent or uncommitted team member can become a bottleneck in Agile projects. This risk factor could result in subpar performance and output, putting project outcomes in jeopardy.

Mitigation

Pre-empt this risk by conducting a thorough vetting process when assembling the team. Post-formation, invest in ongoing training programs and workshops to continuously uplift the team's skill level and commitment.

Project Management Style: Risk and Mitigation

Risk

When the management style doesn't resonate with the Agile team's expectations or capabilities, it can create conflicts and hamper productivity. For instance, a highly directive style may stifle a mature, self-organizing team.

Mitigation

Assess the team's maturity and tailor your management style accordingly. Less experienced teams might require a more directive approach, while mature teams could benefit from a facilitating or coaching style. This alignment enhances the team's efficiency and job satisfaction.

Describing Business Needs: Risk and Mitigation

Risk

In Agile frameworks, late or ambiguous communication of business needs can result in deliverables that don't meet expectations. This misalignment can lead to rework, causing delays and cost overruns.

Mitigation

For effective communication of business needs, utilize frameworks like User Stories or Business-Driven Development (BDD). These methods enable clear articulation of requirements while leaving room for adaptability. Constant engagement with business representatives ensures that updates are integrated in real-time.

Conclusion

By digging deeper into these select risk categories, we can appreciate the complexities involved in managing risks in Agile projects. The key is to understand the nuances of each risk and to apply tailored strategies for mitigation, thereby enhancing the project's chances of success.

Extensive Analysis of DSDM's Risk Mitigation Strategies

DSDM's strength in risk mitigation comes from its structured yet agile approach, offering both flexibility and governance. Here, we delve deeper into the nuances of how DSDM deals with different kinds of risks.

Strategic Alignment for Risk Mitigation

One of the most challenging aspects of project management is ensuring that the project aligns with organizational strategy and culture. Failure to achieve this alignment could lead to risks that are strategic in nature. DSDM tackles this through its Project Approach Questionnaire and Instrumental Success Factors, which help to determine how well the project fits within the organizational context right from the outset. This ensures that there is strong business ownership and commitment, thereby reducing the strategic risks associated with misalignment.

Agile Governance for Flexibility and Control

DSDM provides a framework for governance that allows for the right balance between agility and control. For example, it employs Timeboxing and MoSCoW prioritization as tools to maintain schedule and budget. By focusing on essential features and conducting frequent stakeholder reviews, it ensures that the project remains on track, thereby mitigating risks associated with time and cost overruns.

Handling Uncertainties Through Collaboration and Incremental Builds

Uncertainty is an inherent part of any project and can be a major source of risk. DSDM's emphasis on collaboration, especially through roles like the Business Visionary and Business Ambassador, ensures that there's constant dialogue to clarify requirements. This is bolstered by an incremental build strategy, which allows for prototypes and early versions to be reviewed and refined. This iterative process significantly reduces the risk of ending up with a final product that doesn't meet expectations.

Dynamic Response to Market Volatility

In a rapidly changing business environment, adhering strictly to initially laid out plans can be risky. DSDM handles this by allowing for change and flexibility through its MoSCoW prioritization technique. This ensures that changes in the market or business direction can be accommodated, even mid-project, without causing a derailment. This agility helps mitigate the risks associated with a volatile business environment.

Last Responsible Moment Decision-Making

DSDM advocates making decisions at the 'last responsible moment', allowing the project to maintain flexibility while still ensuring that choices are made with the maximum available information. This principle helps mitigate risks associated with the uncertainty or lack of detailed requirements at the beginning of the project.

By adopting these multi-faceted approaches for risk mitigation, DSDM offers a robust framework that is particularly beneficial for projects that require both agility and strong governance.

Case Study: Utilizing DSDM for Effective Risk Mitigation in a Financial Services Project

In a competitive landscape, a global financial services company embarked on a mission to develop a next-generation trading platform. Due to the need for rapid market entry and high-quality requirements, the company opted for DSDM as the project delivery framework. This case study explores how

DSDM's risk mitigation strategies were instrumental in the project's successful completion.

Identifying Risks

Right from the start, several risks were identified, including rapidly changing regulations, complex stakeholder requirements, and tight deadlines for market entry.

DSDM's Approach:

The company used DSDM's Project Approach Questionnaire to align the project with its broader strategic goals and risk appetite, ensuring strong business commitment.

Managing Uncertainties

As the project progressed, changes in the financial markets and emerging regulatory challenges created uncertainties in project requirements.

DSDM's Approach:

DSDM's collaborative and iterative development model, involving frequent workshops and prototype reviews, helped in adapting to new requirements. Roles like the Business Visionary were crucial in this dynamic setting.

Budget and Schedule Management

Due to the complexities involved, there was a risk of budget and schedule overruns.

DSDM's Approach:

Timeboxing and MoSCoW prioritization techniques were used. By focusing on high-priority features first and using Timeboxing to allocate fixed periods for each development phase, the project managed to stay on course financially and temporally.

Quality Assurance

Given the sensitivity of the financial data involved, the risk related to data integrity and security was high.

DSDM's Approach:

DSDM's incremental build strategy allowed for regular quality reviews, both technical and business, to ensure the platform met all security and compliance guidelines.

Stakeholder Management and Final Sign-off

With diverse stakeholders, from internal teams to external regulatory bodies, the risk of not meeting all requirements was significant.

DSDM's Approach:

Regular reviews with all stakeholder groups were conducted to ensure alignment. This made the final sign-off a mere formality, as all stakeholders had been engaged throughout the project lifecycle.

Conclusion

The application of DSDM's risk mitigation strategies resulted in the successful completion of the trading platform project, meeting both the regulatory requirements and market deadlines. The project became a benchmark within the company for how to manage complex financial projects effectively.

By taking a structured yet flexible approach to risk mitigation, DSDM proved to be invaluable for this high-stakes financial services project.

Risks and Considerations in DSDM Implementation: An Extended Discussion

The Pivotal Role of Continuous Risk Monitoring

Why It's Essential

Continuous risk monitoring in the DSDM framework isn't just a feature but a necessity. Project variables such as scope, timeline, and resource availability are highly dynamic, and a one-time risk assessment is insufficient. The continuous oversight helps to capture new risks and reevaluate existing ones in real-time, allowing for immediate action and minimizing negative impacts.

Tools and Methods for Continuous Risk Monitoring

DSDM recommends various practices like Daily Stand-Ups, regular reviews, and Timebox retrospectives for the continuous monitoring of risks. These practices act as feedback loops, providing real-time insights into project health. Moreover, the use of metrics and Key Performance Indicators (KPIs) can add a quantitative aspect to this continuous monitoring, making it more objective and reliable.

The Criticality of Stakeholder Engagement

Understanding the Complex Web of Stakeholder Interests

Stakeholder engagement isn't just about keeping everyone in the loop; it's about understanding and aligning diverse interests and expectations. This can be a considerable challenge given the varying perspectives stakeholders bring into a project. Neglecting this aspect can lead to unsatisfactory outcomes and conflicts.

Strategies for Effective Stakeholder Engagement

Clear role definitions are vital, but so are facilitated workshops and targeted communication strategies. Methods like Business Process Modeling (BPM) can be used in workshops to arrive at a common understanding among stakeholders. In DSDM, roles such as the Business Visionary, Technical Coordinator, and Project Manager are meticulously designed to serve as engagement conduits between the project and its stakeholders.

Dealing with Organizational Alignment Issues

The Inevitable Conflict Between Framework and Culture

Every organization has its unique culture and operating procedures, which can sometimes be at odds with DSDM's agile principles. This misalignment is not just a project risk but can be considered an organizational risk.

Navigating through Cultural Conflicts

Organizational assessments and readiness reviews can be very revealing. They identify potential hotspots where the DSDM framework may clash with existing norms. Once identified, these areas can be the focus of change management strategies or framework tailoring to ensure that DSDM is not just implemented but ingrained into the organizational fabric.

In conclusion, while DSDM inherently carries robust risk mitigation features, the implementation of the framework is not devoid of risks. Recognizing and addressing these meta-risks head-on is crucial for achieving the project and organizational objectives the framework is designed to facilitate.

DSDM Implementation in a Financial Services Organization: A Case Study

Background and Context

The Challenge

A leading financial services organization was struggling with its project deliveries, mainly due to a lack of a structured project management approach. The leadership decided to adopt the DSDM framework to improve their project outcomes. However, implementing DSDM came with its challenges, including stakeholder alignment, adherence to principles, and reconciling with the existing organizational culture.

Identifying and Addressing Key Risks

Risk: Lack of Professionalism and Discipline

The employees were accustomed to a more traditional project management approach and resisted the change to DSDM initially.

Mitigation:

Training programs were rolled out, and adherence was audited through a series of compliance checks.

Risk: Incomplete Understanding of DSDM Principles

It was evident from early Project Approach Questionnaires (PAQs) that there were gaps in understanding.

Mitigation:

The organization engaged DSDM experts to run workshops, ensuring a more complete understanding and correct implementation of DSDM principles.

Risk: Inadequate Stakeholder Engagement

Initially, key stakeholders were not adequately involved, leading to misaligned objectives.

Mitigation:

The organization ensured proper role definitions and used facilitated workshops to improve stakeholder engagement, thereby aligning everyone to the project's goals.

Risk: Unmonitored Changes and Adaptations

Excessive changes began to be introduced, leading to scope creep.

Mitigation:

The team was re-trained on the importance of MoSCoW prioritization and Timeboxing, and additional governance measures were introduced.

Results and Takeaways

Outcome

Following these risk mitigation strategies, the organization successfully completed several DSDM projects and has now adopted it as their standard approach for project management.

Lessons Learned

- Continuous risk assessment is crucial.
- Stakeholder engagement requires more than just regular updates; it requires a structured approach and clear communication channels.
- Cultural misalignment can be a substantial risk, and strategies should be in place to manage this at an organizational level.

The case study underscores the importance of identifying and proactively managing the inherent risks associated with implementing DSDM. It also highlights the fact that while DSDM is powerful, its successful implementation requires a well-thought-out approach that takes into account both project and organizational intricacies.

Mastering Risk Management in DSDM Projects: A Guide for Agile Project Managers

Effective risk management is an integral aspect of successful project management—more so in Agile environments that leverage frameworks like the Dynamic Systems Development Method (DSDM). While the Project Manager serves as the focal point for risk management, the exercise is largely collaborative, involving various stakeholders across different phases of the project. Below, we delve into tips that Agile Project Managers can employ to master risk management in DSDM projects.

Tips for Risk Management

Tip 1: Harness the Power of the Project Approach Questionnaire (PAQ)

Rationale:

The PAQ is a cornerstone tool that enables early identification and assessment of risks by evaluating the alignment with DSDM Principles and Instrumental Success Factors (ISFs).

Action Steps:

- Complete the PAQ during both the Feasibility and Foundations phases.
- Utilize the PAQ findings to flag risks related to DSDM Principles and ISFs.

Tip 2: Make PAQ Completion a Team Activity

Rationale:

Completing the PAQ collaboratively garners a more holistic understanding of risks.

Action Steps:

- Involve key roles like the Business Visionary and the Technical Coordinator in the PAQ completion process.

Tip 3: Maintain a Realistic Approach to Risk Assessment

Rationale:

Either exaggerating or downplaying risks can lead to misguided strategies.

Action Steps:

- Undertake a balanced and objective risk assessment.

Tip 4: Keep Tabs on Adherence to DSDM Principles

Rationale:

Non-compliance with DSDM principles can be a significant roadblock to project success.

Action Steps:

- Regularly conduct audits to check adherence to DSDM Principles.

Tip 5: Foster Team-wide Risk Awareness

Rationale:

A well-informed team can proactively contribute to risk management.

Action Steps:

- Keep the team abreast of key risks, using methods like a risk wall or regular team briefings.

Tip 6: Don't Overlook Timebox-Specific Risks

Rationale:

Each Timebox can bring its own set of risks that require immediate attention.

Action Steps:

- Spotlight Timebox-specific risks during the Timebox Kick-Off meeting.
- Transfer ownership of these risks to the Team Leader for the duration of the Timebox.

Tip 7: Promote Open Dialogue on Risks

Rationale:

Regular team discussions can serve as an early warning system for emerging risks.

Action Steps:

- Encourage Solution Development Teams to openly discuss risks during planning and review sessions.

Tip 8: Keep the Risk Register Updated

Rationale:

Continuous risk monitoring is essential for proactive management.

Action Steps:

- Reassess risks during Timebox Close-Out and reassign them to project-level roles for further evaluation.

Conclusion

Managing risks in a DSDM project demands a concerted and continuous effort from the entire team, with the Agile Project Manager orchestrating the various activities. By rigorously applying these tips, Project Managers can create a resilient environment capable of identifying, assessing, and mitigating risks effectively, thereby steering the project toward success.

A Case Study: Managing Risks in a DSDM Project for a FinTech Company

Introduction

In this case study, we will explore how a FinTech company utilized the Dynamic Systems Development Method (DSDM) framework for its project and how the Agile Project Manager successfully implemented the tips mentioned earlier for effective risk management.

Project Overview

The company aimed to develop a digital payment gateway to expand its market presence. Being a complex and high-stakes project involving multiple stakeholders and a fixed regulatory deadline, the Agile Project Manager chose to employ DSDM for its comprehensive approach to risk management.

Risk Management Strategies Employed

Utilizing the Project Approach Questionnaire (PAQ)

Implementation:

The Agile Project Manager involved all key stakeholders to collaboratively complete the PAQ during the Feasibility phase. This helped in identifying various risks, such as potential non-compliance with regional payment laws.

Collaborative Completion of PAQ

Implementation:

The Business Visionary and the Technical Coordinator were specifically involved in completing the PAQ, ensuring that both business and technical risks were equally considered.

Realistic Risk Assessment

Implementation:

An objective risk assessment was undertaken, eliminating any optimistic biases that could undermine the significance of risks like data breaches.

Monitoring Adherence to DSDM Principles

Implementation:

The Project Manager scheduled weekly audits to ensure that DSDM principles were being adhered to, especially concerning regular communication and iterative development.

Team-wide Risk Awareness

Implementation:

The identified risks were displayed on a "Risk Wall" that was visible to all team members, keeping everyone aware of what needed to be managed or mitigated.

Timebox-Specific Risks

Implementation:

During the Timebox Kick-Off meetings, the Project Manager highlighted the risks specific to that Timebox, such as the potential delays in integration testing.

Open Dialogue on Risks

Implementation:

Each sprint review included a dedicated time for discussing any newly identified risks or changes to existing ones, facilitating proactive risk management.

Risk Register Update

Implementation:

At the end of every Timebox, risks were reassessed and updated in the project's risk register, which was then reviewed in a meeting involving all project-level roles.

Conclusion

By diligently applying the risk management tips outlined earlier, the Agile Project Manager was able to navigate the complexities of developing a digital payment gateway in a regulated environment. Through collaborative efforts and disciplined adherence to DSDM principles, the project was completed on time, within budget, and met all regulatory compliance requirements. This case study serves as an exemplar for how robust risk management practices can lead to successful project outcomes.

Chapter Twenty-One

Tailoring Based on Practitioner Insights and Risk Assessment

Tailoring DSDM: A Deeper Exploration Based on Practitioner Insights and Risk Assessment

Tailoring the Dynamic Systems Development Method (DSDM) to fit specific project requirements is a nuanced process that relies heavily on practitioner insights and risk assessment tools like the Project Approach Questionnaire (PAQ). This chapter expands on the role of the PAQ in identifying risks and tailoring DSDM to match a project's unique characteristics, while ensuring that the core principles of the framework are maintained.

The Significance of the Project Approach Questionnaire (PAQ)

Purpose and Utility

The PAQ is instrumental in shaping the DSDM implementation strategy for a project. Its dual role is to:

Negotiate Changes: In non-ideal conditions, the PAQ can serve as a negotiation tool for modifying project variables to make DSDM more suitable.

Guide Tailoring: When certain variables cannot be changed, the PAQ assists in making informed decisions about adapting the DSDM methodology.

Decision-Making Criteria

The PAQ findings can indicate varying levels of risk, directing the extent to which tailoring is needed:

Low Risk: Consensus with 'Strong Agreement' or 'Agreement' on all PAQ statements suggests minimal risk, making it likely that the standard DSDM approach suffices.

High Risk: Any form of 'Disagreement' flags potential risks that necessitate corrective actions or more elaborate tailoring.

Circumstances Warranting DSDM Tailoring

Environmental Constraints

Tailoring becomes indispensable when the organizational environment is not conducive to Agile methodologies. This can range from unsupportive management to rigid operational constraints.

Organizational Barriers

Existing corporate culture, policies, or hierarchical structures that clash with Agile principles may necessitate modifications in the DSDM approach.

Complexity of Project Requirements

Projects with intricate or unique features may demand adaptations in the DSDM methodology to accommodate these specific needs.

The Importance of Mindset Over Methodology

Cultivating an Agile Culture

Before embarking on extensive tailoring, project leaders should aim to align team and stakeholder mindsets with Agile philosophies. The first line of action should be fostering an environment that values empowerment, collaboration, and iterative development.

Avoiding Over-Adaptation

The essence of DSDM should not be diluted through excessive tailoring, as this undermines its inherent advantages. The objective is to adapt without compromising on core principles.

Conclusion

Tailoring DSDM is a delicate balance between adhering to its core tenets and adapting to specific project conditions. Decisions on tailoring should be data-driven, informed by risk assessment tools like the PAQ and backed by the seasoned insights of DSDM practitioners. Yet, it's imperative to remember that the ultimate value of any Agile methodology lies in its philosophy, not just its procedures. Adapt carefully, and only after all possibilities to align the project with Agile methodologies have been thoroughly examined.

Case Study: Tailoring DSDM for a Financial Services Project

Introduction

In this case study, we delve into a real-world example of how a financial services company tailored DSDM to meet the challenges posed by stringent regulatory compliance and a conservative corporate culture.

Initial Risk Assessment with PAQ

The Scenario

During the Feasibility phase, the PAQ revealed multiple areas of 'Disagreement,' particularly related to stakeholder engagement and the flexibility to adapt to changes. The project involved developing a new fraud detection system, and there were concerns about sensitive data and regulatory scrutiny.

Interpretation and Decision-Making

Given the high-risk indicators from the PAQ, it was evident that a straightforward DSDM approach would not suffice. The project management team decided to tailor DSDM to meet these unique challenges.

Tailoring Actions

Adapted Timeboxing

Given the regulatory requirements, the team decided to extend the standard timeboxing periods, allowing for a more thorough compliance review process within each Timebox.

Specialized Stakeholder Workshops

To address the identified risk of insufficient stakeholder engagement, the team organized workshops specifically aimed at educating stakeholders about Agile and DSDM.

Enhanced Documentation

To align with regulatory needs, an additional layer of documentation was included without undermining Agile principles.

Mindset Changes

Internal Advocacy

Senior team members took on the role of internal Agile advocates, educating other departments and stakeholders on the merits of Agile methodologies.

Training Programs

An organization-wide training initiative was launched to align the team and stakeholders with Agile philosophies, aiming to minimize the need for tailoring in future projects.

Outcome and Lessons

Successful Implementation

By aligning DSDM's principles with the organization's unique risk profile and constraints, the project was executed successfully, meeting both compliance standards and performance goals.

Institutional Learning

The project served as a blueprint for future endeavors, demonstrating how DSDM could be adapted while retaining its core principles. It also highlighted the need for pre-project education to mitigate the need for extensive tailoring.

Conclusion

This case study illustrates that while DSDM offers a robust framework for Agile project management, real-world complexities often necessitate careful tailoring. However, even when adaptations are made, maintaining fidelity to DSDM's core principles is crucial for realizing its full benefits. Tailoring should be informed by comprehensive risk assessment tools like the PAQ and should be viewed as an evolving approach that adjusts according to the project's demands and lessons learned.

Delving Deeper: The Intricacies of Tailoring DSDM in Agile Projects

The Importance of Discernment in Tailoring

Methodology Versus Adaptability

One might argue that methodologies exist to provide a structured approach to project management. However, the essence of Agile—and, by extension, DSDM—is adaptability. The challenge lies in striking a balance between sticking to a methodological framework and adapting it to meet the unique requirements and challenges of a project.

The Role of Risk Assessment in Tailoring

Risk assessment is not a one-time event but a recurring process that permeates the project lifecycle. The Project Approach Questionnaire (PAQ) can be considered a foundational risk assessment tool, but its utility goes beyond initial evaluations. It provides a mechanism for ongoing, dynamic risk assessments that shape the tailoring process.

In-depth Exploration of Key Tailoring Mechanisms

Stakeholder Engagement

High-quality stakeholder engagement is more than mere involvement; it is about creating a collaborative environment where opinions are valued and information flows freely. Effective engagement directly correlates with more realistic and actionable PAQ assessments.

Dynamic Risk Management

In a fast-paced, Agile environment, risks evolve as quickly as project requirements. Therefore, risk management must be responsive and dynamic. This entails frequent reassessments, continuous monitoring, and perhaps most importantly, a proactive approach to identifying potential future risks.

Synchronizing with Existing Methodologies

While DSDM is a comprehensive framework, it is often implemented alongside other methodologies like PRINCE2 or Scrum. This multi-methodology environment can introduce additional complexities, requiring thoughtful integration strategies that uphold the core principles of each contributing methodology.

The Undeniable Importance of Human Factors

Mindset and Behavior

The successful tailoring of any Agile methodology, including DSDM, hinges significantly on human behavior and mindset. The concepts of shared ownership, proactive communication, and a genuine willingness to adapt are more than just desirable traits; they are prerequisites for effective tailoring.

Training and Skills Enhancement

Tailoring doesn't merely involve adapting processes or activities; it often necessitates skillset adjustments or enhancements. Any tailoring strategy should account for training needs, be they in technical areas, soft skills, or Agile principles.

Conclusion: The Art and Science of Tailoring

The act of tailoring DSDM to suit a specific project's needs is a complex interplay of many factors, ranging from risk assessment and stakeholder engagement to methodological integration and human behavior. It's both an art and a science that demands a deep understanding of Agile principles, the unique challenges of the project at hand, and the nuances of human interaction. This intricate task falls largely on the shoulders of the Agile Project

Manager, whose expertise and leadership are pivotal in navigating the complexities involved.

Case Study: Tailoring DSDM for a Complex Healthcare Project

The project involved developing a patient management system for a network of hospitals. The initial assessment suggested a high level of complexity, a mix of stakeholders with varied interests, and a regulatory landscape that necessitated strict compliance measures. Given these complexities, it was apparent that DSDM, though an excellent starting point, would require significant tailoring.

The Role of PAQ in Initial Assessment

Identifying High-Impact Risks

The PAQ was utilized to identify areas where the project had high risks, especially concerning stakeholder alignment and regulatory compliance. It helped in framing the initial dialogue around what aspects of DSDM would need tailoring.

Facilitating Stakeholder Engagement

The PAQ served as a vehicle for engaging key stakeholders early in the project, thus ensuring that their concerns were integrated into the tailoring process.

Dynamic Risk Management

Iterative Re-assessments

As the project progressed through its various phases, the PAQ was revisited. New risks were added to the register, and some initially identified risks were re-evaluated and adjusted.

Contingency Measures

The dynamic nature of risk management enabled the project team to enact contingency measures proactively. This was particularly important in managing risks associated with regulatory compliance.

Methodological Integration

Synchronizing DSDM with PRINCE2

Given that the organization had been using PRINCE2 for project governance, it was essential to ensure that DSDM did not conflict with existing processes. A detailed mapping exercise was carried out to align DSDM practices with PRINCE2 governance mechanisms.

Human Factors: Training and Behavior Modification

Mindset Training

A series of workshops were conducted to educate the team about the Agile mindset, aiming to bridge the gap between traditional project management ideologies prevalent in the organization and the Agile principles integral to DSDM.

Skill Enhancement

Training sessions were organized to enhance the team's understanding of DSDM practices and how they would be tailored for this particular project.

Conclusion

The successful completion of the project reaffirmed the belief that DSDM could be effectively tailored to suit the complexities and unique challenges of a large-scale healthcare project. The meticulous approach to dynamic risk management, facilitated by the PAQ, played a significant role. Equally crucial were the efforts to integrate DSDM with existing methodologies and the focus on human factors, such as mindset and skill development. This multi-faceted approach to tailoring DSDM proved instrumental in delivering a project that was both efficient and compliant.

Chapter Twenty-Two

Historic Background: Pioneering Agile Project Management

The Evolutionary Synergy: DSDM, AgilePF, and The Pulse of Corporate Flexibility

The Evolutionary Milestones: DSDM to Agile Business Consortium

The inception of the Dynamic Systems Development Method (DSDM) in 1994 marked a pivotal moment in the domain of project management. Created as a balanced counterpoint to traditional project management and Rapid Application Development (RAD), DSDM sought to harmonize essential aspects of speed, quality, and control. As the methodology matured, its custodianship evolved into what is now known as the Agile Business Consortium. This transition widened the framework's scope and democratized its accessibility, ensuring that its intellectual principles remained within universal reach.

Unveiling AgilePF: An Evolution, Not a Revolution

The Agile Project Framework (AgilePF) emanates as a progressive adaptation of its predecessor, DSDM Atern®. Rather than shattering the established paradigms, it fortifies the core tenets and roles while assimilating more seamlessly with contemporary Agile philosophies. This includes a refined approach to process management, emphasizing lean methodologies, value-driven outcomes, and judicious documentation.

The Corporate Relevance of DSDM & AgilePF

Aligning With Project-Centric Approaches

One of the significant facets of DSDM and AgilePF is their focus on the 'project' as a holistic entity, rather than just the 'product'. This orientation synergizes exceptionally well with corporate ecosystems that frequently involve the orchestration of complex, multi-layered projects.

Unambiguous Role Definition

Clearly defined roles are not just a footnote but a cornerstone in DSDM's structure. This granularity in role demarcation is invaluable in expansive corporate settings where role clarity is pivotal to preventing misunderstandings and function overlap.

The Adaptive Leverage of Documentation

AgilePF places particular emphasis on evolving its approach to documentation. By adopting an adaptive and streamlined documentation methodology, AgilePF amplifies its adaptability index, allowing for seamless implementation across a diverse range of corporate terrains without relinquishing the core Agile principles.

Conclusive Remarks

DSDM and AgilePF serve as robust scaffolding for project management paradigms, offering a sturdy yet agile structure that is indispensable in the modern, fast-paced corporate environment. The Agile Business Consortium plays a crucial role in nurturing and adapting these frameworks, ensuring they stay abreast of the dynamically evolving landscape of project management methodologies.

Case Study: Implementing AgilePF in a Multinational Corporation for Optimized Project Management

The Challenge

A multinational corporation with a diversified portfolio was grappling with inconsistencies in project management outcomes across different departments. The company had historically used traditional project management models but was keen on switching to Agile methodologies to boost efficiency and responsiveness.

The Solution: AgilePF Implementation

To address the inconsistency and inefficiency issues, the company opted to adopt AgilePF as its primary project management framework. This decision was influenced by AgilePF's focus on both project and product aspects, its role clarity, and its adaptive documentation framework—qualities that aligned perfectly with the corporation's complexity and scale.

Comprehensive Onboarding and Training

To ensure a smooth transition, the company initiated a comprehensive onboarding and training program. Staff at all levels were educated about the AgilePF's principles, roles, and documentation protocols.

Role Demarcation and Structuring

The project management teams went through a rigorous process of role definition, assigning specific Agile roles based on AgilePF's guidelines. This step eradicated ambiguities and clarified the responsibilities of each team member.

Streamlined Documentation

AgilePF's adaptive documentation framework was implemented. By focusing on value-driven and lean documentation, the company was able to enhance cross-departmental communication and collaboration.

The Outcome

The company experienced a substantial improvement in project delivery timelines and consistency. Metrics related to project success and stakeholder satisfaction saw marked improvements. Moreover, the structured yet flexible approach of AgilePF allowed the company to adapt swiftly to market changes and disruptions.

The Takeaway

The implementation of AgilePF provided the multinational corporation with a structured yet agile framework that was well-suited to its complex project management needs. The framework's alignment with corporate requirements for role clarity and adaptive documentation made it an apt choice for driving efficiency and consistency across the organization's diverse projects.

Chapter Twenty-Three

Choosing Your Agile Approach: Considerations and Benefits

RAD and Agile: Navigating the Evolutionary Spectrum with DSDM as the Lighthouse

The Historical Context: Waterfall and RAD Dilemmas

During the early 1990s, the business environment was largely oriented towards the 'Waterfall' model for project management. This sequential approach, while robust in certain aspects, led to protracted timelines, misaligned communications, and vaguely defined deliverables. Rapid Application Development (RAD) was later adopted as a countermeasure to overcome these challenges, prioritizing speed and agility. However, RAD was not without its pitfalls, notably issues concerning scalability and long-term applicability.

The Emergence of DSDM: Bridging Two Worlds

In this complex landscape, the Dynamic Systems Development Method (DSDM) emerged in 1994 as a reconciliatory framework. DSDM aimed to blend the precision and quality control of traditional models with the swift, adaptive elements of RAD. The framework aspired to deliver both immediate value and long-term viability, tailoring itself to the ever-changing contours of contemporary business practices.

DSDM and the Agile Ecosystem: An Inextricable Bond

DSDM as a Foundational Pillar

DSDM has been a cornerstone in the formation and growth of the Agile ecosystem. As a founding member of the Agile Alliance in 2001, DSDM played a pivotal role in crafting the Agile Manifesto. While the Manifesto initially centered around software development projects, DSDM broadened its reach to encapsulate a more diverse range of projects.

Attributes of 'Mature Agile'

DSDM sets itself apart as a 'mature Agile' methodology for several reasons:

Scalability: The framework is architectured to manage both small and expansive projects effectively.

Inclusivity: DSDM transcends the confines of IT and software development, offering applicability across various solution types.

Project-Centric: Unlike many Agile methodologies that are primarily product-focused, DSDM emphasizes the complete project, making it particularly adept for corporate environments.

Theoretical Exploration: Practical Application

In a scenario like a financial institution aiming to upgrade its systems, DSDM could be the optimal choice. It would allow the organization to initiate the project with well-defined scope and objectives while preserving alignment with long-term business goals. Iterative cycles would facilitate swift development and testing within predefined quality criteria, ensuring both agility and enduring quality.

Final Thoughts

DSDM's emergence as a harmonizing force in project management brings together the strengths of traditional and RAD methodologies. Its seminal contribution to the Agile paradigm elevates it as a preferred methodology for organizations aiming to attain a balanced, mature, and scalable approach to Agile project management.

Case Study: Revitalizing a Financial Institution with DSDM Methodology

Initial Challenges

A prominent financial institution faced significant pressure to modernize its legacy systems and improve customer experience. While traditional project management approaches presented the risk of stagnation and inflexibility, Rapid Application Development (RAD) seemed prone to overlook crucial elements like scalability and long-term maintainability.

Solution: DSDM Implementation

Predefined Scope and Objectives

Adopting the DSDM framework, the institution commenced the project with a clearly delineated scope and set of objectives. This initial phase ensured alignment with long-term business goals, providing a solid foundation for the subsequent project stages.

Rapid and Iterative Cycles

As the project proceeded, the DSDM methodology enabled rapid, iterative cycles for the development and testing of new functionalities. These were executed within the boundaries of predefined quality criteria, ensuring that while the project remained agile, it did not compromise on long-term objectives or quality standards.

Multidimensional Focus

The DSDM framework's holistic, project-centric approach allowed the institution to consider various critical aspects concurrently: customer experience, data security, scalability, and long-term viability.

The Results

Improved Customer Experience

Upon project completion, the institution observed marked improvements in customer satisfaction metrics, confirming the project's alignment with consumer expectations.

Scalability and Long-term Viability

The methodology's intrinsic scalability features allowed for seamless expansion and adaptation, ensuring the new systems' longevity and relevance in an evolving financial market.

Cost Efficiency

By maintaining a balance between speed and quality, DSDM helped to optimize resource allocation, thereby achieving cost-efficiency without compromising on the project's overall quality.

Conclusions

The DSDM methodology enabled the financial institution to strike a balance between rapid development and long-term objectives. Its capability to adapt to varying project sizes and types makes it a quintessential choice for organizations aiming for a mature, balanced, and scalable Agile project management approach.

DSDM: The Harmonizing Framework in the Spectrum of Traditional and Agile Methodologies

Divergence from Traditional Approaches: The Agile Paradigm in DSDM

Iterative Development

In stark contrast to traditional methodologies that emphasize upfront planning and exhaustive documentation, DSDM subscribes to iterative and incremental development. This approach allows projects to remain fluid, adjusting as new information becomes available.

Deferment of Detail

While traditional methodologies necessitate detailed specifications from the get-go, DSDM adopts a more agile approach. The focus is on defining just enough to progress to the next stage, optimizing resources and focus for what is immediately critical.

Immediate Needs Over Future Requirements

Traditional project management often falls into the trap of trying to anticipate all conceivable future requirements. This leads to bloated, complex solutions. DSDM, in contrast, zeroes in on immediate and imminent business needs, offering a more agile and cost-effective strategy.

Lower Total Cost of Ownership (TCO)

DSDM acknowledges that development cost is just a fragment of the Total Cost of Ownership (TCO). As such, it aims for simplified, more manageable solutions, diverging from traditional models that often inflate TCO through complexity and over-engineering.

Divergence from Other Agile Approaches: DSDM's Unique Propositions

Early Foundations

Unlike some Agile methodologies that leap into development phases, DSDM insists on early agreement concerning the basic foundations of the project. This becomes invaluable in large or complex projects where initial clarity can mitigate risks and streamline subsequent phases.

Holistic Role Definition

While many Agile frameworks adopt a minimalist stance on defined roles, DSDM charts a broader landscape. It outlines a comprehensive set of roles that allow for better alignment with corporate governance structures, without compromising agility.

Extending the Agile Manifesto

DSDM adheres to the principles espoused in the Agile Manifesto but goes a step further. It extends these principles beyond the realm of software development, making the methodology more versatile and applicable across diverse project types.

Theoretical Example: Healthcare Records Management System

When tasked with developing a healthcare records management system, DSDM could serve as an optimal methodology. It would commence with an agreed foundation, clearly outlining scope, constraints, and governance measures. Subsequent iterative cycles would then focus on fulfilling immediate healthcare needs while retaining adaptability for future regulations or technological shifts.

Concluding Remarks

DSDM emerges as a balanced, nuanced approach to project management, capable of bridging the gaps between traditional and Agile methodologies. It maintains Agile's iterative advantages while incorporating elements of strategic planning. This hybrid nature makes it particularly relevant for complex or large-scale corporate projects. DSDM not only embraces but extends the core principles of the Agile Manifesto, positioning it as a uniquely flexible yet structured methodology.

Case Study: Implementing DSDM in Healthcare Records Management

Setting the Scene: The Challenge

A regional healthcare provider faced mounting challenges related to records management, such as inefficient processes, regulatory compliance issues, and poor data integrity. Traditional methodologies seemed overly rigid and slow, whereas pure Agile approaches lacked the structure needed for such a critical project subject to stringent regulations.

Solution: Choosing DSDM as the Methodology

Establishing Foundations

Adopting DSDM as its methodology, the healthcare provider started with a foundation phase. This involved outlining the project's scope, constraints, and governance measures, which was essential given the regulatory environment in healthcare.

Iterative Development

DSDM's iterative approach allowed the team to focus on immediate requirements like improving data accuracy and access controls. Each iteration was designed to deliver tangible improvements, tested against predefined quality criteria.

Holistic Role Definition

DSDM's comprehensive set of roles provided a framework for clear responsibilities and decision-making. Roles like Business Sponsor, Business Visionary, and Technical Coordinator were explicitly defined, aligning well with the organization's governance requirements.

Results and Impact

Regulatory Compliance

The DSDM methodology ensured that the project met all compliance regulations, given its foundational focus on governance and scope.

Operational Efficiency

Due to the iterative approach, the healthcare provider could quickly realize benefits at each phase of the project. This led to a steady increase in operational efficiencies and staff satisfaction.

Cost-Effectiveness

By focusing on immediate needs and avoiding over-engineering, the project managed to keep the Total Cost of Ownership (TCO) low, a crucial factor given budget constraints often faced by healthcare providers.

Conclusions

DSDM proved to be the perfect fit for this complex healthcare project. Its balanced approach allowed the organization to address immediate needs iteratively while ensuring alignment with long-term objectives and compliance requirements. The methodology's focus on early foundations and holistic role definition added layers of structure that were invaluable in a regulated environment like healthcare.

Unpacking the Value Proposition of DSDM: A Decision-Making Guide

Advantages of Choosing DSDM

Holistic Approach to Project Management

DSDM stands apart for its comprehensive focus on both the product and the project. This dual emphasis ensures that not just the immediate development tasks but the larger project objectives and business goals are met.

Flexibility and Versatility

DSDM is flexible enough to be deployed as an independent project management framework or to augment other Agile frameworks like Scrum. This malleability makes it a versatile choice suitable for a wide variety of organizational needs.

Interoperability with Established Standards

The framework is designed with pragmatic interoperability in mind. It can be seamlessly integrated with other industry standards like PRINCE2, ITIL, ISO, CMMI, and PMO frameworks without causing disruptions to existing processes.

Wide Applicability

Whether the aim is to develop new solutions or enhance existing ones, DSDM can be applied effectively. This broadens its reach beyond niche or new projects, making it a versatile tool in any project manager's kit.

Summation of Key Benefits

Enhanced Stakeholder Engagement

One of the standout features of DSDM is the emphasis on continuous stakeholder engagement. This ensures that the project remains aligned with business objectives and allows for real-time adjustments, fostering greater ownership and satisfaction among stakeholders.

Priority-Driven Outcomes

DSDM employs the MoSCoW prioritization technique, which categorizes project tasks into Must-haves, Should-haves, Could-haves, and Won't-haves. This methodical approach ensures that critical features are developed and deployed first, thus increasing the project's likelihood of timely delivery without sacrificing quality.

Risk Mitigation

DSDM's iterative development and constant stakeholder interaction serve as built-in risk mitigation strategies. They collectively ensure that the project is closely monitored and adjusted, reducing the likelihood of end-product misalignment with business objectives.

Efficient Deployment

The collaborative approach of DSDM simplifies the transition from development to live use, making the deployment process efficient and reducing the time to market.

Concluding Remarks

Choosing DSDM as your Agile approach provides a host of benefits that extend beyond the scope of most other Agile frameworks. Its adaptability, holistic view of project management, and built-in risk mitigation techniques make it a compelling choice for organizations seeking a robust, comprehensive, and flexible Agile framework.

A Deep Dive into the Practical Application of DSDM: The FinTech Scenario

Context and Project Scope

Imagine a financial technology (FinTech) company aiming to create a groundbreaking portfolio management tool. The stakes are high, given the rapid technological changes and regulatory requirements in the financial sector.

Traditional Scrum Approach: A Limited Scope

In a Scrum-only approach, the focus would primarily be on development cycles, known as sprints, and the product backlog. While this ensures rapid development and quick delivery, it lacks a holistic view that considers business alignment, risk assessment, and broader governance parameters.

Adding DSDM to the Mix: A Hybrid Model

When integrated with Scrum, DSDM can provide the missing pieces. Before diving into development, DSDM would establish a robust foundation, outlining the project's scope, constraints, and governance guidelines. It ensures that the FinTech tool aligns not only with the technical requirements but also with broader business objectives, risk profiles, and compliance mandates.

The Symbiosis: DSDM and Scrum

In this combined approach, Scrum can take care of what it does best: managing the rapid and efficient development cycles, while DSDM offers a more panoramic view of the project. Scrum can focus on the backlog and specific feature development, whereas DSDM ensures the overall business alignment and risk mitigation.

Outcomes and Key Benefits

By adopting this hybrid model, the FinTech company stands to gain in multiple ways:

Business Alignment

The tool is developed with a clear understanding of the business objectives, ensuring that it serves not just a technical need but a business one.

Risk Mitigation

Through continuous monitoring and stakeholder involvement, any deviations from the business objectives or regulatory requirements can be quickly identified and corrected.

Scalability and Governance

The project can scale smoothly, courtesy of DSDM's built-in scalability features. Additionally, governance and compliance issues are continually addressed, reducing any legal or operational risks.

Concluding Insights

The hybrid approach of DSDM and Scrum offers a nuanced and comprehensive project management methodology that caters to both immediate development needs and long-term business objectives. For a sector as complex and rapidly evolving as FinTech, such an approach provides the much-needed balance between speed, quality, and strategic alignment.

Printed in Great Britain
by Amazon

37715452R00364